Programming in Pascal

Programming in Pascal

Nell Dale
The University of Texas at Austin

D. C. Heath and Company
Lexington, Massachusetts   Toronto

Acquisitions Editor: Peter C. Gordon
Developmental Editor: Katherine Pinard
Production Editor: Andrea Cava
Production Coordinator: Mike O'Dea
Photo Researcher: Martha Shethar

Cover Photo: Les Moore/Uniphoto
Cover Design: Dustin Graphics

Photo Credits: p. 4(middle) Official U.S. Navy Photograph; p. 4(right) Official U.S. Navy Photograph/James S. Davis, Photographer; p. 5(left) Courtesy of Eidgenössische Technische Hochschule, Zürich; p. 5(middle) Courtesy of Apple Computer, Inc.; p. 5(right) Susan Griggs Agency Ltd.; 1-2 Sperry Corporation; 1-3 Cray Research Inc.; 1-4 The Institute for Advanced Study, Princeton, NJ; 1-9 IBM; 1-10 IBM; 1-11a IBM; 1-11b Sun Microsystems Inc.; 1-11c Digital Equipment Inc.; 1-11d IBM; 1-12 IBM; 1-13 3M; 1-15 AT&T Archives; 1-18 Digital Equipment Corporation; 1-20a Intel Corporation; 1-20b Apple Computer Inc.; 1-20c IBM; 1-20d Cray Research Inc.

Published simultaneously in Canada.

Printed in the United States of America.

International Standard Book Number: 0-669-20042-5

Library of Congress Catalog Card Number: 89-84414

10 9 8 7 6 5 4 3 2 1

*This book is dedicated to you the reader
with the hope that the 4-Cs will constitute
the cornerstones of your computing career.*

Preface

Pascal burst onto the computer science educational scene in the early 1980s. Two independent events caused this popularity explosion: The revised ACM guidelines for Computer Science I advocated teaching good programming habits through the use of a block structured language like Pascal, and an Advanced Placement Exam in Computer Science, offered for the first time, required a knowledge of Pascal.

Pascal has since moved from computer science departments across campuses to engineering, business, education, and mathematics departments—in fact, to all departments where computing is taught. It has also moved from the academic community into business and industry.

Programming in Pascal reflects this increased use of Pascal in today's world. The examples used in the text cross all disciplines, yet rely on the knowledge of none. The only prerequisites are high school algebra and an interest in learning how to write programs.

Text Organization

This book follows the pedagogical tradition of the highly successful *Introduction to Pascal and Structured Design* by Nell Dale and David Orshalick, but it differs in several important respects.

Chapter Organization

The first chapter traces the evolution of computer software and hardware from the perspective of the author (whose first program was written on first-generation hardware). It is important for students brought up on PacMan and DonkeyKong to have a sense of the history of computing.

It is not enough to teach students to write programs; we must teach them to write *good* programs right from the beginning. Chapter 1 concludes with a definition of what is meant by a "good" program: a good program is *clear*, *concise*, *complete*, and *correct*. Each chapter ends with a discussion of these 4-Cs of good programming as applied to the concepts presented in the chapter.

Chapter 2 introduces the concept of an identifier, which can name both a place (variable) and an action (procedure). WRITE and WRITELN statements and assignment statements are covered. Various problem-solving strategies are defined and discussed. A short but complete program is presented to illustrate the anatomy of a Pascal program.

Chapter 3 builds on the problem-solving techniques introduced in Chapter 2 with a discussion of top-down design methodology. It also covers interactive and file input and points of style for writing prompting messages.

Chapter 4 covers the selection construct of programming represented in Pascal by the IF-THEN and IF-THEN-ELSE statements. Chapter 5 covers the looping or iteration construct of programming represented in Pascal by the WHILE statement. Count-controlled loops and event-controlled loops are defined and illustrated with many short examples. The emphasis is on teaching the students a technique for constructing correct loops rather than on introducing the various syntactic constructs for loops.

Chapter 6 covers procedures and the flow of program control through VAR and value parameters. Scope rules are also covered. The concepts of program design are expanded to cover interface design between program parts. Interface design charts are presented as one method of designing clear interfaces.

Chapter 7 is a collection of a variety of topics, including functions, recursion, and numerical accuracy. The CASE, REPEAT, and FOR statements, "ice cream and cake" constructs (i.e., constructs that are not necessary but are nice to have), are presented.

Chapter 8 formally defines the concept of TYPE as applied both to simple types and structured types. Scalar, ordinal, and array types are defined, and the built-in functions on ordinal types are presented.

One-dimensional arrays can often be another stumbling block for beginning students. Students tend to confuse an array with the list of items stored in the array. The goal of Chapter 9 is to make the students comfortable with processing lists of items represented in a one-dimensional array. Sorting, searching, and merging are covered along with the use of parallel arrays and arrays in which the indexes have semantic content. Strings (PACKED ARRAYS OF CHAR) are presented at the end of the chapter, and the point is made that any of the algorithms discussed can also be applied to lists of strings.

Chapter 10 covers multidimensional arrays and stresses their use as a means to represent data that is logically organized in tables. Chapter 11 covers records. Both Chapters 10 and 11 have sections that discuss how to choose an appropriate data structure.

Chapter 12 covers TEXT files, which are introduced in Chapter 3, in more depth. The concept of a file is extended to cover binary files and the concept of the file buffer variable. The only unstructured composite type, the SET, is also presented.

Chapter 13 introduces the pointer data type and referenced variables. Linked structures are presented as an alternative way of representing items in a list. The chapter concludes with a brief overview of stacks, queues, and binary search trees.

Recurring Themes

Construct Presentation: Each Pascal construct is presented with a syntax diagram and a detailed verbal description, illustrated with short, relevant examples, and used in complete programs. Once a construct has been presented, it is used consistently thereafter.

Problem Solving: Programs are not written in isolation; they are written to solve problems. Each chapter contains several sample problems that serve as case studies on program decomposition and design. The students are carefully walked through the problem statement, possible alternative approaches to the solution, the development of the top-down design, the choice of data types, the design of the interfaces, and finally, the coded, well-documented program. The problems are carefully chosen to illustrate and reinforce the concepts represented in the chapter.

Writing Good Programs: The *4-Cs* section at the end of each chapter reinforces the concepts of good programming. These sections can be thought of as mini-lectures on software engineering as applied to small programs. Testing and debugging are covered in these sections.

Pedagogy

Goals

The goals for each chapter are listed at the beginning of the chapter. These goals are then tested in the Exercises and Pretests.

Color

Throughout the book, color is used effectively to highlight both figures and text. Definitions of important terms are displayed and highlighted, and the comments in the sample programs are in color to easily distinguish them from program syntax. Sample problems have color tabs on the outside margins throughout the problem discussion so that students instantly know if they are looking at a sample problem.

End-of-Chapter Material

Summary: A summary at the end of each chapter restates the major topics covered in the chapter.

Exercises and Pretests: Exercises and Pretests test the student's understanding of the concepts and syntax introduced in the chapter. Answers to the

Exercises are in the back of the book. Answers to the Pretests are in the Instructor's Guide.

Programming Assignments: Students are given specifications to write complete programs that solve problems drawn from everyday experience.

Supplements

Instructor's Guide

The Instructor's Guide includes a summary of chapter topics, teaching notes including tips on teaching difficult topics, answers to the Pretests, and a complete solution and discussion of at least one programming assignment per chapter.

Test Item File

The Test Item File contains over 1,200 possible test questions. It is available in HeathTest Plus, a computerized test generator, for the IBM PC and the Apple.

Also Available

Lab Manual

A Laboratory Course in Pascal by Nell Dale, a pedagogical tool, contains practical, hands-on exercises and problems. A disk containing program "shells" is included so that students spend valuable lab time working on the body of each exercise rather than keying in general information for each program. The first chapter contains tutorials for Turbo Pascal, Versions 3.0 and 4.0/5.0. The programs and exercises in the rest of the chapters are written in ISO standard Pascal with special notes for Turbo users.

Acknowledgments

Thank-you's usually fall into three categories: professional colleagues who reviewed the manuscript, staff members at the publisher, and long-suffering friends and family members. I will not break with tradition.

To Chip Weems, Glen Richards, Mickey Moldenhauer, and Al Dale, thanks for your tremendous help with the manuscript. Chip, your suggestions are always right on target; Glen, you are the most meticulous reader I know; Mickey, when I asked you to work on the exercises, I had no idea that I would get your editorial expertise as well; and Al, thanks for knowing all about SIMDs and MIMDs.

To Peter Gordon, Kitty Pinard, Andrea Cava, and all the other super people at D. C. Heath, thanks for making the manuscript a reality. Peter, your energy put me to shame; Kitty, your view from two perspectives was most useful; and Andrea, your calm professionalism made working with you a pleasure. A very special thanks must go to an unnamed freelance editor who played havoc with my prose and my pride. When I got over being appalled at the amount of red ink, I found that the changes usually made the material stronger.

To Nancy and all my other friends, thank you for not looking bored when this book dominated my conversation. To Chris, thank you for taking care of the house, leaving me to take care of the book. To Nyda, our ancient yellow lab who sleeps under my computer, thank you for your silent companionship. To the extended Dale family—Judy, June, Bobby, Susan, Sarah, Phil, Maricarmen, Tom, Baby Kate, Baby John Alexander, and most especially Al—thanks for always being there when I needed you and leaving me alone when I needed to work.

N.D.

Brief Contents

Contents

7 Functions, Additional Control Structures, and Real Numbers   *231*

Sample Problems

Programming in Pascal

An Overview of Hardware, Software, and Programming

- To be able to define and to distinguish between hardware and software.

- To be able to describe and discuss the five elements of the von Neumann architecture:

    Memory unit
    Arithmetic/logic unit
    Control unit
    Input unit
    Output unit

- To be able to characterize the four generations of the modern computer in terms of both hardware and software tools.

- To be able to define the programming process.

- To be able to define the four properties of a good program.

Most of you who will be studying from this book have grown up during the age of the personal computer. *Hardware, software, program,* and *programming* are probably familiar words to you. Some of you can define these and many other computer-related words explicitly, while others may have only a vague, intuitive understanding of them.

The primary goal of this chapter is for each of you to begin Chapter 2 with an understanding of the terms we will be using. A secondary goal is that you will develop an appreciation for the evolution of modern computing systems, both hardware and software. Finally, we hope that you will be challenged to apply the principles of good programming now and throughout your career.

A Historical Perspective of Computing

Early History

The early history of computing is the story of the search for a faster, more reliable device to manipulate numbers. It makes fascinating reading, not because of the devices (they rarely worked), but because of the great men and women who devoted themselves to the problem. Figure 1–1 (pp. 4–5) is a time line that includes their contributions.

The early history begins with the abacus and ends when the first commercial computer, the Remington Rand UNIVAC I, was delivered to the Bureau of the Census in Washington, D.C., in 1951. The UNIVAC I was the first computer used to predict the outcome of a presidential election (Figure 1–2, p. 6). With the delivery of that machine, the dream of a device that could rapidly manipulate numbers was realized; the search was ended. Or was it?

> A generation ago experts announced that one or two large computers would suffice for the computational needs of mankind. They failed to realize that the ability to calculate rapidly and to process large quantities of information would change the fabric of mathematics, physics, engineering, economics and a variety of other fields so radically that their assessment of what *needed to be calculated* would become entirely invalid.*

After 1951 the story becomes one of the ever-expanding use of computers to solve problems in all areas. From that point, the search has focused not only on building faster, bigger devices (Figure 1–3, p. 6), but on the development of tools to allow us to use these devices more productively.

Modern History

In the nearly forty years since the delivery of that first commercial machine, the architecture (theoretical organization) of what we now call a *computer* has

---

*P. Grogono and S. H. Nelson, *Problem Solving and Computer Programming* (Reading, Mass.: Addison-Wesley, 1982), p. 92. Emphasis added.

changed little. It is helpful, then, to describe this architecture and show how it operates before we continue with our discussion of the history of modern computers.

von Neumann Architecture

John von Neumann (Figure 1–4, p. 7), a Hungarian-born American mathematician, is credited with the development of two very important concepts. The first is that the instructions that operate a machine should be stored in the machine along with the data to be operated on. The second is that data (and instructions) should be represented in the binary number system rather than the decimal number system. In the **binary** (base 2) **number system**, all data is represented by patterns of 1s and 0s. A single binary digit is called a **bit**.

The organization or architecture of the computer is based on von Neumann's ideas and bears his name. The essence of this architecture is *sequentiality*. That is, instructions (a program) are stored in sequential memory locations in binary form and are executed in sequence, one after the other.

The von Neumann architecture consists of five basic units: memory, arithmetic/logic, control, input, and output. The von Neumann architecture is shown in Figure 1–5 (p. 7).

The **memory unit** is the internal storage device of a computer. **Memory** is an ordered sequence of storage cells, each containing a unit of information. It is similar to an old-fashioned post office with a bank of pigeonholes for mail. Memory storage cells are known variously as *memory cells*, *memory locations*, *words*, *bytes*, or *places in memory*. Each memory cell has a distinct **address** by which it is referenced in order to store information in it or retrieve information from it, and each memory cell contains a fixed number of binary digits.

Memory Unit
The internal storage device of a computer.

We've been a little loose about using the words *information* and *data* interchangeably. **Information** is any knowledge that can be communicated. **Data** is information in a symbolic form that can be used by a computer.

Memory contains both data and programs (Figure 1–6, p. 8). The same pattern of binary bits in a memory cell can be interpreted as various types of data (numbers or alphanumeric characters) or as an instruction in a program. The computer is instructed how to interpret a pattern by the program it is **executing**. Memory does not know or care what's contained in a cell; it's simply a storage place.

The **arithmetic/logic unit (ALU)** is made up of one or more *registers*. A value can be retrieved from a place in memory and put into a register, a value can be retrieved from a place in memory and added to (or subtracted from, multiplied by, or divided by) the value in a register, or the value in a register can be stored in a place in memory.

1642   *Blaise Pascal* builds first digital calculator

1835   *Charles Babbage* builds Analytical Engine, the first digital computer

1842   *Augusta Ada Byron*, Countess of Lovelace, develops programming loop

1859   *George Boole* develops symbolic logic

1890   *Herman Hollerith's* punch cards are used to classify and count data for the U.S. Census Bureau

1924   *Thomas J. Watson, Sr.*, forms IBM from Hollerith's Computer Tabulating Company

1937   *Alan Turing* writes specifications for a theoretical, universal computer known as the Turing machine

1944   *Howard Aiken* creates the Harvard Mark I, the first fully automated computer

1945   The first "bug," a moth that was caught in the Mark I hardware, is pasted by *Grace Hopper* into her notes

1946   *John Presper Eckert, Jr.*, and *John W. Mauchly* build the ENIAC, the first large, all-purpose computer

1948   *William B. Shockley, Walter H. Brattain*, and *John Bardeen* invent the transistor at Bell Labs

1951   *John Presper Eckert, Jr.*, and *John W. Mauchly* build the UNIVAC I, the first electronic commercial computer

1957   *John Backus* develops the FORTRAN programming language for solving scientific problems

1959   *Grace Hopper* is a leading member of the committee that creates the COBOL programming language to do data processing for businesses

FIGURE 1–1

Blaise Pascal

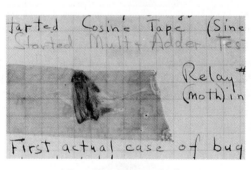

Grace Hopper's notebook

Grace Hopper

1960   *John McCarthy* creates the LISP programming language to manipulate lists of data and abstract symbols

1965   *John Kemeny* and *Thomas Kurtz* develop the BASIC programming language for beginning programmers

1968   *Edsger Dijkstra* writes definitive article on structured programming criticizing the use of the GOTO statement

1971   *Ted Hoff* develops the Intel 4004, the first microprocessor

1971   *Ken Thompson* and *Dennis Ritchie* develop the UNIX operation system

1971   *Niklaus Wirth* creates the Pascal programming language for teaching structured programming

1972   *Dennis Ritchie* creates the C programming language to be used to develop operating systems

1974   *Bill Gates* and *Paul Allen* found Microsoft Corporation

1977   *Stephen Wozniak* and *Steven Jobs* create the Apple computer and form Apple Corporation

1978   *Seymour Rubinstein* develops WordStar, the first general purpose text-editor

1980   The U.S. Department of Defense sponsors the development of the Ada programming language

1981   IBM introduces the first IBM PC

1982   *Mitch Kapor* founds Lotus Development Corporation

1984   Apple Computer introduces the Macintosh computer

1988   *Steven Jobs* introduces the NeXT computer

FIGURE 1–1   Continued

Stephen Wozniak and Steven Jobs

Niklaus Wirth

Edsger Dijkstra

FIGURE 1–2   The UNIVAC I was used by CBS and Walter Cronkite to predict the outcome of the 1952 presidential election.

Arithmetic/Logic Unit

The computer component that performs arithmetic operations (addition, subtraction, multiplication, division) and logical operations (comparison of two values).

In addition to performing arithmetic operations, the arithmetic/logic unit can compare the contents of two registers, a register and a place in memory, or two places in memory. The result of this comparison then can be used to determine the next instruction to be executed.

FIGURE 1–3   Cray Supercomputer

FIGURE 1–4 John von Neumann was one of the most influential figures in the development of the modern computer.

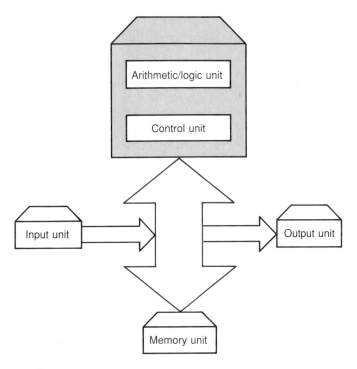

FIGURE 1–5 Key computer components

Memory

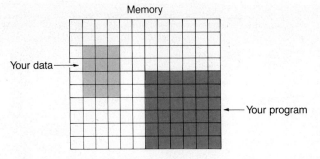

Your data

FIGURE 1-6 Memory

Your program

Every computer has a set of instructions that the hardware is built to execute directly. The set of instructions is called the *machine language* or *machine code* of the machine. These instructions cause actions to take place between memory and the outside world and between memory and the arithmetic/logic unit. When a sequence of instructions is being executed, the **control unit** proceeds step by step through the instruction execution cycle, or the *fetch/execute cycle*:

1. The control unit fetches the next instruction from memory.
2. The instruction is decoded into control signals.
3. Data is fetched (if the instruction requires it).
4. The control signals tell the appropriate unit (memory, arithmetic/logic, or an input/output device) to carry out the instruction.

Control Unit

The computer component that controls the actions of the other components in order to execute instructions (the program) in sequence.

The process starts with the control unit's being given the address in memory of the first instruction. Because execution begins at that address, the content of that memory location is interpreted as an instruction, as are the contents of subsequent memory locations, until the sequence of instructions stops. This cycle is shown graphically in Figure 1–7.

The combination of the arithmetic/logic unit and the control unit is called the **central processing unit (CPU)** (Figure 1–8).

Central Processing Unit (CPU)

The "brain" of a computer which interprets and executes instructions.

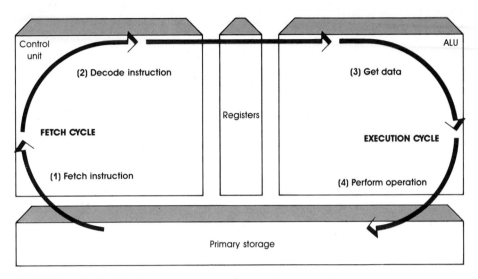

FIGURE I–7 The fetch/execute cycle

An **input unit** is a device through which data and programs from the outside world are entered into the computer. The first input units interpreted holes punched on paper tape or cards. Modern-day input devices include the terminal keyboard and the scanning devices used at supermarkets.

Input Unit
A device that accepts information to be stored in memory.

An **output unit** is a device through which results stored in computer memory are made available to the outside world. The most common output devices are printers and video display terminals.

Output Unit
A device that prints or otherwise displays information stored in memory or makes a permanent copy of information stored in memory on another device.

Figure 1–9 shows some typical input/output devices used with microcomputers. Figure 1–10 shows the basic components of a computer. The dictionary definition of **computer** reflects this architecture.

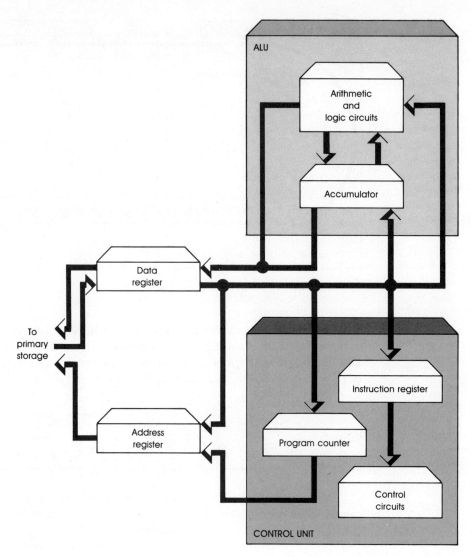

FIGURE 1–8   CPU architecture

> **Computer**
> A programmable electronic device that can store, retrieve, and process data.

The verbs *store*, *retrieve*, and *process* relate to the five basic physical components of the computer: the memory unit, the arithmetic/logic unit, the control
unit, input devices, and output devices. These physical components are
called computer **hardware**. The programs that are available to run on a com-

FIGURE I–9 Typical microcomputer input/output devices. The keyboard is the primary device for entering commands and data, but many microcomputers also use a mouse. The printer is used to produce text and graphics on paper. The display, or monitor, is the most common output device.

FIGURE I–I0 Typical microcomputer hardware

puter are called **software**. Figure 1–11 shows some types of computer hardware. Figure 1–12 is a picture of the inside of a microcomputer with the hardware elements labeled.

Hardware

The physical components of a computer.

Software

Computer programs; the set of all programs available to a computer.

We've gone through four generations in the forty years of computers based on the von Neumann architecture. Each generation is characterized by the components used in the manufacture of the hardware and by the software tools that were developed to use the hardware more productively.

First Generation (1951–1959)

Hardware

Commercial computers of the first generation were built using vacuum tubes that generated a great deal of heat and were not very reliable. The machines required heavy-duty air-conditioning and frequent maintenance. They also required vast amounts of floor space.

(a)

(b)

(c)

(d)

FIGURE 1-11   (a) Microcomputer IBM PS/2 Model 30, (b) workstation Sun-3/60, (c) minicomputer DEC VAX 8200, (d) mainframe IBM 3090/600

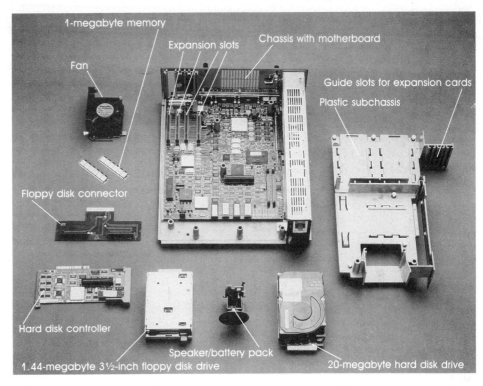

1-megabyte memory

Expansion slots

Chassis with motherboard

Fan

Guide slots for expansion cards

Plastic subchassis

Floppy disk connector

Hard disk controller

Speaker/battery pack

1.44-megabyte 3½-inch floppy disk drive

20-megabyte hard disk drive

FIGURE 1–12 Inside view of an IBM Personal System/2 Model 50

The memory device of this first generation of computers was a magnetic drum that rotated under a read/write head. When the memory cell that was being accessed rotated under the read/write head, the data was written to or read from that place.

The input device was a card reader that read the holes punched in an IBM card (a descendant of the Hollerith card). The output device was either a card punch or a line printer. By the end of this generation, magnetic tape drives had been developed that were much faster than card readers or card punches. **Magnetic tapes** are sequential storage devices. The items on the tapes do not have any sort of addresses associated with them. Each block of information must be read in order to reach the next block on the tape. Although magnetic tapes are slow, there are many applications today that still make effective use of them. Figure 1–13 shows some of these devices.

Devices external to the computer memory that store data in encoded form are called *auxiliary storage devices.* The magnetic tape was the first of these devices. Input units, output units, and auxiliary storage devices became known as **peripheral devices.**

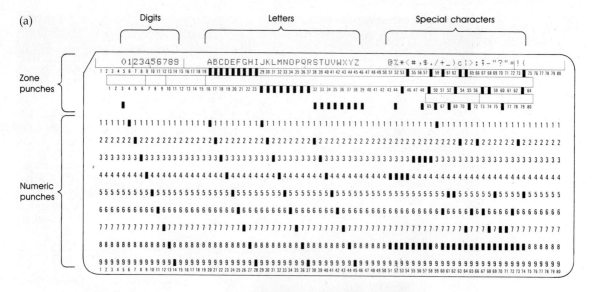

FIGURE 1–13   (a) A computer card, (b) magnetic tape

Software

Software is the set of all programs available to the computer. A **program** is a meaningful sequence of instructions. To be meaningful, a sequence of instructions must be written to perform a specific task.

> **Program**
> A sequence of instructions written to perform a specific task.

The first programs were written using **machine language**, the instructions built into the hardware of a particular computer.

> **Machine Language**
> The set of instructions that is built into the hardware of the computer; also called machine code.

Machine language instructions (and data) are encoded in binary form. The instruction to put the contents of a memory location into a register might look something like 00100011. The instruction to add the contents of another place in memory to the contents of that register might be 11101010. The instruction to store the contents of the register (the result) into a memory location might be 10101110. Even the small task of adding two numbers together uses three binary numbers, and the programmer has to remember which combination of binary digits means what. Clearly this process is both time consuming and prone to errors. No wonder the first programmers were mathematicians!

The first tools developed to help the programmer were assembly languages. **Assembly languages** assign mnemonic letter codes to each machine language instruction. The programmer uses these letter codes in place of binary digits. For example,

LDA might stand for *load* a value into the A register.
ADD might stand for *add* a value to the A register.
STA might stand for *store* the value in the A register in a memory location.

The instructions in an assembly language are much like those you would use to tell someone how to do a calculation on a hand-held calculator. These instructions seem crude, but they are much easier to use than long strings of binary digits.

Because every program that is executed on a computer eventually must be in the form of the computer's machine language, a program called an **assembler** (written in machine language) reads each of the instructions in mnemonic form and translates it into the machine language equivalent. And because each type of computer has a different machine language, there are as many assembly languages and translators as there are types of machines.

Assembler

A program that translates instructions written in an assembly language into the corresponding instructions in machine language.

At the end of the first generation of hardware, the assembly language acted as a buffer between the programmer and the machine hardware (Figure 1–14).

Second Generation (1959–1965)

Hardware

The advent of the transistor (for which John Bardeen, Walter H. Brattain, and William B. Shockley won a Nobel Prize) ushered in the second generation of commercial computers. The transistor replaced the vacuum tube as the main component in the hardware (Figure 1–15). The transistor was smaller, more reliable, faster, more durable, and cheaper.

```
┌─────────────────────────────┐
│    Assembly language        │
│  ┌───────────────────────┐  │
│  │   Machine language    │  │
│  └───────────────────────┘  │
└─────────────────────────────┘
```

FIGURE 1–14 Programming the early computers required a detailed knowledge of the computer's hardware and specific machine code.

The second generation also witnessed the advent of immediate-access memory. When accessing information from a drum or tape drive, the CPU had to wait for the proper place to rotate under the read/write head. The second generation used memory made from magnetic cores, tiny doughnut-shaped devices, each capable of storing one bit of information. These cores were strung together with wires to form cells, which were combined into a memory unit. Because the device was motionless and was accessed electronically, information was instantly available.

The **magnetic disk** (an auxiliary storage device) was also developed during the second generation. The magnetic disk is faster than the magnetic tape because each data item can be addressed by its place on the disk.

Software

As hardware became more powerful, more powerful tools were needed to use it effectively. Assembly languages were certainly a step in the right direction, but the programmer still was forced to think in terms of individual machine

FIGURE 1–15 Transistors were smaller and more reliable than vacuum tubes.

instructions. The second generation of computers saw more powerful languages developed. These **high-level languages** allowed the programmer to write instructions using more English-like statements.

Before we go on, let's formally define what we mean by a **programming language**.

Programming Language

A set of rules, symbols, and special words used to construct a program—that is, to express a sequence of instructions for a computer.

Each programming language has two parts: **syntax**, the part that says how the instructions of the language can be put together, and **semantics**, the part that says what the instructions mean.

Syntax

The formal rules governing the construction of valid instructions in a language.

Semantics

The set of rules that gives the meaning of instructions in a language.

Two of the languages developed during the second generation are still widely used today. They are FORTRAN (a language designed for numerical applications) and COBOL (a language designed for business applications). FORTRAN and COBOL developed quite differently. FORTRAN started out as a simple language and has had additional features, bells and whistles, added to it over the years. In contrast, COBOL was designed first, then implemented. It has changed little over time.*

Another language that was designed during this period and is still in use today is Lisp. Lisp differs markedly from FORTRAN and COBOL and was not as widely accepted. Lisp was used mainly in artificial intelligence applications and research. Dialects of Lisp are among the languages of choice today in the area of artificial intelligence. In fact, Lisp is more widely used now than at any other time.

The introduction of high-level languages provided a vehicle for running the same program on more than one computer. Each high-level language has

---

*Admiral Grace Murray Hopper, who led the team that designed COBOL, retired recently as this country's highest-ranking female naval officer.

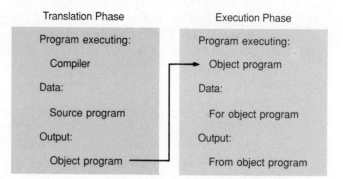

FIGURE 1–16

a translating program that goes with it, a program that takes statements written in the high-level language and converts them to the equivalent machine code instructions. A program written in FORTRAN or COBOL can be translated and run on any machine that has a **compiler** for that language.

Compiler
A program that translates a high-level language into machine language.

A program written in a high-level language is called a **source program** (or *source code*). The machine language version of the source program generated by a compiler is called an **object program** (or *object code*). Source programs (in theory) can be used on any computer with an appropriate compiler; object programs are specific to a particular machine.

The process of running a program written in a high-level language is in two phases: translation, then execution (Figure 1–16). During the *translation phase*, the compiler translates the source program into machine language (the object program). During the *execution phase*, the machine language translation is executed.

A program written in a high-level language is more abstract than the same program written in an assembly language. We can see this in the number of machine instructions needed to code each statement in the program. There is a one-to-one correspondence between assembly language instructions and machine instructions; an instruction in a high-level language may be translated into any number of instructions in machine code.

At the end of the second generation, the programmer was even more insulated from the computer hardware (Figure 1–17). The software surrounding the hardware had become more sophisticated.

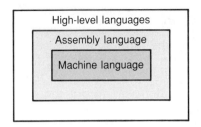

FIGURE 1-17 High-level languages, like FORTRAN and COBOL, formed another layer of language around the machine.

Third Generation (1965–1971)

Hardware

In the second generation, transistors and other components for the computer were assembled by hand on printed circuit boards. The third generation is characterized by *integrated circuits,* solid pieces of silicon that contained the transistors, the other components, and their interconnections. These integrated circuits were much smaller, cheaper, faster, and more reliable than printed circuit boards (Figure 1–18).

Transistors also were used for memory construction. Each transistor represented one bit of information. Integrated-circuit technology allowed memory boards to be built using transistors. The magnetic core did not go away, however, because transistor memory is volatile; that is, the information goes away when the power is turned off.

The terminal, an input/output device with a keyboard and screen, was introduced during this generation. The keyboard gave the user direct access to the computer, and the screen allowed immediate response.

FIGURE 1-18 The integrated circuit was an important development in the third generation of computer hardware.

Software

During the third generation of commercial computers, it became apparent that the human was slowing down the computing process. Computers were sitting idle while waiting for the computer operator to prepare the next job. The solution was to put the computer resources under the control of the computer; that is, to write a program that would determine which programs were run when. This kind of program is called an **operating system**.

During the first two generations, utility programs had been written to handle often-needed tasks. *Loaders* loaded programs into memory, *linkers* linked pieces of large programs together, and *editors* input text in a general form. In the third generation, these utility programs were refined and put under the direction of the operating system. This group of utility programs, the operating system, and the language translators (assemblers and compilers) became known as **systems software**.

The introduction of computer terminals as input/output devices gave the user ready access to the computer, and advances in systems software gave the machine the ability to work much faster. However, inputting and outputting data from keyboards and screens is a slow process, much slower than carrying out instructions in memory. The problem was how to make use of the machine's greater capabilities. The solution was **time sharing**—many different users, each at a terminal, communicating (inputting and outputting) with a single computer all at the same time. Controlling the process was an operating system that organized and scheduled the different jobs.

For the users, time sharing is much like having their own computer. Each user is assigned a small slice of central processing time and then is put on hold while another user is serviced. Users generally aren't even aware that there are other users. However, if too many people try to use the system at the same time, there can be a noticeable wait for a job to be completed.

During the first two generations of computers, it was clear who the computer user was. A problem existed, and a programmer wrote a program in an assembly language or a high-level language to solve the problem. During the third generation, general-purpose application programs were being written. One example was the *Statistical Package for the Social Sciences* (SPSS). SPSS had a special language designed to be used as input to the program. This language allowed the user (who was not a programmer) to describe the data and the statistics to be computed on the data. Books were published describing the system. Suddenly there were computer users who were not programmers in the traditional sense.

The separation between user and hardware was growing wider. The hardware had become only a small part of the picture. A *computer system*—a combination of hardware and software—had emerged (Figure 1–19).

Although the layers of languages kept getting deeper, programmers continued (and still continue) to use some of the very inner layers. If a small

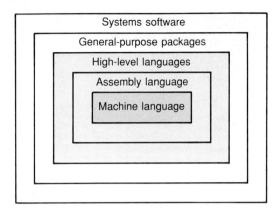

FIGURE 1-19 The layers of software surrounding the hardware continue to grow. However, programmers can still access the inner layers.

segment of code must be made to run as quickly as possible and take up as few memory locations as possible, it may still be programmed in an assembly language or even machine code today.

Fourth Generation (1971–Present)

Hardware

Large-scale integration characterizes this generation. From several thousand transistors to a silicon chip in the early 1970s, we moved to a whole microcomputer on a chip by the middle of the decade. Today, memories are made almost exclusively out of chip technology.

Over the last forty years, each generation of computer has become more and more powerful in a smaller and smaller package at lower and lower cost. And this trend continues, as we can see in Figure 1–20.

By the late 1970s, the phrase *personal computer (PC)* had entered the vocabulary. Microcomputers had become so cheap that almost anyone could have one. And a generation of kids grew up playing PacMan.

The fourth generation found some new names entering the commercial market. The big companies of earlier generations—IBM, UNIVAC, NCR, DEC, Hewlett Packard, Control Data, and Burroughs—were joined by Apple, Tandy/Radio Shack, Atari, Commodore, and Sun. The best-known success story of the personal computer revolution is that of the Apple. Steve Wozniak, an engineer, and Steve Jobs, a high-school student, created a personal computer kit and marketed it out of a garage. This was the beginning of Apple Computer, a multibillion dollar company.

The IBM PC was introduced in 1981 and soon was followed by compatible machines manufactured by many other companies. Apple introduced its very popular Macintosh microcomputer line in 1984. The trademark of the Macin-

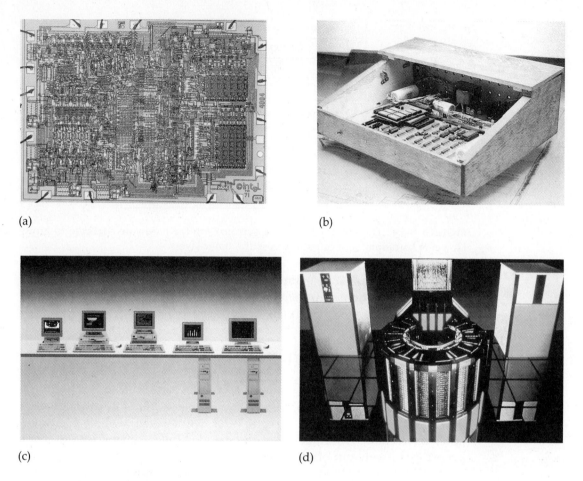

(a)   (b)

(c)   (d)

FIGURE 1–20   (a) The Intel 4004 microprocessor, (b) the original Apple Microcomputer Kit, (c) the IBM PS/2 family of microcomputers, (d) the Cray 2

tosh was ease of use. The line has been continually upgraded, and today the upper-end machines are quite powerful.

The drastic change in the power, size, and cost of computer components was brought home to us at a conference in the summer of 1988. IBM had a manufacturing unit in the exhibit area producing memory chips on the spot. Each chip held a million bits of memory in an element smaller than a thumbnail. These chips were not for sale; they were being given away as a souvenir to anyone who came by the booth!

Software

The 1970s saw the introduction of better programming techniques called *structured programming*, a logical, disciplined approach to programming. (See page 29.) The languages Pascal and Modula-2 were built on the principles of structured programming. And BASIC, a language introduced for third-generation machines, was refined and upgraded in more-structured versions.

Better and more powerful operating systems also were being developed. UNIX, developed at AT&T as a research tool, is now becoming an industry standard. PC-DOS, developed for the IBM PC, and MS-DOS, developed for compatibles, have become standards for personal computers. The operating system for the Macintosh, which accepts commands from a hand-operated device ("mouse") is very easy to use.

High-quality, reasonably priced *applications software packages* became available at neighborhood stores. These programs allow a user with no computer experience to do a specific task. Three typical kinds of application packages are *spreadsheets*, *word processors*, and *data base management systems*. Lotus 1-2-3, a spreadsheet, allows a user with no previous experience to enter and analyze all kinds of data. WordPerfect is a word processor. It was used to produce this text. dBase IV is a system that lets the user store, organize, and retrieve data. (See Figure 1–21.)

The 1980s must be characterized most of all by the changing profile of the user. During the 1950s and 1960s, the computer user was a programmer who wrote programs to solve problems, his or her own or someone else's. During the 1970s, the definition of user grew to include the nonprogrammer who was using general-purpose programs. With the advent of the personal computer, computer games, educational programs, and user-friendly software packages, everyone has become a computer user. The user is a first-grade child learning to read, a high-school student writing a paper, the homemaker planning a budget, a banker looking up a customer's loan record. The user is all of us.

The Future

von Neumann–type machines (sequential machines) have dominated computers for the past forty years. Today, radically new machine architectures are beginning to appear. These parallel architectures consist of a set of interconnected central processing units (each of which is a sequential machine).

One class of parallel machines is organized so that the central processors share the same memory unit. In another, each central processor has its own local memory and communicates with the others over a very fast internal network.

Parallel architectures offer several ways to increase the speed of execution. For example, a given step in a program can be executed simultaneously on each of many processors, with different sections of the data being worked on by each processor. These machines are called SIMD (*s*ingle *i*nstruction, *m*ultiple *d*ata stream) computers. A second class of machines can work on different parts of a program simultaneously. These machines are called MIMD (*m*ultiple *i*nstruction, *m*ultiple *d*ata stream) computers.

The potential of hundreds or even thousands of central processors combined in one machine is enormous. And the challenge to programmers is

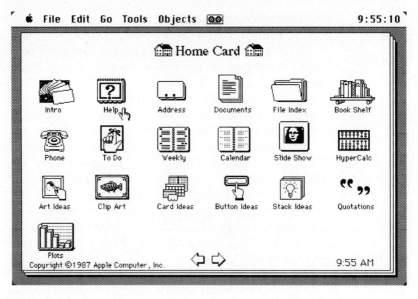

(a)

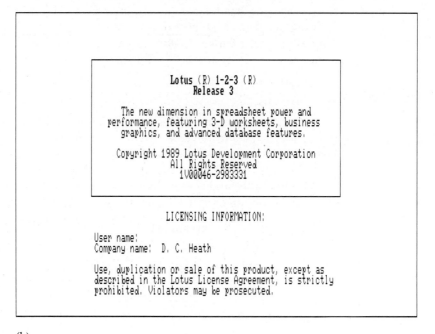

(b)

FIGURE 1–21 Opening screens of some common software packages: (a) the Macintosh Hypercard Software, (b) Lotus 1-2-3, (c) WordPerfect, and (d) dBase IV

```
                    ┌─────────────────────────┐
                    │       WordPerfect        │
                    ├─────────────────────────┤
                    │       Version 5.0        │
                    └─────────────────────────┘

                       (C)Copyright 1982,1988
                         All Rights Reserved
                      WordPerfect Corporation
                         Orem, Utah  USA



   NOTE: The WP System is using C:\WP50



   * Please wait *
```

(c)

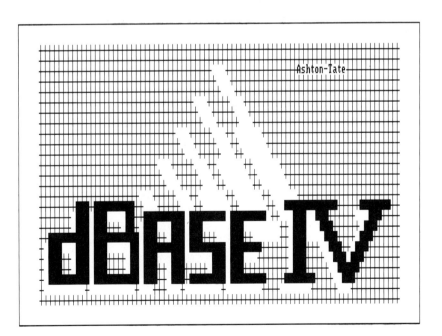

(d)

FIGURE 1–21 Continued

equally enormous. The procedures designed for parallel machines will not be the same as those designed for sequential machines. Programmers will have to rethink the ways in which they approach problem solving and programming in order to exploit parallelism.

The disciplines of algorithm design (problem solving) and program construction that are presented in this book are for sequential machines. But they should give you a foundation on which to tackle the problems of programming for parallel machines in the future.

Programming

What Is Programming?

A program is a sequence of instructions written to perform a specific task. **Programming** is the process of defining the sequence of instructions. There are two phases in this process: determining the task that needs doing and expressing the solution in a sequence of instructions.

> **Programming**
> The process of defining the sequence of instructions that make up a program.

The process of programming always begins with a problem. Programs are not written in isolation; they are written to solve problems. Determining what needs to be done means outlining the solution to the problem. This first phase, then, is the **problem-solving phase**.

> **Problem-Solving Phase**
> 1. *Analysis:* Understand (define) the problem.
> 2. *General solution (algorithm):* Develop a logical sequence of steps to be used to solve the problem.
> 3. *Test:* Follow the steps outlined to see if the solution really solves the problem.

The second phase, expressing the solution in a sequence of instructions, is the **implementation phase**. Here, the general solution outlined in the problem-solving phase is converted into a specific solution (a program in a specific language). Testing is part of both phases. The general solution must be shown to be correct before it is translated into a program.

Implementation Phase

1. *Specific solution (program):* Translate the general solution (algorithm) into statements in a programming language (code the algorithm).
2. *Test:* Have the computer follow the instructions. Check the results and make corrections until the answers are correct.
3. *Use:* Use the program.

The problem-solving and implementation phases interact with each other as shown in Figure 1–22. The programmer analyzes the problem and develops a general solution called an **algorithm**. Understanding and analyzing a problem take up much more time than the figure suggests. They are the heart of the programming process.

Algorithm

A step-by-step procedure for solving a problem in a finite amount of time.

We use algorithms every day. They are simply verbal or written descriptions of logical sequences of actions. Recipes and instructions for defrosting a refrigerator are examples of written algorithms.

When you start your car, you go through a step-by-step procedure. The algorithm might look something like this:

1. Insert key.
2. Make sure transmission is in Park (or Neutral).

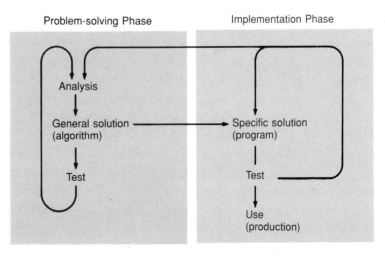

FIGURE 1–22 The programming process

3. Depress the gas pedal.
4. Turn the key to the "start" position.
5. If the engine starts within six seconds, release the key to the "ignition" position.
6. If the engine doesn't start in six seconds, wait ten seconds and repeat Steps 3 through 6 (but no more than five times).
7. If the car doesn't start, call the garage.

Without the phrase "but no more than five times" in Step 6, you could be trying to start the car forever. Why? Because if something is wrong with the car, repeating Steps 3 through 6 over and over again may not start it. This never-ending situation is called an **infinite loop**. If we left "but no more than five times" out of Step 6, our set of steps would not be an algorithm. An algorithm must terminate in a finite amount of time for all possible conditions.

After developing a general solution, we test it, "walking through" the algorithm, performing each step mentally or manually. If the test doesn't produce the correct answers, we repeat the process, analyzing the problem again and coming up with another algorithm. Once we're satisfied with the algorithm, we translate it into a programming language. We use the Pascal programming language in this book. Translating the algorithm into a programming language is called **coding** the algorithm. We test the resulting program by compiling and running it on a computer. If the program fails to produce the results we want, we have to analyze and modify it until it does.

If our definition of a computer program and an algorithm look alike, it's because all programs are algorithms. An algorithm can be in English, but when it is specified in a programming language it is also called a program.

Some students try to take a shortcut in the programming process by going directly from defining the problem to the coding of the program. (See Figure 1–23.) This shortcut is very tempting, and at first it seems to save a lot of time. However, for many reasons that will become obvious to you as you read this book, this approach actually takes more time and effort. By not taking the

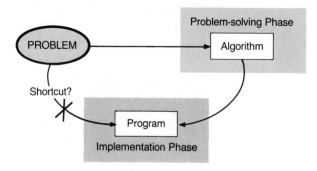

FIGURE 1–23 Programming shortcut?

time initially to think out and polish your algorithm, you will spend a lot of extra time correcting errors (**debugging**) and revising ill-conceived programs. So, think first and code later! The sooner you start coding, the longer it takes to get a correct program.

Pascal Programming

With the advent of third-generation computers, the power of the computer hardware had far outgrown the programmer's ability to manage it; that is, the hardware was capable of executing very large programs very rapidly. Yet the tools that the programmer was using to write these large programs were very primitive.

In a seminal article, "Notes on Structured Programming," published in 1972, Edsger W. Dijkstra pointed out that programmers should be precise and disciplined, that they should use only selected control structures. (**Control structures** are instructions that determine the order in which other instructions in a program are executed.) This article and the others published with it introduced the era of structured programming.* In a **structured program**, each logical unit of the program has just one entry and one exit. The programmer cannot randomly jump in and out of logical units.

The programming language Pascal was designed by Niklaus Wirth in 1968 in response to many of the problems of the programming languages in widespread use at that time. Pascal was formally introduced in 1971. The instructions in Pascal operate much like the control structures Dijkstra described one year later. These control structures are **sequence**, **loop**, **selection**, and **procedure**. We'll discuss these control structures as we learn more about designing good programs.

Although originally intended as a teaching tool for programming concepts, Pascal is now used in industry. Pascal compilers have been implemented on large and small computers. Its simplicity and readability make Pascal one of the best languages for teaching the concepts of programming.

Now, as a preview of coming attractions, let's look at an algorithm and the Pascal program to implement it.

SAMPLE PROBLEM

Problem: Calculate the average rainfall over a period of days.

Discussion: To do the job "by hand," you would write down the number of inches of rain that had fallen each day. Then you would add the figures up and divide the total by the number of days. This is exactly the algorithm we use in the program.

*See O. Dahl, E. W. Dijkstra, and C.A.R. Hoare, *Structured Programming* (New York: Academic Press, 1972).

SAMPLE PROBLEM, CONTINUED

Algorithm:

Average RainFall

Get total inches of rain
IF Total = 0.0
   THEN
      There wasn't any rain
   ELSE
      Average ← total/number of days

Selection construct. One thing is done if there is no rain; another thing is done if there is rain.

Procedure construct. The task of getting the total number of inches is stated in the main algorithm without saying how it is done. This task is expanded separately as a subalgorithm.

Get Total Inches of Rain

FOR number of days DO
   Get inches
   Add to total

Loop construct. The task of getting the number of inches and adding it to the total is repeated for each day.

Sequence construct. The task of getting inches is followed immediately by the task of adding the inches to the total.

The Pascal program that implements this algorithm is given below. Don't worry if you don't understand it. At this stage, you're not expected to. Before long, you will be able to understand all of it.

Incidentally, the information between the symbols (* and the symbols *) is meant for the human reader of the program. This kind of information is called a **comment** and is ignored by the Pascal compiler.

```
PROGRAM AverageRainFall(RainFile, OUTPUT);
(* The average rainfall over a period of days is calculated.   *)
(* The number of days and the rain statistics are on RainFile. *)

VAR
   Average,                 (* average rainfall               *)
   TotalRain : REAL;        (* total accumulated rain         *)
   NumberOfDays : INTEGER;  (* number of days in calculation *)
   RainFile : TEXT;         (* data file                      *)

(* **************************************************************** )
```

```
PROCEDURE GetInches(VAR RainFile : TEXT;
                    VAR NumberOfDays : INTEGER;
                    VAR TotalRain : REAL);
(* INPUT: RainFile                                   *)
(* OUTPUT: NumberOfDays, TotalRain                   *)
(* ACTION: NumberOfDays is read from File RainFile.  *)
(* Rain statistics for NumberOfDays are read and     *)
(* their sum is returned in TotalRain.               *)
(* ASSUMPTION: NumberOfDays is the first value on    *)
(* File RainFile, followed by NumberOfDays REAL      *)
(* values representing inches of rain.               *)

VAR
   Inches : REAL;         (* day's worth of rain     *)
   Counter : INTEGER;     (* loop control variable   *)

BEGIN  (* GetInches *)
  READLN(RainFile, NumberOfDays);
  TotalRain := 0.0;
  Counter := 1;
  WHILE Counter <= NumberOfDays DO
    BEGIN
      READLN(RainFile, Inches);
      TotalRain := TotalRain + Inches;
      Counter := Counter + 1
    END
END;   (* GetInches *)


(***************************************************************)


BEGIN   (* AverageRainFall *)
  RESET(RainFile);
  GetInches(RainFile, NumberOfDays, TotalRain);
  IF TotalRain = 0.0
    THEN
      WRITELN('There was no rain during this period.')
    ELSE
      BEGIN
        Average := TotalRain / NumberOfDays;
        WRITELN('The average rainfall over ', NumberOfDays,
                ' days was ', Average:7:3)
      END
END.    (* AverageRainFall *)
```

Getting Started

There are only three pieces of software that you will need: an editor (to enter your Pascal program), a Pascal compiler (to translate your source program), and an operating system (to allow you to interact with the editor and the compiler).

You can think of the operating system as a hallway that connects all the other pieces of software (Figure 1–24). When you first get on a machine (*log in*), the operating system puts a prompt on the screen. You enter the name of the software you want to use, and the operating system provides it. When you finish using the software, you must come back to the operating system (the hallway) before you can use another piece of software. Each piece of software is like a doorway. The operating system opens the door and ushers you into the room where the software you want to use is kept.

An **editor** is a program that allows you to use your keyboard and screen like a very smart electronic typewriter. In the editor you create a file of written information. A **file** is the information that you type in through the keyboard. It can contain a program or data for a program. You see what you type on the screen. Commands to the editor do what you would do by hand with a typewriter—change and rearrange letters, words, and sentences.

Editor

A program that lets you enter, modify, and save alphanumeric information from the keyboard.

File

An area in secondary storage that has a name and is used to hold a collection of data. The data itself also is referred to as a file.

FIGURE 1–24 The operating system is like a hallway. It connects all the other pieces of software. When you first get on a machine, the operating system puts a prompt on the screen. You enter the name of the software you want to use and the operating system provides it. When you finish using the piece of software, you must come back to the operating system (the hallway) before you can use any other piece of software.

When you are satisfied with what you have typed, you give your file a name and tell the editor to save it for you. Giving a file a name is like putting information into a folder with a label on it. You can pick up the file and carry it with you from one room to another.

When you leave the editor, the operating system comes back with a prompt that says it's ready for you to tell it where you want to go next. If you've created a Pascal program, you say that you want to **compile** (translate) your file (go to the Pascal room). The operating system opens the door, and you hand your file folder to the Pascal compiler.

The Pascal compiler attempts to translate your program. If the program contains grammatical errors (errors in syntax), the compiler tells you so. You then have to go back to the editing room to correct the mistakes. When your source program finally compiles correctly, the Pascal compiler leaves the object program in a file.

You tell the operating system that you are now ready to run the object program. The file containing the machine language program is taken into the execute room, where it is run. It's here, in the execute room, that the problem your program was written to solve actually gets solved.

When you're finished and ready to quit (*log out*), you tell the operating system. It opens the door marked exit, and you can leave.

We've chosen to illustrate this process through an analogy because we can't possibly cover all the many systems in use today. This book is designed to teach you a methodology for problem solving and the syntax (grammar) and semantics (meaning) of the Pascal programming language. It is not designed to teach you how to use an editor or an operating system. You will have to study the documentation of the editor and operating system for the computer you will be using.

The 4-Cs Corner

Although it's very important to have a good structured language, like Pascal, in which to implement a program, good programming begins with good problem solving. A bad solution will be a bad program no matter what language it's coded in. On the other hand, a good solution can be implemented using poor style.

Term papers usually receive two grades: one for content and one for style. A computer program also should be judged on content (correctness) and style. A program can run and even get the correct answer, but still be a bad program. A good program has four properties: clarity, conciseness, completeness, and correctness. Notice that correctness is only one of them.

Clarity. The structure of the solution is apparent from the code. The program is straightforward, precise, and readable. A clear program can be changed and modified easily.

Conciseness. The algorithm is efficient. The code of the implementation is efficient. There are no unnecessary calculations. There is no repetitive code (if code must be repeated, make it into a procedure). Make efficient use of memory; it may be a scarce resource. Remember the old joke "Sorry this letter is so long. I didn't have time to write a short one"? Take the time to write a short program.

Completeness. The algorithm is complete. Each possibility has been taken into consideration. Nothing has been forgotten. All possible error conditions have been anticipated. The program performs checks on all the input data. Because most programs will be modified over time, a complete program is one in which the design anticipates future changes.

Correctness. The program must be thoroughly tested. The tendency in a programming class is to run a program once or twice and say it's correct. This isn't good enough. Testing must be carefully planned. Test cases in which bad data is input to the program must be designed.

Testing is running a program with the intention of finding errors. Even if you've thoroughly tested a program, you can't say that it's correct. All you can say is that it has no known errors. Careful attention to problem solving, algorithm design, and coding is the best way to increase the probability of a program's being correct.

At the end of each chapter, we discuss the concepts presented there in light of these four properties.

One of the major concerns about software in the 1980s has been to define what we mean by a "good" program and to develop tools to help write good programs. Writing a good small program is not difficult; writing a good large program is another question. *Software engineering* deals with developing very large, "good" programs where the code is in the order of millions of lines and hundreds of programmers are working on the project. When the final product is put together, however, success or failure depends on the quality of each small piece of software.

Summary

A computer without any software is about as useful as a house wired for electricity in the middle of the desert. When we say *computer*, we mean "computer system": that is, the hardware (machine) and the software (programs).

The history of modern computing spans four generations, each characterized by the components used to build the hardware and the software tools developed to allow the programmer to make more productive use of the hardware.

Since the mid-1970s, the concept of the user has changed. A person no longer has to be a programmer in order to use a computer system. Software packages that allow someone with no experience to use a computer to perform a specific task (say accounting, word processing, or information management) are available at local computer stores.

In the balance of this book we'll teach you to take a problem that is solvable on a computer, design an algorithm to solve the problem, code the algorithm in the Pascal programming language, and run the program on a machine. That is, we'll teach you to be a programmer. And most important, in doing so we'll constantly focus on the 4-Cs of good programming: clarity, conciseness, completeness, and correctness.

Problem Solving, Syntax/Semantics, and Pascal Programs

- To be able to apply the following problem-solving strategies:

    Ask questions
    Look for things that are familiar
    Divide and conquer

- To be able to interpret syntax diagrams in order to identify and build legal Pascal constructs.

- To demonstrate your understanding of Pascal and memory by being able to define and use the following constructs:

    Identifiers
    Data types (INTEGER, REAL, CHAR, BOOLEAN)
    Constants
    Variables

- To demonstrate your understanding of Pascal and action by being able to define and use the following constructs:

    Assignment statements
    WRITE and WRITELN statements
    Compound statements

- To be able to follow a Pascal program, determining the contents of all the variables after the execution of each statement.

- To be able to write simple Pascal programs using the constructs defined in this chapter.

In Chapter 1 we described the two stages of the programming process: the problem-solving phase and the implementation phase. In the first part of this chapter, we discuss strategies to use in the problem-solving phase. In the second part of the chapter, we describe how you name things in Pascal, what simple data items look like, how to assign a data value to a named place, and how to print something on the screen. In the last part of the chapter, we show you how to put the pieces together to write a complete Pascal program.

Problem-Solving Process

We solve problems every day, often totally unaware of the process we are going through. In a school setting we usually are given most of the information we need: a clear statement of the problem, the given input, and the required output. In real life this usually is not the case; we often have to come up with the problem definition ourselves, then decide what we have to work with and what the results should be. In either case, after we understand the problem (the first step in any problem-solving situation) and analyze the possible approaches, we must come up with a set of steps that will solve the problem. This logical sequence of steps is our algorithm.

Although we work with algorithms all the time, most of our experience with them is in the context of following them. We follow a recipe, play a game, assemble a toy, or take medicine. We are all taught how to follow directions, how to execute an algorithm.

In the problem-solving phase of computer programming you will be designing algorithms, not following them. You will be given a problem and asked to devise an algorithm; that is, to design a set of steps to be carried out in order to solve the problem. Actually, we do this kind of problem solving all the time at an unconscious level. However, we don't write down our solutions; we just execute them.

Problem-Solving Strategies

In learning to program, you have to make conscious some of your underlying problem-solving strategies in order to apply them to programming problems. Let's look at some of the strategies we all use every day.

Ask Questions

If you're given a task verbally, you ask questions until you understand what you're supposed to do. You ask when, why, and where until the task is completely clear. If your instructions are on paper, you might put question marks in the margin; underline a word, phrase, or a sentence; or indicate in some other way that the task is not clear. Perhaps your questions will be answered by a later paragraph. If not, you might have to discuss them with the person who gave you the task.

If the task is one you've set for yourself, this sort of questioning is probably not verbal; it goes on in your head. Here are some typical questions you will be asking in the context of programming:

- What am I given to work with? (What is my data?)
- What does the data look like? What form does it take?
- How much data is there?
- How will I know when I've processed all the data?
- What should my output look like?
- How many times should the process be repeated?
- What special error conditions might come up?

Look for Familiar Things

Never reinvent the wheel. If a solution exists, use it. If you've solved the same or a similar problem before, just repeat the solution. We don't consciously think, "I've seen this before, and I know what to do"; we just do it. Humans are good at recognizing like situations. We don't have to learn how to go to the store to buy milk, then to buy eggs, then to buy candy. We know that going to the store is the same and only what we buy is different.

In programming, you'll see certain problems again and again in different guises. A good programmer immediately recognizes a subtask that's been solved before and uses that solution. For example, finding the daily high and low temperatures is exactly the same problem as finding the highest and lowest grades on a test. You want the largest and smallest numbers in a set of numbers. Many problems include at least one of the following tasks:

- Keeping a cumulative total (summing)
- Keeping a count (counting)
- Calculating an average (averaging)
- Locating the maximum in a list
- Locating the minimum in a list
- Sorting a list into numeric or alphabetical order

Divide and Conquer

We're constantly breaking up large problems into smaller, easier-to-handle units. Cleaning the house or apartment seems overwhelming. But if we take it one room at a time, it seems more manageable. The same principle applies to programming. We break up a large problem into smaller pieces that we can solve individually. The methodology outlined in Chapter 3 for designing algorithms is based on the principle of divide and conquer.

Applying Problem-Solving Strategies

Let's apply these strategies (called *heuristics*) to a specific problem: how to get to a party.

Problem: How can I get to the party?

Questions: Where is the party?
Where am I coming from?
What is the weather like (or likely to be like)?
Will I be walking? Driving a car? Taking a bus?

Once you've answered these questions, you can begin to design your algorithm.

If it's raining, your car is in the shop, and the buses aren't running, your best solution (algorithm) might be to call a taxi and give the driver the address. If you look at a map and see that where you're going is six blocks west of the building where you work, the first part of your algorithm might be to repeat what you do each morning to get to work (assuming you're leaving from home). The next part would be to start walking west, counting each street as you cross it, until you've gone six blocks. This is a technique you'll use frequently in your programs. If you want to repeat a process six times, you'll have to write the instructions to count each time you do the process and check to see when your count reaches six. This is the loop (looping) construct we mentioned in Chapter 1.

If you want to write a set of directions for other people, some leaving from one place and some from another, you would have to have two sets of instructions prefaced by the statement "If you are coming from Place A, follow the first set of directions; otherwise follow the second set of directions." This is an example of the selection (branching) construct we talked about in Chapter 1.

Coming up with a step-by-step procedure for solving a particular problem is seldom cut-and-dried. More often than not the process is one of trial and error, requiring repeated attempts and refinements. We test each attempt to see if it solves the problem. If it does, fine. If it doesn't, we try again.

When designing algorithms for computer programs, it's important to keep in mind that the computer stores, retrieves, and processes data—the information we've reduced to symbolic form. We have described algorithms that require physical actions by a human being. These algorithms clearly are not suitable for use on a computer, which is capable only of electronic actions. Your solution to a problem is the set of instructions you create for the computer to follow to solve the problem.

Our primary concern, then, is how the computer transforms, manipulates, calculates, and processes input data to produce the correct output or results. We can analyze the content (makeup) and form (order or pattern) of the input data, determine the required content and form of the output, and develop an algorithm the computer can follow to transform the input into the output. This is the heart of programming.

After the algorithm is written, we test it by hand, following the steps ourselves using sample data. When we are satisfied that the solution is correct, we code the algorithm in a programming language and run it on the computer.

Program AverageRainFall (see page 30) was coded from an algorithm that paralleled how a person would calculate average rainfall over a given period of time. The algorithm for doing something by hand often can be used with little or no modification as our general solution. Just keep in mind the things a computer can do. Remember what the allowable instructions in a programming language are. This is how you avoid designing an algorithm that is difficult or impossible to code.

We now leave the general topic of problem solving and begin to look at the specifics of the Pascal language. Pascal is the language into which you will convert your general solution (algorithm).

Syntax/Semantics

A programming language is a set of rules, symbols, and special words used to construct a program. There are rules for both syntax (grammar) and semantics (meaning). Syntax rules tell you how to specify an action; semantic rules tell you what actions you can specify.

Syntax Diagrams

There are several formal methods for describing the syntax of a programming language. We use **syntax diagrams** to define the simple syntactic structures of Pascal. To see how syntax diagrams work, let's use one to define a very simple language.

The syntax diagram below shows how to form sentences in this language. A sentence must begin with 'red', 'blue', or 'white' followed by 'car' or 'boat'. The sentence can end here, or 'and' can follow with another 'red', 'blue', or 'white', then 'car' or 'boat'. The pattern either ends or repeats and repeats and repeats.

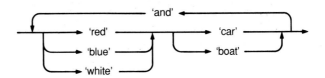

To use a syntax diagram (to generate sentences in a language), we begin at the left and follow the arrows. Where there is a branch, we can go either way. In our simple language, the following are legal sentences:

red car
white car
blue boat and red car
red boat and red car and red boat and white car . . .

We can give names to pieces of the diagram and rewrite the structure like this:

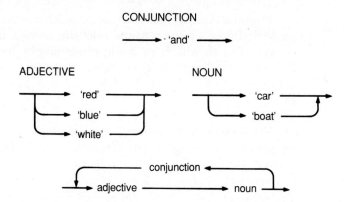

Everywhere there is an adjective, we can replace it with 'red', 'blue', or 'white'. Everywhere there is a noun, we can replace it with 'car' or 'boat'. The process of naming a part of something and using that name to stand for the part is very useful. In Chapter 6 you'll see how this technique can be used to help build a program out of simpler pieces.

From Problem Statement to Running Program

Before we look at individual Pascal constructs, let's look at a simple Pascal program and describe in words what the **statements** (instructions) mean. Because programs are written to solve problems, we begin with the problem statement.

Problem: You've bought a print at the campus bookstore. You decide to frame it yourself. How much wood should you buy?

Discussion: If you were calculating this by hand, you would take a tape measure and get the dimensions of the print. Then you would add twice one side and twice the top. This algorithm is exactly what we use in our program.

```
PROGRAM FrameCost(OUTPUT);

(* Amount of wood needed to frame a *)
(* print is calculated and printed. *)

CONST
   Side = 18;                  (* vertical dimension in inches   *)
   Top  = 24;                  (* horizontal dimension in inches *)
```

```
VAR
   InchesOfWood : INTEGER;      (* inches of wood needed           *)

BEGIN    (* FrameCost *)
   InchesOfWood := Side + Side + Top + Top;
   WRITELN('You need to buy ', InchesOfWood, ' inches of wood.')
END.     (* FrameCost *)
```

There are two basic parts to any Pascal program: instructions to the Pascal compiler and instructions that define the necessary processing. The instructions between the BEGIN-END pair (called *executable statements*) describe the processing. The statements above them give the compiler the information it needs to translate the source program into machine language.

The first line names the program. The word OUTPUT following the name tells the compiler that there will be printed output on the screen. The semicolon is a **statement separator**; it tells the compiler where one instruction ends and another begins in a program.

The statement CONST Side = 18 tells the compiler to set aside a place in memory, give it the name Side, and place the integer number 18 there. The statement Top = 24 tells the compiler to set aside a place in memory, give it the name Top, and place the integer number 24 there. The semicolon after the number 18 separates the two statements.

The statement VAR InchesOfWood : INTEGER tells the compiler to set aside a place in memory and give it the name InchesOfWood. The compiler puts nothing in that place; when the program is executing, one of the statements will cause an integer value (a positive or negative whole number) to be put in that place. InchesOfWood is a *variable*. The value to be put in that place is not known, but its type is; that is, it can contain only an integer value.

The action part of the program is between the BEGIN-END pair. These statements are translated by the compiler into instructions that the computer executes when the program is run. InchesOfWood is assigned the result of adding the values in Side and Top twice.

The statement beginning with the word WRITELN causes a message to be written on the screen. The characters between single quotes are written exactly as shown. Where the word InchesOfWood appears, the content of the place in memory called InchesOfWood is written to the screen.

Semicolons are used to separate Pascal statements. The period after END signals the end of the program.

The Pascal compiler takes this program as input and translates it into machine code. A stylized version of the translated program is shown below. Memory cells are labeled in the upper left-hand corner. The statements in single quotes represent the translated versions of the statements.

MEMORY

Side
18
Top
24
InchesOfWood
?
'InchesOfWood := Side + Side + Top + Top'
'WRITELN(...)'

During the compilation (translation) phase, the compiler sets aside three memory locations and gives them the names Side, Top, and InchesOfWood. The values 18 and 24 are stored in Side and Top respectively. The content of InchesOfWood is undefined, which is indicated by a question mark. The statements between the BEGIN-END pair are translated into machine language and stored in consecutive places in memory.

During the execution phase, the translated instructions are carried out. The content of Side is copied into a register (a calculator). The content of Side is added into the same register. The content of Top is added into the same register. And the content of Top is added into the same register. The content of this register is stored in the place named InchesOfWood. Finally, the following sentence is written to the screen:

```
You need to buy 84 inches of wood.
```

We now look in detail at how to construct names, how to name a place in memory, how to specify the value that should go there (if it is a constant), how to specify the type of the value that can go there (if it is a variable), how to construct an assignment statement, and how to write output from the program to the screen.

Identifiers

Identifiers are used in Pascal to name things. Some identifiers—like CONST and VAR—are defined in the language and reserved for specific uses. Any other names can be defined for your own use. Identifiers are formed with letters and digits. FrameCost, Side, Top, and InchesOfWood are identifiers in Program FrameCost.

> ### Identifiers
> Names that are associated with processes and objects and used to refer to those processes and objects. Identifiers are made up of letters (a–z, A–Z) and digits (0–9) but must begin with a letter.

IDENTIFIER

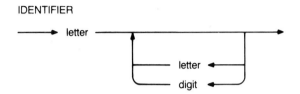

The following are examples of valid identifiers:

BoxScore   Average   Get3Data   Counter1   Sum

Pascal is not case sensitive. This means that DATA, data, and Data are all the same identifier. For us, a meaningful mixture of uppercase and lowercase is easier to read; the computer doesn't care. Identifiers can be any length, but some compilers ignore all but the first few characters. For example, the identifiers

DataItem1   DataItem2

are both valid, but the compiler may treat them as the same identifier. Possible solutions might be

Data1   Data2

or

Data1Item   Data2Item

In Program AverageRainFall (see page 30), the user-defined identifiers listed below were used. Notice that the names we chose convey information about them. (The other identifiers in the program are predefined in Pascal.)

Identifier	How It Is Used
AverageRainFall	Name of the program
Average	Average rainfall
TotalRain	Total number of inches of rain
NumberOfDays	Number of days to be averaged
RainFile	File containing the statistics
GetInches	Name of program unit that inputs the data
Inches	Number of inches of rain in a day
Counter	Keeps track of the number of times an action is repeated

Pascal and Memory

Memory

Memory is divided into a large number of separate locations, each of which can hold a piece of data. Each memory location has an address that can be used to refer to it when data is stored in it or retrieved from it. We can visualize memory as a set of post office boxes, with the box numbers as the addresses used to designate particular locations (Figure 2–1).

We could refer to memory locations by their addresses, as machine language programmers do. But how would you like to try to keep track of data stored in location 101101101? Or was it location 1011011001? Fortunately, Pascal and other high-level languages offer an alternative. In Pascal we can use identifiers as the names of memory locations. The computer keeps track of the address that corresponds to each name. It's as if we put only the names on our letters and left the post office to look up the addresses.

We can use identifiers for both *constant* and *variable* names. In other words, an identifier can be the name of a memory location whose content never changes or the name of a memory location whose content can change.

Each word or cell in memory contains a fixed number of binary digits. The pattern of bits in a word can be interpreted as a machine instruction, a number in one of several forms, alphabetic information, or a value that is either true or false. How does the machine know how to interpret a bit pattern? If the content of a memory location is placed in an instruction register, it is interpreted as a machine language instruction. In all other cases, the programmer tells the system how to interpret the content of the memory location by defining the type of data that can be stored there.

The type of a data object is the general form of the class of object. In Chapter 8 we formally define data type. Here we content ourselves with an intuitive definition of the types of data objects that are so common that they are built into the Pascal language.

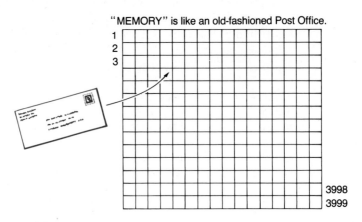

"MEMORY" is like an old-fashioned Post Office.

FIGURE 2–1   Memory

Data Types

Pieces of data are symbols that represent information. A computer program operates on data (stored internally in memory, stored externally on a file on tape or disk, or input from a terminal or electrical sensor) and produces output. When we write a program, the data is our "given"; it is what we must process to produce what we want to produce.

In Pascal each item must be of a specific *type*. The data type affects the representation and processing of the piece of data. In addition to some basic built-in data types, Pascal allows users to define new data types. (We discuss user-defined data types in Chapter 8.)

There are four simple types of data values that come up so often that Pascal has built-in rules about what they look like and what we can and cannot do with them.

INTEGER

Integers are positive or negative whole numbers (no fractional part). They are made up of a sign and digits:

+22   −16   1   −426   0   4600

When the sign is omitted, the integer is assumed to be positive. Commas are not allowed.

Theoretically, integers can be any size, but computer hardware and practical considerations place limits on them. Because these limits vary among machines, Pascal has a predefined identifier—called **MaxInt**—whose value is set to the largest integer number that can be represented in a given computer. If MaxInt is 32767, the range of integers allowed is

−MaxInt through MaxInt

or

−32767 through 32767

MaxInt may be different for your machine, so you should print it to see how large it is. (This requires a Pascal program that you'll be able to write by the end of this chapter.)

NumberOfDays, the identifier for the number of days in Program AverageRainFall is of type INTEGER.

REAL

Real numbers are decimal numbers. We cover them in detail in Chapter 7. What you need to know now are two things:

1. When writing real numbers in your program or inputting them as data, always use a decimal point with at least one digit on either side. Scientific notation (see page 57) is also acceptable.

Valid	Not Valid
3.1415	.42
−111.011	16.
76.43	.2
0.43	−.374
−1.0	

2. Beware of comparing real numbers. Just as there is a limit on the size of an integer number, there is a limit on how accurate real numbers can be. For example, we know that $\frac{1}{3} + \frac{1}{3} + \frac{1}{3}$ add up to 1. Even though $\frac{1}{3}$ is a repeating fraction, in a computer 0.333 stops when there are as many digits (3s) as that particular machine can represent. Therefore, if we summed three real numbers each containing the result of dividing 1 by 3 and asked if the sum were equal to 1.0, the answer would be *no* (0.333 + 0.333 + 0.333 = 0.999).

In Program AverageRainFall, the identifiers Average, TotalRain, and Inches are all of type REAL because they are identifiers for things that logically have decimal points.

CHAR

Data type **CHAR** describes data that consists of one alphanumeric character. **Alphanumeric characters** are letters, digits, and special symbols. For example,

'A'　'a'　'8'　'2'　'+'　'−'　'$'　'?'　'*'　'□'

Every machine has a **character set**, a set of alphanumeric characters that it can represent. (See Appendix I for the three most common character sets.) Your machine may not support both uppercase and lowercase letters. If not, you have to use uppercase only. Notice that each character is enclosed in single quotes. The Pascal compiler needs the quotes to differentiate between the character '8' or '+' and the integer 8 or the addition sign. Notice also that blank, '□', is a character.

You can't add '8' and '3', but you can compare data values of type CHAR. The character set of every machine is ordered in what is known as the **collating sequence**. Although this sequence varies from one machine to another, it is comforting to know that 'A' is always less than 'B', 'B' is always less than 'C', and so forth. Also '1' is always less than '2', '3' is always less than '4', and so on. Later we discuss a program that prints out the collating sequence for your machine. None of the identifiers in Program AverageRainFall are of type CHAR.

BOOLEAN

BOOLEAN is a data type with just two values: TRUE and FALSE. This type is associated with data created within your program and is used to represent the answers to questions. The importance of type BOOLEAN will become clearer in Chapter 4, where we discuss conditions and how decisions are made by the computer. The ability to choose alternate courses of action (selection) is an important part of a programming language. BOOLEAN data cannot be read in as data, as the other types can, but it can be printed out.

The *B* in Boolean is always capitalized because it is named for George Boole (1815–1864), an English mathematician who invented a system of logic using variables with just two values, TRUE and FALSE. When we talk about a BOOLEAN data type in Pascal, however, we capitalize the whole word.

We have defined identifiers that are the names of data objects or actions. We have defined four types of data objects that can be stored in memory. Now we examine how to tell the compiler to associate a name (an identifier) with a place in memory and store a permanent value in that place.

Constants

All the specific instances of values that are legal for a data type are called the **constants** for that type. For example, any integer number that is written down and is within the range of −MaxInt to MaxInt is a constant in the Pascal data type INTEGER. A number that is written down with a decimal is a REAL constant. An alphanumeric character that is written down between single quotes and is in the character set of a particular machine is a CHAR constant. The words TRUE and FALSE are the constants in data type BOOLEAN. Pascal also recognizes a type of constant called a **string constant**, a series of alphanumeric characters written within single quotes.

Constants
All the specific instances of values that are legal for a data type.

Here are examples of each type:

3, 5, 1001, 32000, −4	INTEGER constants
0.006, 32000.0, −1.1	REAL constants
'a', 'A', '1', '*'	CHAR constant
TRUE, FALSE	BOOLEAN constants
'This is a string', 'Ant'	String constants

Notice that the CHAR and string constants are in single quotes. This is to differentiate them from identifiers. 'Ant' (in quotes) is the character string made up of the letters *A*, *n*, and *t* in that order. Ant (without the quotes) is an identifier, the name of a place in memory. To include an apostrophe (single-quote character) within a string, we use two apostrophes (single quotes) with no space between them. For example, 'Mary''s book' is a string that contains an apostrophe.

The Pascal construct that instructs the compiler to set aside a memory cell (perhaps more than one in the case of a string constant) and store a constant in that place is the section of a program headed by the word CONST. The syntax diagram looks like this:

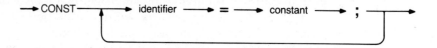

Notice that an = appears between the identifier and the literal (value) in the definition. Here is an example of a valid CONST section:

```
CONST
  Comma = ',';
  Pi = 3.1416;
  NumberOfBlanks = 5;
  TaxRate = 37.0;
  Label = 'Average rainfall for the month of January';
```

Notice the semicolon that follows each constant definition to separate it from the following one.

Constants also can be written directly into statements within the action part of a program. That is, if we were doing a tax calculation, we could say

```
Tax := NetSalary * TaxRate;
```

or

```
Tax := NetSalary * 37.0;
```

In the first statement, TaxRate is a **named constant**, a location in memory referenced by an identifier whose value cannot be changed. In the second statement, the value 37.0 is a **literal constant** or simply a literal; it has a specific value. There are two reasons for using named constants instead of literal constants. First, named constants make programs easier to read. Second, only one line has to be changed if the value changes. For example, if the tax rate changes, only the line in the CONST definition section needs changing if a named constant is used. If we use a literal constant, we would have to change each line in the program where that constant appears. When we use the word *constant*, we usually are referring to a named constant.

Named Constant

A location in memory where a data value that cannot be changed is stored.

Literal Constant

A constant value written in a program.

Variables

Your program operates on data. This data can be of one of the simple types we've discussed: INTEGER, REAL, CHAR, or BOOLEAN. Data is stored in memory. While a program is running, different values can be stored in the same memory location at different times. We call the memory location a **variable**, and its content the *value of the variable*. The symbolic name that we assign to this memory location (variable) is called a *variable name* or *variable identifier*.

Variable

A location in memory, referenced by a variable name (identifier), where a data value can be stored (this value can be changed while the program is being executed).

We refer to the variable name as the variable and say that its value changes. Actually, the memory location is the variable and its content is what changes.

In a Pascal program, variables must be "declared" in the **declaration section**, one of the sections that precedes the action part of the program. A **variable declaration** specifies both the name of the variable and its data type. It tells the compiler to name a memory location whose content will be of a specific type. The type of a variable determines the operations that are allowed on that variable and the way its content is represented in the machine.

Pascal is a strongly typed language. This means that only data values of the specified type can be stored in a variable. By checking for the correct type, the compiler can also catch syntax errors such as an attempt to add a variable of type CHAR to a variable of type INTEGER.

This is the syntax diagram of a variable declaration:

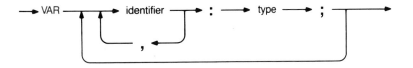

Notice that a colon appears between the identifier and the data type specification. These are valid variable declarations:

```
VAR
   Counter : INTEGER;
   Cost, Discount : REAL;
   Initial : CHAR;
   IsFound : BOOLEAN;
```

The reserved word VAR denotes the beginning of the variable declarations. Although we can have string constants, we cannot have string variables because string is not a built-in data type in standard Pascal. Some compilers do support this type, however. (In Chapter 9, we discuss a way to create variables that contain alphanumeric strings.)

Let's look at the VAR section of Program AverageRainFall:

```
VAR
   Average,                 (* average rainfall            *)
   TotalRain : REAL;        (* total accumulated rain      *)
   NumberOfDays : INTEGER;  (* number of days in calculation *)
   RainFile : TEXT;         (* data file                   *)
```

This section tells the compiler to set up locations in memory for one variable called NumberOfDays, which will contain an INTEGER value, and for two variables called Average and TotalRain, which will contain REAL values. Notice that one or more variable identifiers can be listed with commas between them for a given data type and that a semicolon follows each data type to act as a separator. (Type TEXT is explained in Chapter 3.)

Constant definitions (if there are any) come before variable declarations, as shown in Program FrameCost. As a general rule, all identifiers in Pascal, including constants and variables, must be defined or declared before they are used. This is why the declaration section comes before the main body of the program.

Pascal and Action

Assignment Statements

We change the value of a variable through an **assignment statement**. For example,

```
NumberOfDays := 31;
```

assigns the value 31 to the variable NumberOfDays (places 31 in the memory location called NumberOfDays). This is the syntax diagram of an assignment statement:

$$\longrightarrow \text{variable} \longrightarrow := \longrightarrow \text{expression} \longrightarrow$$

The **assignment operator** : = is read "becomes"; the variable *becomes* the value of the expression. An **expression** is made up of variables and constants combined with appropriate operators.

Expression

A sequence of identifiers (variables and constants) separated by compatible operators.

An assignment statement is not like an equation in mathematics (for example, $x + y = z + 4$); only one variable can be on the left-hand side of an assignment statement. The expression (what's on the right-hand side of the : =) is evaluated, and that value is stored in the single variable on the left of the assignment operator. The value assigned to a variable must be of the same type as that variable. For example, given the following definitions and declarations,

```
CONST
  RealRate = 0.0515;

VAR
  Count1 : INTEGER;
  RealValue : REAL;
  Character : CHAR;
  TestResult : BOOLEAN;
```

the following are valid assignment statements:

```
  Count1 := 0;
  RealValue := RealRate;
  Character := 'A';
  TestResult := FALSE;
```

These are not valid assignments:

```
  Count1 := RealValue;      Count1 is INTEGER; RealValue is REAL.
  Character := 0;           Character is CHAR; 0 is INTEGER.
  TestResult := 0;          TestResult is BOOLEAN; 0 is INTEGER.
```

Variables keep their assigned values until they are changed by another assignment statement (or until we read another value into them, as shown in Chapter 3).

Expressions are made up of constants, variables, and **operators** (symbols that indicate what operation should be performed). The following are all valid expressions:

```
Count1 + 1
RealValue * RealRate
RealValue - 3.0
Count1
TestResult
```

The operators allowed in an expression depend on the data type of the constants or variables in the expression. The **arithmetic operators** are

+	Addition
−	Subtraction
*	Multiplication
/	Division
DIV	Integer division (quotient with no fractional part)
MOD	Modulus (remainder from integer division)

You're familiar with most of these operators, but let's take a closer look at DIV and MOD. When we divide one integer by another integer, we get an integer quotient and an integer remainder. DIV gives only the integer quotient with no fractional part; MOD gives only the remainder.

$$
\begin{array}{cc}
3 \leftarrow 7\ \text{DIV}\ 2 & 2 \leftarrow 8\ \text{DIV}\ 3 \\
2\,\overline{)7} & 3\,\overline{)8} \\
\underline{6} & \underline{6} \\
1 \leftarrow 7\ \text{MOD}\ 2 & 2 \leftarrow 8\ \text{MOD}\ 3
\end{array}
$$

Here are some more examples of how arithmetic operators work:

Expression	Value
3 + 6	9
3 − 6	−3
2 * 3	6
9 DIV 2	4
9 DIV 8	1
9 DIV 9	1
5 DIV 7	0
8 MOD 8	0
8 MOD 9	8
8 MOD 7	1
0 MOD 4	0

Be careful; anything MOD 0 and anything DIV 0 will give an error. You cannot divide by zero.

Because variables are allowed in expressions, the following are valid assignments:

```
RealValue := RealRate * RealRate;
Count1 := Count1 + 1;
Count1 := Count1 MOD 2;
```

Notice that the same variable can appear on both sides of the assignment operator. In the case of

```
Count1 := Count1 + 1;
```

the 1 is added to the value stored in Count1 and the result is placed back into Count1.

REAL values are added, subtracted, and multiplied just like INTEGER values. However, DIV and MOD have no meaning when applied to REAL values. To divide with REAL values, we use the division operator /.

If one operand is REAL and one is INTEGER, the INTEGER value is converted to REAL before the operation is performed. If you use / between two INTEGER variables, both are converted to REAL before the division is done. The result is REAL.

It is valid to assign INTEGER values to REAL variables because it is clear what you want done. Any INTEGER value can be exactly represented in REAL form. For example, 2 can be 2.0, 42346 can be 42346.0. However, you cannot assign a REAL value to an INTEGER variable because it is not clear what you want done with the fractional part. If the REAL value is 1.7, what happens to the .7? If something is ambiguous, it's illegal.

Given the declarations

```
VAR
  A, B : INTEGER;
  X : REAL;
```

the following statements are valid:

Statement	Result
A := B + 2;	B + 2 gives an INTEGER result that is stored in an INTEGER place.
X := A + B;	A + B gives an INTEGER result that is automatically converted to REAL to be stored in a REAL place.
X := A DIV B;	A DIV B gives an INTEGER result that is automatically converted to REAL to be stored in a REAL place.
X := A / B;	A / B gives a REAL result. No conversion is necessary.
X := 2 + 2.3;	An INTEGER plus a REAL gives a REAL result that can be stored in a REAL place.

The following statements are *not* valid:

Statement	Result
A := B + 2.0;	An INTEGER plus a REAL gives a REAL that cannot be stored in an INTEGER place.
B := A - X;	An INTEGER minus a REAL gives a REAL result that cannot be stored in an INTEGER place.
A := A / B;	An INTEGER / an INTEGER gives a REAL that cannot be stored in an INTEGER place.
A := X DIV B;	The operands on either side of DIV must be INTEGER.
B := A + 2 / B;	The / gives a REAL result that cannot be stored in an INTEGER place.

Table 2–1 summarizes the resulting type, given the operator and the types of the operands. Remember that you can assign an INTEGER result to a REAL variable, but you *cannot* assign a REAL result to an INTEGER variable.

Look at the last example of statements that are not valid. It brings up another question. If we rewrite the statement so that it's correct (X : = A + 2 / B;), which is done first, the addition or the division?

The order in which arithmetic operations are performed in Pascal is the same as in standard arithmetic: left to right in order of **precedence**. Three scans are involved:

1. A left-to-right scan is made and all exponentiation is done.
2. A left-to-right scan is made and all multiplications and divisions are done (including DIV and MOD) in the order in which they appear.
3. A left-to-right scan is made and all additions and subtractions are done in the order in which they appear.

Parentheses can be used to override the natural order of precedence. The calculations within parentheses are always done first. In Pascal, there is no exponentiation operator, so only the last two scans are necessary. Here are some examples:

TABLE 2–I

	Types of Operands			
Operator	REAL REAL	REAL INTEGER	INTEGER REAL	INTEGER INTEGER
+	REAL	REAL	REAL	INTEGER
−	REAL	REAL	REAL	INTEGER
*	REAL	REAL	REAL	INTEGER
/	REAL	REAL	REAL	REAL
DIV	error	error	error	INTEGER
MOD	error	error	error	INTEGER

10 DIV 2 * 3 = 15
10 MOD 3 − 4 DIV 2 = -1
5 * 2 / 4 * 2 = 5.0
5 * 2 / (4 * 2) = 1.25
5 + 2 / (4 * 2) = 5.25

Output Statements

Because a computer rarely produces answers (output) just for other computers, programming languages always provide a way for the computer to return information in a form for human consumption. The WRITE statement is one of the Pascal instructions to produce this output. It is one of a set of built-in standard **subprograms**, called *standard procedures*, that do common tasks.

The **parameter list** is a list of the expressions whose contents the user wants to have printed on the screen. (Remember, variables and constants are also expressions.)

Integer and String Expressions

String constants are used to generate text messages. Remember to enclose them in single quotes to differentiate them from identifiers. Each parameter in the list is separated by a comma. The number of spaces an integer expression occupies on the output line depends on the default value built into the compiler. (The **default value** is the value the compiler assumes when no specific value is assigned by the program.) In the following examples we assume that value is five character positions. (On page 58, we show you how to set the number of positions yourself.)

Statement	What Is Printed (□ is a blank)
Data1 := 3; Data2 := 7; WRITE(Data1); WRITE('Data1:', Data1); WRITE('Sum = ', Data1 + Data2); WRITE(Data1 * Data2);	 □□□□3 Data1:□□□□3 Sum□=□□□□10 □□□21

All the parameters of successive WRITE statements are output on one line. In fact, the output of the program segment above is actually

□□□□3Data1:□□□□3Sum□=□□□□10□□□21

The WRITELN statement is similar to the WRITE statement, but it has the added feature of causing the *next* output to be printed on the following line. For example,

```
WRITE('Play');
WRITE(' it ');
WRITE('again Sam');
WRITE('.');
```

produces

```
Play it again Sam.
```

whereas

```
WRITE('Play');
WRITELN(' it ');
WRITE('again Sam');
WRITELN('.');
```

produces

```
Play it
again Sam.
```

You can use the WRITELN statement to generate blank lines:

```
WRITELN('Play it again,');
WRITELN;
WRITELN('Sam.');
```

produces

```
Play it again,

Sam.
```

Both WRITE and WRITELN statements print what is specified on one line, but the WRITELN causes subsequent output to start on the following line (it generates a line feed). Think of a line of output being accumulated, ready to be written. Both WRITE and WRITELN put the values to be written to the right of those already on the line. A pointer is left by one WRITE or WRITELN telling the next WRITE or WRITELN where to begin to put values on the output line. WRITE leaves the pointer where it left off. WRITELN leaves the pointer at the beginning of the next line.

Character Expressions

Because data type CHAR is defined as one alphanumeric character, writing out the content of a place defined to be of type CHAR writes exactly one character. If Ch1 is 'A' and Ch2 is 'b',

```
WRITE(Ch1, Ch2);
```

produces

```
Ab
```

If you want a blank to appear in your output, you must specifically indicate that a blank should be written by leaving a blank space within the single quotes. For example,

```
Grade := 'A';
WRITE('Your grade is', Grade);
```

produces

```
Your grade isA
```

which is not very readable.

```
WRITE('Your grade is ', Grade, '.');
```

is better. It produces

```
Your grade is A.
```

Real Expressions

```
RealValue := 32.7;
WRITE(RealValue);
```

produces

```
3.2700000000000E+001
```

which looks rather strange. This representation of real numbers is called **scientific notation**. The number after the E is the power of 10 by which the first part of the number must be multiplied to get the actual value. The number of digits to the left of the E is set as a default and can be changed. The number of digits in the exponent (the number to the right of the E) is set by the compiler and depends on how the particular machine represents real numbers. (We say more about this in Chapter 7.)

Formatting Output

Integer Numbers and Alphanumeric Characters. You can control what your output looks like by indicating the number of *columns* you want a variable or constant to occupy in the output line. You do this by inserting a colon (:) followed by an integer value after the variable or constant name. The integer following the colon (:) says how many columns (character positions) on the line the printed value of the variable or constant should occupy. The number of character positions you specify is called the **fieldwidth specification**.

When it is printed, the value of a variable or constant aligns at the right of the specified fieldwidth (number of columns), with blanks to the left, filling up the specified number of columns. Let's look at an example:

Answer = 33 (INTEGER)
Number = 7132 (INTEGER)
Letter = 'Z' (CHAR)

WRITE (statement parameters)	OUTPUT (□ is a blank)
a. (Answer:4, Number:5, Letter:3)	□□33□7132□□Z
b. (Answer:4, Number:4, Letter:1)	□□337132Z
c. (Answer:6, Letter:2, Number:5)	□□□□33□Z□7132
d. (Letter:6, Number:4)	□□□□□Z7132
e. (Answer:1, Number:1, Letter:1)	337132Z

In (a) the value 33 is printed with 2 blanks to the left; the value 7132 is printed with 1 blank to the left; and Z is printed with 2 blanks to the left. In (b) the values 33, 7132, and Z all run together, making them difficult to read. In (c) there are extra blanks for readability; in (d) there are none. In (e) the fieldwidth is not large enough for the number. In this case the number of columns is automatically extended so that all the digits are printed.

In addition to lining up the output, you must be sure to explain each item of output; that is, to insert column headings or explanatory statements to identify each output value.

The same spacing convention holds true for literals. For example:

WRITE (statement parameters)	OUTPUT (□ is a blank)
a. ('The answer is':16)	□□□The□answer□is
	16 columns
b. ('□':5, '#':4)	□□□□□□□□#
	9 columns

In (a) 3 blanks are inserted at the left to make up the 16 character positions. In (b) the first 5 blanks come from '□':5 and the next 3 are filled in to make '#':4 cover 4 positions. Note that '#':4 does not make four copies of '#'; '#' is in the fourth position with 3 leading blanks.

Our examples use INTEGER constants to specify fieldwidth, but INTEGER variables and expressions also can be used.

Real Numbers. The default option for printing real numbers is scientific notation. There are various ways to format scientific notation (see Chapter 7). Here we show you how to format real numbers in the form that most people are used to: the whole number, decimal point, and fractional part.

As in the representation of integers and characters, a colon (:) is used to indicate the number of column positions the real number should occupy. With real numbers we also can specify how many decimal places we want to show. This is done with a second colon (:) following the fieldwidth specification. That is, Answer:10:5 says that the total fieldwidth should be 10 character positions and that 5 decimal places should be printed.

Value = 310.0
Percent = 0.13

WRITE (statement parameters)	OUTPUT (□ is a blank)
a. (Value:10:2)	□□□□310.00
b. (Value:10:5)	□310.00000
c. (Value:8:5)	310.00000
d. (Percent:8:3)	□□□0.130
e. (Percent:8:1)	□□□□□□0.1

In (a) the value 310.0 is printed with 4 leading blanks and 2 decimal digits in the fractional portion. In (b) the value 310.0 is printed with 1 leading blank and 5 decimal digits after the decimal point. In (c) the fieldwidth is 8 but the number of digits that it must print plus the decimal point is 9; therefore, the fieldwidth was expanded to 9. If the content of Value had been −310.0, the fieldwidth would have been expanded to 10 to accommodate the minus sign.

In (d) the value 0.13 is printed with 3 leading blanks and 3 digits after the decimal point. In (e) the last digit of the fractional portion is not printed because the number of digit positions after the decimal point is adhered to explicitly; this field is never expanded.

Compound Statements

The executable statement section of a program (the part between the BEGIN-END pair) is called a **compound statement**. This is the syntax diagram for a compound statement:

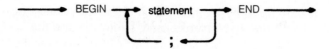

And this is the syntax diagram for a statement:

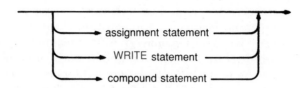

A statement can be the null statement (empty statement), an assignment statement, a named action (like WRITE or WRITELN), or another compound statement. This is important because wherever a statement can be used, a compound statement can be used. We will be using compound statements often, especially as part of other statements.

The BEGIN-END pair sets the limits of a compound statement. Leaving out a BEGIN-END pair can dramatically change the meaning as well as the execution of a program.

Tracing Program Variables

The computer is a literal device—it does exactly what we instruct it to do, not necessarily what we intend for it to do. We can try to make sure that our program does what we want by tracing the action part of the program before we run it (this is also useful during debugging). **Tracing** means following the logical flow of a program and determining the value of variables after each instruction. This technique is known by many names: *playing computer, desk checking, doing a dry run,* or *doing a code walk-through.*

To trace the execution of a program, take a copy of the program and, to the right, make a column for each constant and variable in the program. Put the name of each constant and variable in the column when it is defined or declared. On the line associated with the first BEGIN, write the value of each constant and variable. Constants, of course, have values at this point; variables are undefined (use a question mark). Number each line in the program for easy reference.

Once you have set up the table, go through the execution part of the program by hand. After each statement, fill in the values for each constant and variable. Here's an example:

Line	Statement	Constant	Variables
1	PROGRAM Trace(INPUT, OUTPUT);		
2	CONST		
3	X = 5;	X	

```
 4      VAR
 5         A, B, C : INTEGER;                          A    B    C
 6      BEGIN    (* Trace *)          5               ?    ?    ?
 7         B := 1;                    5               ?    1    ?
 8         C := X + B + 2;            5               ?    1    8
 9         A := C + 4;                5              12    1    8
10         A := C + A;                5              20    1    8
11         B := C;                    5              20    8    8
12         A := A + B + C;            5              36    8    8
13         C := C MOD X;              5              36    8    3
14         B := 0;                    5              36    0    3
15         A := B MOD C;              5               0    0    3
16         WRITELN(A, B, C)           5               0    0    3
17      END.     (* Trace *)
```

This trace illustrates several important points. The first is that constants never change—that's why they're called constants. The second is that only one column changes at a time, the column for the variable on the left-hand side of the assignment statement. The third is that variables maintain their value until they are explicitly changed by being placed on the left-hand side of an assignment statement. In Chapter 3, you'll see that there is one other way to change the value of a variable: reading a value into it from outside the program.

Anatomy of a Pascal Program

Now that we have all the pieces, we can define what we mean by a program. Informally, a program has three parts:

- The name of the program and the the files to be used
- The definitions and declarations
- The statements that define the action to be done

Formally, the first part of the program is the **heading**. The heading is made up of the word PROGRAM followed by the program name (identifier) and a list of identifiers in parentheses:

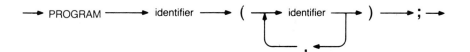

These identifiers are files that are used by the program; they set up communication between the program and the outside world. INPUT and OUTPUT are the standard identifiers for the standard input and output devices. INPUT is usually a terminal keyboard; OUTPUT, a terminal screen.

The definition and declaration sections and the statement section of a program (the second and third elements of our informal definition) make up what's known as a **block**:

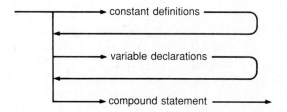

Notice that constant definitions and variable declarations are optional, but if they are present, they must precede the compound statement in the order shown.

A program, then, is a heading followed by a block, followed by a period:

Program FrameCost is repeated below. The heading and the block are clearly visible. The first line names the program. The identifier OUTPUT in the parameter list of the heading lets the compiler know that there will be written output. The CONST definitions and the VAR declaration are part of the block, as is the action part of the program, the code between the BEGIN-END pair. The period ends the program.

```
PROGRAM FrameCost(OUTPUT);
(* Amount of wood needed to frame a *)
(* print is calculated and printed. *)

CONST
   Side = 18;            (* vertical dimension in inches    *)
   Top  = 24;            (* horizontal dimension in inches *)

VAR
   InchesOfWood : INTEGER;      (* inches of wood needed *)

(******************************************************)

BEGIN   (* FrameCost *)
   InchesOfWood := Side + Side + Top + Top;
   WRITELN('You need to buy ', InchesOfWood, ' inches of wood.');
END.    (* FrameCost *)
```

Remember that the words between (* and *) are comments meant for the reader of the program; the compiler ignores them. Comments can appear anywhere in a program.

The CONST definitions and the VAR declaration give the compiler the information it needs to translate the action part of the program, the statement section. During the execution phase, these translated instructions are carried out.

Notice that the statements are separated by a semicolon (except before END, where it's not necessary). Semicolons are separators; they are not part of a statement. The Pascal program always ends with a period.

SAMPLE PROBLEM

Problem: What is the cost per square foot of my 100 × 80 foot dream lot if the price is $40,000?

Discussion: Cost per square foot is calculated by dividing the price by the area. We know the price is $40,000. How do we find the area? Well, we are given the dimensions of the lot (100 feet by 80 feet). Area is the product of these dimensions.

To execute this algorithm (or plan) by hand, we would multiply two numbers together (the width and length of the lot), then divide the result (the area) into the price of the lot for the cost per square foot. To express this algorithm in a computer program requires two additional steps. We have to let the program know what we know, and we have to let it tell us what it knows. What we know is the size of the lot and the price. We give this information to the program by setting constants equal to these values. What the program will know that we don't is the answer. If we calculate the cost per square foot by hand or with a calculator, the answer is there for us to see. If this value is calculated by a program, the result must be written out.

Here is the solution expressed in Pascal:

```
PROGRAM LotCost(OUTPUT);
(* Program calculates the cost per square *)
(* foot of a lot.*)

CONST
   Width = 100;            (* Sets width to 100 feet      *)
   Length = 80;            (* Sets length to 80 feet      *)
   Price = 40000;          (* Sets price to 40000 dollars *)

VAR
   Area : INTEGER;
   CostPerSqFt : REAL;
```

SAMPLE PROBLEM, CONTINUED

```
BEGIN (* LotCost *)
   Area := Width * Length;      (* Calculates the area              *)
   CostPerSqFt := Price / Area;  (* Calculates cost per square foot *)
   WRITELN('Cost per square foot is ', CostPerSqFt:5:2)
END.  (* LotCost *)
```

The CONST section assigns the names Width, Length, and Price to three memory locations. And it assigns the values 100, 80, and 40000 to those locations. The VAR section assigns the names Area and CostPerSqFt to two memory locations, but no values are put into these places. They are needed to hold the results of future calculations.

The statements between BEGIN and END are translated into a machine language the computer can execute. This language varies from machine to machine.

Once the translated version of the program is in memory, control is turned over to the first statement after BEGIN. In other words, what our program says to do is actually done. The calculations are carried out and the following line is printed on the screen:

```
Cost per square foot is  5.00
```

The 4-Cs Corner
Clarity

There are three main ingredients to writing a clear program. The first is to use meaningful identifiers. Identifiers name objects and actions. The names you choose should reflect what the item or object is and what the action does. For example, Top and Side are the constant identifiers in Program FrameCost for the horizontal and vertical dimension of the print. InchesOfWood is the variable identifier for the place where the answer is stored.

WRITE and WRITELN are examples of identifiers associated with actions. They describe the action that takes place. It's a good idea in choosing identifiers to use nouns for items and verbs for actions.

The second ingredient in a well-written program is the use of named constants. We noted that there are two types of constants, named and literal. A named constant is defined in the CONST section of your program. A literal constant is defined in the expression in which it appears. Named constants are easier to understand and easier to change.

The third ingredient is formatting. Formatting refers to the place on a line where you begin a statement or declaration and the places where you insert extra blanks for readability. Pascal syntax is free format, which means that the number of blanks before and after a construct is not important. Actually, this statement is a little misleading. The Pascal compiler doesn't care how statements look in relation to one another, but the human reader of the program most assuredly does. The principle of clarity requires that your programs be readable, both for your sake and the sake of anyone else who has to read them.

When you write an outline in English, you use a certain format (style, indention) to make it readable. There are recommended formatting rules for Pascal programs too. (See Appendix H.) Use them when you are writing a program.

The following is a copy of Program AverageRainFall that does not conform to any formatting standards. Need we say more?

```
PROGRAM AverageRainFall(RainFile, OUTPUT);(* The average rainfall over a
period of days is calculated. *)(* The number of days and the rain statistics
are on RainFile. *)VAR Average, (* average rainfall *) TotalRain : REAL; (*
total accumulated rain *) NumberOfDays : INTEGER; (* number of days in
calculation *) RainFile : TEXT; (* data file*)
(********************************************************)
PROCEDURE GetInches(VAR RainFile : TEXT; VAR NumberOfDays : INTEGER; VAR
TotalRain : REAL);(* INPUT: RainFile *) (* OUTPUT: NumberOfDays, TotalRain
*)(* ACTION: NumberOfDays is read from File RainFile. *)(* Rain statistics
for NumberOfDays are read and *)(* their sum is returned in TotalRain. *) (*
ASSUMPTION: NumberOfDays is the first value on *)(* File RainFile, followed
by NumberOfDays real *)(* values representing inches of rain. *)VAR Inches :
REAL;(* Day's worth of rain *) Counter : INTEGER; (* loop control variable
*)BEGIN (* GetInches *) READLN(RainFile, NumberOfDays); TotalRain := 0.0;
Counter := 1; WHILE Counter <= NumberOfDays DO BEGIN READLN(RainFile,
Inches); TotalRain := TotalRain + Inches; Counter := Counter + 1 END END;
(* GetInches *)
(*********************************************************)
BEGIN (* AverageRainFall*) RESET(RainFile); GetInches(RainFile, NumberOfDays,
TotalRain); IF TotalRain = 0.0 THEN WRITELN('There was no rain during this
period.') ELSE BEGIN Average := TotalRain / NumberOfDays;
WRITELN('The average rainfall over ', NumberOfDays,' days was ', Average:7:3)
END END. (* AverageRainFall *)
```

Correctness

Testing appears twice in our model of the programming process: once in the problem-solving phase and once in the implementation phase. Testing means following the exact steps of either the algorithm or the program to see if the correct results are produced.

In the sample programs in this chapter, testing is quite easy. We just do the calculations by hand and see if the program produces the same results. In the next chapter, we introduce a way of making programs much more general by reading values into the program rather than setting the values as constants. When we do this, testing becomes more complex. We have to show that the program works correctly on sets of different data values. Still, no matter how simple the program, testing should be an integral part of the process. Otherwise we cannot say that the program is correct.

Correctness Hints

1. Three symbols are often confused: = , :, and : = . The equal sign separates a constant name and its value in a constant definition. The colon separates the variable name and its type in a variable declaration. The assignment operator is used to change the value of a variable by assigning the value of an expression to that variable. Before compiling your program, check to be sure that you have used these syntactic symbols correctly.
2. Semicolons separate statements in a Pascal program. Before compiling your program, scan down the right-hand side to check for semicolons.
3. When writing an arithmetic expression, use parentheses to clarify the order in which operations should be executed.
4. DIV and MOD are operations defined on INTEGER values. If one or both of the operands (constants or variables) are REAL, an error will occur.

Summary

Writing a computer program involves a problem-solving phase and an implementation phase. We analyze the problem and devise a workable algorithm. This algorithm is coded into a programming language and tested. We repeat this process until our program is correct, until it solves the problem.

The syntax (grammar) of the Pascal language is defined by syntax diagrams. Identifiers are used to name both items and actions in Pascal, some of which are predefined in the language and some are defined by the user.

The basic predefined data types of Pascal are INTEGER, REAL, CHAR, and BOOLEAN. Constants and variables are defined to be one of these types and occupy a place in memory. The values stored in constants do not change; variables can be assigned different values of their defined types while the program is being executed.

WRITE and WRITELN statements are used to display the output of a program. A WRITE or WRITELN statement prints the values of the expressions listed in its parameter list. A fieldwidth specification following a constant or variable on the parameter list of a WRITE or WRITELN statement can be used to specify the number of character positions that a constant or variable should occupy on the output line.

A program consists of a heading and a block. A block is made up of optional definitions and declarations and a compound statement. The elements within a heading and a block must appear in a specific order. By formatting programs with proper indention and spacing, we make them easier to read and understand—we make them clear.

EXERCISES

1. Mark the following identifiers either valid or invalid:

		Valid	Invalid
a.	Item#1	____	____
b.	Data	____	____
c.	Y	____	____
d.	1Set	____	____
e.	Investment	____	____
f.	Bin-2	____	____
g.	Num5	____	____
h.	SQ FT	____	____

2. Given these syntax diagrams:

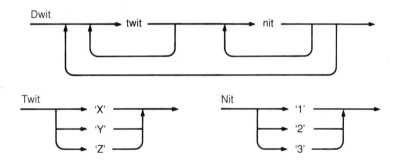

Mark the following "Dwits" either valid or invalid.

		Valid	Invalid
a.	XYZ	____	____
b.	123	____	____
c.	X1	____	____
d.	23Y	____	____
e.	XY12	____	____
f.	Y2Y	____	____
g.	ZY2	____	____
h.	XY23X1	____	____

3. Compute the value of each legal expression below. Indicate whether the value is REAL or INTEGER. If an expression is not legal, indicate why.
   a. 10 / 3 + 5 * 2
   b. 10 MOD 3 + 5 MOD 2
   c. 10 DIV 3 + 5 DIV 2

d. 12.5 + (2.5 / (6.2 / 3.1))
e. −4 * (−5 + 6)
f. 13 MOD 5 / 3
g. (10 / 3 MOD 2) / 3

4. Compute the value of the following expressions to find Result.
   a. `Result := 15 MOD 4;`
   b. `Result := 7 DIV 3 + 2;`
   c. `Result := 2 + 7 * 5;`
   d. `Result := 45 DIV 8 * 4 + 2;`
   e. `Result := 17 + (21 MOD 6) * 2;`
   f. `Result := 4 * (2 + 2);`

5. Mark the following assignments either valid or invalid.

	Valid	Invalid
a. `A := TEMP$;`	____	____
b. `B := S%;`	____	____
c. `C := VARIABLE;`	____	____
d. `D := CONST;`	____	____
e. `CONST A := 7;`	____	____

6. Write a constant definition for InchesPerFoot.

7. Write declarations for the REAL variables Rate and Weight.

8. What is the value of the variable Sum after the following program segment is executed?

```
A := 2;
B := 7;
C := B DIV A;
Sum := A + C;
```

9. Choose meaningful names and write a single VAR declaration for the following values:
   a. Your year of birth
   b. Your grade-point average
   c. A variable indicating whether something is marked or not
   d. A one-character grade code
   e. A four-digit ID number

10. Write a compound statement that would print the following:

    DANGER
    Overvoltage Condition

11. Good program formatting is important because it improves the readability of a program. True or False?

12. Correct any Pascal syntax errors in the following:
    a. `A + B = C;`
    b. `Y = Contents;`
    c. `X := * B;`
    d. `PROGRAM One(INPUT,OUTPUT)`
    e. `CONST X := 18;`

13. A block consists of an optional declarations part and a compound statement. True or false?

14. Create a WRITELN statement to print both the value of an INTEGER variable called Amount (with instructions for formatting the number) and a description in comment form of Amount (make one up).

15. Given the following program, what should the output look like?

```
PROGRAM Exercise(OUTPUT);
(* The program is an exercise in reading a program. *)

CONST
  Pounds = 10;

VAR
  Price, Cost : INTEGER;
  Character : CHAR;

BEGIN    (* Exercise *)
  Price := 30;
  Cost := Price * Pounds;
  Character := 'A';
  WRITELN('Cost is ');
  WRITELN(Cost:6);
  WRITELN('Price is ', Price:2, 'Cost is ', Cost:3);
  WRITE('Grade ', Character, ' costs ');
  WRITELN(Cost);
END.     (* Exercise *)
```

16. Match each of the following terms to the correct definition. There is only one correct answer for each item.
    - _____ a. Program
    - _____ b. Identifier
    - _____ c. Constant
    - _____ d. Semantics
    - _____ e. Problem-solving phase
    - _____ f. Implementation phase
    - _____ g. Computer
    - _____ h. Card reader
    - _____ i. Hardware
    - _____ j. Software
    - _____ k. Assembler

    (1) A place in memory where a data value can be stored
    (2) A place in memory where a data value that cannot be changed is stored
    (3) The part of a computer that holds both program and data
    (4) An input device to a computer
    (5) The time spent planning a program
    (6) Grammar rules
    (7) A looping construct
    (8) Meaning

(9) A program that translates assembly language instructions into machine code

(10) When the machine code version of a program is being run

(11) A name made up of letters and digits that must begin with a letter

(12) When a program in a high-level language is translated into machine code

(13) A program that takes a program written in a high-level language and translates it into machine code

(14) A step-by-step outline for solving a problem

(15) A sequence of instructions to a computer to perform a particular task

(16) When an algorithm is translated into a programming language, then tested and used

(17) A programmable electronic device that can store, retrieve, and process data

(18) The physical components of a computer

(19) Computer programs; the set of all programs available to the computer

PRETEST

1. Mark the following identifiers either valid or invalid.

		Valid	Invalid
a.	R2D2	_____	_____
b.	145R	_____	_____
c.	R*2	_____	_____
d.	Time	_____	_____
e.	X − Y	_____	_____

2. Given these syntax diagrams:

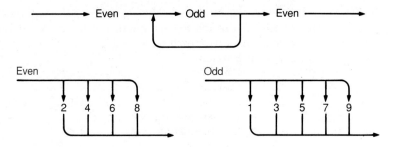

Mark the following either valid or invalid.

		Valid	Invalid
a.	212	_____	_____
b.	333	_____	_____
c.	03330	_____	_____
d.	6135798	_____	_____

3. Compute the value of each of the following expressions. If the value is REAL, be sure to put in a decimal point.

   a. 10 MOD 3   _____

   b. 10 DIV 3   _____

   c. 16 MOD 8 + 16 DIV 8   _____

   d. 13 / 4   _____

     e. 5 * 6 / 15   ____

     f. 13 MOD 5 / 3   ____

     g. 3 + 2 − 4 * 5 DIV 2   ____

4. Mark the following either valid or invalid.

	Valid	Invalid
a. `A := TEMP$;`	____	____
b. `CONST A := 7;`	____	____
c. `VAR X = INTEGER;`	____	____
d. `CONST A + B = 7;`	____	____
e. `VAR X : INTEGER;`	____	____

5. Create a WRITELN statement to print the value of an INTEGER variable Degrees (include formatting instructions) after the words *The angle is.*

6. Formatting a program incorrectly will cause an error. True or false?

7. Mark the following either valid or invalid.

	Valid	Invalid
a. `X x Y = C;`	____	____
b. `Y := CON;`	____	____
c. `CONST X = 10;`	____	____
d. `VAR X : INTEGER;`	____	____
e. `A := B MOD C;`	____	____

8. Create a WRITELN statement to print the value of an INTEGER variable Balance (with formatting instructions) after the words *Your balance is.*

9. Write a Pascal statement to create a constant called MaxNum that contains the number 100.

10. Write a Pascal statement to set up storage for an INTEGER variable called Answer.

11. Given the following program segment:

```
X := 17;
Y := X * 10;
Z := 19 + Y;
W := Z + X;
```

What are the value of the variables?
a. W   ____
b. X   ____
c. Y   ____
d. Z   ____

12. Given the following program segment:

```
Price := 10;
NoBooks := 12;
Bill := Price * NoBooks;
Change := 150 − Bill;
```

What are the values of the variables?
a. Price   ____
b. NoBooks   ____

    c. Bill   ____

    d. Change   ____

13. Match each of the following terms to the correct definition. There is only one correct answer for each item.

  ____ a. Program

  ____ b. Algorithm

  ____ c. Compiler

  ____ d. Identifier

  ____ e. Translation phase

  ____ f. Execution phase

  ____ g. Variable

  ____ h. Constant

  ____ i. Memory

  ____ j. Syntax

  ____ k. Semantics

  (1) A place in memory where a data value can be stored

  (2) A place in memory where a data value that cannot be changed is stored

  (3) The part of a computer that holds both program and data

  (4) An input device to a computer

  (5) The time spent planning a program

  (6) Grammar rules

  (7) A looping construct

  (8) Meaning

  (9) A program that translates assembly language instructions into machine code

  (10) When the machine code version of a program is being run

  (11) A name made up of letters and digits that must begin with a letter

  (12) When a program in a high-level language is translated into machine code

  (13) A program that takes a program written in a high-level language and translates it into machine code

  (14) A step-by-step outline for solving a problem

  (15) A sequence of instructions to a computer to perform a particular task

14. Given the following program, what should the output look like?

```
PROGRAM LetsPrint(Output);
(* This program is designed as an exercise. *)

CONST
   Price = 65;

VAR
   Number, Total : INTEGER;
   Letter : CHAR;

BEGIN (* LetsPrint *)
   Number := 3;
   Total := Price * Number;
   Letter := 'a';
   WRITE ('If ', Letter, ' dress costs $', Price:2);
   WRITELN;
```

```
    WRITE('Then ', Number:5, ' dresses cost', Letter,
          'lot: $');
    WRITELN(Total:3)
END.  (* LetsPrint *)
```

PROGRAMMING ASSIGNMENTS*

1. Input and run the following program. You should fill in the lowercase information requested in parentheses at the beginning of the program.

```
PROGRAM One(INPUT, OUTPUT);
(* Programming Assignment 1    *)
(* (your name)                 *)
(* (date copied and run)       *)
(* (description of the problem) *)

CONST
   Debt = 300.0;        (* Original value owed  *)
   Payment = 22.4;      (* Payment              *)
   Interest = 0.02;     (* Interest rate        *)

VAR
   Charge,              (* Interest times debt   *)
   Reduction,           (* Amount debt is reduced *)
   Remaining : REAL;    (* Remaining balance      *)

BEGIN    (* One *)
   Charge := Interest * Debt;
   Reduction := Payment - Charge;
   Remaining := Debt - Reduction;
   WRITELN('Payment ', Payment, ' Charge ', Charge,
           ' Balance owed ', Remaining)
END.      (* One *)
```

2. Input and run the following program. Fill in the comments using the pattern shown in Assignment 1. (Notice how hard it is to tell what the program is doing without the comments in the code.)

```
PROGRAM Two(INPUT, OUTPUT);
```

*The programming assignments in this book have been collected over a period of years. As they have been used, revised, and used again, the original authors have been forgotten. We therefore want to acknowledge collectively the people who have taught the courses where the assignments have been used: Angus Pearson, Dick Edmiston, Mike Smith, Larry Mahaffey, Woody Bledsoe, Joyce Brennan, Sarah Barron, Tom Rowan, and Bill Bulko.

Note: Several of the programming assignments in this book make use of random numbers. Most Pascal compilers have random-number generators. Because they vary in name and input, we leave the description to the instructor or specific system documentation.

```
CONST
  TotalCost = 600;
  Pounds = 10;
  Ounces = 11;

VAR
  TotalOunces,
  UnitCost : REAL;

BEGIN    (* Two *)
  TotalOunces := 16.0 * Pounds;
  TotalOunces := TotalOunces + Ounces;
  UnitCost := TotalCost / TotalOunces;
  WRITELN('Cost per unit ', UnitCost)
END.    (* Two *)
```

3 Design Methodology and Communication Between the Program and the Outside World

- To be able to apply the top-down methodology to solve a simple problem.

- To be able to code a top-down design in Pascal.

- To be able to properly document a simple Pascal program.

- To be able to determine the contents of variables assigned values in a given READ or READLN statement.

- To be able to write a READ or READLN statement to input a series of data values.

- To be able to use READ and READLN with the standard input device.

- To be able to use READ and READLN with an external file.

Chapter 3 is organized in much the same way as Chapter 2. We begin with a discussion on the general topic of problem solving and end with the specifics of more Pascal constructs. In Chapter 2 we discussed strategies for problem solving; here we outline a methodology to use when applying those strategies.

In Chapters 2 and 3, we've chosen to talk about problem solving and methodology first, then the Pascal constructs. This organization reflects our belief that the general theoretical material is the "meat and potatoes" and the Pascal particulars are the "ice cream and cake." If you are someone who likes to eat dessert first, turn to page 82 and start there. Just be sure to come back to the section on methodology.

Top-Down Design Methodology

We've said that the programming process is made up of two phases: the problem-solving phase and the implementation phase. We warned you not to bypass the problem-solving phase even when small problems don't seem to require it and you're sure that you can write a program directly.

There are good reasons why we insist that you go through the complete process. Even small problems have a large number of details, and a methodical approach is the best way to ensure that nothing is forgotten. Top-down design is a methodical approach. Applying it to small problems will prepare you to tackle larger programming problems that you cannot solve directly. As a by-product, your programs will be readable and understandable *(clear)*, easy to debug *(correct)*, and easy to modify *(complete)*.

The Top-Down Approach

We structure our approach to programming through a well-organized method or technique known as **top-down design**. Also called **stepwise refinement** and **modular programming**, this technique is based on *divide and conquer*, one of the problem-solving strategies we discuss in Chapter 2. When using this methodology, we divide a problem into ever-smaller subproblems. By solving all these subproblems, we reach a solution to the overall problem.

The top-down approach to problem solving involves determining the input to the problem, determining the output that must be produced, and determining a process that will convert the input into the output (Figure 3–1).

If the problem description is vague, then the first step is to create a functional problem description—a description that clearly states what the program should do. In many cases, this means a dialogue between the person with the problem and the programmer. (We try to make this unnecessary in this text!)

The next step is to get a clear picture of the **input**. What data do we have to analyze or transform to get the output? Is the data already in machine-readable form so that we have to access it in a certain way? Is the data on

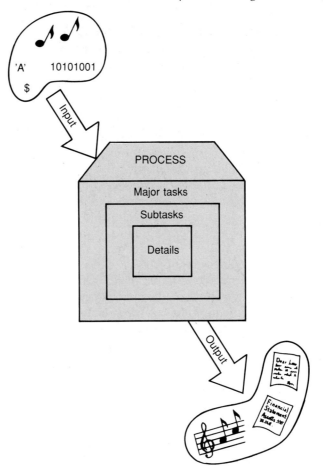

FIGURE 3–1 Top-down design. The three steps to a top-down approach are to determine (1) input to process, (2) output from process, and (3) process to transfer input into output. Design by successive levels of details.

paper so that we must convert it to machine-readable form ourselves? Is the data available at all or do we have to generate it?

Next is the **output**. What form should it take? Are the results of the program going to be read by the chairman of the board? A programmer? Another computer? The answers to these questions determine what the output must look like. Once we have determined our input and output, we have to identify a process for converting one to the other. This is the hard part.

We begin by stating the major tasks that must be done to convert the input into the output (solve the problem). Then we break down each major task into subtasks. The process stops when we do not need to break any subtask down further; we've specified exactly how to do each of the subtasks.

What we are doing in top-down design is working from the abstract (our description or specification of the problem) to the particular (our algorithm).

The process of subdividing tasks stops when each subtask is specified in such a way that we can directly translate the algorithm for it into the statements of a programming language (Pascal in this case).

Modules

In top-down design, we call each task and subtask that we create in the process of breaking down a problem a **module**. The breakdown (decomposition) into smaller and smaller modules creates a hierarchical structure of tasks and subtasks. Modules at one level can call on the services of modules at a lower level. Modules are the basic building blocks of our programs.

By dividing our problem into modules or segments, we can solve each module fairly independently of the others. For example, one module could get data values; another could print values after processing. Various processing modules might keep a cumulative total, keep a count of data values, detect error conditions, or do calculations.

The task at one level becomes the name of the module that solves that task at the next level. A **module design chart** is a picture of the module names by level; it illustrates the successive levels of refinement necessary to solve the problem (Figure 3–2). The top level, or Level 0, is our functional description of the problem; the lower levels are our successive refinements.

How do we divide the problem into modules? Think for a moment about how we usually approach any big problem. We spend some time thinking about the problem in a general sort of way, then we jot down the major steps.

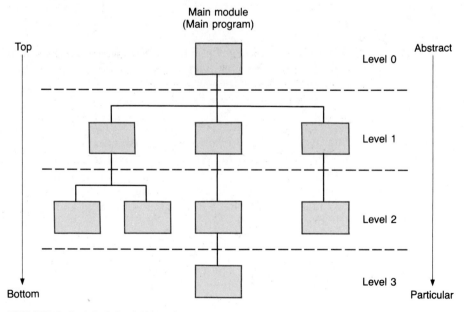

FIGURE 3–2 Module design chart

Next we examine each of the major steps, filling in the details. If we don't know how to accomplish a specific task, we go on to the next one, planning to come back and take care of the one we skipped later, when we have more information.

This is exactly how you should approach a programming problem. Think about how you would solve the problem by hand. Write down the major steps. This becomes your main module. Now begin to develop the details of the major steps as Level 1 modules. If you don't know how to do something, or feel overwhelmed by details, give the task a name and go on. You can expand that name later as a lower module. (We call this the "Scarlett O'Hara technique." If a task is cumbersome or difficult, think about it tomorrow—put off the problem to a lower level.) The process continues for as many levels as it takes to expand every task to the smallest detail.

Applying Top-Down Design

Let's apply the top-down process to the pleasant task of planning a large party. A little thought reveals that there are two main tasks: inviting the people and preparing the food.

One approach to inviting the people would be to reach for the phone book and start calling our friends. However, we'd soon be confused. Who did we reach? Whose line was busy? Who said what? A much better approach would be to make a list of the people we want to invite, then put the list aside and check it over tomorrow to see which of our best friends we've forgotten. Then, with the list in hand, we can go through and fill in the telephone numbers. Now we begin to call, marking down people's responses. It may take a while to reach everyone, but we'll know where we stand. By the time we have an estimate on the number of guests, we can start thinking about the food.

Heaven help us if we just run in and start cooking! Without planning, the job would be overwhelming. Instead, let's break down this task into planning the menu and preparing the food.

We can save a lot of time and effort here if we take advantage of what others have done and look at suggested menus in cookbooks. (In programming we would look in the literature to see if algorithms already exist to solve this problem.) Once we choose a menu, we can put off until later a careful examination of the recipes. The time to do that is when we're preparing the shopping list. (Defer details until later.)

The module design chart in Figure 3–3 shows the process to this point. Notice that a module at each level expands a statement (task) at the level above. We probably could work directly from the Level 2 descriptions. For a computer program, we would have to break the modules down into much finer detail. For example, "Write down names" would have to be at the following level of detail:

Do you have paper?
 No, get paper.

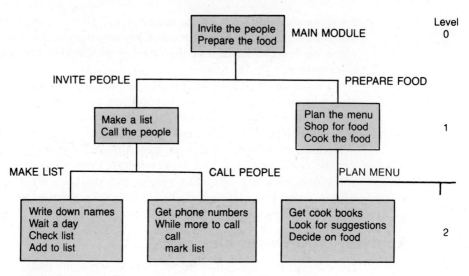

FIGURE 3–3   Planning a party

> Do you have a pen?
>   No, get a pen.
> Pick up pen.
> Put pen to paper. . . .

Your top-down design for giving a party might be very different. Perhaps you have a great little delicatessen down the block, so you have the party catered. Your main module would be

```
Invite the people
Call the delicatessen
```

No two top-down designs are exactly alike. There is no set way of writing a design. Your design reflects your own individual style. However, a good design is modular, with tasks grouped into functional units. A "good" design, like a "good" program, meets the test of the 4-Cs: It is clear, concise, complete, and correct.

Let's leave the social analogy and look again at the process applied to programming. Remember, the domain is new but the process is one you've used all your life.

The main module specifies the names of tasks. Each name (task) must be expanded at a lower level until there's a one-to-one correspondence to a Pascal statement. This is true at each level. There should be as many modules at

Level 1 as there are names of tasks at Level 0, and so on for each successive level.

If you make sure that each module works by going through it carefully by hand with sample data, then your program should work when you put all the modules together. A little effort spent in testing each module can save a lot of effort spent in correcting your program.

Remember that *the idea is to defer details*. Push the actual code to as low a level as possible. When you don't have to worry about the actual implementation, you can concentrate more on functional divisions and algorithms. As you travel down the levels of your design, you make a series of design decisions. If a decision proves awkward or incorrect (and many times it will!), it's easy to backtrack (back up to a previous level) and try something else. At least you don't have to scrap your whole design, only the small part you're working on. There may be many intermediate steps and trial solutions before you reach your final design.

Spend most of your time analyzing and designing your solution. Coding will then take very little time, and debugging should take even less.

Writing a top-down design is like writing an outline for an English paper. You can use English sentences or **pseudocode** (a mixture of English and programming language control structures) to describe each task or subtask. For example, here's a main module for the fairly simple problem of finding the average of a list of numbers:

```
Initialize Sum to 0
Initialize Count to 0
WHILE more data DO
   Get a data value
   Add data value to Sum
   Add 1 to Count
Average = Sum / Count
Print Average
```

The WHILE-DO is a looping control structure. The tasks

```
Get a data value
Add data value to Sum
Add 1 to Count
```

are done over and over again until there is no more data (numbers in the list). Because this is such a simple problem, we can code from this module (each statement can be translated directly into a Pascal statement). Although this example demonstrates pseudocode, it doesn't really show off the beauty of top-down design, the way in which we can simplify a problem by dividing it into subproblems (modules).

"This was your first effort at TOP-DOWN design, wasn't it?"

Cartoon by M. Lad. Topolsky

Communication Between a Running Program and the Outside World

In Program FrameCost (see page 40), we wrote the dimensions of the print into the program as constants. Program FrameCost is very specific. It calculates the amount of wood needed to frame a particular print. We could have calculated it much faster in our heads! If computers could only calculate answers for specific questions with given sets of values, computers would long ago have gone the way of the Pet Rock.

Computer is shorthand for "general-purpose digital computer." It is the fact that computers can solve general problems, not just specific ones, that makes them so valuable. They do this by having programs ask for the data values they need for a calculation while they are running. Let's rewrite Program FrameCost as a general program to calculate the amount of wood needed to frame a print of any dimensions. Then we'll look at the mechanism that allows us to do this.

```
PROGRAM FrameCost(INPUT, OUTPUT);
(* The user is prompted to input values    *)
(* representing the dimensions of the       *)
(* print from the keyboard. The amount      *)
(* of wood needed for the frame is printed  *)
(* on the screen.                           *)
```

```
VAR
  Side,                    (* vertical dimension in inches   *)
  Top,                     (* horizontal dimension in inches *)
  InchesOfWood : INTEGER;  (* inches of wood needed          *)

BEGIN    (* FrameCost *)
  (* Prompt for and read the first dimension. *)
  WRITELN('Enter the vertical dimension of your print.');
  WRITELN('The dimension should be in whole inches.',
          '  Press return.');
  READLN(Side);

  (* Prompt for and read the second dimension. *)
  WRITELN('Enter the horizontal dimension of your print.');
  WRITELN('The dimension should be in whole inches.'
          '  Press return.');
  READLN(Top);

  (* Calculate and print the amount of wood needed. *)
  InchesOfWood := Side + Side + Top + Top;
  WRITELN('You need to buy ', InchesOfWood:3, ' inches of wood.')
END.     (* FrameCost *)
```

This program is an **interactive program**. The user must input two INTE-GER values representing the dimensions of the print in inches. The key word INPUT on the program heading tells the program that the data values it has to read will be on the standard input device (the keyboard). The key word OUTPUT on the program heading indicates that the standard output device (the terminal) will be used. The words that are printed give a message to the person who is running the program.

The user is prompted to press return (the enter key) after entering each dimension. The line following that prompt is the statement that causes the running program to go to the keyboard and get the numbers that have just been keyed in. The instruction READLN(Side) tells the computer to read the number that was keyed in for the vertical dimension and to store that number in the place named Side. The instruction READLN(Top) tells the computer to read the number that was keyed in for the horizontal dimension and to store it in the place named Top. The values for Side and Top are now available for the instruction that calculates the amount of wood needed (InchesOfWood). The last statement prints the result back on the screen for the user to see.

This program can be run again and again to calculate the amount of wood needed to frame any print. It is general because the data values are not built into the program but are input each time the program is run. The program is compiled just once, but it can be run any number of times to calculate the amount of wood needed to frame any number of pictures.

READ and READLN

There are two ways to assign a value to a variable. One is with an assignment statement, as we discussed in Chapter 2; the other is by reading in the value as data, as we've just shown you.

A program needs data on which to operate. Data is not part of a program; it has to be input. In Pascal we input data by using a READ or READLN statement. Both READ and READLN tell the running program to go to the standard input device and read data values. The standard input device is assumed to have the values organized on one or more lines. Although the semantics of READ and READLN are slightly different, their syntax diagrams are identical:

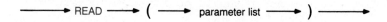

The parameter list is made up of variable identifiers, which tell the program where to put the values that it reads. These variables must be declared in the VAR section of the program. The data values must agree in type with the variables into which they will be stored. The parameters are separated by commas. The program will try to read as many data values as there are places named on the parameter list.

How READ and READLN operate depends on the form—numeric, character, or mixed—of the data values.

Numeric Data

The semantics of READ where the parameters are numeric (either REAL or INTEGER) are as follows:

1. Get a number from the standard input device.
2. Store the number in memory in the first place named in the parameter list.
3. Is there another place still left in the parameter list? If so:
    *   Get a number.
    *   Store the number in the next place named in the parameter list.
    *   Repeat Step 3.
    If not, READ is completed.

Numeric data values may be on one or more lines and are separated by one or more blanks. Although different values can appear on different lines, any given numeric value is assumed to be complete on one line; that is, a single number cannot span lines. Clearly, the key to reading correctly is consistency among the declarations, the READ statement, and the data values on the line. Let's look at an example. To make clear what the line looks like, we show the character positions.

```
VAR
  First : REAL;
  Second : INTEGER;
  .
  .
READ(Second, First);
```

		4	2		2	.	3		. .

We've created two variables: First (REAL) and Second (INTEGER). Nothing is put into these places during **compile-time** (while the program is being translated). However, they are marked REAL and INTEGER respectively, and only values of the proper type can be stored in them.

The READ statement says that two values should be read from the input line. The first value is INTEGER; it should be stored in Second. The second value is REAL; it should be stored in First. At **run-time**, when the translated version of this READ statement is executed, the input line is scanned, past the blanks, for the first numeric character. This character begins the value for Second. The order of the variables on the parameter list indicates their order on the input line. The order in which they are declared in the VAR section is immaterial. The blank after the digit 2 signals the end of the data value to be stored in Second. It is important to note that the blank ends the number; the blank character itself is not read.

There is still a variable identifier on the parameter list that does not have a value, so the scan continues with the blank that ends the previous read. The digit 2, in the sixth position on the line, begins the data value that will be stored in First. The period ends the whole-number part and the blank ends the fractional part of the number. The real number 2.3 is stored in First. The READ knows that First is a REAL variable and is looking for the two parts.

The table below gives additional examples of READ statements, data values, and what value gets assigned to what place. The blanks on the data line are indicated by □. Data1, Data2, and Data3 are of type INTEGER; RData1 is of type REAL.

READ(statement parameters)	Data Line(s)	Contents After READ
a. (Data1)	32	Data1: 32
b. (Data1, Data2, Data3)	3□□□4□□□60	Data1: 3 Data2: 4 Data3: 60
c. (Data1, Data2)	24	Data1: 24 Data2: 76
	76	
d. (Data1, RData1)	(blank line)	Data1: 46 RData1: 32.4
	46□32.4	

What is the difference between the statements READ(Data1) followed by READ(Data2) and the statement READ(Data1, Data2)? Absolutely nothing. Using a list of variable identifiers is only a convenience for the programmer.

What about our second input statement, READLN? READLN differs from READ in one major respect: After the variables in the parameter list have had values put into them, READLN skips to the next line. If there are any numbers remaining on the previous line, they will never be read. Here's an example:

```
READLN(Second);
READ(First);
```

| 4 | 2 | | 2 | . | 3 | | . . |

| | | 4 | . | 6 | | . . |

READLN(Second) reads and stores the value 42 in Second; then skips the rest of the line. The next READ or READLN executed starts looking for values at the beginning of the next line. READ(First) reads and stores the value 4.6 in First; the value 2.3 on the first line is not read.

Suppose we have two INTEGER data items on each line of input separated by two blanks:

```
10   20
15   16
22   21
```

The following sets of statements read the same values into A, B, C, D, E, and F:

a. `READ(A, B);`   b. `READ(A);`   c. `READ(A, B, C, D, E, F);`
   `READ(C, D);`   `READ(B, C, D);`
   `READ(E, F);`   `READ(E, F);`

d. `READLN(A, B);`   e. `READLN(A, B, C, D, E, F);`
   `READLN(C, D);`
   `READLN(E, F);`

Variable	Value Read
A	10
B	20
C	15
D	16
E	22
F	21

Notice that (a) and (d) are the same with READ and READLN interchanged, as are (c) and (e). But if the READs in (b) are replaced by READLNs, an error message occurs. Look what happens:

READLN(A);	10 is stored in A.
READLN(B, C, D);	15 is stored in B.
	16 is stored in C.
	22 is stored in D.
READLN(E, F);	There are no values left to be put into E and F.

The second value on the first line is not read because after the value is read into A, the balance of that line is skipped. The same is true of the second value on the third line.

Imagine a pointer moving along the input line as values are being read. READ leaves the pointer ready to begin with the next column. READLN performs the read, then moves the pointer to the beginning of the next line. Each input line has an **end-of-line marker (<eoln>)** to tell the computer where one line ends and the next begins. The READ or READLN crosses the <eoln> to find as many values as there are identifiers in its parameter list.

Suppose we have three lines of input data:

```
123 456 789<eoln>
987 654 321<eoln>
888 777 666<eoln>
```

Given that A, B, C, and D are variables of type INTEGER, the table below shows how READ and READLN operate. (Each example is independent.)

Input Statements	Values Read	Pointer (↑) Position After READ/READLN
a. READ(A, B);	A: 123 B: 456	123 456 789<eoln> ↑
READ(C, D);	C: 789 D: 987	987 654 321<eoln> ↑
b. READLN(A, B);	A: 123 B: 456	987 654 321<eoln> ↑
READLN(C, D);	C: 987 D: 654	888 777 666<eoln> ↑
c. READ(A, B);	A: 123 B: 456	123 456 789<eoln> ↑
READLN(C, D);	C: 789 D: 987	888 777 666<eoln> ↑
d. READLN(A, B);	A: 123 B: 456	987 654 321<eoln> ↑
READLN(C);	C: 987	888 777 666<eoln> ↑
READLN(D);	D: 888	At the beginning of the next line

continued

Input Statements	Values Read	Pointer (↑) Position After READ/READLN
e. READLN(A);	A: 123	987 654 321<eoln> ↑
READ(B);	B: 987	987 654 321<eoln> ↑
READLN(C);	C: 654	888 777 666<eoln> ↑
READ(D);	D: 888	888 777 666<eoln> ↑

Although we have used INTEGER data values in the table, REAL data values are read exactly the same way.

Look back at Program AverageRainFall (p. 30) and examine the READ statements. NumberOfDays and Inches are each read with a separate READLN statement. This implies that the data items are each on a separate line.

Character Data

READ and READLN treat character data differently from numeric data. A CHAR variable holds just one alphanumeric character. So when values are read into variables declared to be of type CHAR, only one character is read. Again, let's look at an example.

```
VAR
   Chl, Ch2, Ch3, Ch4 : CHAR;
   .
   .
   .
READ(Chl, Ch2, Ch3, Ch4);
```

A	2		x		

Remember, reading character data differs from reading numeric data. Each variable of type CHAR can contain only one character. Therefore, when the variables on the parameter list are CHAR variables, exactly one character is read for each variable identifier on the parameter list. READ(Ch1, Ch2, Ch3, Ch4) inputs exactly four characters. 'A' is stored in Ch1; '2' is stored in Ch2; ' ' (a blank) is stored in Ch3; and 'x' is stored in Ch4. *Don't forget that a blank is a character.*

The table below shows the results of READ and READLN statements given that X, Y, and Z are CHAR variables and the following data:

```
A10<eoln>
BBB<eoln>
999<eoln>
```

Again, each example is independent.

Input Statement	Values Read	Pointer (↑) Position After READ/READLN
a. READLN(X, Y, Z);	X: 'A' Y: '1' Z: '0'	A10<eoln> ↑
b. READLN(X);	X: 'A'	BBB<eoln> ↑
READLN(Y);	Y: 'B'	999<eoln> ↑
READ(Z);	Z: '9'	999<eoln> ↑
c. READLN(X, Y);	X: 'A' Y: '1'	BBB<eoln> ↑
READLN(Z);	Z: 'B'	999<eoln> ↑

Notice that there are no single quotes around the character data values shown. In our program we have to put quotes around character constants to differentiate them from identifiers or numeric constants. When reading in data values, there is no ambiguity. The type of variable in which a value is to be stored determines how the value is interpreted.

Mixed Numeric and Character Data

Before the first READ in a program and after every READLN, the pointer is at the first position on a line. After a READ, the pointer is at the next character position on the line. This causes problems when reading *mixed data*, numeric data followed by character data.

Let's look at an example:

```
VAR
  Ch1, Ch2 : CHAR;
  One, Two : INTEGER;
  .
  .
  .
  READ(Ch1, One, Two, Ch2);
```

	2			3	4		· ·

Because Ch1 is a CHAR variable, the value in the first character position of the line (a blank) is stored in Ch1. One is an INTEGER variable, so the scan continues until the digit 2 is found. The blank following the 2 ends the value for One. Two is also an INTEGER/variable, so the scan continues until the digit 3 is found. The two-digit number 34 is stored in Two. The blank following the digit 4 is examined and ends the value for Two *but is not read as part of the INTEGER variable.* Therefore, the blank that ends Two is read as a CHAR variable and is stored in Ch2.

The table below contains some more examples of mixed reads. Ch1 and Ch2 are of type CHAR, and P and Q are of type INTEGER. The data is

```
24 36 A<eoln>
```

Input Statement	Values Read	Pointer (↑) Position After READ/READLN
a. READ (P, Q);	P: 24 Q: 36	24 36 A<eoln> ↑
READ (Ch1);	Ch1: ' '	24 36 A<eoln> ↑
READ (Ch2);	Ch2: 'A'	24 36 A<eoln> ↑
b. READ (Ch1, Ch2);	Ch1: '2' Ch2: '4'	24 36 A<eoln> ↑

The thing to remember is that a READ involving a type CHAR variable always reads only one character and moves the pointer one character to the right. Because the integer read in (a) left the pointer under the blank after the 6, the next character is a blank. So Ch1 has a blank stored in it, and Ch2 has the letter A. In (b), Ch1 is '2' and Ch2 is '4'; these are the alphanumeric characters '2' and '4', not the integers 2 and 4.

Where does <eoln> come from? What is it? The first question is easy. If you're working at a terminal, you generate an <eoln> yourself when you hit the return or enter key. The answer to the second question varies from computer system to computer system. <eoln> is a special control character that the system recognizes. When your program is reading in values, READ and READLN treat <eoln> as a blank. If your program is reading in a variable of type INTEGER or REAL, it skips over the <eoln> as it would any blank. If your program is reading in a variable of type CHAR, it reads <eoln> as a blank and stores the blank in that variable.

When you use WRITELN, you are actually writing an <eoln> character after the variables listed in the parameter list. The printer or screen goes to a new line when it recognizes this character.

Files

In Chapter 1 we described a file as a named place, usually in secondary storage, where we store data, programs, or any other information in machine-readable form. In everyday usage, a file is both that place and its contents.

The statements READ and READLN and WRITE and WRITELN tell the computer to read or write information. The program heading tells the system *from where* to read the information and *to where* it should be written. When we want data to be read from or written to the standard input and output devices, usually the keyboard and the screen, we use the words INPUT and OUTPUT in the program heading.

When we use a terminal for input and output, we assume that the program is interactive, that a person is sitting at the terminal and interacting with the program. When input data is needed, the program prompts the user to enter it using the keyboard. The program reads this data, processes it, and writes the result to the screen where the user can see it.

There are many times, however, when this is not practical. Input data may be produced at one place to be read at another. There may be too much data to be input at the keyboard while the program is running. The input data may be needed by several different programs. The output may be in the form of a large report that needs to be saved. The output from one program may be needed as input to another program.

So Pascal allows input and output to be read from and written to a file rather than from the standard input and output devices (the default options for READs and READLNs and WRITEs and WRITELNs). If your input data is on a file, you must tell the system so by putting the file name as the first parameter on the READ or READLN parameter list. If you want your output written to a file, you must use the name of the file as the first parameter on the parameter list for the WRITE or WRITELN.

You tell the system to expect to use files by listing their names on the program heading and declaring them in the VAR section of the program. Files that are broken up into lines are called **TEXT files** (which are the kinds of files word processors produce). Not surprisingly, the built-in Pascal data type for files is type TEXT. In addition to <eoln>, TEXT files have a special character called the **end-of-file character (<eof>)**, which follows the last <eoln> in the file. In Chapter 5 we show how the <eoln> and the <eof> can be used to control reading.

Finally, before we can use files instead of the standard input/output devices, we have to prepare the files for processing. The statements (standard procedures) used to prepare files are listed in the table below.

Command	Action
`RESET(FileName);`	Prepare (open) the file for reading. Put the reading pointer at the first character.
`REWRITE(FileName);`	Prepare (open) the file for writing. Any previous contents are lost.
`ASSIGN(FileName, 'SomeName');`	FileName is the file identifier in the program; SomeName is the external name of the file, the name by which the operating system knows the file.
`CLOSE(FileName);`	Save this file.

Before you use a file in a program, it must be opened. That is, the file must be initialized so the reading pointer (for an input file) or the writing pointer (for an output file) is positioned at the beginning of the file. To do this, RESET(FileName) is used before the first READ or READLN and REWRITE(FileName) is used before the first WRITE or WRITELN. RESET opens the file and puts the pointer at the beginning of the file. REWRITE puts the pointer at the beginning of the file ready to write to it, thereby erasing any previous contents of the file.

RESET and REWRITE are done automatically for standard input and output devices. RESET(INPUT) at the beginning of the program is redundant because the system already has done so. If you RESET(FileName) after you've already read some data from FileName, the reading pointer just returns to the beginning of the file. Because INPUT is always the standard input device and OUTPUT is always the standard output device, REWRITE(INPUT) or RESET(OUTPUT) will cause an error.

All user-defined files can be either input or output depending on whether they were opened for reading or opened for writing. While a program is running, a file can be used for both input and output. We show examples of this in later chapters.

ASSIGN and CLOSE are not standard Pascal statements, but they show up in so many Pascal implementations that we include them here. The Pascal run-time support system that is present when your program is running must use the operating system to go and get the file that you are reading from. There must be some mechanism for connecting the file identifier in your program with the file out on secondary storage somewhere. Some systems simply require that they have the same name; others use an ASSIGN statement to make the connection, then a CLOSE statement to save the file in secondary storage. Check the documentation on your Pascal compiler to see if you need to use ASSIGN and CLOSE statements.

The following example reads three data values from one file and writes them to another file in reverse order.

```
PROGRAM ReverseData(FileIn, FileOut, OUTPUT);
(* Three INTEGER values are read from FileIn   *)
(* and written out in reverse order to FileOut. *)

VAR
   Data1, Data2, Data3 : INTEGER;   (* values to be read  *)
   FileIn, FileOut : TEXT;          (* input/output files *)

BEGIN (* ReverseData *)
   RESET(FileIn);
   REWRITE(FileOut);
```

```
  READLN(FileIn, Data1, Data2, Data3);
  WRITELN(FileOut, Data3, Data2, Data1)
END.    (* ReverseData *)
```

FileIn and FileOut are listed on the program heading. OUTPUT is also listed so that the run-time support system knows to use the standard output device for run-time error messages. FileIn and FileOut are listed in the VAR section as TEXT files. Both the READLN and WRITELN statements have a file name listed as the first parameter.

There is no ambiguity about the first parameter. The compiler checks to see the data type of the first parameter. If it is a file, then the input or output is from or to that file. If the first parameter is not a file, the standard input or output device is assumed. If you want part of your input to come from the terminal and part from a file, just be sure that you have INPUT on the program heading and use the file name as the first parameter for the READs that you want to come from that file.

Identifiers Revisited

Identifiers are used in Pascal to specify variables, constants, and processes. The identifiers a programmer can use are restricted to those not reserved by the Pascal language.

Reserved Words and Standard Identifiers

Reserved words are words whose values or meanings are predefined in a programming language. These identifiers *cannot* be used for other than their intended purpose. You've already seen several reserved words in Pascal:

```
BEGIN   CONST   DIV   END   MOD   PROGRAM   VAR
```

See Appendix A for a complete list of reserved words.

Other identifiers—called **standard identifiers**—also are predefined but can be redefined by the programmer. These include the names of built-in types, certain system constants, and the names of the standard input and output devices (see Appendix B). For example,

```
BOOLEAN   CHAR     FALSE   INPUT   INTEGER
MaxInt    OUTPUT   REAL    TEXT    TRUE
```

are all standard identifiers.

Remember that Pascal is not case sensitive. With one exception, we use uppercase for reserved words and standard identifiers in this text. The exception is MaxInt. For some reason, MaxInt looks better in upper- and lowercase.

We are not quite sure why this is so, but we will break our own convention when referring to MaxInt.

Standard Functions and Procedures

Pascal has a set of built-in standard subprograms called *standard procedures* and *standard functions*. The difference between a procedure and a function is syntactic; we explain it in another chapter. For the moment, just think of these standard subprograms as program parts that accomplish tasks that are required so often that they're provided for you. Their names are also standard identifiers. You've already seen six standard procedures:

```
READ   READLN   RESET   REWRITE   WRITE   WRITELN
```

Communication between your program and one of the standard subprograms is accomplished by means of a parameter list. You've seen how this works. The subprogram expects to find the variables it is to work with listed on the parameter list. The user of the subprogram is responsible for listing them in the proper order. For example, the predefined standard functions ROUND and TRUNC expect to be given a parameter (either a variable or a constant) of type REAL. Each returns a value of type INTEGER:

```
ROUND(3.7) = 4      Rounds to nearest integer
TRUNC(3.7) = 3      Truncates decimal part
```

Where it is invalid to assign a REAL value to an INTEGER variable, we can use ROUND or TRUNC to achieve an approximation. (Appendix B lists all the standard subprograms with the parameters they expect.)

SAMPLE PROBLEM

Problem: Find the weighted average of three test scores. This should be an interactive program in which the user is prompted to enter the data in the form of an integer test score followed by its associated weight. Three pairs should be requested.

Discussion: It's common practice to give different weights to tests to arrive at a student's grade in a course. For example, if there are two tests worth 30 percent each and a final exam worth 40 percent, we would take the first test grade and multiply it by 0.30, take the second test grade and multiply it by 0.30, and take the final grade and multiply it by 0.40. Then we would add up these three values to get a weighted average. This by hand algorithm is exactly how we approach this problem.

Input: Three groups of data each composed of TestScore (INTEGER) and Weight (REAL).

Output: Echo-print the input.
Print the weighted average with an appropriate label.

Echo printing means that the values of all variables that are read are immediately written back out. In an interactive program, this means that the user can see that the values are keyed properly. When the output is on a file, a record of the value that was read is on the file with the output. The person examining the output then can check to be sure that the proper values were read.

Assumptions: The three weights add up to 1 and the input data is correct (no error checking).

MAIN MODULE   Level 0

The main module lists the tasks to be performed.

```
Get data
Calculate Average
Print Average
```

GET DATA   Level 1

```
Get Test 1 data
Get Test 2 data
Get Test 3 data
```

GET TEST 1 DATA   Level 2

```
Write 'Enter Test 1 score (INTEGER) and weight (REAL).',
   ' Press return.'
Read Test1Score, Weight1
Write 'Test 1 score and weight are ', Test1Score, Weight1
```

SAMPLE PROBLEM, CONTINUED

GET TEST 2 DATA

Write 'Enter Test 2 score (INTEGER) and weight (REAL).',
  ' Press return.'
Read Test2Score, Weight2
Write 'Test 2 score and weight are ', Test2Score, Weight2

GET TEST 3 DATA

Write 'Enter Test 3 score (INTEGER) and weight (REAL).',
  ' Press return.'
Read Test3Score, Weight3
Write 'Test 3 score and weight are ', Test3Score, Weight3

CALCULATE AVERAGE   Level 1

Average ← Test1Score * Weight1 + Test2Score * Weight2
  + Test3Score * Weight3

PRINT AVERAGE

Write 'Weighted average is ' Average

Module Design Chart:

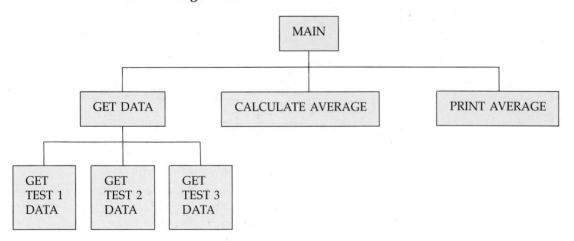

```
PROGRAM WeightedAverage(INPUT, OUTPUT);
(* Weighted average of three tests is *)
(* calculated and printed. This is    *)
(* an interactive program.            *)

VAR
   Test1Score, Test2Score, Test3Score : INTEGER;
   Weight1, Weight2, Weight3 : REAL;
   Average : REAL;

BEGIN (* WeightedAverage *)
   (* Get data *)
   (* Get Test 1 data *)
   WRITELN('Enter Test 1 score (INTEGER) and weight (REAL).',
          '  Press return.');
   READLN(Test1Score, Weight1);
   WRITELN('Test 1 score and weight are ',
          Test1Score:5, Weight1:5:2);

   (* Get Test 2 data *)
   WRITELN('Enter Test 2 score (INTEGER) and weight (REAL).',
          '  Press return.');
   READLN(Test2Score, Weight2);
   WRITELN('Test 2 score and weight are ',
          Test2Score:5, Weight2:5:2);

   (* Get Test 3 data *)
   WRITELN('Enter Test 3 score (INTEGER) and weight (REAL).',
          '  Press return.');
   READLN(Test3Score, Weight3);
   WRITELN('Test 3 score and weight are ',
          Test3Score:5, Weight3:5:2);

   (* Calculate Average *)
   Average := Test1Score * Weight1 +
              Test2Score * Weight2 +
              Test3Score * Weight3;

   (* Print Average *)
   WRITELN('Weighted average is ', Average:10:2)
END.  (* Weighted Average *)
```

The following is a copy of the screen from a run of Program WeightedAverage. The values that were input at the keyboard are in color.

SAMPLE PROBLEM, CONTINUED

```
Enter Test 1 score (INTEGER) and weight (REAL). Press return.
90 0.3
Test 1 score and weight are    90 0.30
Enter Test 2 score (INTEGER) and weight (REAL). Press return.
85 0.25
Test 2 score and weight are    85 0.25
Enter Test 3 score (INTEGER) and weight (REAL). Press return.
78 0.45
Test 3 score and weight are    78 0.45
Weighted average is       83.35
```

The 4-Cs Corner

Clarity

In the last chapter we said that there were three main ingredients in a well-written program. All three of these ingredients—meaningful identifiers, named constants, and formatting—are part of a program's documentation. **Documentation** consists of the written descriptions (including the top-down design), specifications, development, and actual code of a program.

Good documentation helps us read, understand, and modify (maintain) software. If you haven't looked at a program for six months and need to haul it out and make some changes, you'll be happy that you documented it well. Of course, if someone else has to use and modify your program, the documentation is indispensable!

Documentation external to the program includes the specifications, development history, and top-down design. Internal documentation includes program formatting, comments, and **self-documenting code**. You can use the pseudocode from your top-down design as comments in your program. Keep documentation up to date. Be sure to record all changes made in the program in all the pertinent documentation.

> **Self-Documenting Code**
> A program containing meaningful identifiers, named constants, and judiciously used clarifying comments.

The documentation we have discussed is fine for the person who's reading and maintaining your programs. However, if a program is released to be used by others, you must provide a user's manual as well.

Ideally, even a nonprogrammer should be able to read a Pascal program. In Appendix G we discuss some program documentation conventions.

Completeness

Old programs never die; they just get modified. This means a program is not complete unless you've allowed for future modifications. Good documentation and good modularization are two key features of a complete program.

Conciseness

In Program WeightedAverage, the user is instructed three times to input data values. We could shorten the program by printing the instructions for keying the data just once, with a reminder that three sets of values are needed. Another way to make the program more concise is to name the task of prompting the user and reading in data values, then refer to the name in the program. We show you how to do this in Chapter 6.

Correctness

Communication between the program and the outside world is the part of a program that is most error prone. Three things must be consistent: the description of what the data will look like, the statements that do the actual inputting, and the data itself. To make things more complex, data can be input in real time in an interactive program or prepared in advance and stored in a file. The combination of things that can go wrong is frightening. The best advice we can give you is *be careful*. Listed in the Correctness Hints below are some suggestions about things that need special attention.

Correctness Hints

1. The data on the input line (whether from the keyboard or a file) must be in the order in which the names of where to put the data are listed in the parameter list.
2. The types of data must be the same as the types of variables into which the data will be stored.
3. If the data is on a file, be sure that the file name is the first parameter on the input statement. If not, the system assumes that the data is on INPUT. When you run a program and nothing seems to be happening, the program may be waiting for input from the keyboard (that is, you may have forgotten to put the file name on the input statement).
4. If the program is interactive, be sure that the user is prompted with enough information to form the input properly. If a value could be either REAL or INTEGER, be sure that the user is told which to use.
5. Mixing character and numeric data values on one line can be hazardous to your health. Don't do it if you can possibly avoid it.

Summary

The top-down methodology presented in this chapter may be the most important thing you will learn from this book. Use the guidelines below when you're writing programs.

The top-down design method can be broken down as follows:

1. **Analyze the problem.**

   Understand the problem. Understand what is given (input) and what is required (output). Specify input and output formats. List assumptions (if any). Think. How would you solve the problem by hand? Develop an overall algorithm or general plan of attack.

2. **Write the main module.**

   Use English or pseudocode to restate the problem in the main module. Use module names to divide the problem into functional sub-problems. If this module is too long (more than ten to fifteen statements), you're at too low a level of detail. Introduce any control structures (such as looping or selection) that are needed at this point. Resequence logically if needed. Postpone details to lower levels. The main module may change during further refinement.

   Don't worry if you don't know how to solve an unwritten module at this point. Come back to it later. All you have to do in the main module is give the names of lower-level modules that provide certain functions (solve certain tasks). Use meaningful module names.

3. **Write the remaining modules.**

   There is no fixed number of levels. Modules at one level can specify more modules at lower levels. Each module must be complete, although it can reference unwritten modules. Make successive refinements through each module until each statement can be translated directly into a Pascal statement.

   If you do not know yet how to do a task, give it a name and go on. Later you can come back and fill in the details. If you're overwhelmed by details, step back and look at what you're trying to do. Write down those tasks to be developed later at a lower level, and go on.

4. **Resequence and revise as necessary.**

   Plan for change. Don't be afraid to start over. Several attempts and refinements may be necessary. Try to be clear. Express yourself simply and directly.

We use this outline for our top-down designs:

Input Description
Output Description
Assumptions (if any)
Data Structures (starting in Chapter 8)
Main Module
Remaining Modules

All the remaining sample problems in this book follow this outline.

Programs operate on data. Data and programs are separate. (The same program can be run with many different sets of input data.) A READ or READLN statement inputs data from a file or a terminal and stores the input in memory in the variables specified in its parameter list.

There are certain tasks that are done so often in Pascal programs that Pascal provides a library of subprograms to do them. These subprograms are called standard procedures and functions. Although we talk about READ statements and WRITE statements, they actually are procedures built into the Pascal language. When the compiler sees READ, it knows that this is one of its subprograms, and it goes and gets it for you to use.

A program communicates with its subprograms by means of parameter lists. A subprogram expects to be given a list of the variables and constants that it will need. The main program provides these each time it uses a subprogram. For example, READ(NumberOfDays) has one identifier listed on the parameter list. The READ procedure looks at this list and knows that it must go out and read one data value and store it in the place NumberOfDays.

In Chapter 6, you will learn how to write your own procedures and functions to do specific tasks.

EXERCISES

1. Modularization can be thought of as a building block approach to problem solving. True or false?

2. Write input commands to read in the following data, using meaningful identifiers. Assume that the variables have been declared.
   a. A file (Payroll) containing an employee identification number followed by a department number (INTEGER), and, on the next line, a deductions code (CHAR), hours worked (INTEGER), and overtime hours (INTEGER).
   b. A file (GradeSheet) containing a student identification number (INTEGER), a classification code (CHAR), and four letter grades (CHAR). Each data item is separated by a blank.

3. Label each of the following identifiers as reserved words (R) or user-defined identifiers (U).
   a. TEMP   ____
   b. VAR   ____
   c. BEGIN   ____
   d. CONST   ____

e. CONSTANT ____
f. SIGNAL   ____
g. FLAG   ____
h. PROGRAM ____

4. If A = 5 and B = 2, what does each of the following statements produce?

a. `WRITELN('A = ', A, ' B = ', B);`
b. `WRITELN('Sum = ', A + B);`
c. `WRITELN(A DIV B);`
d. `WRITELN(B - A);`

5. Given these input instructions:

```
VAR
  A, B, C, D : INTEGER;
  .

  .
  READ(A);
  READLN(B, C);
  READ(D);
```

and this data: 24 72
                   46 55
                   18   4

What is the value of
a. A? ____
b. B? ____
c. C? ____
d. D? ____

6. Trace the values of the variables in the following program. Use a question mark (?) if the value is undefined; repeat the value if it is the same.

```
PROGRAM Trace(INPUT,OUTPUT);
VAR
  X, Y, Z: INTEGER;              X   Y   Z
BEGIN    (* Trace *)
  READ(X, Y, Z);                ___ ___ ___
  X := X + Y + Z;               ___ ___ ___
  X := X MOD Z;                 ___ ___ ___
  Z := Y DIV 2;                 ___ ___ ___
  Y := X * X + 10;              ___ ___ ___
  X := (X - 10) * 3;            ___ ___ ___
  WRITELN (X, Y, Z)             ___ ___ ___
END.     (* Trace *)            ___ ___ ___
```

Data: 25 20
          2 10

7. For each of the following sets of input instructions and data, determine the values or the variables. All variables are of type INTEGER.

a. READLN(A);
   READ(B, C);
   READLN(D);

   Data: 42 17
               24 15
               31 43
   A: ____
   B: ____
   C: ____
   D: ____

b. READLN(A);
   READ(B, C, D);

   Data: 19 22
               25 16
               13
                 4
   A: ____
   B: ____
   C: ____
   D: ____

c. READLN(A);
   READLN(B);
   READLN(C);

   Data: 17 cost of yard of fabric
               24 width of window
               58 length of window
   A: ____
   B: ____
   C: ____

8. Write input commands to read in the described data. Assume the variables have been declared. Use meaningful identifiers.
   a. An inventory control file containing the stock number of the item in Columns 7–10 (INTEGER), the cost in Columns 30–37 (REAL), and the sale price in Columns 49–56 (real) of each line. (Assume blanks everywhere else.)
   b. A file containing a pumping station identification number (INTEGER) on one line followed by a line containing a one-character code in Column 2 (G for gasoline, K for kerosene, D for diesel) (CHAR), followed by the number of gallons of that type of petroleum product pumped (INTEGER).

9. Name two things that contribute to readable programs.

10. In PASCAL, write the expression

$$\frac{A + B}{C + D}$$

a. for a REAL result.

b. for an INTEGER result.

11. Using correct syntax and program structure, and self-documenting code, write a Pascal program that reads an input line containing an invoice number, quantity ordered, and unit price (INTEGER) and computes total price (INTEGER). Write out the invoice number, quantity, unit price, and total price with identifying phrases. Use top-down methodology and show your modules.

12. Reserved words can be used as variable names. True or false?

13. Given the following program fragment, what values would the variables contain after execution?

```
VAR
    Ch1, Ch2, Ch3, Ch4 : CHAR;
    .
    .
    READ(Ch1, Ch2, Ch3, Ch4);
```

Data:

	A	2		X		

a. Ch1 _____

b. Ch2 _____

c. Ch3 _____

d. Ch4 _____

14. Modify the following program to read from a file (FileA) and write to another file (FileB).

```
PROGRAM ChangeIt(INPUT, OUTPUT);

VAR
    Item1, Item2 : INTEGER;

BEGIN    (* ChangeIt *)
    READLN(Item1, Item2);
    WRITELN(Item2, Item1)
END.      (* ChangeIt *)
```

PRETEST

1. Trace the values of the variables in the following program. Use a question mark (?) if the value is undefined; repeat the value if it is the same.

```
PROGRAM Test3(INPUT,OUTPUT);
CONST
    N = 4;
```

```
VAR
    A, B, C : INTEGER;                      A    B    C
BEGIN  (* Test3 *)
    A := 5;                                ____ ____ ____
    B := A * N;                            ____ ____ ____
    C := A MOD N;                          ____ ____ ____
    A := C;                                ____ ____ ____
    B := A + C;                            ____ ____ ____
    WRITELN(A, B, C)                       ____ ____ ____
END.       (* Test3 *)                     ____ ____ ____
```

2. For the following sets of input instructions and data, determine the values of the variables. All variables are of Type INTEGER.

   a. READLN(A);
      READ(B, C);
      READLN(D);

      Data: 24 72
               46 55
               18   4
      A: ____
      B: ____
      C: ____
      D: ____

   b. READLN(A);
      READLN(B);
      READLN(C);

      Data: 17 cost of gallon of paint
               14 width of room
               18 length of room
      A: ____
      B: ____
      C: ____

   c. READ(A);
      READ(B, C);
      READ(D);

      Data: 24 17
               22 13
               12 14
      A: ____
      B: ____
      C: ____
      D: ____

3. Write input commands to read in the described data. Assume the variables have been declared. Use meaningful identifiers.

a. A sales discount file containing the stock number of the item in Columns 5–8 (INTEGER), the original price in Columns 20–27 (REAL), and the sale price in Columns 29–36 (REAL).

b. A file containing a service station identification number (INTEGER) on one line followed by a line containing a one-character code in Column 1 (P for premium, L for lead-free, R for regular (CHAR), followed by the number of gallons of that type gas sold (INTEGER).

4. For each of the following sets of input instructions and data, determine the values of the variables. All variables are of type INTEGER.

a. `READ(A, B, C);`
   `READLN(D);`

   Data: 42 17
            24 15
            31 43

   A: ____
   B: ____
   C: ____
   D: ____

b. `READ(A);`
   `READLN(B, C);`
   `READLN(D);`

   Data: 42 17
            24 15
            31 43

   A: ____
   B: ____
   C: ____
   D: ____

c. `READLN(A);`
   `READLN(B);`
   `READLN(C);`

   Data: 16 cost of square yard of carpet
            24 width of room
            13 length of room

   A: ____
   B: ____
   C: ____

5. Write input commands to read in the described data. Assume the variables have been declared. Use meaningful identifiers.

a. A file containing an identification number (INTEGER) followed by two grades (INTEGER).

b. A file containing a record identification number (INTEGER) on one line followed by a line containing a one-character code in Column 2 (C for classical, R for rock, J for jazz) (CHAR), followed by the number sold (INTEGER).

6. Name two things that contribute to the readability of a program.

7. In Pascal, write the expression

$$\frac{A + B}{C}$$

   a. for a REAL result.
   b. for an INTEGER result.

8. Mark each of the following identifiers either reserved or user-defined identifiers.
   a. PROGRAM   ____
   b. VAR   ____
   c. FLAG   ____
   d. CONST   ____
   e. THEEND   ____

9. Given the following program fragment, what values would the variables contain after execution?

```
VAR
    Ch1, Ch2, Ch3, Ch4 : CHAR;
.
.
.
READ(Ch1):
READLN(Ch2, Ch3);
READ(Ch4);
```

Data:

B		3	X		
7		C	2		

   a. Ch1 ____
   b. Ch2 ____
   c. Ch3 ____
   d. Ch4 ____

10. Modify the following program to read from a file (GetIt) and write to another file (PutIt).

```
PROGRAM Switch(INPUT, OUTPUT);

VAR
    One, Two : INTEGER;

BEGIN    (* Switch *)
    READLN(One, Two);
    WRITELN(Two, One)
END.     (* Switch *)
```

PROGRAMMING ASSIGNMENTS

1. In Assignment 1 in Chapter 2, the values for Debt, Payment, and Interest were set as constants. Rewrite that program so that Debt, Payment, and Interest are read in. You will need to make the following adjustments:

- Change your comments.
- Add Interest, Debt, and Payment to the VAR section (after removing them from the CONST section).
- Prompt the user to input the proper data.
- Read values into Interest, Debt, and Payment.

2. Write a program to calculate the cost of glasswork and metal stripping for rectangular windows. All windows, no matter what size, use the same quality of glass and aluminum strips, therefore the unit prices are *constants* for all windows:

> Glass : 50 cents per square inch (unit area)
> Aluminum : 75 cents per inch (unit length)

The length and width of a window should be read as input data. Select *any one* of the following three sets of data (all measured in inches) as your input data:

> 60 30
> 55 24
> 25 18

Output: (all properly labeled)
    (1) Echo-print the input data.
    (2) The total cost, the sum of the costs of glasswork and metal strips can be expressed in cents.

Note: Area = length × width
        Perimeter = 2 × (length + width)
        100 cents = 1 dollar

3. You know the formula for conversion from Fahrenheit to centigrade:

$$C = \frac{5}{9} * (F - 32)$$

But it takes too long to calculate. Your friend says that a good approximation when converting Fahrenheit to centigrade is to take half the Fahrenheit temperature and subtract 15. How good an approximation is it?

Write a Pascal program that reads in a temperature given in Fahrenheit, computes the centigrade equivalent by the actual formula, computes the approximation, and computes the percentage difference between the two. Remember to prompt for the input, and be sure the output is properly labeled.

Input: Temperature in Fahrenheit

Output: (1) Temperature in Fahrenheit
          (2) Correct temperature in centigrade
          (3) Approximated version of temperature in centigrade
          (4) Percentage difference between approximation and actual temperature

4. Write a program to compute and print the area and perimeter of the following:
  a. A triangle (sides 3, 4, and 5 inches)
  b. A rectangle (sides 7 and 9 inches)
  c. A circle (6 inches in diameter)

5. Read in three integers representing the blast-off time of a rocket expressed in hours, minutes, and seconds on a twenty-four-hour clock. Then read another integer giving the rocket's flight time in seconds. Use these data values to calculate the time of day at which the rocket will return to earth, then print out this time in a readable format. Assume that the rocket returns on the same day.

    Input: Four integers

    Output: The expected time of return

    Data: 3 47 32 45678

    Remarks: (1) Always echo-print the input data.
                (2) Always label your output properly.

 **Selection**

- To be able to construct a simple Boolean expression to evaluate a given condition.
- To be able to construct a complex Boolean expression to evaluate a given condition.
- To be able to construct an IF-THEN statement to perform a specific task.
- To be able to construct an IF-THEN-ELSE statement to perform a specific task.
- To be able to construct a set of nested IF statements to perform a specific task.
- To be able to debug a Pascal program with errors.

The order in which you enter your statements at the keyboard is the *physical order* of your program. So far the execution of your program has paralleled this physical order. The second statement is executed after the first, the third is executed after the second, and so on. But what if you want to execute one statement *or* another statement depending on what's happened before? What if you want to execute your statements in a *logical order* that differs from the physical order? To do this, you must have the capability to ask questions about what has happened so far in the execution of the program.

The IF statement gives us this capability. It allows us to ask a question and do one thing if the answer is yes (TRUE) and another thing if the answer is no (FALSE).

The first part of this chapter deals with how to ask questions; the second part deals with the IF statement itself.

Boolean Expressions

In a programming language the only kind of question we can ask is one with a yes or no answer. This may seem like a severe restriction; however, you'll quickly become adept at phrasing what seem to be complex questions in a way that can be answered yes or no.

The idea is to phrase a question in the form of an assertion about the state of one or more of the variables in your program. If the assertion is true, the answer is TRUE (yes). If the assertion is not true, the answer is FALSE (no). For example, to compare the values of two variables to see if the first is less than the second, you assert First < Second. The program examines the values stored in First and Second to see if this assertion is true. If the content of First is less than the content of Second, the assertion is evaluated as TRUE. If the content of First is greater than or equal to the content of Second, the assertion is evaluated as FALSE. These assertions are called **Boolean expressions**.

> **Boolean Expression**
> A sequence of identifiers, separated by compatible operators, that evaluates to TRUE or FALSE.

In Chapter 2 we defined arithmetic expressions. The identifiers name numeric variables or constants, and the compatible operators are the arithmetic operators. An illegal expression is one where operands and operators do not match (for example, real numbers with DIV or MOD). Here we introduce two additional sets of operators—relational and Boolean—and show how they can be used to form complex Boolean expressions.

A Boolean expression is one of the following:

- A BOOLEAN variable or constant
- An arithmetic or character expression followed by a relational operator, followed by an expression of the same type

- A Boolean expression followed by a Boolean operator, followed by a Boolean expression

A BOOLEAN constant is a constant that has been set to either TRUE or FALSE. A BOOLEAN variable is a variable declared to be of type BOOLEAN. This means that the contents of this variable can be either TRUE or FALSE. BOOLEAN variables differ from variables of type INTEGER, REAL, or CHAR because values cannot be read into them; they must be set within the program by an assignment statement. For example, given the following definitions and declarations:

```
CONST
  TestRun = TRUE;

VAR
  TestResult : BOOLEAN;
  .
  .
BEGIN
  TestResult := TRUE;
```

TestRun is a BOOLEAN constant and TestResult is a BOOLEAN variable set to TRUE.

```
TestResult := FALSE;
```

sets the BOOLEAN variable TestResult to FALSE.

Arithmetic expressions with a relational operator between them are another form of Boolean expression. A **relational operator** is one of the following:

=	equal to
<>	not equal to
<=	less than or equal to
>=	greater than or equal to
>	greater than
<	less than

If Data1 is 5 and Data2 is 10, then the following Boolean expressions are all TRUE:

Data1 < Data2	5 is less than 10.
Data1 <= Data2	5 is less than or equal to 10.
Data1 <> Data2	5 is not equal to 10.
Data2 > Data1	10 is greater than 5.
Data2 >= Data1	10 is greater than or equal to 5.

Character expressions with a relational operator between them also form a Boolean expression. If Data1 is 'M' and Data2 is 'P', then the same expressions are TRUE because $<$, when referring to characters, means "comes before in the collating sequence of the computer." Of course, we must be careful to compare like things—numbers with numbers (REAL or INTEGER) and characters with characters (CHAR).

Relational operators *compare* things such as numbers and letters. **Boolean operators** are the special operators AND, OR, and NOT. AND and OR are used to *combine* Boolean expressions; NOT is used to *negate* a Boolean expression. Because Boolean expressions can only take on two values, TRUE and FALSE, we can define the Boolean operators by showing the result of every possible case:

AND	TRUE	FALSE	OR	TRUE	FALSE	NOT	
TRUE	TRUE	FALSE	TRUE	TRUE	TRUE	TRUE	FALSE
FALSE	FALSE	FALSE	FALSE	TRUE	FALSE	FALSE	TRUE

The AND table says:

- If both expressions are TRUE, the result is TRUE.
- If one expression is TRUE and one expression is FALSE, the result is FALSE.
- If both expressions are FALSE, the result is FALSE.

The OR table says:

- If both expressions are TRUE, the result is TRUE.
- If either expression is TRUE, the result is TRUE.
- If both expressions are FALSE, the result is FALSE.

And the NOT table says:

- If the expression is TRUE, the result is FALSE.
- If the expression is FALSE, the result is TRUE.

AND and OR are **binary operators**; they go between two Boolean expressions (operands). The NOT operator is a **unary operator**.

Just as there is an order of precedence among arithmetic operators, there is an order of precedence among Boolean operators. NOT has the highest precedence, AND is next, and OR is third. For example, look at this Boolean expression:

```
A AND NOT B OR C
```

NOT B is evaluated first. The result is then AND-ed with A. Finally, the result of this operation is OR-ed with C.

Relational operators have the lowest precedence of all, they are the last to be evaluated. This can cause problems. For example, if you want to make the statement (ask the question) that A is equal to 24 and B is less than 10, you might write the expression

```
A = 24 AND B < 10
```

But this statement is syntactically incorrect. Because AND has higher precedence than =, the expression 24 AND B is evaluated first. AND is a Boolean operator and 24 and B are integers. We can solve the problem by using parentheses:

```
(A = 24) AND (B < 10)
```

In mathematics, we use the notation $X < Y < Z$ to indicate that Y is greater than X and less than Z. This is illegal in Pascal. Instead we have to write out the expression as follows:

```
(X < Y) AND (Y < Z)
```

If we leave off the parentheses, we get a syntax error again.

Appendix D shows the order of precedence for the operators: Boolean (logical), relational (comparison), and arithmetic. Remember, parentheses override the order of precedence of all operators.

```
A AND B OR C
```

is the same as

```
(A AND B) OR C
```

but not the same as

```
A AND (B OR C)
```

Here are some more examples of valid assignments to BOOLEAN variables:

```
Flag := TRUE;
Check := FALSE;
Test := Flag AND Check;
Check := Counter > 0;
Flag := DataItem = LastItem + 1;
Found := (DataValue >= DataItem) OR (Counter >= MaxValue);
```

The first three are straightforward. Let's take a closer look at the last three:

```
Check := Counter > 0;
```

This statement sets Check to TRUE if the current value of Counter is greater than zero and to FALSE for any value of Counter less than or equal to zero.

```
Flag := DataItem = LastItem + 1;
```

This sets Flag to TRUE for any pair of values for DataItem and LastItem where DataItem is one more than LastItem. For any other pair of values for DataItem and LastItem, Flag is set to FALSE.

```
Found := (DataValue >= DataItem) OR (Counter >= MaxValue);
```

Found is TRUE if either of the two expressions is TRUE. The first is TRUE for any pair of values DataValue and DataItem in which DataValue is greater than or equal to DataItem. The second expression is TRUE for any pair of values for Counter and MaxValue in which Counter is greater than or equal to Max-Value. If neither expression is TRUE, Found is FALSE.

The Selection Control Structure

The ability to make decisions, to execute instructions conditionally, is necessary for the practical application of computers. In Pascal, as in other programming languages, the structure that provides this control is called an IF statement. There are two basic forms of IF statements: IF-THEN and IF-THEN-ELSE.

IF-THEN Statement

Now that we have the capability to ask questions, we can use the answers to change the order in which program statements are executed.

```
IF Boolean expression
   THEN
      Statement1A;
Statement2;
```

means "If the Boolean expression is TRUE, execute Statement1A and continue with Statement2. If the Boolean expression is FALSE, skip Statement1A and continue with Statement2." Figure 4–1 illustrates the **flow of control** (the order in which statements are executed) of the IF-THEN statement.

Suppose you want to test to see if a data value is positive and write an error message if it is not. The code would look like this:

```
IF Data < 0
   THEN
      WRITELN('Bad data');
```

Figure 4–2 illustrates the flow of control of this statement.

As the program is executing, the Boolean expression Data < 0 is evaluated. If the content of the place named Data is less than zero, the Boolean expression is TRUE and the words *Bad data* are printed. If the content of Data is not less than zero, the expression is FALSE and the WRITELN is not exe-

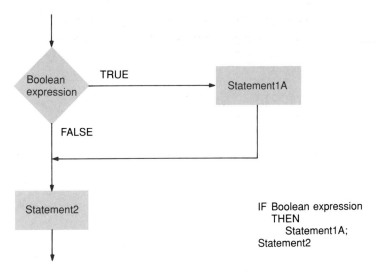

FIGURE 4–1 IF-THEN structure diagram

cuted. In either case, execution continues with the statement following the WRITELN.

What if we need to set the value of Data to zero whenever we print the error message? This would require two statements, but the syntax says Statement1A. That's easy to fix. We just put a BEGIN-END pair around the two statements, making them into one compound statement:

```
IF Data < 0
    THEN
      BEGIN (* a single (compound) statement *)
        WRITELN('Bad data');
        Data := 0
      END;
```

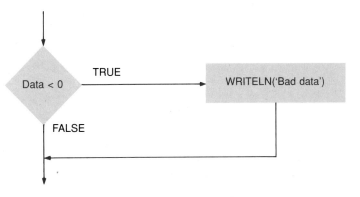

FIGURE 4–2

The test Data < 0 is made as before. If Data does contain a negative value, the statements between the BEGIN-END pair are executed in sequence. After Data has been set to zero, the program continues with the statement following the END.

IF-THEN-ELSE Statement

```
IF Boolean expression
    THEN
        Statement1A
    ELSE
        Statement1B;
Statement2;
```

The IF-THEN-ELSE statement means "If the Boolean expression is TRUE, execute Statement1A and continue with Statement2. If the Boolean expression is FALSE, execute Statement1B and continue with Statement2" (Figure 4–3).

The following Pascal fragment prints either *Tennis anyone?* or *Too cold for tennis.* depending on the value of the INTEGER variable Temperature.

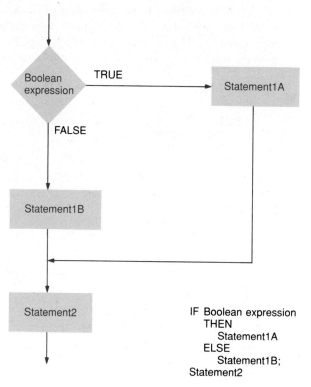

```
IF Boolean expression
    THEN
        Statement1A
    ELSE
        Statement1B;
Statement2
```

FIGURE 4–3 IF-THEN-ELSE structure diagram

```
IF Temperature >= 50
   THEN
      WRITELN('Tennis anyone?')
   ELSE
      WRITELN('Too cold for tennis.');
```

Look back at Program AverageRainFall on page 30. The following IF-THEN-ELSE statement is used there:

```
IF TotalRain = 0.0
   THEN
      WRITELN('There was no rain during this period.')
   ELSE
      BEGIN
         Average := TotalRain / NumberOfDays;
         WRITELN('The average rainfall over ', NumberOfDays,
                 ' days was ', Average:7:3)
      END;
```

The IF-THEN-ELSE statement is used to determine if any rain has fallen during the time period. If it has not, no calculation is necessary and an appropriate message is printed. If there has been rain, the average is calculated and the result is printed out.

SAMPLE PROBLEM

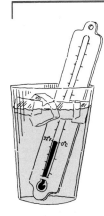

Problem: The metric system is here to stay! You kept thinking that it would go away if you ignored it, but it hasn't. You decide to write a program that allows you to input a number in Fahrenheit, convert the number to centigrade, and print the result. On reflection, you realize that this is only half the solution. You also need to be able to input a number in centigrade, convert it to Fahrenheit, and print the result. These are the conversion formulas:

$C = 5 * (F - 32)\ \mathrm{DIV}\ 9$ From Fahrenheit to centigrade

$F = (9 * C + 160)\ \mathrm{DIV}\ 5$ From centigrade to Fahrenheit

Discussion: How will the program know which conversion to do? You have to input a code letter to tell the program whether the input is in centigrade or Fahrenheit. The program will have to examine the code letter (how about a C or an F?) and decide which conversion should be done.

Input: 'C' or 'F'
         An integer number (call it Temp)

SAMPLE PROBLEM, CONTINUED

Output: Temp, " in Fahrenheit is ", ConTemp, " in centigrade."
or
Temp, " in centigrade is ", ConTemp, " in Fahrenheit."

Assumptions: Temperatures are INTEGER values.

MAIN MODULE   Level 0

```
Get data
IF Letter is a C
    THEN
        Convert from centigrade to Fahrenheit
    ELSE
        Convert from Fahrenheit to centigrade
Print output message
```

GET DATA   Level 1

```
Prompt user for input
Read Letter
Read Temp
```

CONVERT CENTIGRADE TO FAHRENHEIT

```
ConTemp ← ((9 * Temp + 160) DIV 5)
```

CONVERT FAHRENHEIT TO CENTIGRADE

```
ConTemp ← (5 * (Temp − 32) DIV 9)
```

PRINT OUTPUT MESSAGE

```
IF Letter is a C
    THEN
        Write centigrade to Fahrenheit message
    ELSE
        Write Fahrenheit to centigrade message
```

PROMPT USER FOR INPUT   Level 2

> Writeln 'INPUT MENU'
> Writeln
> Writeln 'F : Convert from Fahrenheit to centrigrade'
> Writeln 'C : Convert from centigrade to Fahrenheit'
> Writeln
> Writeln 'Type a C or an F, then press return.'
> Writeln 'Type an integer number, then press return.'

Module Design Chart:

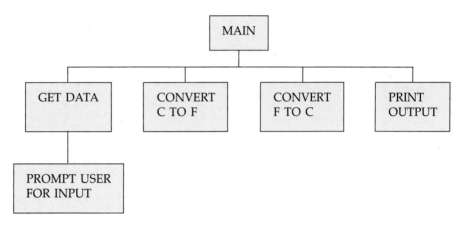

```
PROGRAM TemperatureConversion(INPUT, OUTPUT);
(* The user is prompted to enter either a 'C' or an        *)
(* 'F' and an integer number.  If the letter is a 'C',     *)
(* the number is converted from centigrade to Fahrenheit.  *)
(* If the letter is not a 'C', the number is converted from *)
(* Fahrenheit to centigrade.  In either case the converted *)
(* temperature is printed.                                 *)

VAR
   Letter : CHAR;          (* letter that controls processing *)
   Temp,                   (* temperature to be converted     *)
   ConTemp : INTEGER;      (* converted temperature           *)
```

SAMPLE PROBLEM, CONTINUED

```
BEGIN   (* TemperatureConversion *)
  WRITELN('INPUT MENU');
  WRITELN;
  WRITELN('F : Convert from Fahrenheit to centigrade');
  WRITELN('C : Convert from centigrade to Fahrenheit');
  WRITELN;
  WRITELN('Type a C or an F, then press return.');
  WRITELN('Type an integer number, then press return.');
  READLN(Letter);
  READLN(Temp);
  IF Letter = 'C'
     THEN
       ConTemp := ((9 * Temp + 160) DIV 5)
     ELSE
       ConTemp := (5 * (Temp - 32) DIV 9);
  IF Letter = 'C'
     THEN
        WRITELN(Temp, ' in centigrade is ', ConTemp,
                      ' in Fahrenheit.')
     ELSE
        WRITELN(Temp, ' in Fahrenheit is ', ConTemp,
                      ' in centigrade.')
END.      (* TemperatureConversion *)
```

A copy of the screen from two runs is shown below. Input from the keyboard is shown in color.

```
INPUT MENU

F : Convert from Fahrenheit to centigrade
C : Convert from centigrade to Fahrenheit

Type a C or an F, then press return.
Type an integer number, then press return.
F
32
32 in Fahrenheit is 0 in centigrade.

INPUT MENU
F : Convert from Fahrenheit to centigrade
C : Convert from centigrade to Fahrenheit

Type a C or an F, then press return.
Type an integer number, then press return.
C
0
0 in centigrade is 32 in Fahrenheit.
```

We examine this program in more detail in the 4-Cs Corner at the end of this chapter.

Nested IF Statements

There are no restrictions on what the statements in an IF statement can be; therefore, an IF within an IF is okay. In fact, an IF within an IF within an IF is legal. The limiting factor is us. Humans can't follow a structure that's too involved. A clear program is a program that people can follow, that they can read and understand.

SAMPLE PROBLEM

Problem: Read in a temperature and print out the sport that is appropriate for that temperature using the following guidelines.

Sport	Temperature
Swimming	Temp > 85
Tennis	$70 < \text{Temp} \le 85$
Golf	$32 < \text{Temp} \le 70$
Skiing	$10 < \text{Temp} \le 32$
Chinese checkers	$\text{Temp} \le 10$

Discussion: The temperature must be compared with the limits of each sport. When the proper place is found, that sport is printed. This comparison can be done with the IF statement.

Input: Integer temperature (Temperature).

Output: Prompt user for temperature.
Print the appropriate sport.

MAIN MODULE   Level 0

```
Get Temperature
Print Sport
```

SAMPLE PROBLEM, CONTINUED

GET TEMPERATURE   Level 1

> Write 'Enter an integer temperature (Fahrenheit).'
> Writeln ' Press return.'
> Read Temperature

PRINT SPORT

> Write 'The appropriate sport for ', Temperature, ' degrees is '
> IF Temperature > 85
>   THEN
>   Print 'swimming'
> IF Temperature ≤ 85 AND > 70
>   THEN
>   Print 'tennis'
> IF Temperature ≤ 70 AND > 32
>   THEN
>   Print 'golf'
> IF Temperature ≤ 32 AND > 10
>   THEN
>   Print 'skiing'
> IF Temperature ≤ 10
>   THEN
>   Print 'Chinese checkers'

The algorithm for PRINT SPORT uses five IF statements. In all but the first and last, the Boolean expression has a compound condition. A careful look at these expressions shows that the first test in each one is actually testing the opposite of the IF statement above it; that is, the first part of the second IF is asking if Temperature is less than or equal to 85. The first IF is asking the opposite: Is Temperature greater than 85? This means that the five IFs can be combined into one IF-THEN-ELSE, where the first condition in the second, third, and fourth IFs don't need to be asked. That is, we wouldn't be at this point if the first condition was not true.

PRINT SPORT can be coded as one nested IF-THEN-ELSE statement. This is the first concrete example of what we mean by a program (or code segment) being concise. The first version of this algorithm makes unnecessary tests.

Module Design Chart:

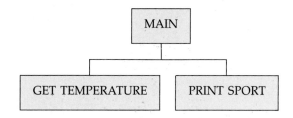

```
PROGRAM Sport(INPUT, OUTPUT);
(* The user is prompted to input a temperature.  *)
(* The appropriate sport is printed.             *)

VAR
   Temperature : INTEGER;     (* input temperature *)

BEGIN    (* Sport *)
   WRITE('Enter an integer temperature (Fahrenheit).');
   WRITELN('  Press return.');
   READLN(Temperature);
   WRITE('The appropriate sport for ', Temperature:1,
         ' degrees is ');
   IF Temperature > 85
      THEN
        WRITELN('swimming.')
   ELSE IF Temperature > 70
      THEN
        WRITELN('tennis.')
   ELSE IF Temperature > 32
      THEN
        WRITELN('golf.')
   ELSE IF Temperature > 10
      THEN
        WRITELN('skiing.')
      ELSE
        WRITELN('Chinese checkers.')
END.    (* Sport *)
```

If you input −30, the output will be

```
The appropriate sport for −30 degrees is Chinese checkers.
```

SAMPLE PROBLEM, CONTINUED

If you input 100, the output will be

```
The appropriate sport for 100 degrees is swimming.
```

Figure 4–4 shows exactly how the flow of control works in this example.

SAMPLE PROBLEM

Problem: Many universities require that freshmen who are in danger of failing a class be sent a warning notice. You are to calculate the average of three test grades and print out the student's ID number, the average, and whether the student is passing or not. Passing is a 60-point average or better. If the student is passing with less than a 70 average, indicate that he or she is marginal. The data is on File Grades.

Discussion: To calculate the average, you have to read in the three test scores, add them up, and divide by 3. To print the appropriate message, you have to determine if the average is 60 or above or if it is below 60. If it is 60 or above, you have to determine if it is less than 70.

In doing this calculation by hand, you'd probably notice if a test grade was negative and question it. If the semantics of your data imply that values should be positive, then your program should test to be sure they are. Here we test to be sure each grade is positive and use a BOOLEAN variable to report the result of the test.

Input: Student ID (INTEGER) followed by three test grades (INTEGER). Data is on File Grades.

Output: Output should be on File Report.
Echo-print input data.
Message containing student ID, passing/failing, average grade, possible marginal indication, or error message if any of the test scores are negative.

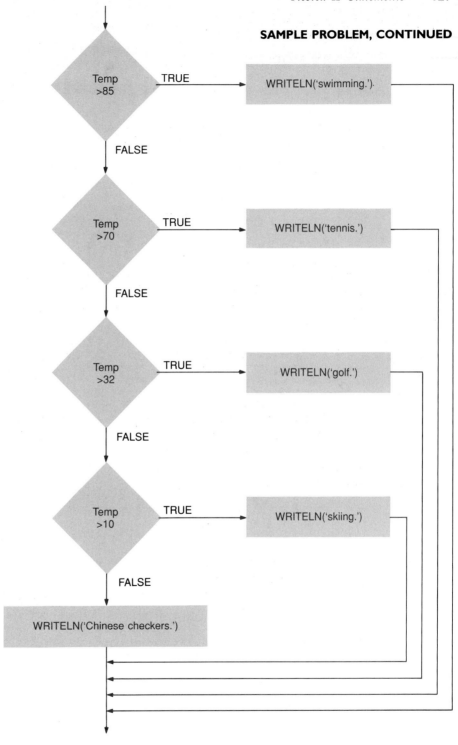

FIGURE 4–4

SAMPLE PROBLEM, CONTINUED

MAIN MODULE   Level 0

```
Get data
Test data
IF data OK
    THEN
        Calculate Average
        Print message
    ELSE
        Print error message
```

GET DATA   Level 1

```
Read StudentID, Test1, Test2, Test3
Print StudentID, Test1, Test2, Test3
```

TEST DATA

```
IF (Test1 < 0) OR (Test2 < 0) OR (Test3 < 0)
    THEN
        DataOK ← FALSE
    ELSE
        DataOK ← TRUE
```

CALCULATE AVERAGE

```
Average ← (Test1 + Test2 + Test3) / 3
```

PRINT MESSAGE

```
Write Average, StudentID
IF Average ≥ 60.0
    THEN
        Write 'Student is passing'
        IF Average < 70.0
        THEN
            Writeln ' but marginal'
    ELSE
        Write 'Student is failing'
Write '.'
```

Module Design Chart:

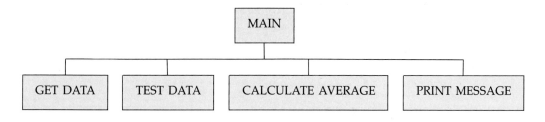

```
PROGRAM Notices(OUTPUT, Grades, Report);
(* Program to determine a student's average grade *)
(* and passing/failing/marginal status.          *)

VAR
  Average : REAL;        (* average of three grades *)
  StudentID,             (* identification number   *)
  Testl,
  Test2,
  Test3 : INTEGER;       (* three test grades        *)
  DataOK : BOOLEAN;      (* TRUE if data is correct  *)
  Grades,                (* input file               *)
  Report : TEXT;         (* output file              *)

BEGIN   (* Notices *)
  RESET(Grades);
  REWRITE(Report);
  READLN(Grades, StudentID, Testl, Test2, Test3);
  WRITELN(Report, StudentID, Testl, Test2, Test3);
  IF (Testl < 0) OR (Test2 < 0) OR (Test3 < 0)
     THEN
       DataOK := FALSE
     ELSE
       DataOK := TRUE;
  IF DataOK
     THEN
       BEGIN
         Average := (Testl + Test2 + Test3) / 3;
         IF Average >= 60.0
            THEN
              BEGIN
                WRITE(Report, 'Student is passing');
                IF Average < 70.0
                   THEN
                     WRITE(Report, ' but marginal')
```

SAMPLE PROBLEM, CONTINUED

```
                END
            ELSE
                WRITE(Report, 'Student is failing');
            WRITELN(Report, '.')
        END
    ELSE
        WRITELN(Report, 'Invalid data.')
END.    (* Notices *)
```

Program Notices tests the grades to be sure they are positive. This type of data checking is important. If you know something must always be true about your data, put a test in your program to be sure that your data is valid.

There are three IF-THEN-ELSE statements and one IF-THEN statement in Program Notices. To test each branch, take the following sets of values for Test1, Test2, and Test3 and calculate what happens by hand.

```
100  100  100
 60   60   60
 50   50   50
-50   50   50
```

The first set is valid and gives an average of 100, which is passing and not marginal. The second set is valid and gives an average of 60, which is passing but marginal. The third set is valid and gives an average of 50, which is failing. The fourth set has an invalid test grade (-50), so an error message would be printed.

There is one point of confusion when nesting IF statements: To which IF does an ELSE belong? For example, let's change the problem definition slightly for Program Notices. If a student's average is 70 or greater, print nothing. If it is between 60 and 69, print *Passing but marginal*; print *Failing* if it is below 60. Coding this slight change gives us an IF-THEN-ELSE nested within an IF-THEN:

```
IF Average < 70
    THEN
        IF Average < 60
            THEN
                WRITE(Report, 'Failing')
            ELSE
                WRITE(Report, 'Passing but marginal');
```

How do we know that *Passing but marginal* will be written when Average is between 60 and 69 and not when Average is 70 or above? In other words, how do we know to which IF the last ELSE belongs? The rule is that an ELSE is paired with the closest IF that does not have a matching ELSE and has not been terminated by an END. In this example we formatted the code to reflect this pairing. However, formatting does not affect the code. If the ELSE had been lined up with the first THEN, it still would belong with the second IF.

Look at the existing IF-THEN-ELSE statement in Program Notices:

```
IF Average >= 60.0
    THEN
      BEGIN
        WRITE(Report, 'Student is passing');
        IF Average < 70.0
            THEN
              WRITE(Report, ' but marginal')
      END
    ELSE
      WRITE(Report, 'Student is failing');
```

We use a compound statement in the THEN branch because we want to execute two statements in that branch. However, even if we removed one of the WRITE statements, we would still need the BEGIN-END pair. Why? Because we want the ELSE branch as part of the first IF statement, not the second. The BEGIN-END pair around the nested IF statement indicates that the nested IF statement is complete, so the ELSE is matched up with the outside IF statement.

We would like to make one other point before leaving Program Notices. We assigned a value to DataOK in an IF statement. We could have done this another way, by simply saying

```
DataOK := NOT ((TEST1 < 0) OR (TEST2 < 0) OR (TEST3 < 0));
```

In fact, we can reduce the code even more. How about:

```
IF (Test1 >= 0) AND (Test2 >= 0) AND (Test3 >= 0);
```

in place of IF DataOK. To convince yourself that these two variations work, try them by hand with the test data.

The 4-Cs Corner

Correctness

In Chapter 1 we described the two phases of programming: problem solving and implementation. Testing is an integral part of both phases. This is as it should be; testing is an integral part of demonstrating the correctness of our programs. Let's apply testing at both phases on the problem for Program TemperatureConversion.

Testing at the problem-solving phase involves looking at each level of the top-down design and saying, "If the levels below this are expanded correctly, will this level do what needs to be done?" In this case, if (1) GET DATA correctly inputs a 'C' or an 'F', (2) both CONVERTs correctly convert one temperature to the other, and (3) PRINT OUTPUT MESSAGE prints the proper message, then the main module is correct.

The next step is to examine each module at Level 1 and ask the same question: "If the Level 2 modules are assumed to be correct, will this module do what it's supposed to do?" Notice that there is no code in the top-down design. We could just as easily translate the design into FORTRAN (another widely used high-level language) as into Pascal.

GET DATA calls on Module PROMPT USER FOR INPUT and reads in Letter and Temp. If PROMPT USER FOR INPUT correctly prompts the user for 'C' or 'F', then GET DATA is correct. *But is it really?* What happens if someone keys in a value other than a 'C' or an 'F'? There is no internal data checking in this module. Whatever value is keyed in is the value that is returned to the previous module to use.

This type of error can be very hard to detect. Look what happens if the user keys in an incorrect letter. The main module checks only for a 'C'; it treats any other character as an 'F'. This means that the error could go undetected for years. The program does not crash because of bad data; it simply gives the wrong answer! The main module must be redesigned:

```
Get data
IF Letter = 'C'
    THEN
        Convert from centigrade to Fahrenheit
    ELSE IF Letter = 'F'
        THEN
            Convert from Fahrenheit to centigrade
        ELSE
            Write 'Character input was not a C or an F.'
```

Our algorithm walk-through continues with PROMPT USER FOR INPUT, which uses a *menu* to prompt the user for input. The options are listed for the user, and the user inputs a code that indicates which of the options should be used. Notice that the form of the input is clearly specified and the user is told when to hit the return key.

But there is one problem with these instructions. If the menu option must be keyed in as either uppercase or lowercase, this point should be made explicitly. The directions show uppercase letters, but if the program only recognizes one form or the other, that is not enough. The user must be warned. The other option is to let the IF statement in the main module check for both uppercase and lowercase letters.

CONVERT CENTIGRADE TO FAHRENHEIT correctly converts 0° C to 32° F and 100° C to 212° F. CONVERT FAHRENHEIT TO CENTIGRADE correctly converts 32° F to 0° C and 212° F to 100° C. This is sufficient for the algorithm level.

Once you've desk-checked the algorithm, the next refinement is coding the instructions. This is part of the implementation phase.

Testing at the implementation phase is done at several different points. After you've coded the algorithm, you should carefully go over the code, checking to make sure you've reproduced the top-down design faithfully. At this stage you should take some actual values and calculate what the output should be by doing a code walk-through (tracing the program). Later, you can use these same values as input and check the results.

Remember that a program is first compiled, then executed. The program you've coded is now ready for compilation. The Pascal compiler takes the program coded in Pascal and translates it into machine code, a language that the machine you're using can execute.

There are two distinct outputs from the compilation phase: a listing of the program with error messages (if any) and the translated version of the program ready to be executed (if there are no errors). (See Appendix F for a list of the errors that can occur during the compilation phase.)

When the compiler no longer gives you any error messages, the translated version of your program is ready to be executed. Here, the tasks you want to be done are done—a line is read, a value is tested, a message is printed.

You are now in the debugging phase. This is where you locate and correct all errors (called **bugs**) in your program. Errors are of two types: syntactic or semantic. Syntactic errors are errors in Pascal syntax and usually are caught by the compiler. Semantic errors are more difficult to locate; they usually surface when the program is executing. These are errors that give you the wrong answer. An error can be an undetected bug in your top-down design or a keying error that creates a syntactically correct but meaningless statement.

Always run a program with more than one set of data. A program may work on the end cases but not be correct on values in the middle. For example, in Program TemperatureConversion, cases that we know the answer to—like the boiling point and freezing point of water—work fine. But try running the program to convert 84° F and 28° C. You will find that 84° F converts to 28° C, but that 28° C converts to 82° F. Is there an error in the conversion algorithm? No, what you're seeing is a truncation error because the conversion algorithms use DIV instead of /. With DIV the remainder is thrown away. (We have more to say about this type of error in Chapter 7.)

Figure 4–5 pictures the programming process we have just discussed. The figure indicates where syntax and semantic errors occur and where they can be corrected.

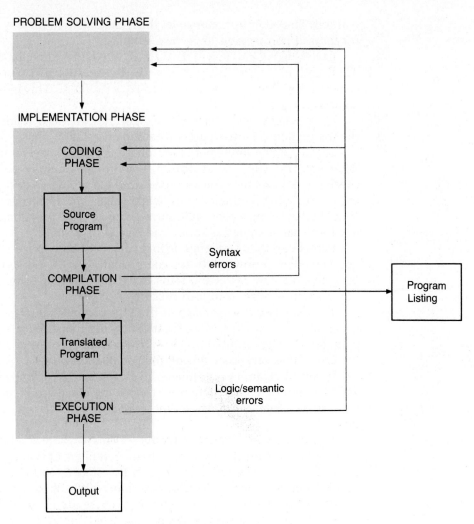

PROBLEM SOLVING PHASE

IMPLEMENTATION PHASE

CODING
PHASE

Source
Program

COMPILATION
PHASE

Syntax
errors

Translated
Program

Program
Listing

Logic/semantic
errors

EXECUTION
PHASE

Output

FIGURE 4–5 Programming process

Correctness Hints

1. Echo-print all input data. Put a corresponding WRITELN immediately below each READ or READLN statement. This way you know your input data is what you want it to be.
2. Test for bad data in your program. If a data value must be positive, put an IF statement in to test the value. If it is negative, print an error message, otherwise continue with the processing. For example, in Program Sport the following statement should be inserted after the first WRITE (echo print):

```
IF (Temperature > 120) OR (Temperature < -25)
   THEN
     WRITELN('Temperature data is in error.')
   ELSE
     BEGIN
       (* balance of program *)
     END
```

This IF statement tests the limits of reasonable temperatures and only continues if the data is reasonable. Note that the parentheses are necessary; otherwise the order of precedence would impose

```
Temperature > (120 OR Temperature) < -25
```

which would give a syntax error. This leads us to the next hint.

3. Use parentheses to make your Boolean expression clear and correct.
4. Remember, semicolons *separate* statements. An IF-THEN-ELSE is one statement. A semicolon before the ELSE would tell the compiler that it had reached the end of an IF-THEN statement. The compiler would then expect the next word, ELSE, to begin a new statement. Because it is not the first word in any statement and is a reserved word, an error occurs.
5. Check your declarations to be sure each variable name used has been declared.
6. Take sample data values and try them by hand as we did for Program Notices. (There is more on this in Chapter 5.)
7. If an answer produced by your program does not agree with the value you calculated by hand, try the following suggestions:
   - Redo your arithmetic.
   - Recheck your input data.
   - Carefully check the section of code that does the calculation. If you're in doubt about the order of operations, insert clarifying parentheses.
   - Check for integer overflow. The value of an INTEGER variable may have exceeded MaxInt during calculation. Many systems give you an error message when this happens; others do not.
8. If you're using files, be sure to RESET the input file and REWRITE the output file.

Completeness

Completeness and correctness go hand in hand. In testing Program TemperatureConversion we discovered that it was not correct because it was not complete; that is, the input data was not checked to be sure that it met the specifications of the problem. Checking the input for correctness is essential to the completeness of any program. Verifying the validity of input data is called **data validation**.

Clarity

In Program TemperatureConversion the variable identifier for the input temperature is Temp and the variable identifier for the converted temperature is ConTemp. In Program Sport the variable identifier for the input temperature is Temperature. This was not done to confuse you, but to make a point about meaningful identifiers.

Although Temperature is certainly clearer than Temp in isolation, there is no confusion as to the meaning of Temp within the context of Program TemperatureConversion. Whether you use a complete word for an identifier or a meaningful abbreviation is a matter of taste. There clearly is a break-even point; an overly long identifier is a distraction. Also, the longer the word, the more chances there are of a keying mistake. The moral is to be thoughtful in your choice of identifiers and to be consistent.

Summary

In Chapter 4 we have described a way of asking questions about the execution of a program as it runs. A Boolean expression is evaluated: It is TRUE if the expression is true and FALSE if the expression is not true.

The IF statement allows the program to take different alternatives based on the value of a Boolean expression. IF-THEN allows the program to choose whether or not to take one particular action. IF-THEN-ELSE allows the program to choose between two courses of action. The branches of an IF-THEN or IF-THEN-ELSE can be any statement, simple or compound. They can even be (or include) another IF statement.

EXERCISES

1. One form of Boolean expression involves comparison. Look at this comparison:

   ```
   MinimumAge <= Age < MaximumAge
   ```

   a. Is it a legal comparison in Pascal?
   b. If not, how can it be expressed properly?

2. Write a statement containing a comparison that sets BOOLEAN variable Available to TRUE if NumberOrdered is less than or equal to NumberOnHand less Number-Reserved.

3. Declare Eligible to be a BOOLEAN variable. Assign it the value TRUE.

4. Given the following values for BOOLEAN variables A, B, C, and D, evaluate the Boolean expressions below.

   A = TRUE   B = FALSE   C = FALSE   D = TRUE

   a. (A AND B) OR (A AND D)
   b. NOT C AND D AND A

c. NOT (A AND D) OR (C OR D)

d. (A OR B) AND NOT (C OR D)

5. Write a statement containing a Boolean expression that assigns TRUE to BOOL-EAN variable Candidate if SATScore is greater than or equal to 1100, GPA is not less than 2.5, and Age is greater than 15. Otherwise Candidate should be FALSE.

6. Given the following declarations:

```
VAR
   LeftPage : BOOLEAN;
   PageNumber : INTEGER;
```

Write a statement that sets LeftPage to TRUE if PageNumber is even.

7. Simplify the following program segment so that fewer comparisons are necessary.

```
IF Age > 64
   THEN
      WRITE('Social Security');
IF Age < 18
   THEN
      WRITE('Exempt');
IF (Age >= 18) AND (Age < 65)
   THEN
      WRITE('Taxable');
```

8. Write an IF-THEN-ELSE statement that assigns to the variable Largest the greatest value contained in variables A, B, and C. Assume the three values are distinct.

9. What would the following program segment write in a case where

a. Height exceeds MinHeight and Weight exceeds MinWeight?

b. Height is less than MinHeight and Weight is less than MinWeight?

```
IF Height > MinHeight
   THEN
      IF Weight > MinWeight
         THEN
            WRITELN('Eligible to serve.')
         ELSE
            WRITELN('Too light to serve.');
```

10. Use top-down design to write a Pascal program segment that reads three integer numbers corresponding to the day, month, and year of a person's birth, followed by three integer numbers corresponding to today's date. Compute the person's age in years (disregarding additional months and days). Write out the birthdate and age in years with identifying phrases.

11. In the following program, correct the syntax errors.

```
PROGRAM Exercise(INPUT,OUTPUT)

CONST
  A = 10
  B = 5
  C = 6

VAR
  D:E;F:INTEGER

BEGIN     (* Exercise *)
  READ(D,E F)
  IF (D > A)
     THEN
        D = A + D;
     ELSE
        D = A
  E := D + F
  WRITE('This program does not make any sense,
          E, F D)
  END;     (* Exercise *)
```

12. Given the following declarations, what is the value of Equal after execution?

```
PROGRAM A2(INPUT, OUTPUT);

CONST
  A = 5;
  B = 6;
  X = 11;

VAR
  Y : INTEGER;
  Equal : BOOLEAN;

BEGIN     (* A2 *)
  Y := X;
  Equal := (A >= B) OR (X >= Y)
END.     (* A2 *)
```

13. Write a program that reads a day of the month followed by a temperature. Write out the day of the month, followed by *Cool* if the temperature is less than 75 degrees, *Warm* if it is 75 to 90 degrees, and *Hot* if it is 90 degrees or higher.

14. Correct the syntax errors in the following program.

```
PROGRAM M4V3(INPUT=OUTPUT);

CONS
  A = 29

VAR
  I J K: INTEGER;
```

```
START     (* M4V3 *)
  READ(K)
  I := 29 DIV A
  J := 9
  IF K = I OR J
     THEN
        K = 0
     ELSE
        WRITE('Nope')
  READ(I,J);
  IF I = J
     THEN
        WRITELN('Equal')
  J := I + K + J + A
END.      (* M4V3 *)
```

15. Given the corrected version of Exercise 14 and the following data:

    Data: 12   7   10

    a. What are the values of variables I, J, and K at the end of execution?
    b. What is written?

PRETEST

1. Look at Boolean expressions (a) and (b). They are logically equivalent, but only (b) is legal in Pascal. True or false?

   a. `TotalIncome >= NetIncome > TaxAmount`
   b. `(TotalIncome >= NetIncome) AND (NetIncome > TaxAmount)`

2. Given the following values for BOOLEAN variables X, Y, and Z, evaluate the Boolean expressions. Circle T if the result is TRUE, F if the result is FALSE.

   X = TRUE   Y = FALSE   Z = TRUE

a. `(X AND Y) OR (X AND Z)`	T	F
b. `(X OR NOT Y) AND (NOT X OR Z)`	T	F
c. `X OR Y AND Z`	T	F
d. `NOT (X OR Y) AND Z`	T	F

3. Write an IF statement that assigns to the variable Biggest the greatest value contained in variables I, J, and K. Assume all three values are distinct.

4. Write a program that reads a package number followed by a weight in ounces. Write out the package number, followed by *Class1* if the package weighs less than 32 ounces, *Class2* for 32 up to 128 ounces, and *Class3* for 128 ounces and over.

5. Correct the syntax errors in the following program.

```
PROGRAM Pretest(INPUT=OUTPUT);

CONST
   W = 5
```

```
VAR
  Four, One, Zero := INTEGER;

BEGIN    (* Pretest *)
  READ(Four; Zero; One)
  Four = Four + Zero + W
  IF Four =< One
     THEN
        Four = One
     ELSE
        One = Four
  IF Zero < 0
     THEN
        WRITE('Zero is negative.')
  WRITELN(' It is over.')
BEGIN.    (* Pretest *)
```

6. Given the corrected version of Problem 5 and the following data:

   Data: 13   16   17

   a. What are the values of variables Four, One, and Zero at the end of execution?
   b. What is written?

7. Given the following declarations, what is the value of Answer after execution?

```
PROGRAM One(INPUT, OUTPUT);

CONST
  I = 300;
  J = 200;
  M = 100;

VAR
  N: INTEGER;
  Answer: BOOLEAN;

BEGIN    (* One *)
  N := I + J;
  Answer := (I >= J) AND (M >= N)
END.    (* One *)
```

8. Write an IF statement that assigns to the variable Smallest the smallest value contained in variables I, J, and K. Assume all three values are distinct.

9. Write a program that reads a student ID number followed by a grade point. Write out the ID number, followed by *Unacceptable* if the grade point is less than 2.0, *O.K.* for 2.0 up to 3.0, and *Good* for 3.0 and over. Use a procedure to get the data.

10. Correct the syntax errors in the following program.

```
PROGRAM M4V3(INPUT=OUTPUT);

CONST
  W := 7
```

```
VARIABLE
   C, A, B = INTEGER;

BEGIN     (* M4V3 *)
   READ A, B, C;
   IF A < B
      THEN
         A = A + C;
      ELSE
         A = B
   B = 2B
   IF A < B
      THEN
         WRITELN('A is small.')
   WRITELN('A is not small.')
END;      (* M4V3 *)
```

PROGRAMMING ASSIGNMENTS

1. You want to find the minimum number of rolls of coins (quarters, dimes, nickels, pennies) in a given amount of money. You also want to calculate the minimum number of coins in any amount left over. Use only integer arithmetic in solving this problem.

    Input: A REAL value representing the total amount of money. Use 66.69.

    Output: (1) Echo-print and label the input.
    (2) Print a line for each coin, giving the number of rolls of that coin. If there are none, print an appropriate message. Label each line.
    (3) Print the amount left over in cents, then the minimum number of coins to make up that amount. Be sure to label the output.

    Note: The amount in dollars for a roll of each coin:

Quarters	$10.00
Dimes	5.00
Nickels	2.00
Pennies	.50

2. Prompt for and read in two numbers, Debt and Received. Debt is the balance due on a customer's charge account. Received is the amount received from the customer. Compare these two numbers. If they are equal, print the message *Nothing owed*. If the amount received is greater than the amount due, give the customer credit toward the account. Print out the credit balance. If the amount received is less than the amount owed, the new balance is computed by adding a 1.5 percent service charge to the unpaid amount. Print that amount.

3. Your great-grandmother wants you to paint the floor of her gazebo without wasting any paint. She knows from experience that it takes 1 quart of paint to cover 37 square feet of surface area. If the gazebo floor is 10 feet in diameter, how much paint should she buy? (Remember that a gazebo is round and that the area of a circle is πR^2.) Your answer should be in quarts.

4. The Local Pizza Parlor advertises a giant pizza (15 inches in diameter) for $9.52 and a large pizza (10 inches in diameter) for $4.40. Susy and Sarah have decided that two 10-inch pizzas are a better buy than one 15-inch pizza. Write a program to determine if they're right.

5. You can use the following information to compute the date of any Easter Sunday; X = the year

   A = the remainder of the division of X by 19
   B = the remainder of the division of X by 4
   C = the remainder of the division of X by 7
   D = the remainder of the division of (19A + 24) by 30
   E = the remainder of the division of (2B + 4C + 6D + 5) by 7

   Easter Sunday = March (22 + D + E). (This can give a date in April.)
   Use this information to determine and print out the date for Easter Sunday 1991.

5 Looping

GOALS

- To be able to construct syntactically correct WHILE loops.

- To be able to construct count-controlled loops with a WHILE statement.

- To be able to construct event-controlled loops with a WHILE statement.

- To be able to construct loops to do the following tasks:

    Count events
    Sum values
    Calculate averages

- To be able to use function EOLN to control the input of character data.

- To be able to use function EOF to control the input of data.

We introduced in Chapter 4 the concept of logical ordering. The physical order of a program is the order in which the statements are written; the logical order is the order in which the statements are executed.

The IF statement is a way of making the logical order different from the physical order. If a condition (or set of conditions) is TRUE, then one statement is executed. If a condition (or set of conditions) is not true, then another statement is executed or, in the case of IF-THEN, no statement is executed.

In this chapter we talk more about the loop (repetition) construct mentioned in Chapter 1. This construct allows a program to repeat a statement as long as a Boolean expression is TRUE. When the Boolean expression becomes FALSE, the statement is not repeated again. The Pascal statement that implements the loop construct is the WHILE statement. With the introduction of the WHILE statement, you have all the control structures you will ever need. Pascal does have some additional control structures, but they are merely for convenience.

WHILE Statement

The WHILE statement, like the IF statement, tests a condition.

```
WHILE Boolean expression DO
   Statement1;
Statement2;
```

means "If the Boolean expression is TRUE, execute Statement1. After the execution of Statement1, go back to test the Boolean expression again." This process continues until the Boolean expression becomes FALSE. At that time Statement1 (which could be a compound statement) is skipped and execution continues with Statement2, the first statement following the loop. Statement1 is often called the *body of the loop*. Figure 5–1 illustrates the flow of control of the WHILE statement.

At first glance, the IF statement and the WHILE statement look alike. They do have similarities, but a careful examination shows their fundamental differences (see Figure 5–2). In the IF, either Statement1A *or* Statement1B is executed exactly once. In the WHILE, Statement1 is executed zero or more times (zero times if the Boolean expression is FALSE to start with).

The flow of control returns to test the Boolean expression in the WHILE; in the IF it does not. The IF is used to *choose between* two courses of action. The WHILE is used to *repeat* a course of action. Remember that Statement1, Statement1A, Statement1B, and Statement2 can all be compound statements.

Loops Using the WHILE Statement

We can classify loops on the basis of the Boolean expressions that control them. There are two basic types: *count-controlled loops*, in which the Boolean expression tests whether or not the loop has been repeated a required number

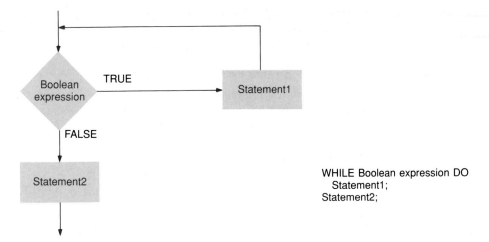

WHILE Boolean expression DO
    Statement1;
Statement2;

FIGURE 5–1   WHILE structure diagram

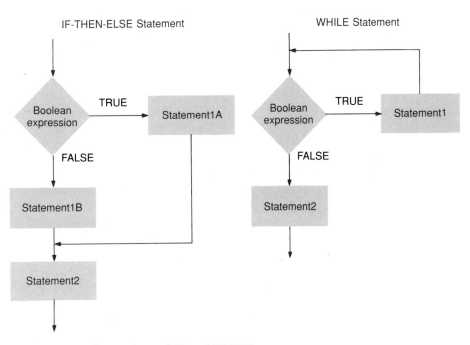

FIGURE 5–2   Comparison of IF and WHILE

of times; and *event-controlled loops*, in which the Boolean expression tests whether or not a particular event has occurred.

Count-Controlled Loops

Count-controlled loops are loops where we know how many times a process or action should be executed. The looping mechanism simply counts each time the process is repeated, then tests to see if it's finished before beginning again. Remember our example of counting each street as you cross it in order to keep track of how many blocks you've gone? If you need to go six blocks, a count of six streets tells you when you're there.

To implement a count-controlled loop using a WHILE statement, three things must be done:

1. The variable that is going to be used as a counter must be **initialized** (set to a starting value).
2. A Boolean expression that compares this counter to the number of times you want to repeat the process must be used as the expression in the WHILE statement.
3. The counter must be incremented within the body of the WHILE statement.

Let's say we want to repeat a process ten times. The loop looks like this:

```
(* Execute a process 10 times. *)
Counter := 1;                          ← Initializes Counter
WHILE Counter <= 10 DO                 ← Tests Counter
  BEGIN
    Statement;
    Counter := Counter + 1             ← Increments Counter
  END;
(* next statement to be executed *)
```

Counter is the **loop control variable.** It is set to 1 *outside* the loop. The WHILE statement tests the expression Counter <= 10 and executes the compound statement, the statements between the BEGIN-END pair, as long as the expression is TRUE. Statement represents the action we want the loop to repeat. The last statement in the compound statement, Counter : = Counter + 1, increments Counter by adding 1 to it. When the loop has repeated ten times, the value of Counter is 11. The expression Counter <= 10 is no longer TRUE, so control passes to the statement directly below the loop.

A WHILE statement always tests the condition first. If the expression is FALSE to begin with, the body of the loop is never executed. It's the programmer's responsibility to see that the condition to be tested is set correctly (initialized) before the WHILE statement begins.

The loop control variable in a count-controlled loop doesn't have to be initialized to 1, but it makes things easier. You don't have to agonize over which relational operator to use; the test is always the loop control variable less than or equal to the number of repetitions wanted. If you vary from this pattern, you can create an "off-by-1" error (the loop executing one more time or one less time than you want it to).

You must be sure that the loop control variable is incremented *within* the loop so that the expression becomes FALSE at some point or you will never exit from the loop. (This is called an *infinite loop*.)

In our example we use a literal constant in the loop control expression. A named constant or variable works in exactly the same way.

Event-Controlled Loops

Event-controlled loops are loops in which the number of repetitions is controlled by an event that occurs within the body of the loop itself. To implement an event-controlled loop using a WHILE statement, there are again three things that must be done.

1. The event must be initialized.
2. A Boolean expression must be constructed to test the event. This expression must be the expression in the WHILE statement.
3. The event must be updated within the body of the loop.

Here is an example:

```
(* Repeat a process as long as Event is TRUE. *)
Event := (* initial value *);        ← Initializes Event
WHILE Event DO                        ← Tests Event
  BEGIN
    Statement;
    Event := (* update event *)       ← Updates Event
  END;
```

Statement represents the process being repeated. When the event that is controlling the loop changes, the WHILE expression becomes FALSE, and control passes to the statement immediately below the loop. Notice that Event is *not* initialized to TRUE. There may be a time in the flow of your program when you want to skip this loop. Therefore, the skeleton code segment simply says to initialize the event.

The count-controlled loop is very straightforward: The process is repeated a specified number of times. The event-controlled loop is less clear-cut. Let's look at a concrete example: reading and writing data values until a negative value is encountered. (We ignore prompts in this example.)

```
READ(DataValue);
DataPositive := (DataValue >= 0);
WHILE DataPositive DO
  BEGIN
    WRITE(DataValue);
    READ(DataValue);
    DataPositive := (DataValue >= 0)
  END;
```

The first two statements initialize DataPositive, the Boolean expression (the event) that controls the loop. The WHILE statement tests DataPositive. If DataPositive is TRUE, the loop body is executed. DataValue is printed, and the last two statements in the loop update DataPositive.

To verify that the loop does what it's supposed to do, let's do a code walk-through. A data value (DataValue) is read. DataPositive is set to TRUE if DataValue is positive; DataPositive is set to FALSE if DataValue is negative. If DataPositive is TRUE, the loop is entered and DataValue is printed. A new DataValue is read and DataPositive is reset. If the current value of DataValue is negative, DataPositive becomes FALSE and the loop does not execute again. The negative value that stops the process is not printed. If DataValue is negative originally, the loop is never entered and nothing is printed.

Each repetition of either a count-controlled loop or an event-controlled loop is called an *iteration* of the loop.

Practice with Constructing Loops

Loops are never constructed in the abstract; they are constructed to perform a task. When we construct a loop, there are two questions we must ask about the task:

1. *What type of repetition are we dealing with?* Is it a count-controlled repetition, where we know how many times the process should be repeated, or is it an event-controlled repetition, where an event occurring within the execution of the task itself controls the repetition?
2. *What task has to be done within each repetition?*

Now let's look at several tasks, ask these questions, and arrive at the loops that implement the tasks.

Problem 1:   Add up the numbers from 1 through 10.

Type of loop: There are ten numbers between 1 and 10 (inclusive), so the loop is adding ten values and must be executed once for each value. This is a count-controlled loop. We must remember to initialize the counter outside the loop, test it in the WHILE expression, and increment it within the loop.

Task of the loop: Our task is to add up the numbers 1 through 10. We need a place to put the running sum (sum so far). Sum seems a meaningful identifier for this variable. Sum must be initialized to zero outside the loop. Within the loop, we have to add the number 1 to Sum during the first repetition, the number 2 during the second, the number 3 during the third, and so on. Notice that the number we are adding is the value of the loop counter before it has been incremented.

Solution:

```
Counter := 1;
Sum := 0;
WHILE Counter <= 10 DO
  BEGIN
    Sum := Sum + Counter;
    Counter := Counter + 1
  END;
```

Comments on the solution: Counter is the variable we're using to keep track of the number of times the loop has been repeated. Counter is initialized to 1 outside the loop. Sum is the place where the sum of the numbers is being accumulated. Sum is initialized to 0 outside of the loop.

Counter is compared to 10 in the Boolean expression. As long as Counter is less than or equal to 10, the loop is repeated. When Counter becomes greater than 10, control passes to the statement immediately below the WHILE statement.

Within the body of the loop, the task (adding the numbers from 1 through 10) is done with the statement

```
Sum := Sum + Counter;
```

Counter is incremented with the statement

```
Counter := Counter + 1
```

The loop control counter must be incremented *after* the counter is added to the sum in order for the values to come out right. If the counter is incremented at the beginning of the loop, the answer is wrong. If the statements were reversed, a 1 would have to be subtracted from Sum at each iteration to make the answer come out right.

Problem 2: Read in and sum values until a negative number is read. Do not include the negative number in the sum.

Type of loop: We do not know how many numbers should be read and summed. A negative number will tell us when to stop reading and summing. Therefore, this loop is an event-controlled loop. When the number that has just been read is less than zero, the loop terminates. That sounds just like the loop we used to demonstrate event-controlled loops. In fact, we can take that looping structure and just replace the task. (Look for familiar patterns; never reinvent the wheel!)

Notice that we have to read the first value outside the loop in order to initialize the Boolean expression that controls the loop. Reading the first data value outside a loop is called a *priming read*.

Task of the loop: This problem is similar to the last one. We have to sum some numbers. However, we don't know what the numbers are; they have to be read from the keyboard or a file. Since no file is given with the problem, we assume the keyboard. We are going to need a place to keep the sum, and this place must be initialized to 0.

Solution:

```
READ(DataValue);
DataPositive := (DataValue >= 0);
Sum := 0;
WHILE DataPositive DO
  BEGIN
    Sum := Sum + DataValue;
    READ(DataValue);
    DataPositive := (DataValue >= 0)
  END;
```

Comments on the solution: The Boolean expression must be TRUE for the loop to be executed. If we frame our event expression so that it reflects when we wish to stop repeating the loop, we must put NOT before the expression in the WHILE loop. For example, the following code fragment is logically identical to the one above, and both are equally correct. In the solution below, because our event expression is TRUE when we want to stop reading (DataValue is negative), we have to use the Boolean operator NOT before the event. The semantics of the identifier chosen for the event (DataNegative instead of DataPositive), force the Boolean expression used in the WHILE statement to be negated.

```
READ(DataValue);
DataNegative := (DataValue < 0);
Sum := 0;
WHILE NOT DataNegative DO
  BEGIN
    Sum := Sum + DataValue;
    READ(DataValue);
    DataNegative := (DataValue < 0)
  END;
```

Problem 3:   Count the number of positive numbers and the number of negative numbers in a file of integers (File Numbers). A zero value ends the data file.

Type of loop: We have to count the number of positive integers and the number of negative integers in a file of integers. How many integers are there? We don't know. Therefore, this cannot be a count-controlled loop; it must be an event-controlled loop.

The event that is controlling the loop is the value of the last integer read. As long as that value is not zero, the loop continues. When the number read is zero, the loop terminates. The expression controlling the WHILE loop must be initialized outside the loop. This means the first value must be read outside the loop as it is in Problem 2.

Task of the loop: We have to count two things: positive numbers and negative numbers. This means that we have to set up two places in which to keep these counts. Let's call them PositiveCt and NegativeCt. Each time we read a positive integer, PositiveCt must be incremented. Each time we read a negative integer, NegativeCt must be incremented. PositiveCt and NegativeCt are called *event counters* because they keep track of how many times an event occurs.

Solution:

```
PositiveCt := 0;
NegativeCt := 0;
READ(Numbers, DataValue);
NonZero := (DataValue <> 0);
WHILE NonZero DO
  BEGIN
    IF DataValue > 0
      THEN
        PositiveCt := PositiveCt + 1
      ELSE
        NegativeCt := NegativeCt + 1;
    READ(Numbers, DataValue);
    NonZero := (DataValue <> 0)
  END;
```

Comments on the solution: The loops in Problems 1 and 2 are called *summing loops* because their task involves summing values. The loop in Problem 3 is called a *counting loop* because events are being counted. Notice the difference between count-controlled loops and counting loops. *Count-controlled* refers to the type of termination condition used in the loop; *counting* refers to the task being done within the loop.

Input Loops Using **EOLN** and **EOF**

In Problems 2 and 3, data values are read and processed in some way. This is such a common occurrence that Pascal has two standard functions that we can use to control reading in data: EOLN and EOF. Loops using these standard functions are event-controlled loops. The event being tested is the position of the reading pointer of the standard input device or a file.

Function **EOLN**

In Chapter 3 we discussed the end-of-line symbol (<eoln>) that is inserted at the end of each line in a TEXT file. We can use this symbol to control input, and we have access to it through a built-in standard function called EOLN.

EOLN allows us to ask the question "Have we read the last character in a line?" If the reading pointer is under <eoln>, EOLN is TRUE. If the reading pointer is under any other character, EOLN is FALSE.

Function EOF

EOF is the standard function in Pascal that asks the question "Have we read the last data value in a file?" EOF becomes TRUE when the next character to be read is the end-of-file character (<eof>). This is the last character in a data file. It follows the last <eoln> in a TEXT file. You do not have to worry about putting in the <eof> character when you're creating a file. The system does it for you. If you're working interactively, the end-of-file character is probably a Ctrl-Z. This is not a standard, however, so you should check the documentation on your system.

Notice that EOF returns TRUE if the next character to be read is <eof>. We have to be careful when we use EOF to control a loop because we want to continue the loop as long as there is more data in the file. This means that we must use NOT EOF to control the WHILE loop.

When reading from a file, the file identifier must be a parameter for EOF and EOLN. If these functions are used without parameters, the standard input device is assumed.

Practice with EOLN and EOF Loops

Problem 4: Count the number of lines of text in File Info.

Type of loop: This can't be a count-controlled loop because the problem is to count the number of lines. There is nothing in the problem to tell us when to stop reading; therefore, we must keep reading until we run out of data. This implies an EOF-controlled loop.

Task of the loop: The files that we have been reading from or writing to are TEXT files; that is, they are broken up into lines. Each line ends with <eoln>. The problem here is to recognize and count this symbol, to continue reading and testing EOLN. As in any counting loop, we must remember to initialize the counter outside the loop.

Solution:

```
LineCount := 0;
WHILE NOT EOF(Info) DO
  BEGIN
    READ(Info, Character);
    IF EOLN(Info)
       THEN
         BEGIN
           LineCount := LineCount + 1;
           READLN(Info)
         END
  END;
```

Comments on the solution: Notice that we use the name of the file as a parameter for EOF, EOLN, READ, and READLN. If the file name is left off, the standard input device is assumed.

Problem 5: File Data is a file of integers organized like this:

<value>	<value>	<value>	<eoln>
<value>	<value>	<value>	<eoln>
<value>	<value>	<value>	<eoln>
<value>	<value>	<value>	<eoln>
<eof>			

Calculate the average of the values on File Data.

Type of loop: We use the EOF function to control READ loops where we do not know in advance how many sets of data values we have to read in. Because there are three integers on a line, we can use READLN and read one line at a time. READLN leaves the pointer ready to read the first character at the beginning of each new line, which is the < eof > character when the data has all been read in.

Task of the loop: To calculate an average we must have two pieces of information: the sum of the values and the number of values. The average is the sum divided by the number of values. Our tasks, then, are to sum and count the number of values. We've done both of these tasks before. There is one problem that we have to look out for: If Data is empty (has no data values), the sum and the count will both be zero. Calculating the average when the count is zero will cause an error because trying to divide by zero is always an error condition.

Solution:

```
Sum := 0;                              ← Initializes running sum
Count := 0;                            ← Initializes counter
WHILE NOT EOF(Data) DO
  BEGIN
    READLN(Value1, Value2, Value3);
    Sum := Sum + Value1 + Value2 + Value3;
    Count := Count + 3                 ← Increments counter
  END;
IF Count = 0
  THEN
    Average := 0.0
  ELSE
    Average := Sum / Count;
```

Comments on the solution: We can use a READLN here because we know how our data is organized on lines. There are times when this is not the case and we must use a READ. Could we simply replace the READLN, which takes three parameters, with a READ, which takes one, and increment Count by 1 instead of 3? No. This would *not* work. Let's do a code walk-through using a READ instead of a READLN, with the following data:

24 36<eoln>
27<eoln>
<eof>

The first two data values are read with no problem. The third data value is read, and 27 is added to Sum. Count is 3. The loop test EOF(Data) asks if there is any more data on File Data. We would expect the answer to be no because there are no more data values. Actually, the answer is yes. The <eoln> hasn't been read yet. EOF is only TRUE if the reading pointer is at the <eof>. In this case, the reading pointer is at the <eoln>.

What happens? The loop is repeated one more time, but there are no more values to be read. This is clearly an error. How this error is handled depends on your system. More often than not, you will get an error message such as TRIED TO READ PAST EOF.

The best advice we can give you is not to use EOF in combination with a READ. If you do not know how many data values there are or how your numeric data is organized, use a special data value (called a **flag** or **sentinel**) to signal the end of the data. Problem 2 uses a negative value, and Problem 3 uses a zero value to *signal* or *flag* the end of the data.

Although our examples use files, interactive input should behave the same way. We say *should* rather than *will* because each Pascal run-time system is just a little different when it comes to input and output. If you have difficulty with interactive input on your particular system, read the manual for your system or talk with your instructor.

SAMPLE PROBLEM

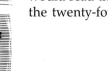

Problem: Take hourly outdoor temperature readings for a twenty-four-hour period. Find the average temperature for the day and the day's high and low temperatures.

Discussion: To do this task without a computer is easy. Each hour, we would read the thermometer and write down the temperature. At the end of the twenty-four-hour period, we would compute the average.

We know how to take an average. It involves a summing loop and a counter that contains the number of data values.

To find the day's high by hand, we would scan the list of numbers looking for the largest. To find the day's low, we would scan the list for the smallest number. How can we do this on the computer?

Well, let's look a little more carefully at what we are actually doing. To find the largest number in a list of numbers, we compare the first with the second and remember which number is larger. Then we compare this number with the third one. Again we remember the larger number and compare it with the fourth. This process continues until we run out of numbers. The one we remember is the largest. The process of finding the smallest number is the same, only we remember the smaller number, not the larger one.

Now that we understand the process, we can design an algorithm to do it. We declare two variables, HighSoFar and LowSoFar, in which we save ("remember") the largest and smallest numbers we've seen so far. As we look at each new temperature, we compare it to HighSoFar and LowSoFar. If it is larger than HighSoFar, it becomes the new value of HighSoFar; if it is smaller than LowSoFar, it becomes the new value of LowSoFar.

Now we are ready to write the design for the program. We assume that someone else has already recorded the temperatures, which are ready to be input to our program from File TempData. The program will read and process each temperature.

Input: Twenty-four integer numbers representing hourly temperatures

Output: Echo-print the temperatures.
Print the average temperature.
Print the day's high temperature.
Print the day's low temperature.

MAIN MODULE   Level 0

```
Initialize variables
WHILE more hours DO
   Get Temperature
   Add Temperature to Sum
   Update HighSoFar
   Update LowSoFar
   Increment HourCounter
Compute Average
Print results
```

The loop could be a count-controlled loop going from 1 to 24 or an event-controlled loop using EOF(TempData). The count-controlled loop is a better

SAMPLE PROBLEM, CONTINUED

choice here. If an error has been made in recording the data and there are only twenty-three temperatures, the count-controlled loop would give us a read error. The EOF loop would not give an error; it would just give the wrong answer.

INITIALIZE VARIABLES   Level 1

> Reset data file
> Sum ← 0
> HourCounter ← 1
> HighSoFar ← − MaxInt
> LowSoFar ← MaxInt

At first glance, the way we've initialized HighSoFar and LowSoFar seems backwards, but it's not. We want the first value to become both HighSoFar and LowSoFar. We ensure this by initializing HighSoFar to the *smallest* possible integer and LowSoFar to the *largest* possible integer.

GET TEMPERATURE

> Read Temperature from File TempData
> Echo-print Temperature

ADD TEMPERATURE TO SUM

> Sum ← Sum + Temperature

UPDATE HIGHSOFAR

> IF Temperature > HighSoFar
>   THEN
>   HighSoFar ← Temperature

UPDATE LOWSOFAR

> IF Temperature < LowSoFar
>   THEN
>   LowSoFar ← Temperature

INCREMENT HOURCOUNTER

> HourCounter ← HourCounter + 1

COMPUTE AVERAGE

> Average ← Sum / 24

Although our design shows 24 as a literal constant, we should make it a named constant in our program.

PRINT RESULTS

> Print 'Average temperature is ' Average
> Print 'High temperature is ' HighSoFar
> Print 'Low temperature is ' LowSoFar

Module Design Chart:

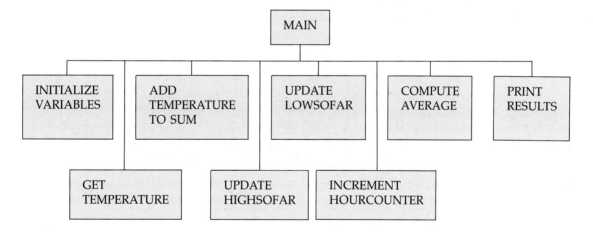

```
PROGRAM TemperatureStatistics(TempData, OUTPUT);
(* The day's average, high, and low temperatures *)
(* are calculated and printed to the screen.     *)
(* The data is on File TempData.                  *)
```

SAMPLE PROBLEM, CONTINUED

```
CONST
  HoursInDay = 24;

VAR
  Temperature,            (* an hourly temperature reading *)
  HighSoFar,              (* highest reading so far        *)
  LowSoFar,               (* lowest reading so far         *)
  Sum,                    (* running sum                   *)
  HourCounter : INTEGER;  (* loop control counter          *)
  Average : REAL;         (* average daily temperature     *)
  TempData : TEXT;        (* data file                     *)

BEGIN   (* TemperatureStatistics *)
  Reset(TempData);
  Sum := 0;
  HourCounter := 1;
  HighSoFar := -MaxInt;
  LowSoFar := MaxInt
  WHILE HourCounter <= HoursInDay DO
    BEGIN
      READ(TempData, Temperature);
      WRITELN(Temperature:10);
      Sum := Sum + Temperature;
      IF Temperature > HighSoFar
        THEN
          HighSoFar := Temperature;
      IF Temperature < LowSoFar
        THEN
          LowSoFar := Temperature;
      HourCounter := HourCounter + 1
    END;
  Average := Sum/HoursInDay;
  WRITELN('Average temperature is ', Average:6:1);
  WRITELN('High temperature is ', HighSoFar:9);
  WRITELN('Low temperature is ', LowSoFar:10)
END.    (* TemperatureStatistics *)
```

Given this input data:

45 47 47 47 50 50 55 60 70 70 72 75
75 75 75 74 74 73 70 70 69 67 65 50

The output looks like this:

```
                    45
                    47
                    47
```

```
                    47
                    50
                    50
                    55
                    60
                    70
                    70
                    72
                    75
                    75
                    75
                    75
                    74
                    74
                    73
                    70
                    70
                    69
                    67
                    65
                    50
Average temperature is      63.5
High temperature is           75
Low temperature is            45
```

What would happen if we updated HighSoFar and LowSoFar in one IF-THEN-ELSE instead of two IF-THENs?

```
IF Temperature < LowSoFar
   THEN
     LowSoFar := Temperature
   ELSE
     IF Temperature > HighSoFar
        THEN
          HighSoFar := Temperature
```

This certainly looks more efficient. After all, why bother to ask if a temperature is larger than HighSoFar if we know it's smaller than LowSoFar? Logically we shouldn't have to, but because of the way HighSoFar and LowSoFar have been initialized, we would get the wrong answer if the highest temperature was the first value read in. We could initialize these variables by reading the first value outside the loop and setting HighSoFar and LowSoFar to this first value. If we did this, the IF-THEN- ELSE structure shown above would work correctly.

Nested Logic

Nested logic is a control structure contained within another control structure. In Chapter 4 we described nested IF statements. Both WHILE and IF statements contain statements and are themselves statements. The body of a WHILE statement or the branch of an IF statement can contain other WHILE or IF statements. Remember that any statement can be replaced with a compound statement. Nesting, then, can be extended to create complex control structures.

Can we extend the previous algorithm we used to calculate a day's temperature statistics for a year? Yes, by putting a count-controlled loop around the body of Program TemperatureStatistics:

Initialize DayCounter
WHILE more days DO

> Initialize variables
> WHILE more hours DO
>   Get Temperature
>   Add Temperature to Sum
>   Update HighSoFar
>   Update LowSoFar
>   Increment HourCounter
> Compute Average
> Print results

Increment DayCounter

The two loops are coded like this:

```
DayCounter := 1;
WHILE DayCounter <= DaysInYear DO
BEGIN
  .
  .
  HourCounter := 1;
  WHILE HourCounter <= HoursInDay DO
    BEGIN
      .
      .
      HourCounter := HourCounter + 1
    END;
  .
  .
  DayCounter := DayCounter + 1
END;
```

Notice that each loop has a counter that is initialized to 1 and is incremented at the end of the loop.

Let's take a closer look at the general pattern of a nested loop. OutCounter is the counter for the outer loop, InCounter is the counter for the inner loop, and OutLimit and InLimit are the number of times each loop should be executed.

```
OutCounter := 1;
WHILE OutCounter <= OutLimit DO
  BEGIN
    .
    .
    InCounter := 1;
    WHILE InCounter <= InLimit DO
      BEGIN
        .
        .
        InCounter := InCounter + 1
      END;
    .
    .
    OutCounter := OutCounter + 1
  END;
```

Although both of these loops are count-controlled loops, the same pattern can be used for event-controlled loops or a combination of count-controlled and event-controlled loops. Let's do a code walk-through of a program fragment that has a loop within a loop.

The fragment below shows an EOLN loop where characters are read and printed, nested within an EOF loop.

```
LineCount := 0;                      1
WHILE NOT EOF(Info) DO               2
  BEGIN
    WHILE NOT EOLN(Info) DO          3
      BEGIN
        READ(Info, Character);       4
        WRITE(Character)             5
      END;
    READLN(Info);                    6
    LineCount := LineCount + 1;      7
    WRITELN                          8
  END;
```

For this walk-through we need some simple notation, so we've numbered each line (omitting the BEGINs and ENDs). As we go through the program using our walk-through table (Table 5-1), we indicate the first time line 1 is

Data: T□<eoln>
D2<eoln>
<eof>

NOTE: There are two characters on the first line: a 'T' and a blank.

TABLE 5–1 Code Walk-Through

	Variables		Expressions		
Statement	LineCount (INTEGER)	Character (CHAR)	EOLN	EOF	Output
1.1	0	?	—	—	
2.1	0	?	—	F	
3.1	0	?	F	—	
4.1	0	T	—	—	
5.1	0	T	—	—	T
3.2	0	T	F	—	
4.2	0	□	—	—	
5.2	0	□	—	—	□
3.3	0	□	T	—	
6.1	0	□	—	—	
7.1	1	□	—	—	
8.1	1	□	—	—	<eoln>
2.2	1	□	—	F	
3.4	1	□	F	—	
4.3	1	D	—	—	
5.3	1	D	—	—	D
3.5	1	D	F	—	
4.4	1	2	—	—	
5.4	1	2	—	—	2
3.6	1	2	T	—	
6.2	1	2	—	—	
7.2	2	2	—	—	
8.2	2	2	—	—	<eoln>
2.3	2	2	—	F	

Output: T□<eoln>
D2<eoln>

executed by 1.1, the second by 1.2, and so on. We use a box (□) to stand for a blank. We bracket the iterations of the loops on the left.

Because LineCount and Character are variables, their values remain the same until they are explicitly changed. The values of the Boolean expressions EOF(Info) and EOLN(Info), however, exist only when a test is made. This is indicated by a dash in those columns at all times except during a test.

The data itself is made up of two lines of characters, each with two characters. Notice that a blank (□) is a character and that the 2 in the data is a character but that the number 1 in line 7 is an integer 1 and can be added to LineCount. Although the 2 and 1 both look like numbers to us, they are represented in memory in two entirely different ways.

How does the Pascal compiler know what we mean? The program tells the compiler which data type it is. Because Character is of type CHAR, the 2 is read as an alphanumeric 2. Because line 7 is an arithmetic assignment statement, the 1 is assumed to be a numeric 1.

SAMPLE PROBLEM

Problem: You are sitting with a month's worth of sales receipts from the local supermarket. As usual your checkbook balance is flirting with zero. Where does all the money go? How much do you spend on food? How much do you spend on other items? You decide to write a program to take the sales receipts as input and calculate how much money you spend on food and how much money you spend on nonfood items at the supermarket.

Discussion: In your state, all nonfood items are taxed. Each taxable item is marked on the sales receipts with an asterisk. Total tax and total sales appear at the bottom of each receipt. There are three ways to solve the problem:

- Sum all the taxable items and sum all the nontaxable items.
- Sum the taxable items and sum the total sales, then subtract the taxable sum from the total sales sum to calculate the nontaxable sum.
- Sum both the tax totals and the sales totals. Next calculate the amount of money spent on taxable items from the tax totals. The total sales minus the amount spent on taxable items gives the amount spent on food items.

Let's use the third method because it requires the least amount of input.

Input: This is an interactive program. We can use a menu to prompt for input, with 'T' for tax total, an 'S' for sales total, and a 'Q' for quit reading. After each 'T' or 'S' the user should input a real dollar amount.

Output: Total amount spent
Total amount of sales tax paid
Total amount spent on food
Total amount spent on nonfood items

Assumptions: None

SAMPLE PROBLEM, CONTINUED

MAIN MODULE   Level 0

```
Initialize variables
WHILE more receipts DO
   Get data
   Add Amount to correct sum
Calculate nonfood costs
Calculate food costs
Print results
```

INITIALIZE VARIABLES   Level 1

   The main loop is an event-controlled loop. The event that stops the reading of input is a 'Q' input from the keyboard. Because the first value is not read in until the loop is entered, the variable used to hold the input character has to be initialized outside the loop. This variable (we call it MenuCode) can be initialized to either a 'T' or an 'S'; it doesn't matter which.

```
TaxTotal ← 0.0
Salestotal ← 0.0
MenuCode ← 'T'
```

GET DATA

```
Prompt user for input
Read MenuCode, Amount
```

ADD TO CORRECT SUM

```
IF MenuCode is a 'T' or a 't'
     THEN
        TaxTotal ←TaxTotal + Amount
     ELSE IF MenuCode is an 'S' or an 's'
        THEN
           SalesTotal ← SalesTotal + Amount
```

CALCULATE NONFOOD COST

Because the amount of tax is some percentage of the total of the taxable items (that is, TaxTotal = NonFoodCost * TaxRate), we simply solve for NonFood-Cost in this equation where the tax rate is represented as a decimal percentage.

$$\text{NonFoodCost} \leftarrow \text{TaxTotal / TaxRate}$$

CALCULATE FOOD COST

$$\text{FoodCost} \leftarrow \text{SalesTotal} - \text{NonFoodCost}$$

PRINT RESULTS

Write 'Total amount spent this month ' SalesTotal
Write 'Total amount of tax this month ' TaxTotal
Write 'Total amount spent on food ' FoodCost
Write 'Total amount spent on nonfood items ' NonFoodCost

PROMPT USER FOR INPUT   Level 2

```
Write '****************************************'
Write '************** MENU **************'
Write '* T : total taxes on receipt        *'
Write '* S : total sales on receipt        *'
Write '* Q : last data value read          *'
Write '****************************************'
Write '* Input a T or an S and a dollar *'
Write '* amount (include decimal).        *'
Write '* Input a Q to quit processing.  *'
Write '****************************************'
```

Module Design Chart:

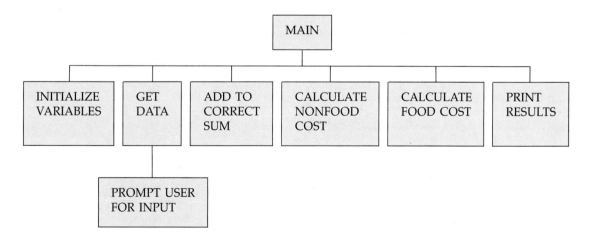

SAMPLE PROBLEM, CONTINUED

```
PROGRAM SalesReceipts(INPUT, OUTPUT);
(* The amount of money spent on taxable and *)
(* nontaxable items at the supermarket       *)
(* is calculated from sales receipts.        *)

CONST
  TaxRate = 0.08;

VAR
  MenuCode : CHAR;           (* 'T', 'S', or 'Q'              *)
  TaxTotal,                  (* total tax paid               *)
  SalesTotal,                (* total amount spent           *)
  Amount,                    (* dollar amount                *)
  FoodCost,                  (* amount spent on food         *)
  NonFoodCost : REAL;        (* amount spent on other items *)

BEGIN   (* SalesReceipts *)

  (* Initialize variables *)
  TaxTotal := 0.0;
  SalesTotal := 0.0;
  MenuCode := 'T';
  WHILE(MenuCode <> 'Q') AND (MenuCode <> 'q') DO
    BEGIN

      (* Get data (Prompt user) *)
      WRITELN('***********************************');
      WRITELN('************* MENU ***************');
      WRITELN('*  T  :   total taxes on receipt   *');
      WRITELN('*  S  :   total sales on receipt   *');
      WRITELN('*  Q  :   last data value read     *');
      WRITELN('***********************************');
      WRITELN('*  Input a T or an S and a dollar *');
      WRITELN('*  amount (include decimal).      *');
      WRITELN('*  Input a Q to quit processing.  *');
      WRITELN('***********************************');
      READLN(MenuCode, Amount);

      (* Add to correct sum *)
      IF (MenuCode = 'T') OR (MenuCode = 't')
          THEN
            TaxTotal := TaxTotal + Amount
          ELSE IF (MenuCode = 'S') OR (MenuCode = 's')
            THEN
              SalesTotal := SalesTotal + Amount
    END;
  NonFoodCost := TaxTotal / TaxRate;
  FoodCost := SalesTotal - NonFoodCost;
```

```
(* Print results *)
 WRITELN('Total amount spent this month ', SalesTotal:10:2);
 WRITELN('Total amount of tax this month ', TaxTotal:10:2);
 WRITELN('Total amount spent on food ', FoodCost:10:2);
 WRITELN('Total amount spent on nonfood items', NonFoodCost:10:2)
END.    (* SalesReceipts *)
```

We test Program SalesReceipts in the 4-Cs Corner.

The 4-Cs Corner

Clarity

Specifying Fieldwidth with Variables and Constants

In Chapter 2 we described how to specify fieldwidth (the number of column positions that a numeric or character variable should occupy on an output line). There we used a literal integer to specify the number of columns. We can also specify fieldwidth using a variable or constant identifier. This can be useful. For example, the following program segment plots a graph of an item's sales history:

```
READ(ItemFile, UnitSales);      ← Inputs the number of unit sales
EndData := UnitSales < 0;
WHILE NOT EndData DO
  BEGIN
    (* Print (UnitSales - 1) blanks followed by an asterisk. *)
    WRITELN('*':UnitSales);
    READ(ItemFile, UnitSales);
    EndData := (UnitSales < 0)
  END;
```

The statement WRITELN('*':UnitSales) says to print an asterisk using the value of UnitSales as the fieldwidth specification.*

How does it work? Suppose this is the data on File ItemFile:

5 7 8 9 10 9 8 9 10 9 <eof>

The output to the screen would look like this:

---

*Of course, if UnitSales is larger than the number of columns on a page, an appropriate scaling factor should be used.

```
      *
       *
        *
         *
          *
           *
            *
             *
              *
               *
                *
```

Documenting Output

A combination of WRITEs and WRITELNs can be used to center headings, line up columns, and make your output clear and readable. Just as comments in the program document the code, your headings and explanatory material document your output.

The first step is to decide exactly what you want printed. We use the temperature data problem to illustrate the process by setting up the WRITE and WRITELN statements to create a table with a year's worth of daily high, low, and average temperatures. The table should contain a heading that describes what is in the table, column headings that describe the temperature values being printed, and the temperature values themselves.

The next step is to take a pencil and paper (graph paper is useful here) and make a sketch of how the table should look. Line up headings and put in

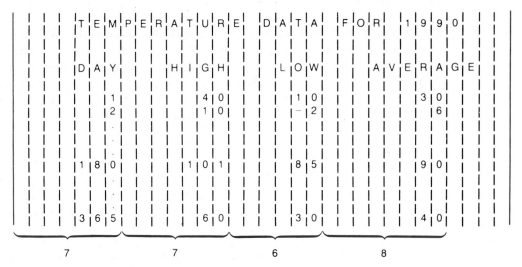

FIGURE 5–3 Output formatting

some actual values. After several tries, we might come up with the layout in Figure 5–3. Notice that we have added a column that shows the day of the year for each set of temperatures. Once we have lined things up the way we want them, we mark off the number of character positions needed for each heading or data value.

In our format, the table heading takes up 25 character positions; the column headings take up 26. If we want 4 blanks to the left of each heading line, we would use fieldwidth specifications of :29 and :30 respectively. To line up the values in each column, we count the number of character positions from the end of the previous column to the last character position in the column we're working with. This count becomes the fieldwidth. In this case the fieldwidths are :7, :7, :6, and :8 respectively.

```
WRITELN('TEMPERATURE DATA FOR 1990':29);
WRITELN;
WRITELN;
WRITELN('DAY    HIGH    LOW    AVERAGE':30);
WRITELN;
        .
        .
        .
WHILE DayCounter <= DaysInYear DO
        .
        .
   WHILE HourCounter <= HoursInDay DO
        .
        .
   WRITELN(DayCounter:7, HighSoFar:7, LowSoFar:6,
             ROUND(Average):8);
```

Notice that the table headings and the column headings are printed before the program enters the nested loops. The values to be printed in the columns are computed within the inner loop and then printed at the bottom of the outer loop. In Program TemperatureStatistics, Average is of type REAL. People usually think of temperatures as integers, so we use the standard function ROUND to convert Average from a REAL value to an INTEGER for printing.

Program Readability

Program SalesReceipts is hard to read! Although the top-down design separates the tasks into meaningful units, the modularization is completely lost in the program code. The user prompts take up so much room that the code for the loop is hard to find. There is nothing we can do about the length of the program, but we can do something about the modularization of the program. We can write our modules as procedures and functions. That process is the topic of the next chapter.

Correctness

Testing

As the programs we write get more complex, the task of testing them gets more difficult. So far we have taken sample data, calculated what the results should be by hand, run the program, and compared the program's output with our hand-calculated results. For a complicated program, many data sets have to be designed in order to test all parts of the program.

For Program SalesReceipts we have an alternate way to check the results. In the discussion of the problem, we pointed out that there were several approaches to the solution. We chose to use the one with the least input. We can check the results by calculating what the answer should be using the "brute force" method. That is, we can take our sales receipts and add up all the taxable items, the food items, the tax paid, and the total sales. Now we can check the program's output against these figures, which we know to be correct.

Figure 5–4 shows data from three sales receipts. Let's use the information on them to test the program. Working by hand with the data in Figure 5–4, we come up with these totals:

Total amount spent: 160.56
Total sales tax paid: 4.02
Total spent on food: 106.29
Total spent on nonfood items: 50.25

When we ran Program SalesReceipts using the same data, this was the printed output:

```
Total amount spent this month        160.56
Total amount of tax this month          4.02
Total amount spent on food      110.31
Total amount spent on nonfood items       50.25
```

Several things come to mind when we look at this output. The first is that the numbers are not lined up. We can correct this easily by changing the fieldwidth specifications. What about the answers? Are they correct? *No. The amount spent on food is wrong.* We know from adding up the items without stars on the sales receipts that the total spent on food should be 106.29. The output says 110.31.

What went wrong? The first step is to check to be sure that the top-down design was correctly coded into Pascal. It was translated correctly, so we must go back to the algorithm in our design and look for a logic error.

Because the total sales and the total taxes are correct, the error cannot be within the loop. The nonfood total is also correct. Therefore the error must be in the CALCULATE FOOD COST module. There is only one statement in this module, and it says that the cost of the food items is the total sales less the cost of the nonfood items. That's the problem! We forgot to account for the

ORANGE JUICE	2.49		TRASH CAN	11.31*
BAKERY	1.09		GRAPE NUTS	2.49
RED PEPPER	5.01		CAN BACON	3.19
GREEN PEPPER	5.03		RAZOR BLADES	4.99*
WHIP CREAM	.73		FLOWER SHOP	.99*
WHIP CREAM	.73		FLOWER SHOP	.99*
WHIP CREAM	.73		FLOWER SHOP	.99*
CELLO MSHROO	.99		FLOWER SHOP	.99*
CELLO MSHROO	.99		WHT POTATOES	.88
CELLO MSHROO	.99		SPRITE	1.89*
CELLO MSHROO	.99		RMAINE LTUCE	.50
REFLECTOR	5.99*		CALF LIVER	1.15
SHAMPOO	4.79*			
FISH DEPT	3.98		SUBTOTAL	30.36
GREEN ONIONS	.45			
RASPBERRIES	1.89		TAX PAID	1.77
STELLADORO	.89			
PRES RED RSP	2.69		TOTAL SALES	32.13
ENG STILTON	3.69			
CHESHIRE	4.57			
PRODUCE	3.99			
MONINI OIL	8.69		OLIVE OIL	5.79
VEAL SCALLPI	20.58		ANCHOVIES	1.19
CHRY TOMATO	1.19		BROWN EGGS	.79
CREST	3.59*		SK ALBACORE	2.55
LAUNDRY DETR	6.75*		C&B CAPERS	3.19
ASPARAGUS	4.02		MILK	2.19
BULK GARLIC	.42		DIET COKE	1.99*
MILK	1.19		FLOWER SHOP	4.99*
BUTTER	2.15		LEMONS	2.22
SUBTOTAL	101.28		SUBTOTAL	24.90
TAX PAID	1.69		TAX PAID	.56
TOTAL SALE	102.97		TOTAL SALE	25.46

FIGURE 5–4 Sales receipts

taxes paid. The cost of the food items should be the total sales less the cost of the nonfood items *less the taxes paid*. That is,

```
FoodCost := SalesTotal − (NonFoodCost + TaxTotal);
```

With this change, the program is correct. Notice that the second way to solve the problem listed on page 63 has the same logical error.

Input Idiosyncrasies

We have pointed out before that input, especially from the keyboard, may be treated differently by different Pascal run-time systems. An example of this occurs in Procedure GetData in Program SalesReceipts. Here's the loop (without the prompts):

```
WHILE (MenuCode <> 'Q') AND (MenuCode <> 'q') DO
  BEGIN
    .
    .
    READLN(MenuCode, Amount);
    IF (MenuCode = 'T') OR (MenuCode = 't')
        THEN
           TaxTotal := TaxTotal + Amount
        ELSE IF (MenuCode = 'S') OR (MenuCode = 's')
           THEN
              SalesTotal := SalesTotal + Amount
  END;
```

The menu instructs the user to enter a 'T' or an 'S' and a dollar amount or to enter a 'Q' to quit processing, but the input statement always reads two values, a letter code, and an amount. Entering a 'Q' by itself (which the instructions imply that we can) should cause an error because there is no value to read into Amount. This is exactly what we did, however, when we were testing this program, and it ran correctly.

Being curious, we broke the READLN into two statements to see what would happen:

```
READ(MenuCode);
READLN(Amount);
```

By definition this should work exactly the same way. You guessed it. It didn't. This combination hung up the keyboard. The moral of this story is twofold: There was a design flaw in the input to this program, and Pascal input/output systems are very idiosyncratic. Just be careful.

Correctness Hints

1. Plan your test data carefully to test all sections of your program.
2. Beware of infinite loops (loops where the expression in the WHILE statement never becomes FALSE). The symptom is a program that doesn't stop. If you're at a terminal, nothing happens. The program just keeps going and going. If you're on a system that monitors the amount of time a program is taking and stops it if it goes too long, the message might be TIME LIMIT EXCEEDED.

If this occurs, check the logic and syntax of your loops. Be sure there is no semicolon immediately after the DO in the WHILE loop, which would cause an infinite loop. Make sure the control variable is incremented or updated within the loop.

3. Treat EOF with great respect. If you know what your data looks like (how it is organized on lines), use READLN to avoid possible EOF errors. If you have to use READs, use a flag to signal the end of the data.

4. If all else fails, use debug WRITE statements. These are WRITE statements inserted in a program to help in debugging. They provide an output message indicating the flow of execution in the program. They also can be used to report the value of variables at certain points in a program.

   For example, if you wanted to know the value of variable Sum at a certain point in a program, you could insert the statement

```
WRITELN('Sum = ', S);
```

If you use this debug WRITE statement in a loop, you will get as many values of Sum printed as the number of times the body of the loop is executed.

After you have debugged your program, you can remove the debug WRITE statement.

Completeness

In the Correctness section in Chapter 4 (page 131), we said that programs with menu options should allow the user to enter either uppercase letters or lowercase letters. Program SalesReceipts is written this way, yet it is still not complete. The loop will just cycle and do nothing if the user enters a wrong letter. We discuss the problem of bad input data in greater detail in later chapters.

Remember, all the documentation for a program must be consistent. All changes made to a program must be made in the design.

Summary

The WHILE statement is a looping construct that allows us to repeat a statement as long as an expression is TRUE. When the expression is FALSE, the statement is skipped and execution continues with the statement following the loop. There are several distinct types of loops that can be constructed using WHILE, and you will use them again and again.

In a count-controlled loop a statement is repeated a specified number of times. Immediately before the WHILE statement, you initialize a variable to be used as a counter to 1. This loop control variable is tested against the limit in the expression of the WHILE. The last statement in the WHILE loop's compound statement should increment the loop control variable.

There are other patterns for count-controlled loops, but the pattern of initializing the loop control variable to 1 and incrementing it at the end of the loop is good style.

In an event-controlled loop an event that occurs within the body of the loop determines whether the loop repeats again. The loop expression reflects the event. If the loop should be repeated, the loop expression should be TRUE. If the loop should not be repeated, the loop expression should be FALSE. The loop expression should be initialized outside the loop and updated within the loop.

EOF and EOLN are standard functions that ask questions about the state of the input file (or standard input device). They can be used to control reading in data.

Like the IF statement, the WHILE statement can contain other WHILE or IF statements. Nested logic is used to create complex control structures.

EXERCISES

1. Write a program that reads in integers from a file, and counts and prints out the number of positive integers and the number of negative integers. If a value is zero, do not count it. There is one integer per line. Continue the process until EOF becomes TRUE.

2. Look at your program in Exercise 1.
   a. What kind of loop have you used?
   b. What is the task?

3. Write a program segment that adds up the even integers between 16 and 26 (inclusive).

4. Write a program segment that processes six data lines stored in a file, each containing five values. Write out the line number and the sum of the five values.

5. Look at your program segment in Exercise 4.
   a. What kinds of loops have you used?
   b. What are the tasks?

6. Write a program segment that reads in ten data values or reads until a negative value is read, whichever comes first.

7. Use top-down design to write a Pascal program that finds the average of N integers, with the value of N being the first number of the data followed by N integers.

8. Look at your program in Exercise 7.
   a. What kind of loop have you used?
   b. What is the task?

9. Write a program segment that sets BOOLEAN variable Overflow to TRUE and stops reading in data if Level (a REAL variable being read in) exceeds 200.0. Use Overflow as a flag to control the loop.

10. Rewrite Program TemperatureStatistics using a different initialization scheme. Read one temperature outside the loop and initialize all values (except Hour-Counter) to the first temperature.

11. Write a program segment that reads in pairs of integers one per line. Use EOF to control your loop.
12. a. Write a statement to create the following headings:

    ```
         SALES
    WEEK1   WEEK2   WEEK3
    ```

    b. Write a statement to print values lined up under each week. The values are stored in Week1, Week2, and Week3. The last digit of each number should fall under the 1, 2, or 3 of the column headings.
13. Write a program segment that reads into REAL variable Data until Data is negative. Use Positive, set to FALSE when Data is negative, as a flag to control the loop.
14. Write a program segment that reads a file of characters until either EOF becomes TRUE or a character is read that is equal to 'A', 'B', or 'C'. After leaving the loop, print *Alphabetic* if one of the specified characters is encountered; otherwise print *Alphanumeric*.
15. Given this program and the following data:

```
PROGRAM Test5(INPUT, OUTPUT);

CONST
  N = 4;

VAR
   I, Sum, Value: INTEGER;
   Flag: BOOLEAN;

BEGIN    (* Test5 *)
   Sum := 2;
   I := 1;
   Flag := FALSE;
   WHILE (I <= N) AND NOT Flag DO
     BEGIN
       READ(Value);
       IF Value > 1
          THEN
             Sum := Sum + Value
          ELSE
             IF Value = 1
                THEN
                   Flag := TRUE;
       I := I + 1
     END;
   WRITELN('End of test', Sum, Value)
  END.      (* Test5 *)
```

Data: 2 2 2 −2 −2 −2 3 −3
a. What is the content of Sum after the program is executed?
b. What is the content of Value after the program is executed?
c. Does this data fully test this program? Explain your answer.

PRETEST

1. Write a program segment that sets a BOOLEAN variable Danger to TRUE and stops reading in data if Pressure (a REAL variable being read in) exceeds 510.0. Use Danger as a flag to control the loop.

2. Look at your program segment in Problem 1.
   a. What kind of loop did you use?
   b. What is the task?

3. Write a program segment that counts the number of times the integer 28 occurs in a file of 100 integers.

4. Look at your program segment in Problem 3.
   a. What kind of loop did you use?
   b. What is the task?

5. Write a program segment that reads a file of grades for a class (any size) and finds the class average. The grades are on FileOfGrades, one grade per line.

6. Write a program segment that reads a file of integers until either a zero value is found or EOF is TRUE. After leaving the loop, print either *Zero occurrence found* or *No zero occurrence*, whichever is the case. The integers are one per line.

7. Write a program segment that reads into REAL variable Speed until Speed is less than 5.0. Use Accelerate, set to TRUE when Speed is less than 5.0, as a flag to control the loop.

8. Write a program segment that reads a file of hourly pay rates for a group of employees and finds the average rate. Negative values should be ignored by the program. The data is on File1, one pay rate per line.

9. Write a program segment that reads a file of characters until either the character 'F' is found or EOF is TRUE. After leaving the loop, print *Problem encountered* if an 'F' was found; otherwise print *Checklist OK*.

10. Given this program and the following data:

```
PROGRAM Pretest(INPUT, OUTPUT);

CONST
  N = 8;

VAR
  I, Sum, Value : INTEGER;
  Flag : BOOLEAN;

BEGIN    (* Pretest *)
  Sum := 0;
  I := 1;
  Flag := FALSE;
  WHILE (I <= N) AND NOT Flag DO
    BEGIN
      READ(Value);
      IF Value > 0
        THEN
          Sum := Sum + Value
```

```
              ELSE
                IF Value = 0
                    THEN
                        Flag := TRUE;
              I := I + 1
           END;
         WRITELN('End of test ', Sum, Value)
      END.     (* Pretest *)
```

Data: 5 6 −3 7 −4 0 5 8 9
a. What is the content of Sum after the program is executed?
b. What is the content of Value after the program is executed?
c. Does this data fully test this program? Explain your answer.

PROGRAMMING ASSIGNMENTS

1. The formula for calculating the date for any Easter Sunday was given in Programming Assignment 5 in Chapter 4. Write a Pascal program that prints out a table showing the dates of Easter Sunday from 1965 to 1995.

   Output: A properly labeled table with two columns, one the year and the other the date of Easter Sunday for that year.

2. Write a program to assign *letter grades* (A, B, C, D, F) to students and to calculate the number of students who received each grade. Letter grades should correspond to the following ranges of numerical grades:

   A Above and including 90,
   B From 80 to 89 (inclusive)
   C From 70 to 79 (inclusive)
   D From 60 to 69 (inclusive)
   F Below 60

   Input: (on File Data)
   (1) First line contains an integer number giving the total number of students in the class.
   (2) Following are as many lines (one for each student) as the total number of students. Each line contains the following data:
       (a) Social security number (INTEGER)
       (b) Numerical grade from zero to 100 (INTEGER)

   Output: Social security number, numerical grade, and letter grade—in tabular form, one line per student. Below this table, there should be five lines of output, one for each letter grade, telling how many students received that grade.

3. You are a programmer for a polling service. The service has just completed a survey of your area. Each respondent was asked which candidate he or she preferred in an upcoming mayoral election. The responses were coded into integer numbers as follows:
   1. Boyd
   2. Nagle

3. Fuller
4. Riley

Your job is to determine the percentage each candidate got in the poll.

> **Input:** One number per data line. The first line in the data is the number of people in the survey. Each succeeding line has a number between 1 and 4 representing a preference.
>
> **Output:** A table showing the candidates' names, how many votes each candidate received, and what percentage of the total votes each received.

4. You do the accounting for a local soft drink distributorship that sells Coke (ID Number 1), Sprite (ID Number 2), Diet Coke (ID Number 3), and Diet Sprite (ID Number 4) by the case. Write a program that does the following:

   - Reads in the case inventory for each brand
   - Processes all weekly sales and purchase records for each brand
   - Prints out the final inventory

   Input:
   (1) First line: eight values representing the initial inventory (ID number followed by number of cases).
   (2) Remainder of data: an ID number and number of cases (a positive integer represents amount bought, a negative integer represents amount sold). Use EOF to determine when you're through.

   Output: Labeled output for each soft drink: name, ID number, number of transactions, and final inventory for the transaction period

5. Write a program that determines the quantity in pounds and ounces of boxes of laundry soap. Each box should be described by two numbers, which represent total price in cents and the unit price per ounce in cents. Prompt the user to enter the two numbers. Calculate the quantity in pounds and ounces, and print the result with an appropriate comment. For example, if the input values are 162 (total price in cents) and 2 (unit price in cents), the output would be

```
This box of soap contains 5 lb 1 oz of detergent.
```

6. In 1626 Peter Minuit purchased Manhattan Island from the Indians for $24 worth of beads and trinkets. If his money had been invested at 7 percent interest and the interest had been compounded annually, what would the investment be worth in 1990?

7. You borrow $1,000 from a banker to buy a stereo. You pay 12 percent interest on this three-year loan, compounded semiannually. At the end of three years, what have you actually paid for the stereo?

8. Most computer systems have a built-in function that generates random numbers. Find out how to call the random number generator on your system. You'll need to use it in this problem. Most orb weaver spiders build their webs at night. Their webs, which are used to capture prey, consist of both spokes and spirals that radiate outward from the center or hub of the web. To be effective, web silk must remain sticky and must be repaired when torn.

   Assume that an orb weaver spider must rebuild its web on three successive evenings because of some disturbance factor (wind, insects). Make the following assumptions:

- Only one web is built each evening.
- The web is complete except for the spiral when the orb weaver begins.
- The spider begins the spiral at the hub.
- Seven successful rounds are needed to complete the spiral of the web.
- Each round is 2 centimeters greater than the size of the previous round.
- The first round closest to the center is 2 centimeters in circumference.
- Continual disturbances during the building of the web (modeled by calling the random generator) impede the spider's building of the spiral.
- Each call to the random generator is equivalent to 1 centimeter if successful (that is, one "spin"), and a round is completed when exactly 2 centimeters is reached for the first round, 4 centimeters for the second round, and so on.
- Numbers generated less than 0.5 or greater than 0.5 are equal in probability. Numbers less than 0.5 are equivalent to unsuccessful spins and numbers greater than 0.5 are equivalent to successful spins. The number 0.5 can be treated as either a successful or an unsuccessful spin.

Input: None

Output: For each of the three evenings:
(1) Print in a readable format the number of spins (each equivalent to 1 centimeter) necessary for the spider to complete each spiral round up to and including the seventh round.
(2) Print the total number of spins necessary to complete all seven rounds of the spiral.
For all evenings:
(1) Print the average number of spins for each successful round.
(2) If on any of the three evenings the spider does not complete the spiral in a total of 110 tries, abort the building of the web and print *The spider will go hungry tonight.*

6 Procedures

GOALS

- To be able to write a program that reflects the structure of your top-down design.

- To be able to write a procedure that can be executed more than once.

- To be able to write a procedure to do a common task and save that procedure to be used again.

- To be able to do the following tasks, given a Pascal program with procedures:
    - Determine whether a parameter is a VAR or value parameter
    - Determine whether a variable is being referenced globally
    - Determine which variables are local variables
    - Determine which variables are defined in each block

- To be able to do the following tasks, given a top-down design for a problem:
    - Determine what the formal and actual parameter lists should be for each procedure
    - Determine which formal parameters should be VAR parameters and which should be value parameters
    - Determine what local variables should be declared for each procedure

- To be able to determine the scope of each variable in a program.

- To be able to avoid side effects.

On page 169, we pointed out that the modularization of our design for Program SalesReceipt was lost when the pieces were collected into a program. If we could name each process, then our program could look like our design. The procedure is the structure that allows us to do this.

Procedures: Independent Processes

Procedure Definitions

A procedure definition names and defines an action. When we want the action to take place, we put the name of the action—the **procedure identifier**—in our program. READ, READLN, WRITE, and WRITELN are procedure identifiers. They name standard procedures in Pascal. Procedure identifiers also can be defined by the programmer.

Because Pascal requires that things be named before they are defined, the name of the action comes first, followed by its definition. Procedure definitions can be quite complex. We introduce them here in abbreviated form. As the programs we write get more complicated, we'll tell you more about procedure definitions.

```
──────▶ PROCEDURE ──────▶ identifier ──────▶ ; ──────▶ compound statement ──────▶ ;
```

Look at the syntax diagram. The reserved word PROCEDURE tells the compiler that we are going to name an action. The identifier is the name of the action that is defined in the compound statement. This procedure definition defines the action of writing a box of asterisks:

```
PROCEDURE WriteBoxOfStars;        ← Name of the action (procedure heading)
(* This procedure writes a box of asterisks, 30 × 3. *)

BEGIN    (* WriteBoxOfStars *)
  WRITELN('******************************');
  WRITELN('*                            *');    } Action
  WRITELN('******************************')
END;     (* WriteBoxOfStars *)
```

Executing a Procedure

We execute the action by putting the name of the procedure in a compound statement in the action part of the program. Here's an example of a program using Procedure WriteBoxOfStars:

```
PROGRAM ShowOffProcedure(OUTPUT);

(***********************************************)

PROCEDURE WriteBoxOfStars;
(* This procedure writes a box of asterisks, 30 × 3. *)

BEGIN    (* WriteBoxOfStars *)
  WRITELN('******************************');
  WRITELN('*                            *');
  WRITELN('******************************')
END;    (* WriteBoxOfStars *)

(***********************************************)

BEGIN    (* ShowOffProcedure *)
  WriteBoxOfStars;
  WRITELN('*          Cary Grant         *');
  WriteBoxOfStars
END,    (* ShowOffProcedure *)
```

The output of Program ShowOffProcedure looks like this:

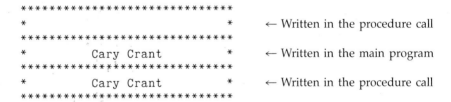

There are two compound statements in the program: The one associated with the procedure heading defines the action of the procedure; the one associated with the program heading defines the action of the main program. During compile-time, both compound statements are translated. The procedure identifier (WriteBoxOfStars) used as a statement in the main program tells the program to execute these steps at run-time:

1. Go to where the translated version of the compound statement associated with this procedure identifier (WriteBoxOfStars) is stored.
2. Execute the statement.
3. When that statement (procedure) has been executed, continue execution with the next statement in the program (here, the WRITELN).

When a procedure identifier is used as a statement, it **calls** or **invokes** the procedure. In our example, Procedure WriteBoxOfStars is invoked twice.

Calling a Procedure

Using a procedure identifier as a statement.

Using Procedures: Syntax

With an understanding of procedure definitions and calls, let's look again at a couple of syntax diagrams. Here's the diagram for a block:

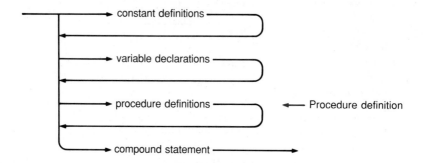

Notice that a procedure must be defined before the compound statement in which it is invoked.

The procedure call changes our syntax diagram of a statement. Where we used a WRITE statement as part of that diagram in Chapter 2, now we can use the more general term *procedure identifier:*

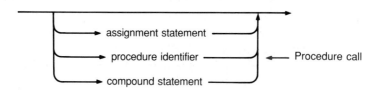

The physical order of the parts of a program is different from the logical order in which the statements are executed. As you can see in the block diagram, the procedure definition comes before the main program's compound statement, but *execution* of the program always begins with the first statement in the compound statement of the main program. Although the action part of the procedure physically precedes the main program, the code is not executed until the procedure is invoked.

Program SalesReceipts Revisited

In The 4-Cs Corner in Chapter 5, we said that Program SalesReceipts is hard to read, that our modular design is lost in the code. Procedures help clarify our programs; they give us a means for retaining the modular structure in our top-down design in the program itself.

Here we've rewritten the design and code for Program SalesReceipts. Look at Module PROMPT USER FOR INPUT. It describes a self-contained task; it does not access any of the program variables; and it is made up exclusively of WRITELN statements. Instead of coding it in-line (as part of the main program), we've made it a procedure.*

MAIN MODULE   Level 0

```
Initialize variables
WHILE more receipts DO
   Get data
      Add amount to correct sum
Calculate costs
Print results
```

INITIALIZE VARIABLES   Level 1

```
TaxTotal ← 0.0
SalesTotal ← 0.0
MenuCode ← 'T'
```

GET DATA

```
Prompt user for input
Read MenuCode
```

---

*We've also modified the design and code to reflect the other changes we talked about in The 4-Cs Corner in Chapter 5.

ADD TO CORRECT SUM

```
IF MenuCode is a 'T' or a 't'
    THEN
        Read Amount
        TaxTotal ← TaxTotal + Amount
    ELSE IF MenuCode is an 'S' or an 's'
        THEN
            Read Amount
            SalesTotal ← SalesTotal + Amount
```

CALCULATE COSTS

```
NonFoodCost ← TaxTotal / TaxRate
FoodCost ← SalesTotal − (NonFoodCost + TaxTotal)
```

When we revised the documentation, we decided to combine modules CALCULATE NONFOOD COST and CALCULATE FOOD COST because they are so short and their meanings are so closely tied together.

PRINT RESULTS

```
Write 'Total amount spent this month ' SalesTotal
Write 'Total amount of tax this month ' TaxTotal
Write 'Total amount spent on food ' FoodCost
Write 'Total amount spent on nonfood items ' NonFoodCost
```

PROMPT USER FOR INPUT   Level 2

```
Write '***************************************'
Write '*************** MENU ***************'
Write '* T:  total taxes on receipt        */
Write '* S:  total sales on receipt        */
Write '* Q:  last data value read          */
Write '***************************************'
Write '* Input a T or an S and a dollar */
Write '* amount (include decimal).      */
Write '* Input a Q to quit processing.  */
Write '***************************************'
```

Module Design Chart:

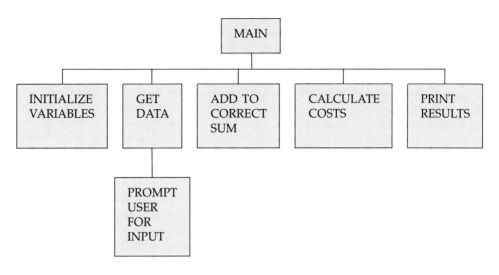

```
PROGRAM SalesReceipts(INPUT, OUTPUT);
(* The amount of money spent on taxable and *)
(* nontaxable items at the supermarket      *)
(* is calculated from sales receipts.       *)

CONST
  TaxRate = 0.08;

VAR
  MenuCode : CHAR;            (* 'T', 'S', 'Q'                   *)
  TaxTotal,                   (* total tax paid                 *)
  SalesTotal,                 (* total amount spent             *)
  Amount,                     (* dollar amount                  *)
  FoodCost,                   (* amount spent on food           *)
  NonFoodCost : REAL;         (* amount spent on other items *)

(*******************************************************************************)

PROCEDURE PromptUserForInput;

BEGIN   (* PromptUserForInput *)
  WRITELN('***********************************');
  WRITELN('************* MENU **************');
  WRITELN('*  T:  total taxes on receipt    *');
  WRITELN('*  S:  total sales on receipt    *');
  WRITELN('*  Q:  last data value read      *');
```

```
  WRITELN('**********************************');
  WRITELN('*  Input a T or an S and a dollar *');
  WRITELN('*  amount (include decimal).      *');
  WRITELN('*  Input a Q to quit processing   *');
  WRITELN('**********************************')
END;    (* PromptUserForInput *)


(***************************************************************************)

BEGIN   (* SalesReceipts *)

  (* Initialize variables *)
  TaxTotal := 0.0;
  SalesTotal := 0.0;
  MenuCode := 'T';
  WHILE (MenuCode <> 'Q') AND (MenuCode <> 'q') DO
    BEGIN

      (* get data *)
      PromptUserForInput;        ← Procedure call
      READ(MenuCode);

      (* Add to correct sum *)
      IF (MenuCode = 'T') OR (MenuCode = 't')
        THEN
          BEGIN
            READLN(Amount);
            TaxTotal := TaxTotal + Amount
          END
        ELSE IF (MenuCode = 'S') OR (MenuCode = 's')
          THEN
            BEGIN
              READLN(Amount);
              SalesTotal := SalesTotal + Amount
            END
    END;

  (* Calculate costs *)
  NonFoodCost := TaxTotal / TaxRate;
  FoodCost := SalesTotal - (NonFoodCost + TaxTotal);

  (* Print results *)
  WRITELN('Total amount spent this month ', SalesTotal:10:2);
  WRITELN('Total amount of tax this month ', TaxTotal:10:2);
  WRITELN('Total amount spent on food ', FoodCost:10:2);
  WRITELN('Total amount spent on nonfood items', NonFoodCost:10:2)
END.    (* SalesReceipts *)
```

The functional parts of the program look a little clearer in this version of Program SalesReceipts, but the program still looks cluttered. The modularization in the top-down design is still not obvious. We can do better, and we will in the next section.

Procedures with Parameters

WRITE and WRITELN take the expressions listed on their parameter lists and print them. READ and READLN return values in the variables listed on their parameter lists. User-defined procedures also can use parameter lists to pass information back and forth between the procedure and the program unit that is invoking it.

The parameter list is part of the procedure heading:

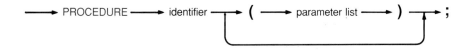

This is the syntax diagram for a parameter list:

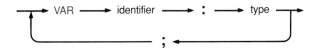

The following procedure has one parameter (Sum). The body of the procedure reads a value from the terminal and adds the value to the parameter.

```
PROCEDURE ReadAndSum(VAR Sum : REAL);
(* A value is read from the terminal and *)
(* added to Sum.                         *)

VAR
   Amount : REAL;       (* a place to read the value into *)

BEGIN   (* ReadAndSum *)
   READLN(Amount);
   Sum := Sum + Amount
END;    (* ReadAndSum *)
```

We can use Procedure ReadAndSum to make the body of Program SalesReceipt less cluttered:

```
WHILE (MenuCode <> 'Q') AND (MenuCode <> 'q') DO
  BEGIN
    PromptUserForInput;
    READ(MenuCode);
    IF (MenuCode = 'T') OR (MenuCode = 't')
      THEN
        ReadAndSum(TaxTotal)
    ELSE IF (MenuCode = 'S') OR (MenuCode = 's')
      THEN
        ReadAndSum(SalesTotal)
  END;
```

Procedure
calls

The parameter list in the procedure heading is called the **formal parameter list.** Each identifier on the formal parameter list has its type specified. The parameter list on the calling or invoking statement is called the **actual parameter list.** These identifiers are defined or declared within the program unit that is invoking the procedure, so their types are not repeated in the procedure call.

> **Formal Parameter List**
> The list of identifiers in the procedure heading.

> **Actual Parameter List**
> The list of identifiers in the procedure call.

When a procedure is executed, the variable listed in the actual parameter list is substituted for the corresponding variable in the formal parameter list. For example, if MenuCode is a 'T' or a 't', ReadAndSum is invoked with TaxTotal as the actual parameter. This means that where Sum (the formal parameter) appears in the code of Procedure ReadAndSum, TaxTotal (the actual parameter) is used.

```
PROCEDURE ReadAndSum(VAR Sum : REAL);

ReadAndSum(TaxTotal);
```

If MenuCode is an 'S' or an 's', ReadAndSum is invoked with SalesTotal as the actual parameter. This means that where Sum (the formal parameter) appears in the code of Procedure ReadAndSum, SalesTotal (the actual parameter) is used.

```
PROCEDURE ReadAndSum (VAR Sum : REAL);

ReadAndSum(SalesTotal);
```

Parameters in Pascal are called *positional parameters*. This means that the parameters on the formal and actual parameter lists are matched up by position. The first parameter on the actual parameter list matches up with the first parameter on the formal parameter list. If there is more than one formal parameter, the second parameter on the actual parameter list matches up with the second parameter on the formal parameter list and so on.

Applying Procedures
Translating Top-Down Design into Code

The process of breaking down a problem stops when each subtask can be coded directly in a programming language. This means that coding the design is a routine task. The main module (Level 0 module) becomes the compound statement associated with the program heading—that is, the main program. The names of tasks in the main module become procedure calls to procedures that implement the lower-level modules.

Should every module be coded as a separate procedure? No, not necessarily. The top-down design reflects not only our algorithm but the decomposition process we went through to get the algorithm. When we translate the algorithm into code, we may decide that the decomposition is too fine. For example, two or more modules, each of which can be translated into one line of code, may be grouped into one procedure if the statements are logically closely related. A group of statements that are closely related are said to be *cohesive*.

There is no general rule about when to make a module a separate procedure. It depends on the problem and on the programming language you are using. Bear in mind that modules are building blocks for algorithms; procedures are building blocks for Pascal programs. The concepts are closely related, but they are not identical.

Interface Design

When translating a top-down design into Pascal code, we need to pay attention to the communication between the procedure and the part of the program that invokes the procedure. This communication is specified in the formal parameter list of the procedure. In determining this specification, there are two questions we ask from the viewpoint of the procedure:

1. What information do I (the procedure) *need* that the invoking part of the program must provide for me?
2. What information am I determining (calculating or reading) that I must *return* to the invoking part of the program?

We can think of the answer to the first question as the *input* to the procedure and the answer to the second question as the *output* from the procedure. Input and output in this case have nothing to do with reading values or printing them (unless the task of the procedure is to read or print). Input means the information that the procedure must have to do its task; output means the information that the procedure must provide for the part of the program that invokes it.

Once we've determined the answers to these two questions, we have to determine variable identifiers and their associated types for each piece of information. The list of these variables becomes the formal parameter list of the procedure.

As a practical matter, the first step in converting a top-down design into Pascal code is to make a list of the identifiers that you've used in your design that must be defined or declared in the program. Be sure to indicate the type of each variable. Refer to this list when you are writing your formal parameter lists.

In many cases the variable identifiers on the formal parameter list are the same as the names of the actual parameters that are given to the procedure (that is, those on your list of identifiers). If there is no explicit reason for not doing so, use the same identifiers for both the formal and the actual parameter lists.

In other cases, the two lists cannot be the same. For example, Procedure ReadAndSum reads a value and adds it to the place named in the formal parameter. ReadAndSum is called twice: The actual parameter is TaxTotal the first time and SalesTotal the second. The formal parameter list and the actual parameter lists cannot use the same identifier.

Determining the formal and actual parameters is called **interface design.** Formally, an **interface** is a shared boundary where independent systems meet and communicate with each other. In the case of a procedure and the part of the program that invokes the procedure, this shared boundary is the parameter list.

Interface Design

Using formal and actual parameters to establish communication between a procedure and an invoking program unit.

It often is useful to describe program variables, along with a list of procedure names and their "needs" (what they need from the invoking unit) and "returns" (what they have to provide for the invoking unit) in an **interface design chart.** We use these charts in our sample problems.

Now we're ready to finish recoding Program SalesReceipts, using parameter lists to communicate between program units. Module CALCULATE COSTS is only two lines long, so we code it in-line, but we code all the other modules as procedures. Notice that we use Procedure ReadAndSum within Procedure AddToSum.

Interface Design Chart:

Program Variables and Constants

Identifiers	Type	Role
MenuCode	CHAR	Identifies the next data value as a tax total (T), a sales total (S), or a flag to quit loop (Q)
TaxTotal	REAL	Total of tax paid on a sales receipt
SalesTotal	REAL	Total of sales on a sales receipt
FoodCost	REAL	Amount spent on food items
NonFoodCost	REAL	Amount spent on taxable items
TaxRate	REAL	Sales tax

Procedures

Identifiers	Needs	Returns
Initialize	Nothing	MenuCode, TaxTotal, SalesTotal
PromptUserForInput	Nothing	Nothing
GetData	Nothing	MenuCode
AddToSum	MenuCode	TaxTotal, SalesTotal
PrintResults	SalesTotal, TaxTotal, FoodCost, NonFoodCost	Nothing

```
PROGRAM SalesReceipts(INPUT, OUTPUT);
(* The amount of money spent on taxable and *)
(* nontaxable items at the supermarket      *)
(* is calculated from sales receipts.       *)

CONST
  TaxRate = 0.08;
```

```
VAR
  MenuCode : CHAR;            (* 'T', 'S', 'Q'                *)
  TaxTotal,                   (* total tax paid              *)
  SalesTotal,                 (* total amount spent          *)
  FoodCost,                   (* amount spent on food        *)
  NonFoodCost : REAL;         (* amount spent on other items *)

(*********************************************************************)

PROCEDURE Initialize(VAR MenuCode : CHAR;
                     VAR TaxTotal, SalesTotal : REAL);
(* Program variables are initialized *)

BEGIN   (* Initialize *)
  TaxTotal := 0.0;
  SalesTotal := 0.0;
  MenuCode := 'T'
END;   (* Initialize *)

(*********************************************************************)

PROCEDURE PromptUserForInput;
(* Menu is printed. *)

BEGIN    (* PromptUserForInput *)
  WRITELN('**********************************');
  WRITELN('************* MENU ***************');
  WRITELN('*  T:   total taxes on receipt   *');
  WRITELN('*  S:   total sales on receipt   *');
  WRITELN('*  Q:   last data value read     *');
  WRITELN('**********************************');
  WRITELN('*  Input a T or an S and a dollar *');
  WRITELN('*  amount (include decimal).      *');
  WRITELN('*  Input a Q to quit processing   *');
  WRITELN('**********************************')
END;     (* PromptUserForInput *)

(************************************************************************)

PROCEDURE GetData(VAR MenuCode : CHAR);
(* MenuCode is read. *)

BEGIN    (* GetData *)
  PromptUserForInput;
  READ(MenuCode)
END;     (* GetData *)

(************************************************************************)

PROCEDURE ReadAndSum(VAR Sum : REAL);
(* A value is read from the terminal and added to Sum. *)
```

```
VAR
  Amount : REAL;

BEGIN    (* ReadAndSum *)
  READLN(Amount);
  Sum := Sum + Amount
END;     (* ReadAndSum *)

(***************************************************************************)

PROCEDURE AddToSum(VAR MenuCode : CHAR;
                   VAR TaxTotal, SalesTotal : REAL);

BEGIN    (* AddToSum *)
  IF (MenuCode = 'T') OR (MenuCode = 't')
     THEN
        ReadAndSum(TaxTotal)
  ELSE IF (MenuCode = 'S') OR (MenuCode = 's')
     THEN
        ReadAndSum(SalesTotal)
END;     (* AddToSum *)

(***************************************************************************)

PROCEDURE PrintResults(VAR SalesTotal, TaxTotal,
                           FoodCost, NonFoodCost : REAL);
(* All the totals are printed. *)

BEGIN    (* PrintResults *)
  WRITELN('Total amount spent this month ', SalesTotal:10:2);
  WRITELN('Total amount of tax this month ', TaxTotal:10:2);
  WRITELN('Total amount spent on food ', FoodCost:10:2);
  WRITELN('Total amount spent on nonfood items ', NonFoodCost:10:2)
END;     (* PrintResults *)

(***************************************************************************)

BEGIN    (* SalesReceipts *)
  Initialize(MenuCode, TaxTotal, SalesTotal);
  WHILE (MenuCode <> 'Q') AND (MenuCode <> 'q') DO
    BEGIN
      GetData(MenuCode);
      AddToSum(MenuCode, TaxTotal, SalesTotal)
    END;
  NonFoodCost := TaxTotal / TaxRate;
  FoodCost := SalesTotal - (NonFoodCost + TaxTotal);
  PrintResults(SalesTotal, TaxTotal, FoodCost, NonFoodCost)
END.     (* SalesReceipts *)
```

Using Procedures: A Rationale

There are three main reasons for using procedures:

- Procedures allow our program to look like our top-down design. A module in our design can be a procedure in our program.
- Procedures save time. We can code a task just once, then use it in the program again and again.
- Procedures are a resource. We can program common tasks once, then save them in a standard format for use in other programs.

In the top-down design method, we solve a problem by breaking it into subproblems. We can give a subproblem or subtask a name, then go on with the rest of the solution without worrying about the details of the subtask. When we are ready to design the next level of detail, we come back to the subtask and design its solution.

Think about the way we design a program. Our modules form a hierarchy, moving down from a general solution to a specific solution. When we translate our modules into procedures, our program reflects this same structure. If we do not use procedures, we end up with a flat representation of our hierarchical solution. Yes, a correct flat representation works properly, but it is harder to read and maintain. Functional units made clear with procedures tend to blend together in a flat representation.

The second reason for using procedures is that they make a program more concise. Program SalesReceipt had two lines of code that were identical except for the variable names. The version without procedures repeated the code twice: once to add the value to TaxTotal and once to add the value to SalesTotal.

In our discussion of problem-solving strategies in Chapter 2, we said to look for things that are familiar; don't reinvent the wheel. The analogy in the implementation phase is don't rebuild the wheel. Once you have implemented a common task as a procedure and have tested the code, save it on a file so that you can use it again. Make your own collection of standard procedures.

Many programming languages allow you to add procedures to the built-in procedure library. Standard Pascal does not have this facility, but you can keep your own file of procedures. When you need one, copy it into the code of the new program. (Copy it electronically; don't rekey it!)

Communication Between Program Parts
Full Anatomy of a Procedure

A procedure is a heading and a compound statement. Actually the body of a procedure, like the body of the main program, is a block. This means that a procedure can define its own constants, declare its own variables, even define its own procedures. Constants, variables, and procedures defined within the block of a procedure are *local* to the procedure. This expansion of the body of a procedure shouldn't surprise you; Procedure ReadAndSum had a VAR section.

We also need to expand our definition of *parameter list*.

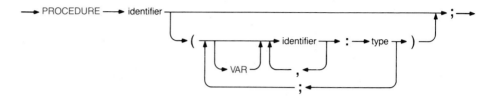

The definition of the parameter list now includes an arrow that bypasses the word VAR. Because we now have two kinds of formal parameters, we need a way to distinguish between them when we refer to them. Parameters with a VAR in front of them are called (not surprisingly) VAR parameters. Those without the VAR are called value parameters.

Parameter Lists: A Review

The concept of parameter lists as a method of communication is very important. Let's review it before we go on. When we want to invoke or call a procedure, we use its name as a statement followed by a list of the variables it will use, enclosed in parentheses. These variables are called **actual parameters**. Because a procedure must be defined before it is called, it does not know which variables from the main program it will be working with. To solve this dilemma, we specify a list of variable names with associated types (again in parentheses) beside the procedure name when it is defined. These variables are called **formal parameters**.

Actual Parameters
The identifiers listed in the procedure call.

Formal Parameters
The identifiers listed on the procedure heading.

The action of the procedure is defined using the identifiers listed on the formal parameter list. When the action takes place, the actual parameters are substituted one by one for the formal parameters. The substitution is done in the order in which the parameters appear on the two lists: The first actual parameter substitutes for the first formal parameter, the second actual parameter substitutes for the second formal parameter, and so on.

The substitution mechanism acts like a message board. When a procedure

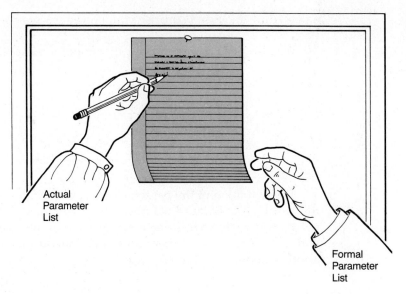

Actual
Parameter
List

Formal
Parameter
List

FIGURE 6–1 Parameter passing

is invoked, a list of the actual parameters is passed (given) to the procedure (put on the procedure's message board) (Figure 6–1). The actual parameters tell the procedure where to find the values it is supposed to use. When a formal parameter is used in the body of the procedure, the procedure accesses it through its relative position on the message board. That is, the procedure looks for its first parameter in the first position on the message board and for its second parameter in the second position on the message board.

There must be the same number of actual parameters in the call as there are formal parameters in the procedure heading, and the parameters must match up in both position and data type. Because the formal and actual parameters are matched by position, their names don't have to be the same. This is very helpful when a procedure is called more than once, with different actual parameters used in each call. Parameters passed in this fashion are often called *positional parameters.*

It's up to the programmer to be sure that the formal and actual parameter lists match up semantically. For example, Procedure AddToTotal in Program SalesReceipts has the following formal parameter list:

```
(VAR MenuCode : CHAR; VAR TaxTotal, SalesTotal : REAL)
```

If the calling statement is:

```
AddToTotal (MenuCode, SalesTotal, TaxTotal);
```

the lists would match up in type and number of parameters so there would be no syntax error, but the output would be incorrect.

VAR and Value Parameters

A variable identifier is a name associated with an address in memory. When a formal parameter is defined as a **VAR parameter**, the calling statement leaves the *address* of the variable for the procedure to work with. When a formal parameter is defined as a **value parameter** (VAR is not placed in front of the identifier on the formal parameter list), the procedure is given a *copy of the content* of that place to work with.

VAR Parameter

A parameter whose address is put on the message board.

Value Parameter

A parameter whose content is copied onto the message board.

This means that a procedure cannot change the content of an actual parameter that is passed as a value parameter; it can only use the copy. If a procedure does contain a statement that redefines the value, the copy is changed, not the original. In contrast, any statement that redefines the value of a VAR parameter redefines the original value.

Let's look at an example. The following program fragment contains a procedure that exchanges the contents of two places. If you wanted to change the contents of two glasses of water, you would need a third glass to hold the content of one temporarily. The same is true when we change the contents of two memory locations. We need to declare a local variable to hold the content of one temporarily.

```
VAR
   Datal, Data2 : INTEGER;

PROCEDURE Swap(VAR Iteml, Item2 : INTEGER);
(* The contents of Iteml and Item2 are interchanged. *)

VAR
   TempItem : INTEGER;    (* used in the swap *)

BEGIN    (* Swap *)
   TempItem := Iteml;
   Iteml := Item2;
   Item2 := TempItem
END;     (* Swap *)


(* ********************************************************* *)
```

```
BEGIN    (* MainProgram *)
  .
  .
  Swap(Data1, Data2);
  .
  .
END.     (* MainProgram *)
```

Memory locations for Data1 and Data2 are set aside at compile-time. The action portion of the main program is translated using the memory locations assigned for Data1 and Data2. Procedures are handled differently. The action portion of a procedure is translated so that all variable references, *both to parameters and local variables*, are relative. When the procedure is called, the addresses of the parameters and local variables are determined.

If a parameter is a VAR parameter, the procedure code is generated to interpret that position on the message board as a place containing information on where to go to get the actual parameter; that is, as a memory address from which a value is retrieved or into which a value is stored. If a parameter is a value parameter, the procedure code is generated to interpret that position on the message board as the actual parameter itself. A procedure cannot access an actual value parameter directly; it can only use its content on the message board while the procedure is executing.

In addition to the parameters, a position on the message board is set aside for each local constant or variable. Each time a procedure is called, an appropriate message board is created. (What we are calling a message board is technically called an activation record.)

Look at Figure 6–2. The parts of the figure in the darker shade of color are defined at compile-time and exist in memory during the entire execution of the program. The variables that are part of what we call the message board exist in memory only as long as Procedure Swap is being executed.

Because the parameters Item1 and Item2 are VAR parameters, the calling statement puts the address of Data1 into the first place in the message board. and the address of Data2 into the second place in the message board. This is indicated by the arrow going from Item1 to Data1 and from Item2 to Data2. A place for the local variable TempItem is created. The action part of Procedure Swap exchanges the contents of Data1 and Data2.

When the procedure has finished executing and control returns to the statement immediately following the call to Procedure Swap, the message board goes away. The local variable TempItem no longer exists . The memory cells used by the message board are available to be used by some other procedure. (You do not have to worry about this. Pascal does it for you automatically.)

Figure 6–3 shows what happens to the message board if we change Procedure Swap's heading as follows:

```
PROCEDURE Swap(Item1, Item2 : INTEGER)
```

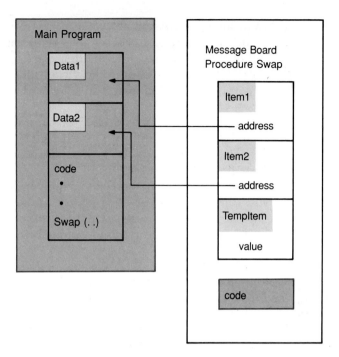

FIGURE 6–2 Memory when Swap is called: VAR parameters

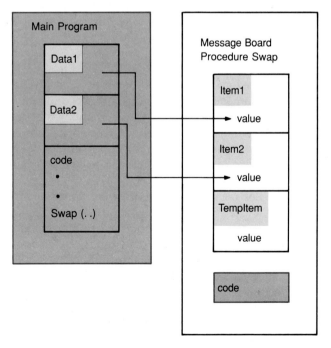

FIGURE 6–3 Memory when Swap is called: value parameters

Here Item1 and Item2 are value parameters. When Procedure Swap is called, the message board is created as before but with several changes: The content of Data1 is copied into the first place in the message board, and the content of Data2 is copied into the second place in the message board. The action part of Procedure Swap swaps the contents of Item1 and Item2, *not the contents of Data1 and Data2.*

What happens when we run Procedure Swap with value parameters? Nothing. Absolutely nothing. The contents of two places on the message board have been changed, but the message board goes away when the procedure has finished executing.

The interface design chart has two columns for procedures: needs and returns. All the variable identifiers listed in the returns column must be VAR parameters. Those that are listed in the needs column should be value parameters. This prevents a procedure from inadvertently changing the value of a variable.

Because the address of a VAR parameter is passed to the procedure, the corresponding actual parameter must be a variable. The actual parameter for a value parameter can be any expression of the appropriate type.

SAMPLE PROBLEM

... Boylan, June;
Weaver, Tom;

Problem: Write a program that reads in names in the form of first name, blank(s), last name, and prints them out last name, comma, blank, first initial, period. There may be leading blanks and any number of blanks between the first name and last name in your input. The names are on File Names. The output is to be on File PrintNames.

Discussion: This would be an easy task to do by hand. We would read the two names and write down the second one, followed by a comma and a blank. We would then go back and write down the first letter of the first name, followed by a period. This is basically how we program the problem. The hard part comes in trying to simulate reading the two names. The program has to read one character at a time, examine it, and decide what to do with it.

Let's analyze the process by going character by character through the input. Starting from left to right, we're going to see a blank or a letter. If it's a blank, we skip over it and get another character. If it's a letter, we need to save it because it's the first initial.

Once we have the first initial, we're not interested in the rest of the first name, so we just continue to read until we reach the last name. How do we recognize the beginning of the last name? It's the first letter after the blank(s) following the first name. Once we find the last name, we continue reading a character and printing it until we find a blank. Then we print a comma followed by a blank and the initial of the first name (which we saved) followed by a period.

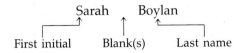

First initial   Blank(s)   Last name

Let's say our input is two names:

June   Boylan
Tom   Weaver

Our output would look like this:

```
Boylan, J.
Weaver, T.
```

Now that we've analyzed the problem, we can do our top-down design.

Input: From File Names, in this form:

First name   Blank(s)   Last name

Output: To File PrintNames, in this form:

Last name   ', '   First initial '.'

Assumptions: Input data is valid and has one name per line.

MAIN MODULE   Level 0

```
WHILE more names DO
   Get Initial
   Print last name
   Write Comma and Blank
   Print Initial
   Write Period
```

GET INITIAL   Level 1

```
Skip blanks
Initial ← First nonblank
```

SAMPLE PROBLEM, CONTINUED

PRINT LAST NAME

```
Find last name
WHILE more letters DO
    Write letter
    Read letter
```

PRINT INITIAL

```
Write Initial
```

SKIP BLANKS   Level 2

```
Get a letter
WHILE letter = Blank
    Get a Letter
```

FIND LAST NAME

```
Skip first name
Skip blanks
```

SKIP FIRST NAME   Level 3

```
Get a letter
WHILE letter <> Blank
    Get a Letter
```

Module Design Chart:

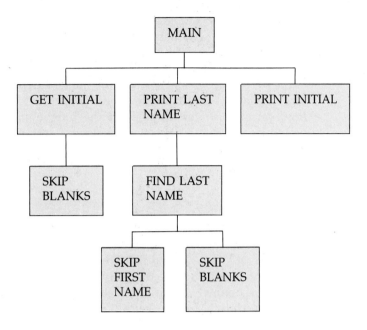

Module PRINT INITIAL is only one line; it should not be a procedure. The other modules should all be coded as procedures.

Interface Design Chart:

Program Variables		
Identifiers	*Type*	*Role*
Initial	CHAR	First letter in first name
Names	TEXT	File of names to be printed
PrintNames	TEXT	File of formatted names
Procedures		
Identifiers	*Needs*	*Returns*
GetInitial	Names	Initial
PrintLast	Names	PrintNames
SkipBlanks	Names	Character (first nonblank)
FindLast	Names	Character (first letter)
SkipFirst	Names	Nothing

SAMPLE PROBLEM, CONTINUED

The identifiers listed in the needs column should be value parameters with one exception: Pascal requires that files passed as parameters must be VAR parameters. The identifiers listed in the returns column must be VAR parameters. If a parameter is both needed and returned, it must be a VAR parameter and should be placed in the returns column.

Now we can code our program. The only constraint on the physical order of the procedures is that a procedure must be defined before it's called; therefore, the lowest-level module should be defined first. Within this constraint, however, it improves readability to have them in logical order. A good order would be

>SkipBlanks
>GetInitial
>PrintLast
>>FindLast
>>>SkipFirst

We've indented FindLast to show that it's embedded within Procedure PrintLast. We've indented SkipFirst even more to show that it's embedded within FindLast. Because the body of a procedure is a block, we can have a procedure defined within a procedure.

Here's the Pascal program that parallels our design.

```
PROGRAM Transpose(OUTPUT, Names, PrintNames);
(* Names are read from File Names and written *)
(* to File PrintNames in the form Last name,  *)
(* comma, blank, first initial, period.       *)

CONST
  Blank = ' ';
  Comma = ',';
  Period = '.';
VAR
  Initial : CHAR;
  Names, PrintNames : TEXT;

(*************************************************************)

PROCEDURE SkipBlanks(VAR DataFile : TEXT; VAR Character : CHAR);
(*  Blanks are skipped.  Character is the first nonblank. *)

BEGIN    (* SkipBlanks *)
  READ(DataFile, Character);
  WHILE Character = Blank DO
    READ(DataFile, Character)
END;     (* SkipBlanks *)
```

```
(***************************************************************)

PROCEDURE GetInitial(VAR Names : TEXT; VAR Initial : CHAR);
(* First nonblank character is returned in Initial. *)

VAR
  Character : CHAR;

BEGIN   (* GetInitial *)
  SkipBlanks(Names, Character);
  Initial := Character
END;    (* GetInitial *)

(***************************************************************)

PROCEDURE PrintLast(VAR Names, PrintNames : TEXT);
(* Last name is read from Names and written to PrintNames. *)

VAR
  Character : CHAR;
  MoreLetters : BOOLEAN;

  (*---------------------------------------------------------*)

  PROCEDURE FindLast(VAR Names : TEXT; VAR Character : CHAR);
  (* First letter of last name is returned in Character. *)

    (*+++++++++++++++++++++++++++++++++++++++++*)

    PROCEDURE SkipFirst(VAR Names : TEXT);
    (* Balance of characters in the *)
    (* first name are skipped.      *)
    VAR

      Character : CHAR;

  BEGIN   (* SkipFirst *)
    READ(Names, Character);
    WHILE Character <> Blank DO
      READ(Names, Character)
  END;    (* SkipFirst *)

    (*+++++++++++++++++++++++++++++++++++++++++*)

  BEGIN   (* FindLast *)
    SkipFirst(Names);
    SkipBlanks(Names, Character)
  END;    (* FindLast *)
```

SAMPLE PROBLEM, CONTINUED

```
  (*————————————————————————————————————————*)


BEGIN    (* PrintLast *)
  FindLast(Names, Character);
  MoreLetters := TRUE;
  WHILE MoreLetters DO
    BEGIN
      WRITE(PrintNames, Character);
      IF NOT EOLN(Names)
        THEN
          READ(Names, Character);
      MoreLetters := (Character <> Blank) AND NOT EOLN(Names)
    END;
  READLN(Names)
END;     (* PrintLast *)


(****************************************************************)


BEGIN    (* Transpose *)
  RESET(Names);
  REWRITE(PrintNames);
  WHILE NOT EOF(Names) DO
    BEGIN
      GetInitial(Names, Initial);
      PrintLast(Names, PrintNames);
      WRITE(PrintNames, Comma, Blank);
      WRITE(PrintNames, Initial);
      WRITELN(PrintNames, Period)
    END
END.     (* Transpose *)
```

Notice that Program Transpose has two procedures nested within procedures: SkipFirst is nested in FindLast; FindLast is nested in PrintLast. To nest or not to nest is a matter of style. We say more about nesting procedures later in this chapter. This problem may seem too simple to need such an involved structure, but we've set it up this way to show you how procedures are used and placed.

Scope of Identifiers
Local and Global Variables

Local identifiers are the variables defined in the VAR section of a procedure. These are variables the procedure needs for itself. For example, counter variables should be local variables.

Local Identifiers
Identifiers that are defined or declared within the block of a procedure.

In Program Transpose, Procedures GetInitial, PrintLast, and SkipFirst all need a place to hold a character. We defined a local variable Character in each case. The fact that they all use the same identifier isn't a problem. Each time a procedure is called, a place for each local variable is set up within the message board for the procedure; local variables are accessed in relation to their position on the message board.

There's no guarantee that the same locations will be chosen for the message board each time a procedure is called, so all local variables must be initialized within the procedure itself. If there is a variable in a procedure that must maintain its value from one call to the next, this variable must be a VAR parameter to the procedure, not a local variable.

Any variable or constant declared or defined in the block associated with the program heading (the main block) is a **global identifier**. Any global identifier is known (and can be accessed directly) by any procedure that does not declare a variable or constant with the same name. In Program Transpose, Blank, Comma, and Period are global constants. Identifier Blank is used in SkipBlanks, SkipFirst, and PrintLast. Although identifiers Comma and Period are used only in the main program, they could be accessed by any of the procedures.

Global Identifiers
Identifiers that are defined or declared within the main block of a program.

The same is true of the variable identifier Initial. We do not have to pass Initial to GetInitial as a parameter; GetInitial can access it directly. Variable Initial is defined in the main block and can be accessed directly by all the procedures in Program Transpose. Notice we say that it *can* be accessed directly, not that it *should* be accessed directly. We discuss later the issue of when to access an identifier globally.

Finally, local identifiers are *nonlocal* but accessible to any procedures nested within the same block. For example, Procedure PrintLast declares a local variable Character. That variable is nonlocal to Procedure FindLast but is accessible to it because FindLast is nested within the PrintLast block. The rules that govern all this business of who can access what where are called *scope rules*.

Scope Rules

Scope is the area within a program in which an identifier is known. The principle of scope is simple: Any identifier (constant, variable, or procedure) defined or declared in a block is known to any procedure within that block. Three basic rules apply this principle:

- The scope of an identifier includes all statements following the definition or declaration of the identifier within the same block.
- The scope of an identifier begins with its most recent definition or declaration.
- The scope of a formal parameter for a procedure is the same as the scope of a local variable for the procedure.

Figure 6–4 shows Program Transpose in terms of blocks. Let's look at it and see just what this means.

In this example every procedure knows (and can therefore access) Names, PrintNames, and Initial because they are defined in the outermost block. The local variables Character and MoreLetters defined in PrintLast are nonlocal to FindLast and SkipFirst because FindLast and SkipFirst are embedded within PrintLast. However, Procedure SkipFirst also has a local variable Character. The second rule says that any references within SkipFirst to Character are to this local variable.

Why, then, do we use parameter lists? Good programming practice dictates that communication between modules of our program should be explicitly stated. This limits the possibility of one module accidentally interfering with another. In other words, each procedure is given only what it needs to know. This is how we write "good" programs. There are a few cases where globally referenced constants and variables are okay. The use of the constant Blank in Program Transpose is one such example.

An identifier cannot be defined more than once in the same VAR section, but the same identifier can be defined in more than one VAR section. **Name precedence** clears up any confusion over multiply defined identifiers: When an identifier is used in the action part of a program or procedure, it refers to the most recently defined variable.

When an identifier is used in a procedure, the compiler first looks to see if the identifier is a local variable, then looks to see if it is a formal parameter. Only if it doesn't find the identifier listed in either place does it look to see if it's declared in the main block. If procedures are nested, the compiler works upward through each level of nesting, looking for the identifier declaration, until the compiler either finds it or gives the compile-time error: UNDECLARED IDENTIFIER.

We cannot define an identifier more than once at the same level in a block, but we can reuse an identifier at any nested level within the block. The scope rules tell us that an identifier can be used only within the block where it's defined or declared, and that it's not known outside of that block.

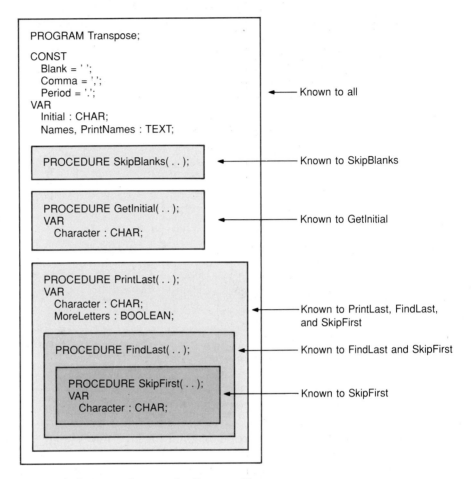

FIGURE 6–4 Scope diagram for Program Transpose

Here is another example to demonstrate the scope rules:

```
PROGRAM ScopeExample(INPUT, OUTPUT);
VAR
   A1 : INTEGER;
   A2 : BOOLEAN;

(*****************************************************)

PROCEDURE Block1(P1 : INTEGER; VAR P2 : BOOLEAN);
VAR
   D1, D2 : INTEGER;
BEGIN   (* Block1 *)
.

.
END;    (* Block1 *)
```

```
(****************************************************)

PROCEDURE Block2;
VAR
  B1, B2: INTEGER;

  (*------------------------------------*)
  PROCEDURE Block3;
  VAR
    C1, B2: INTEGER;
  BEGIN     (* Block3 *)
  .

  .
  END;       (* Block3 *)
  (*------------------------------------*)

BEGIN     (* Block2 *)
.

.
END;       (* Block2 *)

(****************************************************)

BEGIN     (* ScopeExample *)
.

.
END.        (* ScopeExample *)
```

Figure 6–5 is the scope diagram for Program ScopeExample. A1 and A2 are global variables, accessible to all parts of Program ScopeExample, but the identifiers A1 and A2 can be redefined in any of the three procedures in the program.

Variables D1 and D2 are defined in Block1; these local variables are not accessible to any other part of the program. Variables B1 and B2, which are defined in Block2, are local to Block2 but are nonlocal to Block3. Block3 can access B1 from Block2, but Block3 cannot access B2 from Block2 because Block3 has a local variable of the same name.

Block1 can invoke Block1. This is called a *recursive call*, and we define what that means in the next chapter. Block1 cannot invoke Block2 because the procedure name hasn't been defined yet. Block1 cannot invoke Block3 for two reasons. First, its name (identifier) is not known at that level. Second, a nested procedure cannot be called from outside of the block in which it is nested.

Block2 can invoke itself (recursively), Block1, and Block3. The statement within Block2 that invokes Block3 comes in the action part of Block2. Block3 is

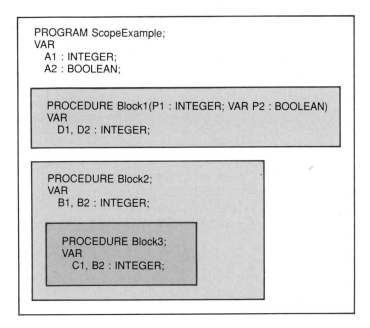

```
PROGRAM ScopeExample;
VAR
  A1 : INTEGER;
  A2 : BOOLEAN;

    PROCEDURE Block1(P1 : INTEGER; VAR P2 : BOOLEAN)
    VAR
      D1, D2 : INTEGER;

    PROCEDURE Block2;
    VAR
      B1, B2 : INTEGER;

        PROCEDURE Block3;
        VAR
          C1, B2 : INTEGER;
```

FIGURE 6–5 Scope diagram for ScopeExample

defined within the declaration portion of Block2. Therefore Block3's name is defined before it appears in a call. Block3 can invoke all of the other blocks.

The 4-Cs Corner
Correctness

Avoiding Side Effects

Procedure parameter lists can be complicated, especially at first. So you may be tempted to reference global variables directly instead of passing them through a parameter list. *Don't!* It's a bad habit that can lead to program bugs that are extremely hard to locate. If communication between program modules is confined to the parameter lists and all nonoutput variables are *value* parameters, each module is isolated from what happens in other parts of the program. In other words, the code in one procedure should not have **side effects** elsewhere in the program, except through the well-defined interface of the parameter list (Figure 6–6).

Another way of saying this is that procedures should use only the variables defined in their *formal* parameter list or in their own VAR section. Create stand-alone modules that communicate through parameter lists. Avoid side effects!

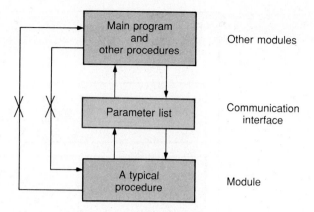

FIGURE 6–6 Proper channels of communication

> I shot an arrow into the air,
> It fell to earth I know not where.
> I looked here, I looked there.
> I sure lose a lot of arrows that way!
> —Anonymous

Here is a short program that runs but produces incorrect results because of side effects:

```
PROGRAM Trouble(INPUT, OUTPUT);
(* This program counts the number of characters   *)
(* on each line of input and the number of lines. *)
(* These totals are printed.                       *)

VAR
  Count : INTEGER;
  Character : CHAR;

(*****************************************************)

PROCEDURE CharCount;
(* Counts and prints the number of characters *)
(* in a line of input.                         *)

BEGIN   (* CharCount *)
  Count := 0;
  WHILE NOT EOLN DO
    BEGIN
      READ(Character);
```

```
      Count := Count + 1
    END;
  WRITELN(' Number of characters on line ', Count)
END;     (* CharCount *)


(********************************************************)

BEGIN    (* Trouble *)
  Count := 0;
  WHILE NOT EOF DO
    BEGIN
      Count := Count + 1;
      CharCount
    END;
  WRITELN( 'Number of lines of input ', Count)
END.     (* Trouble *)
```

Program Trouble is supposed to count and print the number of characters on each line of input. After the last line has been processed, it should print the number of lines. Strangely enough, each time we run the program, the number of lines of input is the same as the number of characters in the last line of input!

If we declare a local variable Count in Procedure CharCount, the program works fine. There's no conflict between the local Count and the global Count; the local Count is a separate variable known only to the block it is local to. Character, of course, should be declared locally in the procedure because it's only used in the procedure.

Creating Correct Interfaces

The errors that occur when we use procedures are usually due to incorrect interfaces between the main program and a procedure or between two procedures. Careful preparation of an interface design chart is the safest way to avoid these kinds of errors.

The identifiers listed in the program variables section of the chart are the global identifiers for the program. These identifiers become the actual parameters for the procedures called from the main block. The formal parameters should use the same identifiers unless there's a reason for being more general. SkipBlanks in Program Transpose is a very general procedure. It is coded with a general name for the file (DataFile) rather than the specific name (Names) used in the problem. Procedure SkipBlanks should be in your personal library of useful procedures.

If Procedure A calls Procedure B, the actual parameters that Procedure A should use in the call are its formal parameters or its local variables. Remember, all communication should be through parameter lists.

Nesting Procedures

Whether or not you nest your procedures is a matter of style and what your top-down design calls for. It's perfectly all right to list all your procedures sequentially without nesting them, as long as you declare a procedure before you call it. Because most programs change during design, testing, and maintenance, it might be better not to nest your procedures.

For example, if in Program Transpose we decide that we want another procedure to call SkipFirst, we would have to rewrite our program or even our design because SkipFirst is nested in FindLast, which is nested in PrintLast. The scope rules prevent a procedure at the same level as PrintLast from calling the nested SkipFirst. On the other hand, we may choose to nest a procedure just to prevent any other procedure from calling it.

If you think that you may want to call a procedure from more than one place, don't nest it. If one procedure is an integral part of another and there is no possibility that it will be needed anywhere else, nest it. Otherwise it doesn't matter. Nesting does sometimes allow your program to reflect your top-down design more accurately.

Correctness Hints

1. Follow the documentation guidelines carefully when writing procedures. As your programs get more complex, it is increasingly important to adhere to the documentation and formatting standards. Label the main BEGIN-END pair of each procedure with the procedure name. If the procedure name doesn't clearly define the process being done, describe that process in comments. Use comments to explain the purpose of all local variables.
2. Be sure to put a semicolon following the procedure heading.
3. Be sure the formal parameter list gives the types of each parameter.
4. Be sure the formal parameter list matches the actual parameter list in order, type of variables, and number.
5. Make sure that variables used as actual parameters are declared in the block where the procedure call is made either in a VAR section or in a Formal Parameter List.
6. Declare a procedure before any calls to that procedure are made.
7. A VAR parameter requires a variable as an actual parameter because an address is put on the message board. A value parameter can have any expression that supplies a value of the correct type (variables or constants, and operators) as an actual parameter.
8. Avoid the side effects of procedures. Use the well-defined interface of the parameter list to communicate with the calling block. Variables used only in a procedure should be declared as local variables. Do not reference global variables directly from inside a procedure.

9. The reserved word VAR must precede each VAR parameter in the formal parameter list. When no symbol is used, the parameter is a value parameter.
10. You can't reference an identifier (variable, constant, procedure) that is outside the scope of the block.

Summary

Pascal has the facility to let you write your program in functional modules; therefore the structure of your program can parallel your top-down design. Your main program (what is between the BEGIN-END pair of the main block) can look exactly like the Level 0 of your top-down design. You do this by writing each functional module as a procedure. Your main program simply executes these procedures in logical sequence.

Communication between the calling program and the procedure is handled by the use of two lists of identifiers: the *formal parameter list*, which is in the procedure heading and includes the type of each identifier, and the *actual parameter list*, which is in the calling statement. These lists of identifiers must agree in position, type, and number.

Part of the top-down design process is determining what data must be given to a lower-level module and what information must be received back. The module interfaces defined become the formal and actual parameter lists, and the module name becomes a call to the procedure.

Pascal has two types of parameters: VAR and value. VAR parameters have the word VAR before them in the formal parameter list; value parameters do not. Parameters that are output parameters from the procedure must be VAR parameters, and files must be passed as VAR parameters. All other parameters should be value parameters. Using value parameters helps us avoid side effects because the procedure is working with a copy of the original value parameter, not the original itself.

Anything declared in the block associated with the program heading is known to all procedures and is called a global identifier. It is not good programming practice to reference global and nonlocal variables directly from within a procedure. All communication between modules of your program should be done through the use of formal and actual parameter lists.

The scope of an identifier refers to the area in which it is known. The rules say an identifier is known in the block in which it is defined or declared and in all of the blocks within that block. If an identifier is redefined, name precedence determines which variable or constant is meant when that identifier is referenced.

EXERCISES

1. Write a top-down design for Exercise 1 in Chapter 5. Convert your design into a structured Pascal program using procedures.

2. a. Write a procedure that adds up the even integers from N to M. The result is left in Answer.

   b. Write a statement to invoke your procedure that sums the even integers from 16 to 26.

3. a. Write a procedure that reads and sums ten positive values. If a negative value is encountered, stop the process and set AllPositive to FALSE.

   b. Write an invoking statement for your procedure.

4. Define the following terms
   a. Procedure call
   b. Parameter list
   c. Positional parameters
   d. Formal parameter
   e. Actual parameter
   f. VAR parameter
   g. Local variable

5. Given this program and the following data:

```
PROGRAM Exercise(INPUT, OUTPUT);

VAR
A, B, C, Sum : INTEGER;

(*************************************)

PROCEDURE Add(VAR X, A, Z, Sum : INTEGER);

BEGIN    (* Add *)
  READ(X, A, Z);
  Sum := X + A + Z
END;     (* Add *)

(*************************************)

BEGIN    (* Exercise *)
  Add(A, B, C, Sum);
  WRITELN(A, B, C, Sum)
END.     (* Exercise *)
```

   Data: 2 4 6 8
   What is your output?

6. Using a VAR parameter, a procedure can obtain the initial value of an actual parameter as well as change the value of the actual parameter in the calling program. True or false?

7. Using a value parameter, the value of a variable can be passed to a procedure and used for computation there, without any modification to the value of the variable in the main program. True or false?

8. A particular procedure is an inner block in the program that contains it, and an outer block to any procedures declared within it. True or false?

9. Identifiers declared at the beginning of a block are accessible to all executable statements that are part of that block, including statements belonging to inner blocks. True or false?

10. We can declare a local variable in a procedure using the name of a variable in the main program without confusing the compiler. Why?

11. Use the following procedure heading and call to answer the questions below.

```
PROCEDURE Parameters(X : INTEGER; VAR Y : INTEGER);
          .
          .
Parameters(A, B);
```

   a. When the procedure is called, a storage location is created for X, then initialized to the value of A. True or false?
   b. Because Y is a VAR parameter, a storage location is created, then initialized to the address of B. Y stands for the variable B itself, and any change in Y changes B. True or false?
   c. X is initialized to the value of A because their positions correspond in the parameter list. True or false?
   d. X and Y can both be used to receive values from the main program, but only X, the value parameter, can be used to return a value to the main program. True or false?

12. Use the following block structure to answer the questions below:

```
PROGRAM ScopeRules(INPUT, OUTPUT);

VAR
   A, B : INTEGER;

(*********************************************)

PROCEDURES Block1;

VAR
   A1, B1 : INTEGER;

   (*-----------------------------*)
   PROCEDURE Block2;

   VAR
      A, A2, B2 : INTEGER;

   BEGIN   (* Block2 *)
         .
         .
   END;    (* Block2 *)
   (*-----------------------------*)

BEGIN    (* Block1 *)
```

```
            .
            .
    END;      (* Block1 *)

    (*********************************************)

    PROCEDURE Block3;

    VAR
      A3, B3 : INTEGER;

    BEGIN    (* Block3 *)
            .
            .
    END;     (* Block3 *)

    (*********************************************)

    BEGIN    (* ScopeRules *)
            .
            .
    END.     (* ScopeRules *)
```

a. A and B are global variables, accessible to all parts of Program ScopeRules, including Procedure Block2. True or false?
b. Because ScopeRules is the outer block, statements in its body can reference all variables declared in inner blocks, including Procedure Block2. True or false?
c. Because Procedure Block2 is the innermost block, its local variables can be accessed by all other blocks. True or false?
d. Variable A1 is nonlocal to Procedure Block2. True or false?
e. Variable B2 is local to Procedure Block1. True or false?
f. The statement A1 : = A would be legal in Procedure Block1. True or false?
g. The statement A3 : = A1 would be legal in Procedure Block3. True or false?
h. Variables A2 and B2 are not defined in any of the outer blocks. True or false?
i. The statement A : = B2 in Procedure Block2 assigns the value of B2 to the local variable A; it does not affect the global variable A. True or false?
j. Variables A1 and B1 are nonlocal to Procedure Block2, local to Procedure Block1, and not defined in the outer block. True or false?

13. Draw a scope diagram for the block structure in Exercise 12.

14. Define the following terms:
    a. Value parameter
    b. Global variable
    c. Scope
    d. Name precedence
    e. Side effects
    f. Nonlocal

15. Read the following program, then answer the questions below.

```
PROGRAM Sample(INPUT, OUTPUT);
```

```
VAR
  A, B : INTEGER;

(*************************************************)

PROCEDURE Change(X: INTEGER; VAR Y : INTEGER);

VAR
  B : INTEGER;

BEGIN (* Change *)
  B := X;
  Y := Y + B;
  X := Y
END;   (* Change *)

(*************************************************)

BEGIN  (* Sample *)
  A := 10;
  B := 7;
  Change(A, B);
  WRITELN(A, B)
END.    (* Sample *)
```

    a. What are the values of Sample variables A and B when Change is called? (Let U indicate an undefined value.)

    b. What are the values of Change variables X, Y, and B when Change is called? (Let U indicate an undefined value.)

    c. What are the values of Sample variables A and B after Change is executed? (Let U indicate an undefined value.)

16. Read the following program, then answer the questions below.

```
PROGRAM One(INPUT, OUTPUT);

VAR
  A, B: INTEGER;

(*********************************************)

PROCEDURE Two(VAR X : INTEGER; Y : INTEGER);

VAR
  B : INTEGER;

BEGIN   (* Two *)
  B := X;
  Y := Y + B;
  X := Y
END;    (* Two *)
```

```
( ************************************************* )

BEGIN    (* One *)
   A := 5;
   B := 4;
   Two(A, B)
END.     (* One *)
```

a. What are the values of One variables A and B when Two is called? (Let U indicate an undefined value.)
b. What are the values of Two variables X, Y, and B when Two is called? (Let U indicate an undefined value.)
c. What are the values of One variables A and B after Two is executed? (Let U indicate an undefined value.)

17. Read the following program, then answer the questions below.

```
PROGRAM Dog(INPUT, OUTPUT);

VAR
   A, B : INTEGER;

( ****************************************** )

PROCEDURE Cat(X, Y : INTEGER);

BEGIN    (* Cat *)
   B := X;
   Y := Y + B;
   X := Y
END;     (* Cat *)

( ****************************************** )
BEGIN    (* Dog *)
   A := 7;
   B := 10;
   Cat(A, B);
   WRITELN(A, B)
END.     (* Dog *)
```

a. What are the values of Dog variables A and B when Cat is called? (Let U indicate an undefined value.)
b. What are the values of variables X, Y, and B when Cat is called? (Let U indicate an undefined value.)
c. What are the values of Dog variables A and B after Cat is executed? (Let U indicate an undefined value.)

PRETEST

1. Because a procedure is a subprogram within a program, it cannot contain input or output instructions or other subprograms. True or false?

2. The parameters listed in the procedure heading are called *formal parameters;* the parameters listed in the invoking statement are called *actual parameters.* True or false?

3. Write a procedure named Increment, with one variable parameter of type INTEGER, which adds 15 to the value received in the parameter and returns the new value to the calling program.

4. a. Write a procedure that reads in heart rate, (INTEGER values) from a file until a normal heart rate (between 60 and 80) is read or EOF becomes TRUE. Normal is a parameter that returns TRUE if a normal heart rate is read or FALSE if <eof> is encountered. You may assume one value per line.

   b. Write the invoking statement for your procedure. (Use the same variable names used in the procedure.)

5. a. Write a procedure that reads grades and counts the number of failing grades (Score ≤ 59) in a set of N grades. N is an input parameter of the procedure; the number of failing grades is an output parameter.

   b. Write an invoking statement for your procedure. (Use N and NFail as your actual parameters.)

6. Given this program and the following data:

```
PROGRAM Pretest(INPUT, OUTPUT);

CONST
   Ten = 10;

VAR
   A, B, C : INTEGER;

(****************************************************)

PROCEDURE Test(VAR Z, X, A : INTEGER);

BEGIN    (* Test *)
   READLN(Z, X, A);
   A := Z * X + A
END;      (* Test *)

(****************************************************)

BEGIN    (* Pretest *)
   Test(A, B, C);
   B := B + TEN;
   WRITELN('The answers are ', B, C, A, TEN)
END.      (* Pretest *)
```

Data: 3 2 4
What is your output?

7. When writing procedures we have to be aware of the declarations for all other blocks, because if we declare a local variable with the same name as a variable in an outer block, we may accidentally modify that variable. True or false?

8. Read the following program, then answer the questions below.

```
PROGRAM Test6(INPUT, OUTPUT);

VAR
  X, Y : INTEGER;

(**************************************************)

PROCEDURE Alter(VAR A : INTEGER; B : INTEGER);

VAR
  Y : INTEGER;

BEGIN    (* Alter *)
  Y := B;
  A := A + Y;
  B := A
END;     (* Alter *)

(**************************************************)

BEGIN    (* Test6 *)
  X := 12;
  Y := 2;
  Alter(Y, X);
  WRITELN(X, Y)
END.     (* Test6 *)
```

a. What are the values of Test6 variables X and Y when Alter is called? (Let U indicate an undefined value.)
b. What are the values of Alter variables A, B, and Y when Alter is called? (Let U indicate an undefined value.)
c. What are the values of Test6 variables X and Y after Alter is executed? (Let U indicate an undefined value.)

9. a. Write a procedure that returns the sum of the squares of three numbers (INTEGER) and a Boolean TRUE if all three numbers are positive. Use variable and value parameters as required.
   b. Write the calling statement for your procedure if the three numbers are A, B, and C.

10. Use the following skeletal program to answer the questions below.

```
PROGRAM ScopeTest(INPUT, OUTPUT);

VAR
  X, Y : INTEGER;

(********************************************)

PROCEDURE Block1(X1 : INTEGER);
```

```
VAR
  X, Y1 : INTEGER;

BEGIN    (* Block1 *)
  .
  .
END;     (* Block1 *)

(************************************************)

PROCEDURE Block2(X2, Y2 : INTEGER);

  (*------------------*)
  PROCEDURE Block3(Y3 : INTEGER);

  VAR
    X3 : INTEGER;

  BEGIN    (* Block3 *)
    .
    .
  END;       (* Block3 *)
  (*----------------*)

BEGIN      (* Block2 *)
  .
  .
END;       (* Block2 *)

(************************************************)

BEGIN      (* ScopeTest *)
  .
  .
END.       (* ScopeTest *)
```

a. X and Y are global variables, accessible to all parts of the program, including Procedure Block1. True or false?

b. Because Procedure Block3 is the innermost block, its local variables can be accessed by all other blocks. True or false?

c. Variable Y1 is local to Procedure Block1 and nonlocal but accessible to Procedure Block2. True or false?

d. The statement X : = X1 in Procedure Block1 would change local variable X of Procedure Block1, but would not affect global variable X of Program ScopeTest. True or false?

e. The statement Y2 : = X3 in Procedure Block2 would be legal. True or false?

11. Given this program and the following data:*

```
PROGRAM ScopeOut(INPUT, OUTPUT);
```

```
VAR
  A, B, C : INTEGER;

(**************************************************)

PROCEDURE One(X, Y : INTEGER; VAR Z : INTEGER);

VAR
  A : INTEGER;

BEGIN    (* One *)
  A := 1;
  B := 7;
  X := Y;
  Z := A + X
END;     (* One *)

(**************************************************)

BEGIN    (* ScopeOut *)
  A := 4;
  B := 5;
  C := 12;
  One(A, B, C);
  WRITELN(A, B, C)
END.     (* ScopeOut *)
```

What is the output?

PROGRAMMING ASSIGNMENTS

1. Write a program that reads in a sequence of grades (ranging from zero to 100) and calculates the following information:

   - The number of grades
   - The average grade
   - The minimum grade
   - The maximum grade
   - The number of failing grades (below 60)
   - The number of passing grades

     Input: A sequence of integer numbers, one per line.
     (Use EOF to determine when you've finished reading the numbers.)

     Output:
     (1) Echo-print the numbers.
     (2) The six values described above properly labeled.

2. Knowing you're a computer whiz, a friend has asked you to write a program that calculates the mileage information for the car he drove on a recent vacation. At each stop for gas he recorded the odometer reading and the amount of gas purchased.

Assume that he filled the tank each time. In addition, assume that he bought gas immediately before he left on the trip and right after he got back, taking odometer readings at each point. Design a program to read the total number of stops made (including the first and last), the odometer readings, and gas purchases. Then compute the following:

- The gas mileage achieved between every pair of stops on the trip
- The gas mileage achieved through the entire trip
- The best gas mileage on a single tank

3. The registrar's office would like a program that processes semester grades and prints a grade report for each student. To determine the grade-point average for each student, use this formula:

$$\text{Grade point average} = \ C(i) * W(i) \ / \ C(i)$$

where C(i) is credits for the course and W(i) is the weight for the grade (4 for A, 3 for B, 2 for C, 1 for D, 0 for F). If the sum of credits for a student is zero, print zero for the grade-point average. All of the records for any one student are together in the input stream.

> **Input:** Each student record indicates the number of courses taken, the course number, credit hours, and grade, and is written in the following form:
> (1) First line: student ID and number of courses taken
> (2) Next lines (one for each course taken): course number, credit hours, and grade (4, 3, 2, 1, 0)

> **Output:** For each student, print a report as follows (double-space between students and label properly):
> (1) First line: student ID
> (2) Next lines (one for each course taken): course number, credit hours, and grade
> (3) Last line: total credits taken, total credits received, and semester grade point average

4. A very popular department on campus has problems with growing enrollment in its classes. The department decides that during registration it will go up to room limit on all of its classes. In fact, because of special permission and errors before registration week, some classes already have exceeded room size. The department would like to have a list for each day of the registration period, showing enrollment figures for each class. You've been asked to write a program to print this kind of list.

> **Input:**
> (1) First line of data: the number of classes on the list
> (2) Other data lines: unique four-digit number, room size, and current enrollment

> **Outline:** Echo-print each line of input, with the following additional information on the same line (whichever applies):
> (1) If the class is full, a statement to that effect
> (2) If the room limit has already been exceeded, a statement to that effect and the number of spaces exceeded
> (3) If space is left in the class, a statement to that effect and the number of spaces left

5. A local savings and loan association is planning to use a computer to prepare statements for its new "save-spend" accounts. For each customer, a set of data entries is prepared that lists the account number, balance forwarded from the previous month, and transaction entries. The transaction entries are arranged one per line, with the customer's account number repeated before each transaction. Deposits appear as positive entries, withdrawals as negative entries. The number of transactions is arbitrary. A new customer's leading entry is detected by a change in the account number.

> **Output:** For each customer, print a report as follows:
> (1) First line: customer ID (account number).
> (2) Second line (headings): item, deposits, withdrawals, and balance.
> (3) Next lines: one line for initial balance and each transaction (deposit or withdrawal) under appropriate heading. Keep a running balance.
> (4) Next line: service charge ($1 per withdrawal) and balance.
> (5) Last line: interest paid (1 percent on any final balance over $1,000) and totals (label each row correctly).

6. A poor soul, considerably intoxicated, stands in the middle of a 10-foot-long bridge spanning a river. He staggers along, toward the left bank, then the right bank, but fortunately cannot fall off the bridge. Assuming that each step he takes is exactly 1 foot long, how many steps will he take before he reaches either bank of the river? Assume that he's just as likely to step toward the left bank as toward the right.
   You must do three things:
   (1) Find how many steps it takes to get off the bridge.
   (2) Tell which bank is reached.
   (3) Let the drunkard go out for five nights and arrive at the same point (the center) of the bridge. Find, on the average, how many steps it takes to get off the bridge.
   You must have a random number generator to solve this problem. (Check with your instructor for the name of the random function in your system.) Assume that it's just as likely to generate a number less than 0.5 as the same or greater. Here's an example of how this function is used:

   ```
   X := Random(0.0)
   ```

   X can be used to determine the direction of the drunkard's next step. If the number of steps exceeds 100, print *He'll have to sleep it off.*

7. The Chargall Company needs a billing system that takes a customer's current balance, computes the interest and adds it to the current balance, adds current purchases, and determines the minimum payment due. The current interest rate varies from month to month, but the minimum payment is always 10 percent of the new balance. Your job is to program the system. The one restriction is that the form of the input data cannot be changed.

   > Position 1–9: Social security number
   > Position 10: ,
   > Position 11 on: Amount (REAL) of sales or credit or current balance

   Before you receive it, the data has been sorted by social security number, with the current balance the last data item. For example:

   456491217, 12.36   Sales or credits
   456491217, −5.00   Sales or credits

456491217, 242.0   Current balance
921007121, 25.00   Sales or credits
921007121, 31.50   Sales or credits
921007121, 300.36   Current balance

Input:
(1) A line containing the interest rate to be charged on INPUT
(2) The data described above on File Data with an <eof> indicating the end of the run

Output: The output should be a table showing the interest rate at the top and a line of output for each customer, showing social security number and the corresponding new balance and monthly payment due.

8. You've just bought a small computer to help out in your computer classes. It would be nice to make some money with it as well, so you and a friend decide to print and sell a weekly list of prices of common products sold at the three largest grocery chains in town. You want your program to print a list of the stores and the times surveyed, the minimum cost of each particular item, and the ID number of the store charging that minimum.

Input:
(1) First entry: number of stores surveyed
(2) Next entries (one line for each store surveyed): name of store (twenty characters), store ID
(3) Last entries (a new line for each item): name of item (twenty characters), store ID, price, store ID, price, store ID, price

Output:
(1) A heading to the list that includes some appropriate title and the list of store names and corresponding IDs
(2) For each item in the list, the name of the item, the minimum cost, and the ID of the store with the minimum price
(3) A final line that prints total savings (accumulation of the savings on each item)

Label appropriately.

9. Summer school is over and it's time for your tour of Europe. However, you're a little concerned about handling all those currencies and want to be able to convert quickly in your head before you go. The last time you looked, these were the rates of exchange:

$$5.9 \text{ French francs} = \$1$$
$$0.55 \text{ British pound} = \$1$$
$$1.7 \text{ German marks} = \$1$$
$$1,306 \text{ Italian lira} = \$1$$

Because this isn't very easy to do in your head, you decide to use the following approximations:

$$6 \text{ French francs} = \$1$$
$$.5 \text{ British pound} = \$1$$
$$2 \text{ German marks} = \$1$$
$$1,000 \text{ Italian lira} = \$1$$

Write a program that reads in a value in francs, pounds, marks, and lira and computes the actual dollar amount for each using the exchange table, then computes the approximation for each and the difference between the two.

Output: A line for each currency that includes the following:
(1) Amount of foreign currency read in
(2) Correct amount in dollars
(3) Approximate amount in dollars
(4) Difference between the two

The output should be labeled properly.

7 Functions, Additional Control Structures, and Real Numbers

- To be able to code and invoke a function for a specified task.

- To be able to recognize a recursive call.

- To be able to use a REPEAT statement to implement a loop.

- To be able to use a FOR statement to implement a count-controlled loop.

- To be able to use a CASE statement for multiway selection.

- To be able to define and use real numbers appropriately.

- To be able to determine where it is appropriate to use a function.

- To be able to determine whether to use a WHILE, RE-PEAT, or FOR statement to implement a loop to perform a specific task.

- To be able to determine whether to use a nested IF or a CASE statement for multiple-way selection.

In this chapter we introduce four Pascal constructs: the function (another form of subprogram), REPEAT and FOR statements (alternate forms of looping structures), and the CASE statement (another form of selection structure). These are the "ice cream and cake" of Pascal. None of these constructs is essential, but they're all nice to have.

We also cover two theoretical topics here: recursion (a different kind of repetition) and the representation of real numbers in a computer.

Functions

A **function** is a subprogram called from within an expression that returns a value through the function name. There are three important things to remember about functions:

- Like a procedure, a function is a subprogram that does a task.
- Unlike a procedure, a function is invoked by using it in an expression.
- Unlike a procedure, a function identifier has two purposes:
   It names the action.
   It is the variable identifier in which the result is returned.

The syntax diagram of a function is very similar to that of a procedure:

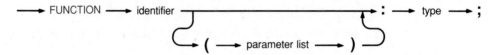

Because the name of a function serves the dual purpose of naming the subprogram and serving as a place to send back a value, the function must be assigned a data type. We do this by putting a colon and the name of a type after the function identifier on the formal parameter list (if there is one).

Let's augment Program WeightedAverage (see page 97) by printing the appropriate letter grade to go with the weighted average that's been calculated. We implement the task of converting from a numeric grade to a letter grade by using a function. The input to the function is the weighted average; the output from the function is the equivalent letter grade.

```
FUNCTION LetterGrade(Average : REAL) : CHAR;
(* Assumption:  Average is a numeric grade     *)
(* between O and 100.  The equivalent letter   *)
(* grade is determined using the usual scale.  *)

BEGIN    (* LetterGrade *)
  IF Average >= 90
     THEN
        LetterGrade := 'A'
  ELSE IF Average >= 80
     THEN
        LetterGrade := 'B'
```

```
    ELSE IF Average >= 70
       THEN
          LetterGrade := 'C'
    ELSE IF Average >= 60
       THEN
          LetterGrade := 'D'
    ELSE
       LetterGrade := 'F'
END;    (* LetterGrade *)
```

In order to print out the letter grade along with the weighted average, we would rewrite the output statements like this:

```
WRITELN('The weighted average is ', Average:10:2, '.');
WRITELN('The corresponding letter grade is ',
        LetterGrade(Average), '.');
              ↑
          Function call
```

Function LetterGrade is defined as a CHAR function. Within the body of the function, the name of the function must be set to the CHAR variable or constant that is to be returned. The use of the function name in an expression causes the function to be invoked. In this case, the name of the function is used in a parameter list for WRITELN. The value that is stored in the function name (identifier) replaces the function call in the expression. In this case, the value that is returned is printed.

In Program Notices on page 129, the input data is checked to be sure that each of the test scores is positive. Variable DataOK is set to TRUE if the three test scores are all positive. This test could have been implemented as a BOOL-EAN function:

```
FUNCTION DataOK(Testl, Test2, Test3 : INTEGER) : BOOLEAN;
(* DataOK is set to TRUE if all three input *)
(* values are positive.                     *)

BEGIN    (* DataOK *)
  DataOK := (Testl >= 0) AND (Test2 >= 0) AND (Test3 >= 0)
END;     (* DataOK *)
```

We would use the function like this:

```
IF DataOK(Testl, Test2, Test3)
    THEN
       .
       .
```

Functions are provided in Pascal to simulate mathematical entities called *functions*. Pascal also provides a set of built-in common mathematical functions. A list of these is in Appendix B.

Function Side Effects

Functions are designed to be used where a single value should be returned. However, if a function has VAR parameters in the formal parameter list, the corresponding actual parameters can indeed be changed. The sending back or changing of more than one value in a function is a side effect of the function and should be avoided.

A good rule of thumb is *never use VAR parameters in the formal parameter list of a function*. If you must have them, then you should be using a procedure, not a function. Of course you can use value parameters as you need them.

Another example of a side effect crops up when a procedure or function references a global variable directly, not through its formal parameter list. (We see this same side effect in procedures.) Remember, communication between program modules should be confined to the actual and formal parameter lists.

This example illustrates the two types of side effects:

```
PROGRAM UnExpected(INPUT, OUTPUT);
(* This program demonstrates a side effect of a function. *)

VAR
  A, B : INTEGER;

(*********************************************)

FUNCTION Side(VAR X, Y : INTEGER) : INTEGER;
(* This function has a side effect. *)

BEGIN    (* Side *)
  X := X + Y;
  A := X + 1;
  Side := X + A
END;     (* Side *)

(*********************************************)

BEGIN    (* UnExpected *)
A := 0;
B := 1;
WRITELN(Side(A, B));
WRITELN(Side(A, B));
WRITELN(Side(B, A));
WRITELN(Side(B, A))
END.     (* UnExpected *)
```

We would expect the first two WRITELN statements to produce the same output and the second two WRITELN statements to produce the same output. That is, we would expect a function to return the same result from duplicate inputs. Unfortunately, Function Side has side effects: It does not return the same value from two successive identical calls. Let's do a code walk-through and see why.

Statement	A	B	X	Y	Side
(initial values)	0	1	?	?	?
Side(A, B) (when entered)	0	1	0	1	?
X := X + Y	1	1	1	1	?
A := X + 1	2	1	2	1	?
Side := X + A	2	1	2	1	4 ← What is printed
Side(A, B) (when entered)	2	1	2	1	?
X := X + Y	3	1	3	1	?
A := X + 1	4	1	4	1	?
Side := X + A	4	1	4	1	8 ← What is printed
Side(B, A) (when entered)	4	1	1	4	?
X := X + Y	4	5	5	4	?
A := X + 1	6	5	5	6	?
Side := X + A	6	5	5	6	11 ← What is printed
Side(B, A) (when entered)	6	5	5	6	?
X := X + Y	6	11	11	6	?
A := X + 1	12	11	11	12	?
Side := X + A	12	11	11	12	23 ← What is printed

Because the function parameters are VAR parameters, when the formal parameter is changed, the actual parameter is changed also. Here, Y is not changed, but X is. Because A is being referenced globally, the function is changing it each time as well. As you can see by the output of Function Side (the values marked with an arrow), not only are different values returned with the same input, but there is no obvious pattern.

Recursion

In the last chapter, we said that a procedure could invoke itself. So can a function. When a subprogram invokes itself, the call is known as a *recursive call*. **Recursion**—the ability of a procedure or function to call itself—is an alternative control structure to repetition (looping).

Recursion is a very powerful tool. Many believe it is too advanced for an introductory text. We bring it up here in parallel with the discussion of functions because functions lend themselves to an error called *inadvertent recursion*. We describe this error here, then show you how to use recursion correctly.

The following INTEGER function is designed to read and sum ten INTEGER values:

```
FUNCTION Sum : INTEGER;
(* Ten INTEGER values are read and summed. *)

VAR
  Number,        (* a place to hold an input value *)
  Count : INTEGER;       (* loop control variable *)

BEGIN    (* Sum *)
  Sum := 0;
  Count := 1;
  WHILE Count <= 10 DO
    BEGIN
      WRITELN('Enter an INTEGER value and press return.');
      READLN(Number);
      Sum := Sum + Number;
      Count := Count + 1
    END
END;     (* Sum *)
```

The problem with this function is that it inadvertently calls itself. The function identifier is Sum. The statement

```
Sum := 0;
```

sets the function identifier variable to zero. That's fine. But the statement

```
Sum := Sum + Number;
```

contains a recursive call. The function identifier Sum is used in an expression on the right side of the assignment statement. When this statement is translated, the code is generated to execute Function Sum. Each time this statement is executed, Function Sum is invoked again, and we end up with an infinite loop (Count is always 1). We can correct this problem by using a temporary variable to hold the running sum of the input values. The last statement in the function can set the function identifier to this value.

```
FUNCTION Sum : INTEGER;
(* Ten INTEGER values are read and summed. *)

VAR
  Number,
  Count,
  TempSum : INTEGER;                    ← Temporary variable
```

```
BEGIN    (* Sum *)
  TempSum := 0;                                    ← Initializes running sum
  Count := 1;
  WHILE Count <= 10 DO
    BEGIN
      WRITELN('Enter an INTEGER value and press return.')
      READLN(Number);
        TempSum := TempSum + Number;    ← Adds to running sum
        Count := Count + 1
    END;
  Sum := TempSum                                   ← Stores in function identifier
END;      (* Sum *)
```

The moral is that unless you mean to use recursion you must not use the name of your function in an expression in the body of that function. The function name can appear any number of times on the left-hand side of an assignment statement in the body of the function. For those of you whose curiosity has been piqued, we include two recursive examples.

Remember that recursion is a control structure that can be used in place of repetition. The error in Function Sum is not with the use of the function identifier on the right side of the assignment statement but with the control structure in which it is embedded. A correct recursive solution to a very similar problem is given below. Instead of reading and summing ten values from the keyboard, this program reads and sums values from File Data until <eof> is reached.

```
PROGRAM RecursiveSumTest(OUTPUT, Data);
(* This program tests recursive Function Sum. *)

VAR
  Data : TEXT;

(*********************************)

FUNCTION Sum : INTEGER;
(* Recursive function to read and sum values until <eof>. *)

VAR
  Number : INTEGER;

BEGIN    (* Sum *)
  IF EOF(Data)
    THEN
      Sum := 0
```

```
      ELSE
        BEGIN
          READLN(Data, Number);
          Sum := Sum + Number
        END
END;      (* Sum *)


(*********************************)


BEGIN    (* RecursiveSumTest *)
  RESET(Data);
  WRITELN('Sum of the values on File Data: ', Sum:10)
END.      (* RecursiveSumTest *)
```

Now Function Sum correctly adds the data values on File Data. Let's do a code walk-through, using the following data:

>   23<eoln>
>   46<eoln>
>   33<eoln>
>   <eof>

Function Sum is called the first time from the WRITELN statement. The calling statement creates the message board. There are no parameters, but there is a local variable, Number. In the case of a function, there also must be a place assigned for the function identifier variable. There is one additional value on the message board that we have neglected to mention: the return address. The *return address* is the address of the next statement to be executed after the subprogram call. Here it's the instruction that prints the value that has been returned.

Data is not at EOF so the ELSE branch is taken. The value 23 is read into Number. The next statement

```
Sum := Sum + Number
```

invokes Function Sum again. Another message board is created with a cell for local variable Number and the function identifier variable Sum. The return address that's put on the message board is different this time; it's the address of the instruction to add the returned value to the local variable Number and store it into Sum.

Data is still not at EOF so the ELSE branch is taken. The value 46 is read into local variable Number. The next statement

```
Sum := Sum + Number
```

again invokes Function Sum. Another message board is created with a cell for local variable Number and the function identifier variable Sum. The return address on the message board returns control to finish the assignment statement.

Data is still not at EOF so the ELSE branch is taken. The value 33 is read into local variable Number. The next statement again invokes Function Sum.

EOF(Data) is now TRUE. The function identifier variable is set to zero, and the last function call is now complete. The value of the function identifier variable is now substituted for the function call in the assignment statement.

```
Sum := 0 + Number
```

can now be completed. Because Number is 33 on this message board, the resulting value of the function identifier variable is 33. This call to Function Sum is now complete, and the value 33 is passed back to replace the function call in the assignment statement.

```
Sum := 33 + Number
```

can now be completed. Number on this message board is 46; the resulting value for Sum is 79. This call to Function Sum is now complete, and the value 79 is passed back to replace the function call in the assignment statement.

```
Sum := 79 + Number
```

can now be completed. Number on this message board is 23; the resulting value for Sum is 102. This call to Function Sum is now complete, and the value 102 is passed back to replace the function call in the WRITELN statement.

```
WRITELN('Sum of the values on File Data: ', 102:10);
```

can now be executed. The following line is written:

```
Sum of the values on File Data:          102
```

The process is illustrated in Figure 7–1. Each box represents the message board for a particular call. Return address R1 stands for the place to return in the original call. Return address R2 stands for the place to return after the recursive call. Values that are underlined are stored on return from the recursive call.

Pascal does not provide an exponentiation operator. In a second recursive example, we write a function to calculate

$$A^n$$

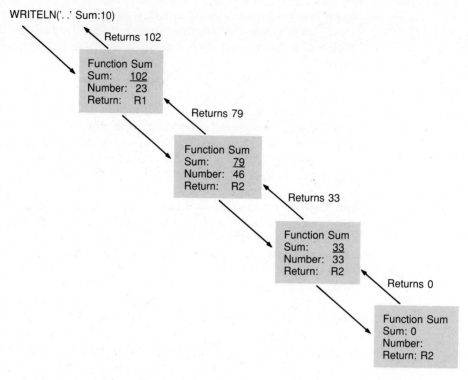

FIGURE 7–1 Message boards for Function Sum

where A and n are both nonzero positive integers. The formula is

$$A^n = \underbrace{A \times A \times A \times \ldots \times A}_{n \text{ times}}$$

Another way of writing this relationship is

$$A^n = A \times \underbrace{(A \times A \times \ldots \times A)}_{(n-1) \text{ times}}$$

If we know what A^{n-1} is, we can calculate A^n because $A^n = A \times A^{n-1}$. In the same way, we can reduce A^{n-1} further:

$$A^n = A \times A \times \underbrace{(A \times \ldots \times A)}_{(n-2) \text{ times}}$$

If we know what A^{n-2} is, we can calculate A^{n-1} and thus calculate A^n because $A^n = A \times A \times A^{n-2}$. We can continue this process until the innermost expression becomes A^1. We know what A^1 is; it's A.

We express this reasoning in Function Power, which has two parameters, A and N:

```
FUNCTION Power(A, N : INTEGER) : INTEGER;

BEGIN    (* Power *)
  IF N = 1
     THEN
        Power := A
     ELSE
        Power := A × Power(A, N−1)
END;     (* Power *)
```

Each call to Function Power creates a new message board with the current actual parameters. The value for A is the same for each version of Power, but the value for N decreases by 1 for each call until N − 1 becomes 1. The call to Function Power where N is 1 stops the calling chain because Power can now be given a value. Power is assigned a value (A to be exact) that is passed back to the version of Function Power that made the last call. The value of Power for that version can now be calculated and passed back to the version that made the previous call. This continues until the value of Power can be passed back to the original call.

Let's see what a call to Power where A is 2 and N is 3 does. The statement

```
Number := Power(2, 3);
```

in the body of the program assigns the value returned by the call to the variable Number. The value returned by Power and assigned to Number should be 8 (2 to the third power or 2 × 2 × 2). Figure 7–2 shows the message

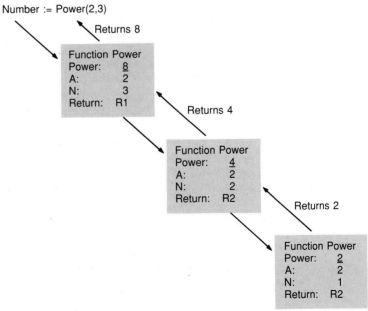

FIGURE 7–2 Message boards for Function Power

boards for the execution of this statement. R1 is the return address from the original call; R2 is the return address from each recursive call.

If you find these examples not only clear but obvious, go ahead and use recursion. It is a powerful way to express algorithms. If not, don't be intimidated. Understanding recursion is not one of the goals of this chapter. If you continue to study computing, you will get into recursion in depth.

Additional Control Structures

Pascal gives us the four basic ways of structuring statements that are mentioned in Chapter 1. We have looked at sequential code, the IF statement for selection, the WHILE statement for looping, and procedures and functions. These are all the control structures we need to write a program. Pascal does have several more for convenience: REPEAT and FOR statements for looping and the CASE statement for multiway selection.

REPEAT Statement

The REPEAT statement, like the IF and WHILE statements, makes use of a Boolean expression:

```
REPEAT
   Statements
UNTIL Boolean expression;
Statement2;
```

Statements are repeated as long as the Boolean expression is FALSE. When the Boolean expression becomes TRUE, the processing continues with Statement2.

The REPEAT statement is actually the REPEAT-UNTIL statement. It's a looping control structure with the loop condition tested at the end of the loop after the reserved word UNTIL. Because UNTIL delimits the statement, a BEGIN-END pair is not necessary around the body of the loop.

The WHILE statement tests the loop condition before executing the body of the loop, so it's called a **pretest loop.** The REPEAT statement tests the loop condition at the end of the loop, so it's called a **posttest loop.** Notice that the semantics of the tests are reversed. The body of the WHILE loop is executed as long as the expression is TRUE; the body of the REPEAT loop is executed as long as the expression is FALSE.

> **Pretest Loop**
> A loop that tests the condition at the beginning of the loop. The loop may be skipped entirely.

Posttest Loop

A loop that tests the condition at the end of the loop. The loop is always executed at least once.

Here is a counting loop implemented with a WHILE statement and with a REPEAT statement:

WHILE

```
Counter := 1;
WHILE Counter <= 10 DO
   BEGIN
      Process;
      Counter := Counter + 1
   END;
```

REPEAT

```
Counter := 1
REPEAT
   Process;
   Counter := Counter + 1
UNTIL Counter > 10;
```

Figure 7–3 compares the structure diagrams of counting loops using WHILE and REPEAT statements.

REPEAT-UNTIL would be the natural choice for the task of skipping blanks that we coded as Procedure SkipBlanks in Program Transpose (see page 207) because we know that the loop should execute at least once.

```
PROCEDURE SkipBlanks(VAR DataFile : TEXT; VAR Character : CHAR);
(* SkipBlanks returns in Character the first  *)
(* nonblank character found on File DataFile. *)

BEGIN    (* SkipBlanks *)
   REPEAT
      READ(DataFile, Character)
   UNTIL Character <> Blank
END;     (* SkipBlanks *)
```

FOR Statement

The FOR statement is a looping construct designed specifically for count-controlled loops. The statement predefines the initial and final values of the loop control variable and automatically increments that variable.

The Boolean expression that controls other looping constructs is implicit in the FOR statement.

```
FOR variable identifier := Expression1 TO Expression2 DO
   Statement1;
Statement2;
```

The variable identifier is initialized to Expression1 and is incremented each time through the loop. Statement1 continues to be executed until the content

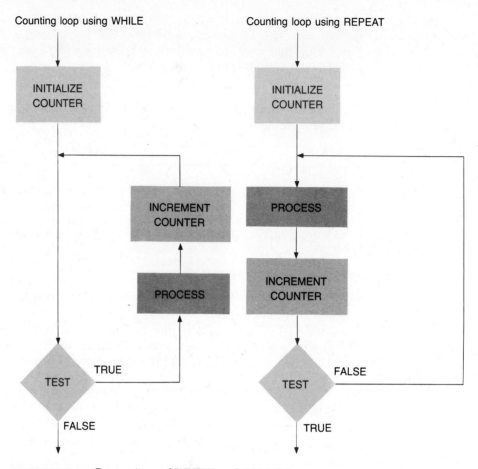

FIGURE 7-3 Comparison of WHILE and REPEAT

of the variable identifier becomes greater than Expression2. At this point, processing continues with Statement2 (Figure 7–4). The variable identifier, Expression1, and Expression2 must be of the same type, either INTEGER or CHAR.

The statement

```
FOR Counter := StartValue TO EndValue DO
  Statement1;
Statement2;
```

is executed like this:

1. Counter is set to StartValue.
2. IF Counter > EndValue, processing continues with Statement2.
3. IF Counter <= EndValue, Statement1 is executed.
4. Counter is either incremented by 1 (if the loop control variable is an inte-

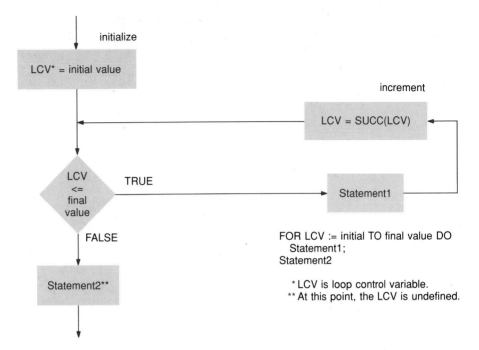

FIGURE 7–4 FOR structure diagram

ger) or set to the next value in the collating sequence (if the loop control variable is an alphanumeric character).

5. The process repeats from Step 2.

The FOR loop above is functionally equivalent to this WHILE loop:

```
Counter := StartValue;
WHILE Counter <= EndValue DO
   BEGIN
     Statementl;
     Counter := Counter + 1
   END;
Statement 2;
```

There is an alternate version of the FOR statement in which the word TO is replaced with DOWNTO. The loop control variable is decremented rather than incremented, and the looping continues as long as the content of the variable identifier is greater than or equal to the second expression. Here is an example of a loop that executes with the loop control variable going from 'Z' down to 'A'.

```
FOR Count := 'Z' DOWNTO 'A' DO
   Statementl;
Statement2;
```

The loop executes twenty-six times, with Count at 'Z', 'A' and all the letters in between.

FOR statements are very convenient, so many students tend to overuse them. Be warned: FOR loops are not *general-purpose* loops. They are designed exclusively for *count-controlled* loops. To use them intelligently, you should remember these facts about FOR loops:

- The loop control variable cannot be changed within the loop. Its value can be used but not changed. That is, the loop control variable can appear in an expression but not on the left side of an assignment statement.
- The loop control variable is incremented or decremented, automatically. If you need to increment or decrement a numeric counter by some other value than 1, you should use a WHILE or REPEAT.
- The loop control variable is undefined at the end of the loop. If you try to use it in an expression in the statement following the FOR loop, you may get a run-time error message. You might expect the loop control variable to be the final value plus 1 or the next character in the collating sequence, but it is not. It is undefined.
- The loop control variable of a FOR statement used in a procedure or function must be a local variable.
- The loop is executed with the loop control variable at the initial value, the final value, and all values in between. If the initial value is greater than the final value, the FOR statement is not executed. If the initial value is equal to the final value, the FOR statement is executed once.
- *You cannot put an additional termination condition in the loop.* The heading must be exactly like this:

```
FOR name := initial value TO final value DO
```

or

```
FOR name := initial value DOWNTO final value DO
```

- Name must be a variable; the initial value and final value can be any valid expressions (variables or constants and operators).

Syntax diagrams for WHILE, REPEAT, and FOR statements are shown in Figure 7–5.

CASE Statement

The IF statement allows us to decide between two courses of action. To decide among several courses of action, we have used a set of nested IF statements. Deciding among multiple courses of action occurs so often that Pascal has a statement that allows us to do this: the CASE statement.

The CASE statement is a selection control structure that allows us to list several alternate courses of action and choose one to be executed at run-time.

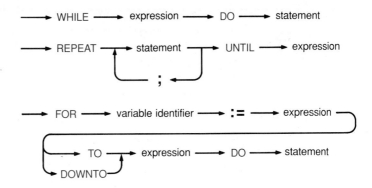

FIGURE 7–5 Syntax diagrams for looping statements

The selection is done by matching up the value of an expression with a constant that identifies a course of action.

```
CASE Expression OF
  Constant1 : Statement1;
  Constant2,
  Constant3 : Statement2;
  Constant4 : Statement3;

    .
    .
    .
END;  (* CASE *)
```

The expression can be of type INTEGER, CHAR, or BOOLEAN; the constants must be of the same type as the expression. The expression is evaluated and the result compared with each of the constants until a match is found. The statement that corresponds to the match is executed. Processing continues with the statement below the END that marks the end of the CASE statement.

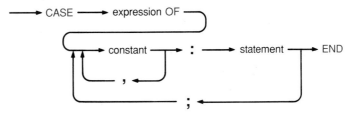

The expression in a CASE statement is called the **case selector;** the constants listed with each statement are called **case label lists.**

Case Selector

The expression whose value determines which case label list is selected.

> **Case Label List**
>
> A list of constants (of the same type as the case selector) listed beside a course of action.

Here's an example:

```
CASE Wins OF
  1, 2, 3 : WRITE('Losing');
  4, 5, 6 : WRITE('Average');
     7, 8 : BEGIN
               WRITELN('!!!!!!');
               WRITE('Super')
            END
END;  (* CASE *)
WRITELN(' Season.');
```

Wins is an INTEGER variable. If Wins contains a 1, 2, or 3, the word *Losing* is printed. If Wins contains a 4, 5, or 6, the word *Average* is printed. If Wins contains a 7 or 8, the line *!!!!!!* is printed followed by the word *Super*. After the CASE statement is executed, the word *Season.* is printed with a blank before it and a period after it.

What happens if the content of Wins is not on one of the case label lists? For example, if the team loses every game? The results are undefined. Some systems skip the CASE statement; others stop with an error message. Some compilers allow an OTHERWISE label, which is matched if the expression is not matched on any of the other lists. Check the documentation for your compiler.

The following program fragment prints an appropriate comment based on a student's grade:

```
CASE Grade OF
  'A', 'B' : WRITE('Good work');
       'C' : WRITE('Average work');
  'D', 'F' : WRITE('Poor work')
END;  (* CASE *)
```

Grade is the case selector and 'A', 'B', 'C', 'D', and 'F' are the constants in the case label lists. If Grade contains an 'A' or a 'B', *Good work* is printed. If Grade contains a 'C', *Average work* is printed. If Grade contains a 'D' or an 'F', *Poor work* is printed.

There are several things to remember about the syntax of the CASE statement:

- The labels are separated from the action by a colon.
- The action can be a simple statement or a compound statement.
- The type of the case selector expression must be the same as the type of the

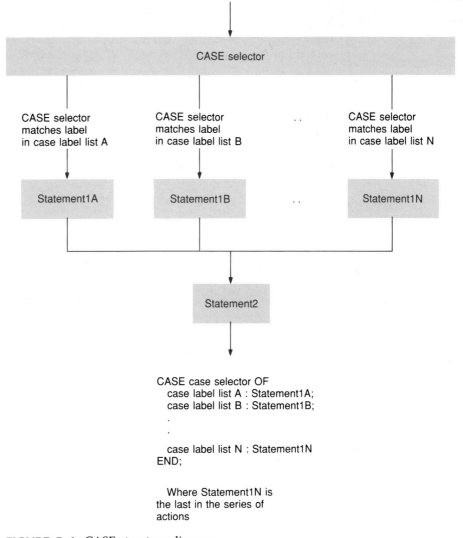

CASE case selector OF
    case label list A : Statement1A;
    case label list B : Statement1B;
    .
    .
    case label list N : Statement1N
END;

    Where Statement1N is
the last in the series of
actions

FIGURE 7–6 CASE structure diagram

case label constants. INTEGER, CHAR, BOOLEAN, and other types that we discuss in Chapter 8 can be used; REAL cannot.

Figure 7–6 shows the flow of control for a CASE statement.

More on Real Numbers
Representing Numbers

Let's assume we have a computer where each **word** (location in memory) is divided up into a sign plus five decimal digits. This means that when a variable is declared or a constant is defined, the cell or location assigned to it consists of five digits and a sign. When an INTEGER variable is declared or an INTEGER constant is defined, the interpretation of the number stored in that place is quite straightforward. When a REAL variable is declared or a REAL constant is defined, the number stored there has both a whole number part and a fractional part. It must be coded in some way to represent both parts.

Let's see what these coded numbers might look like and what this coding does to arithmetic values in our programs. We begin with integers. The **range** of the numbers we can represent with five digits is −99,999 to +99,999:

| − | 9 | 9 | 9 | 9 | 9 | Largest negative number

| + | 0 | 0 | 0 | 0 | 0 | Zero

| + | 9 | 9 | 9 | 9 | 9 | Largest positive number

Our **precision** (the maximum number of digits that can be represented) is five digits, and each number within that range can be represented exactly.

What happens if we allow one of these digits (let's say the leftmost one) to represent an exponent? Thus,

| + | 1 | 2 | 3 | 4 | 5 |

↑
Exponent

represents the number $+2{,}345 \times 10^1$. The range of numbers we can now represent is much larger:

$$-9{,}999 \times 10^9 \text{ to } +9{,}999 \times 10^9$$

or

$$-9{,}999{,}000{,}000{,}000 \text{ to } +9{,}999{,}000{,}000{,}000$$

Now our precision is only four digits. That is, we can represent only four **significant digits** (nonzero digits or zero digits that are exact) of the number itself. This means we can represent any four-digit number exactly in our system. What happens to larger numbers? The four leftmost digits are correct, and the balance of the digits are assumed to be zero. We lose the rightmost, or *least significant*, digits. The table on the top of page 251 shows what happens.

Notice that we can represent 1,000,000 exactly, but not −4,932,416. Our coding scheme limits us to four significant digits; the digits we cannot represent are assumed to be zero.

To extend our coding scheme to represent real numbers we need to be able to represent negative exponents. For example:

Number	Power of 10 notation	Coded representation						Value
		Sign ↓	Exp. ↓					
+99,999	$9,999 \times 10^1$	+	1	9	9	9	9	+99,990
−999,999	$-9,999 \times 10^2$	−	2	9	9	9	9	−999,900
+1,000,000	$+1,000 \times 10^3$	+	3	1	0	0	0	+1,000,000
−4,932,416	$-4,932 \times 10^3$	−	3	4	9	3	2	−4,932,000

$$4,394 \times 10^{-2} = 43.94$$

or

$$22 \times 10^{-4} = 0.0022$$

Because our scheme does not allow for a sign for the exponent, we have to change the scheme slightly. We let the sign that we have be the sign of the exponent and add a sign to the left of it to be the sign of the number itself.

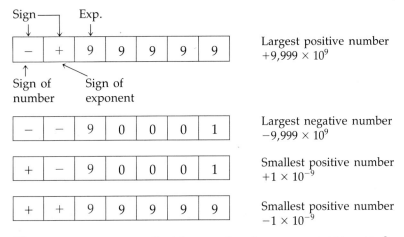

Now we can represent all of the numbers between $-9,999 \times 10^{-9}$ and $9,999 \times 10^9$ accurately to four digits.

Adding negative exponents to our scheme allows us to represent fractional numbers too. For example:

Number	Power of 10 notation	Coded representation Sign	Exp.						Value
0.1032	$1{,}032 \times 10^{-4}$	+	−	4	1	0	3	2	0.1032
−5.4060	$-5{,}406 \times 10^{-3}$	−	−	3	5	4	0	6	−5.406
−0.003	$-3{,}000 \times 10^{-6}$	−	−	6	3	0	0	0	−0.0030
476.0321	$4{,}760 \times 10^{-1}$	+	−	1	4	7	6	0	476.0
1,000,000	$1{,}000 \times 10^{3}$	+	+	3	1	0	0	0	1,000,000

Notice that we still have only four digits of precision. The numbers 0.1032, −5.406, and 1,000,000 can be represented exactly. The number 476.0321 has seven significant digits, but because only four can be represented, we lose the 321.

Most modern computers do not use decimal arithmetic, but real numbers in binary machines are encoded in a scheme similar to the one outlined here, except that the digits are binary, not decimal, digits.

When we use integer arithmetic our results are exact. Real arithmetic, however, cannot be exact. Suppose we want to add three real numbers, X, Y, and Z. We could add X to Y, then add Z to the result. Or we could do it another way, adding Y to Z, then adding X to that result. The associative law of arithmetic says that the two answers should be the same—but are they?

The computer limits the precision (the number of significant digits) of a real number. Using our coding scheme of four significant digits and an exponent, let's add the following allowable values of X, Y, and Z:

$$X = -1{,}324 \times 10^3$$
$$Y = 1{,}325 \times 10^3$$
$$Z = 5{,}424 \times 10^0$$

First let's look at the result of adding Z to the sum of X and Y:

$$
\begin{array}{lr}
\text{(X)} & -1{,}324 \times 10^3 \\
\text{(Y)} & \underline{1{,}325 \times 10^3} \\
& 1 \times 10^3 = 1{,}000 \times 10^0 \\
\\
\text{(X + Y)} & 1{,}000 \times 10^0 \\
\text{(Z)} & \underline{5{,}424 \times 10^0} \\
& 6{,}424 \times 10^0 = 6{,}424
\end{array}
$$

Now, let's see what happens when we add X to the sum of Y and Z:

(Y) $1,325,000 \times 10^0$
(Z) $\underline{5,424 \times 10^0}$
$1,330,424 \times 10^0 = 1,330 \times 10^3$ (truncated to four digits)

(Y + Z) $1,330 \times 10^3$
(X) $\underline{-1,324 \times 10^3}$
$6 \times 0^3 = 6,000 \times 10^0 = 6,000$

Our answers are the same in the thousands' place but are different in the hundreds', tens', and ones' places. This is called **representational error.** The result of adding Y to Z gives us a number with seven digits of precision, but only four digits can be stored.

Real Numbers: Some Definitions

Now let's formally define some of the terms we have used informally in the previous section.

A real number is a number that has a whole part and a fractional part and no imaginary part. Type REAL is limited to the range and precision defined in a specific implementation of Pascal. This is because the number of digits used to represent the exponent and the number of digits used for the number itself (mantissa) vary from machine to machine. When the precision of the result of an arithmetic operation is greater than the precision of the machine, we end up with a representational error.

Range
From the smallest to the largest allowable values.

Precision
The maximum number of significant digits.

Significant Digits
Those digits that begin with the first nonzero digit on the left and end with the last nonzero digit on the right (or a zero digit that is exact).

> **Representational Error**
> An arithmetic error caused by the fact that the precision of the result of our arithmetic operations is greater than the precision of our machine.

REAL is a standard type in Pascal. When you declare a variable to be of type REAL, the value stored in that place is interpreted as a *floating-point number* (the name of the coding scheme we've just described). That is, certain digits associated with that place are assumed to be the exponent, and the remaining digits are assumed to be the number itself.

We call this **floating-point representation** because the number of significant digits is fixed and the decimal point floats. In our coding scheme example, every number is stored as four digits with the leftmost one being nonzero and the exponent adjusted accordingly. 1,000,000 is stored as

+	+	3	1	0	0	0

and 0.1032 is stored as

+	−	4	1	0	3	2

This allows for the maximum precision possible.

There are two ways of expressing real numbers in Pascal, whether they are constants or data. One is by using a decimal point; the other is by using power of 10 notation. Because the keyboard cannot do superscripts, we use an *E* before the exponent. Here's the syntax diagram:

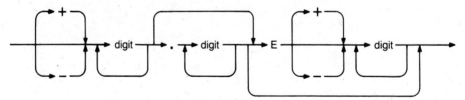

This table shows valid and invalid real numbers.

Valid Reals	Invalid Reals	
1.1	.032	(no digit before the decimal point)
55E5	1.	(no digit after the decimal point)
56.3E+01	5.E−32	(no digit after the decimal point)
1000.0E42	1000	(no *E* or decimal point)
21E-36	21.0E	(no digit after *E*)

There are two standard functions used with real numbers that are quite useful. ROUND **rounds off** a real value to the nearest integer; TRUNC decreases the precision of a number by **truncating** (removing) one or more least significant digits. Both ROUND and TRUNC take a REAL parameter and return an INTEGER value.

Value of Number	ROUND(Number)	TRUNC(Number)
3.41	3	3
3.56	4	3
−5.02	−5	−5
−5.52	−6	−5

Problems with Real Arithmetic

There are two problems to watch out for in real arithmetic: underflow and overflow. **Underflow** is where the absolute value of a calculation gets too small to represent. Going back to our decimal representation, let's look at a calculation involving very small numbers:

$$4,210 \times 10^{-8}$$
$$\underline{\times\ 2,000 \times 10^{-8}}$$
$$8,420,000 \times 10^{-16} = 8,420 \times 10^{-13}$$

This value cannot be represented in our scheme because an exponent of -13 is too large. Our maximum is -9. Therefore the result of this calculation would be set to zero. Any value too small to be represented is set to zero, which is a reasonable thing to do under these circumstances.

Overflow is a more serious problem because there is no logical thing to do when it occurs. For example, the results of this calculation

$$9,999 \times 10^9$$
$$\underline{\times\ 1,000 \times 10^9}$$
$$9,999,000 \times 10^{18} = 9,999 \times 10^{21}$$

cannot be stored. What should we do? To be consistent with underflow, we could set the result to $9,999 \times 10^9$, the maximum REAL value allowed in our scheme. But this seems intuitively wrong. The alternative is to stop with an error message. Pascal does not define what should happen in the case of overflow. Try it with your compiler and see what happens.

Another problem that can occur with real numbers is called **cancellation error**. This happens when numbers of widely differing sizes are added or subtracted. Here's an example:

$$(1 + 0.00001234) - 1 = 0.00001234$$

The laws of arithmetic say this should be true. But what happens when the computer is doing the arithmetic?

$$100,000,000 \times 10^{-8}$$
$$\underline{+\ 1,234 \times 10^{-8}}$$
$$100,001,234 \times 10^{-8}$$

"It gives the answer as 12,621,859.007. But, it says it's just a hunch."
Colossal Computer

With four-digit accuracy, this becomes $1,000 \times 10^{-3}$. Now we subtract 1:

$$
\begin{aligned}
1{,}000 &\times 10^{-3} \\
-1{,}000 &\times 10^{-3} \\
\hline
0
\end{aligned}
$$

The result is zero, not 0.00001234.

We have been discussing problems with real numbers, but integer numbers can overflow both negatively and positively. To see how your compiler handles the situation you should try adding a 1 to +MaxInt and a negative 1 to −MaxInt. On one system we've used, adding a 1 to +MaxInt sets the results to −(MaxInt + 1)!

The moral of this discussion is twofold. First, the results of real calculations often are not what you expect. Second, if you are working with very large numbers or very small numbers, you need more information than this book provides.

The 4-Cs Corner

Clarity

The code of a program is part of the documentation. The more the code mirrors a process, the easier it is to read. In this chapter we've talked about constructs that are alternatives to those we've been using. Here we discuss how to choose among competing alternatives with the clarity of program code as our goal.

Procedures Versus Functions

There are no rules for when to code a module as a procedure and when to code a module as a function, but there are some guidelines:

- If there is more than one output from your module, *do not use a function*.
- If there is only one output from the module and it's a BOOLEAN value, a function is probably called for.
- If there is only one output and that value is going to be used immediately, a function is probably called for.
- When in doubt, use a procedure. Any function can be recoded as a procedure with the function name becoming an output parameter of the procedure.
- If both are acceptable, use the one you feel most comfortable with.

WHILE Versus REPEAT Versus FOR

The WHILE statement is general and can be used anywhere that the other looping statements can be used. There are times, however, when we can express the looping process more succinctly using either a REPEAT statement or a FOR statement.

There are two characteristics that describe the looping process: type of loop (count controlled or event controlled) and placement of the test (at the beginning or end of the loop). The chart below shows where the loops fit into this pattern.

	Count Controlled	Event Controlled
Pretest →	FOR or WHILE	WHILE
Posttest →	REPEAT	REPEAT

Although the FOR is a pretest looping construct designed specifically for counting, it can only be used when the counter is being incremented or decremented by 1.

The other thing to think about when choosing between a WHILE statement and a REPEAT statement is the semantics of the event. If the event is naturally phrased in terms of when the loop should be terminated, the REPEAT statement is clearer. If the event is naturally phrased in terms of when the loop should be continued, the WHILE statement is clearer.

IF Versus CASE

Although both IF and CASE statements allow us to choose an alternative course of action, they are not interchangeable. Any CASE can be recoded as a set of nested IFs, but not every set of nested IFs can be recoded as a CASE. Case label lists must be made up of discrete constants. If the choices cannot be expressed in terms of discrete constants, a CASE statement cannot be used.

For example, Function LetterGrade (page 232) could not be recoded using a CASE statement without listing every possible grade within each interval.

In the cases (no pun intended) where either can be used, the CASE is usually more descriptive. Consider the main module of Program Sales-Receipts (page 166). The input to the program is a letter code and a value. The letter code (called MenuCode) determines what is done with the value. We have recoded this module using a CASE statement (and a REPEAT):

```
BEGIN   (* SalesReceipts *)
  Initialize(TaxTotal, SalesTotal);
  REPEAT
    GetData(MenuCode, Amount);
    CASE MenuCode OF
      'T', 't' : TaxTotal := TaxTotal + Amount;
      'S', 's' : SalesTotal := SalesTotal + Amount;
      'Q', 'q' : ;
    END    (* CASE *)
  UNTIL (MenuCode = 'Q') OR (MenuCode = 'q');
  NonFoodCost := TaxTotal / TaxRate;
  FoodCost := SalesTotal - (NonFoodCost + TaxTotal);
  PrintResults(SalesTotal, TaxTotal, FoodCost, NonFoodCost)
END.    (* SalesReceipts *)
```

The form of the CASE statement makes all the alternatives stand out equally; it clarifies the code.

Conciseness

When we talk about conciseness, we're talking about efficiency. We would be negligent if we didn't point out that the examples that we have used to demonstrate recursion are very inefficient in terms of machine execution time and utilization of memory. Both of the examples could be solved very easily using repetition.

The problem with discussing recursion is that the examples that are simple enough to use as an introduction can all be implemented more efficiently using a looping construct. You'll just have to take it on faith that recursion is a powerful, efficient tool when applied to more complex problems.

Correctness Hints

1. A function heading must include a type. The function name is assigned a value, so it must be typed. (Don't forget to assign a value to the function name.) We give the function name a type by putting a colon and type after the formal parameter list, or after the function name if there is no formal parameter list.
2. Do not use the function name in an expression within the function unless you are deliberately writing a recursive function. If you do this by mistake, you'll probably end up with a syntax error because you have no actual

parameter list. If, however, the function has no parameters and you use the function name in an expression in the function, you'll get a run-time error saying something about STACK OVERFLOW.

3. Avoid comparisons of real numbers when possible. When not possible, consider testing for *close equality* rather than exact equality. Not only does 1/3 + 1/3 + 1/3 not equal 1.0, but .1 + .1 + .1 + .1 + .1 + .1 + .1 + .1 + .1 + .1 does not equal 1.0 on computers that use binary arithmetic!

   We're familiar with this problem in the decimal system. We know that some numbers, like 2/3 and pi, never stop. However, even a simple fraction like 1/10 (0.1 in the decimal system) cannot be represented exactly in the binary system. Because numbers are represented in binary in most machines, this means our tests might not be exact. This is another example of representational error.

   One way of handling this problem is to put in a *tolerance*. For example, if you want to see if A equals B, test to see if the absolute value (ABS) of the difference between A and B is less than some value. For example,

$$ABS(A - B) < 0.01$$

   tests whether A and B are equal to at least two decimal places. The size of the tolerance depends on the data and the situation.

4. Use integer numbers if you know you are dealing only with whole numbers. Any integer can be represented exactly in any base. This means there is no loss of accuracy in converting a decimal integer to binary. Also, on most machines, integer arithmetic is faster.

5. Be aware of rounding and truncation errors.

6. Remember the REPEAT statement is always executed at least once. The WHILE tests the expression at the beginning of the loop and does not execute the body of the loop if the expression is FALSE. The REPEAT tests the expression *after* it has executed the loop body. Remember that the WHILE stops when the expression becomes FALSE; the REPEAT stops when the expression becomes TRUE.

7. The FOR statement is a looping construct that should be used only for count-controlled loops. Go back and review the cautions relating to the FOR statement. We're not against FOR statements. It's just that the FOR statement has a very clearly defined purpose, and we have seen too many students try to use it indiscriminately.

8. Use the CASE statement with caution. Remember that if the selector expression does not match one of the label constants, the results are undefined. This means that your program may run and produce an answer that looks reasonable but is wrong. The label constants cannot be combined into an expression. If you want to take one action if a value is between 1 and 5, you must list 1, 2, 3, 4, and 5.

Summary

A function is a special type of subprogram that sends back its answer in the name of the function. The function, therefore, has to have a type. We invoke a function by using its name in an expression. All the rules about parameters apply to both procedures and functions.

The REPEAT statement is a posttest loop in which the expression is not tested until the loop has been executed at least once. The FOR statement is a pretest loop designed specifically for count-controlled loops. It automatically initializes, increments, and tests the counter. The CASE statement allows us to choose among several courses of action, by matching a selector expression with a label (constant) attached to the action.

Real numbers have a whole and a fractional part. They are encoded in a floating-point format, where the exponent is carried separately. The range for real numbers is much wider than that for integers, but the accuracy can be much less.

EXERCISES

1. Write a function, P5, that returns the fifth power of its REAL parameter.
2. Write a function, Minimum, that returns the minimum of its three INTEGER parameters.
3. Write a function, Accept, that receives a grade point (REAL) and SAT score (INTEGER), and returns TRUE if the grade point is at least 3.4 or the SAT score is at least 1300.
4. Because a function returns a single value through its identifier, it cannot have value parameters that allow values to be passed into the function. True or false?
5. A function call is always a component of an expression, but a procedure call is always a statement in itself. True or false?
6. Both procedures and functions must have a type. True or false?
7. A good rule of thumb is to always use VAR parameters in the formal parameter list of a function. True or false?
8. Rewrite Exercise 1 in Chapter 5 using a REPEAT loop.
9. Rewrite Exercise 6 in Chapter 5 using a REPEAT loop.
10. Convert the following into a CASE statement.

```
IF (Storeys > 4) AND (Storeys <= 10)
   THEN
      WRITELN('Address restrictions')
   ELSE
      IF (Storeys > 0) AND (Storeys < 10)
         THEN
            BEGIN
               WRITELN('No restrictions')
               Inspection := FALSE
            END;
```

11. Write a CASE statement that does the following:
    - If the value of Grade is 'A', adds 4 to Sum
    - If the value of Grade is 'B', adds 3 to Sum

- If the value of Grade is 'C', adds 2 to Sum
- If the value of Grade is 'D', adds 1 to Sum
- If the value of Grade is 'F', prints 'Student is on probation.'

12. Write a CASE statement that does the following:
    - If the value of Error is 1, prints 'Invalid input'
    - If the value of Error is 2, prints 'Results out of range'
    - If the value of Error is 3, prints 'Error Type 3'
    - If the value of Error is 4 or 5, prints 'Undefined error'

13. Mark the following REAL constants either valid or invalid.

	Valid	*Invalid*
a. +0.472	____	____
b. −6.0E7	____	____
c. 3.	____	____
d. .057	____	____
e. −2.4E2.5	____	____
f. 3.141592	____	____
g. +0.029	____	____
h. 47	____	____
i. 7E5	____	____
j. −7.4E − 16	____	____

14. The value of Area is 749.7434126. Show the WRITE statements that would format this value in the following ways:
    a. 7.497434126E + 002
    b. 74.97E + 002
    c. 749.7434126
    d. 749.74

15. Use this program structure to answer questions below. Be sure to read the questions carefully.

```
PROGRAM Modular(INPUT, OUTPUT);

VAR
  A, B, C : INTEGER;
  Q : BOOLEAN;

(*******************************************************)

FUNCTION One(Q1 : BOOLEAN; A1 : INTEGER): INTEGER;

VAR
  B : INTEGER;

BEGIN    (* One *)
  .
  .
END;     (* One *)

(*******************************************************)
```

```
      PROCEDURE Buzz(VAR A2 : INTEGER; B2 : INTEGER);

      VAR
        Q2 : BOOLEAN;

      (*************************************************)
      FUNCTION Two(B3 : INTEGER; Q3 : BOOLEAN): BOOLEAN;

      BEGIN    (* Two *)
         .
         .
      END;     (* Two *)
      (*************************************************)

      BEGIN    (* Buzz *)
         .
         .
      END;     (* Buzz *)


      (*************************************************)

      BEGIN    (* Modular *)
         .
         .
      END.     (* Modular *)
```

    a. The statement One(Q, A) in the body of Program Modular would invoke Function One, initializing Q1 and A1 with the values of Q and A. True or false?

    b. The statement B : = A1 in Function One would assign the value of A1 to local variable B of One and would not affect global variable B of Program Modular. True or false?

    c. The statement A2 : = Two(B2, Q2) in the body of Procedure Buzz would invoke Function Two and assign the result to A2. True or false?

    d. The statement Q1 : = Two(B, Q) in the body of Function One would invoke Two and assign a BOOLEAN value to Q1. True or false?

    e. The statement Buzz(A, B) in the body of Program Modular would invoke Procedure Buzz, would initialize A2 and B2 to the values of A and B, and would return any changes in VAR parameter A2 to the main program in A. True or false?

16. Write a recursive function that computes the factorial of its positive INTEGER parameter.

17. Write a program fragment containing a FOR statement that reads and adds ten scores to SumScore and finds the average.

18. Write a program fragment containing a FOR statement that reads a beginning balance and N (number of checks), counts them from N backward to 1, reads and adds the amount of each check to the check total, and finds the ending balance.

PRETEST

1. Value parameters allow values to be passed into a function but do not return values to the main program. The only way a function can return a value to the main program is through a VAR parameter. True or false?

2. Given the following declaration:

```
VAR
   Income, Deductions : INTEGER;
   .
   .


FUNCTION HighTaxBracket(Inc, Ded : INTEGER) : BOOLEAN;
   .
   .
```

Is the following statement legal in the main program?

```
IF HighTaxBracket(Income, Deductions)
   THEN
      WRITELN('UPPER CLASS');
```

3. Write a function, Rebate, that receives the day, month, and year of a car sale (INTEGER) and returns TRUE if the sale occurred on or before an 8/9/89 deadline.

4. The basic difference between a REPEAT loop and a WHILE loop is that the REPEAT loop is a pretest loop and the WHILE loop is a posttest loop. True or false?

5. Convert the following into a CASE statement.

```
IF (Count = 1) OR (Count = 2) OR (Count = 3)
   THEN
      WRITELN('Low Count')
   ELSE
      IF (Count = 4)  OR  (Count = 5)
         THEN
           WRITELN('Pass')
      ELSE
        IF Count = 6
           THEN
             WRITELN('Pass')
           ELSE
             IF Count = 7
                THEN
                  BEGIN
                    WRITELN('High Count');
                    OK := OK + 1
                  END;
```

6. Use the following program structure to answer the questions below. Be sure to read the questions carefully.

```
PROGRAM PreTest(INPUT, OUTPUT);

VAR
   A, B, C : INTEGER;
   Q: BOOLEAN;

(* ********************************************* )
```

```
FUNCTION Task1(Q1 : BOOLEAN; A1 : INTEGER): INTEGER;

VAR
  B : INTEGER;

BEGIN    (* Task1 *)
     .
     .
END;    (* Task1 *)

(*********************************************)

PROCEDURE Task2(VAR A2 : INTEGER; B2 : INTEGER);

VAR
  Q2 : BOOLEAN;

  (*****************************************)
  FUNCTION Task3(B3 : INTEGER; Q3 : BOOLEAN): BOOLEAN;

  BEGIN    (* Task3 *)
     .
     .
  END;    (* Task3 *)

  (*****************************************)

BEGIN    (* Task2 *)
   .
   .
END;    (* Task2 *)

(*********************************************)

BEGIN    (* PreTest *)
   .
   .
END.    (* PreTest *)
```

a. Function Task3 cannot be invoked from the body of Program PreTest. True or false?

b. The statement A2 : = Task3(A2, Q2) would be legal in the body of Procedure Task2. True or false?

c. The statement B : = Task1(A) would invoke Function Task1 in the body of Program PreTest. True or false?

d. Task2(B, A) in the body of Program PreTest would invoke Task2 and initialize A2 to B and B2 to A. True or false?

e. The statement A1 : = B in the body of Function Task1 would assign the value of local variable B to A1. True or false?

7. Mark the following REAL constants either valid or invalid.

	Valid	Invalid
a. 6.42E − 7.5	____	____
b. .41325	____	____
c. +7E16	____	____
d. 257.5415	____	____
e. −47.9E − 10	____	____

8. Assume a real number representation with six significant decimal digits, underflow of 1.0E−99, and overflow of 1.0E99. What is the sum of 1.0 and 0.000001?

9. Write a program segment that would produce the following output. (Value is REAL and Freq is INTEGER.) Be sure to write both lines of output.

```
Value       Freq
26.33564      7
```

10. Write a program fragment containing a FOR statement that reads twenty-five student ID numbers and birthdates, compares each date with a cut-off date of September 1, 1985, counts those that come before the cut-off date, and writes the student ID to the screen. ID numbers and birthdates are stored in a file with dates (in two-digit numbers) by month, day, and year, with space between the numbers (for example, 09 01 85), one ID and date per line.

11. Write a program fragment containing a FOR statement that adds the even numbers from 100 to 50 and writes the sum to the screen.

PROGRAMMING ASSIGNMENTS

1. A positive integer p is said to be a *prime number* if $p > 1$ and the only positive divisors of p are 1 and p. For example, 2, 3, 5, 7, and 11 are the first five prime numbers. (Notice that 1 is not a prime number.)

    If two positive integers p and $p + 2$ are both prime numbers, we say that each of them is a *twin prime* of the other.

    For any positive integer p, then,

    • if p is not a prime number, it has no twin prime.
    • if p is a prime number, it may have zero, one, or two twin primes.

    For example, 1, 2, 4, 6, 8, and 9 have no twin primes; 3 and 7 each have one twin prime (5); and 5 has two twin primes (3 and 7).

    Given a sequence of positive integers, determine for each whether it is a prime number and, if so, find its twin primes (if they exist).

2. A local bank has instituted a new credit system and would like to have account numbers that are self-checking in order to have some protection against fraud and clerical errors. The bank has devised the following system: The account numbers will be nine digits long. The ninth digit (rightmost) can be calculated by either summing, subtracting, or multiplying all of the preceding digits and finding the rightmost digit of the result.

    Your job is to write a program to check the validity of the account numbers that have been sent to the bank as part of its daily transactions.

> **Input:** An arbitrary number of single-digit operation codes and nine-digit account numbers

In the operation code, 1 is addition, 2 is subtraction, and 3 is multiplication. You will also need to check for the correctness of the operation code.

> **Output:** (1) Echo-print the input.
> (2) Under each echo-printed line, state whether the account number is valid or invalid.

For example, given the following input:

1   123456786

1   represents addition, so

$$1 + 2 + 3 + 4 + 5 + 6 + 7 + 8 = 36$$

6 is the rightmost digit of 36, therefore the account is valid.

3. Redo Programming Assignment 9 in Chapter 6 with the following change. Instead of reading in values in francs, pounds, marks, and lira each time, use the following code to indicate the currency:

'F' French francs
'B' British pounds
'G' German marks
'I' Italian lira

Use a CASE statement to determine which currency you're converting.

4. Recode the WHILE loops in the Programming Assignments in Chapter 5 as REPEAT loops.

5. You are the head programmer at the El Cheapo Manufacturing Company. For years the accounting department has rounded the number of hours worked by each employee to the nearest hour. Now management is considering truncating hours instead of rounding them. You've been asked to write a program that calculates the payroll both ways and compares the total cost to the company.

> **Input:** Update: (1) Employee ID number
> (2) Hours worked
>
> Master: (1) Employee ID number
> (2) Hourly wage
> (3) Number of dependents

> **Output:** (1) A report showing gross pay, tax withheld, net pay based on rounding, and net pay based on truncation
> (2) A summary statement showing how much money would be saved using truncation

> **Processing:** Withholding: 15 percent of gross pay less 10 times the number of dependents

8 Data Types: Simple and Structured

GOALS

- To be able to define and use subrange types.

- To be able to define and use user-defined (enumerated) types.

- To be able to use the predefined ordinal functions PRED, SUCC, ORD, and CHR.

- To be able to define a one-dimensional ARRAY type designed to hold a group of like data objects.

- To be able to declare and use an ARRAY variable.

- To be able to use a one-dimensional ARRAY variable in a program to represent items in a list.

The pattern of bits (binary digits) in a computer word can be interpreted in different ways. The type of the data that is stored in a word dictates how the bit pattern is interpreted. Pascal has several built-in data types: INTEGER, REAL, CHAR, BOOLEAN, and TEXT, which is used to describe information on a file.

We defined these built-in data types by describing what values they could take. In this chapter we formally define what we mean by data type, describe the Pascal facility for defining new data types, look at new data types, and introduce the concept of a structured data type.

Data Types

We can define a data type in two ways: by listing all the constants in that type or by describing the pattern of allowable values. When we defined the built-in data type BOOLEAN, we said that constants or variables of this type can take on one of two values: TRUE or FALSE. That is, we defined type BOOLEAN by listing all its constants. When we defined type INTEGER, we described the pattern of its values: integer numbers in the range −MaxInt to +MaxInt. (We could have listed all these values, but it would have taken up too many pages!)

Each of the types we have discussed has a set of operations that can be applied to data values of that type. Arithmetic and relational operators can be applied to numeric values. Relational operators can be applied to values of type CHAR. Logical operators can be applied to values of type BOOLEAN.

A **data type,** then, is both a description of the objects of that type and the set of operations that can be applied to objects of that type.

Data Type
A description of a set of values and the operations that can be applied to those values.

Type Declarations

One of the strengths of Pascal is that it allows us to create types of our own. We do this in the *TYPE section* of the program. The TYPE section comes between the CONST section and the VAR section in the program block:

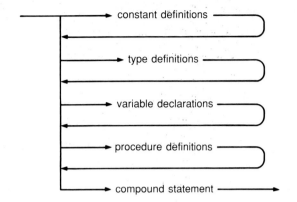

A **type definition** defines a pattern, what something can look like. No object of that pattern exists until one has been declared in the VAR section of the program.

Here is the syntax diagram for a type definition:

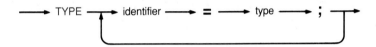

In the next two sections we describe two new types that Pascal allows the user to define: subrange types and user-defined (enumerated) types.

Subrange Types

A **subrange type** is exactly that: a type made up of a subrange of another type (called the *host type*). The subrange is defined by listing the lowest value in the subrange and the highest value in the subrange with two periods between them.

Subrange Type

A continuous subsection of an already defined type (the host type).

Here is the syntax diagram for subrange types:

$$\longrightarrow \text{constant} \longrightarrow .. \longrightarrow \text{constant}$$

For example:

```
TYPE
   LimitType = -3..3;
   Digits = '0'..'9';
   UpperCaseLetters = 'A'..'Z';
   LowerCaseLetters = 'a'..'z';
   NonNegative = 0..MaxInt;
   TestRange = 0..100;

VAR
   Limit : LimitType;
   OneDigit : Digits;
   CapitalLetter : UpperCaseLetters;
   LittleLetter : LowerCaseLetters;
   Counter : NonNegative;
   TestScore : TestRange;
```

LimitType is a type made up of the constants −3, −2, −1, 0, 1, 2, and 3. Limit is a variable that can contain one of the seven constants of type Limit-Type. Digits is a type made up of the characters from '0' to '9'. OneDigit is a variable that can contain one of the ten constants of type Digits. LimitType describes a pattern that's a subset of type INTEGER; Digits, a pattern that is a subset of type CHAR.

UpperCaseLetters and LowerCaseLetters both describe types that are subsets of type CHAR. CapitalLetter and LittleLetter are variables that can contain the values listed as constants in types UpperCaseLetters and Lower-CaseLetters respectively. NonNegative is a type made up of zero and all the positive integer values that a particular machine can represent. Counter is a variable of type NonNegative.

TestRange is a type made up of the integers between zero and 100 (inclusive). TestScore is a variable of type TestRange; only the allowable values of type TestRange can be stored in TestScore. What happens if we key in a negative number or one over 100 when we are reading a value into TestScore? We get a run-time error. The program halts with the error message VALUE OUT OF RANGE. Whenever a value is stored in a variable that has been declared to be of a subrange type, the Pascal run-time support system automatically checks the value before it is stored to be sure it is within the proper subrange. This is called **range checking.**

Using subrange types improves the readability of a program. By telling a reader the range of values that a variable can take, we convey something about how the variable is being used.

User-Defined Types

In Pascal we are able to create a new data type simply by listing all the possible constants of that type. This kind of type is called a **user-defined type** or an **enumerated type.** Both names are equally descriptive. We use them interchangeably.

> **User-Defined Type**
> The ordered set of distinct values (constants) defined as a data type in a program. Also called *enumerated type*.

Here is the syntax diagram for user-defined types:

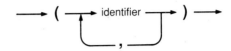

These declarations

```
TYPE
    ZooType = (Mouse, Cat, Dog, Buffalo, Elephant);
    CarType = (Ford, Chevrolet, Plymouth, Jaguar, Nissan, Toyota);

VAR
    Animal : ZooType;
    Car : CarType;
```

create two new user-defined types. Mouse is now a constant in a data type made up of five constants. Mouse is *not* a variable name; it is one of the values that the variable Animal can contain.

Look at this assignment statement:

```
Animal := Mouse;
```

Animal does not contain the character string 'Mouse'; it does not contain the contents of the place named Mouse. It contains the value Mouse. Assuming Animal is of type ZooType, the following IF statement is valid:

```
IF Animal = Mouse
    THEN
        WRITELN('Set trap')
ELSE IF Animal <= Dog
    THEN
        WRITELN('Pet')
ELSE
    WRITELN('Run');
```

Enumerated types can be used in CASE statements as well:

```
CASE Car OF
   Ford, Chevrolet, Plymouth : Tax := Price * DomesticRate;
   Jaguar : Tax := Price * EuroRate;
   Nissan, Toyota : Tax := Price * AsianRate
END;    (* CASE *)
```

The constants that make up an enumerated type must be unique; they cannot be used to define another enumerated type. For example,

```
TYPE
   Vowels = ('A', 'E', 'I', 'O', 'U');
```

is not valid because the constants that make up the type are part of the standard type CHAR. And the declaration

```
TYPE
   Food = (Corn, Fish, Bean, Squash);
   Grain = (Wheat, Corn, Rye, Barley, Sorghum);
```

is not valid because Corn is used in two different type definitions.

Because user-defined types have meaning only within a program, we cannot read them in or write them out. We have to use some sort of code. For example, this fragment reads in an animal using the first letter of its name:

```
READ(Letter);
CASE Letter OF
   'm', 'M' : Animal := Mouse;
   'c', 'C' : Animal := Cat;
   'd', 'D' : Animal := Dog;
   'b', 'B' : Animal := Buffalo;
   'e', 'E' : Animal := Elephant
END;    (* CASE *)
```

If we want to output an enumerated type, we could use a fragment like this:

```
CASE Car OF
   Ford : WRITELN('Ford');
     .
     .
     .
   Toyota : WRITELN('Toyota')
END;    (* CASE *)
```

BOOLEAN is a predefined enumerated type in Pascal. Like enumerated values, a BOOLEAN value cannot be read in. However, unlike user-defined values, BOOLEAN values (TRUE, FALSE) can be printed.

Once we have defined an enumerated type, we can also define a subrange of that type. Notice that enumerated types are enclosed in parentheses but that subrange types are not.

```
TYPE
    Weather = (Rain, Fog, Sleet, Humid, Cold, Hot, Dry);
    WetWeather = Rain..Sleet;
```

Type Classifications
Scalar Data Types

All the data types that we have looked at so far—except type TEXT—have two properties in common: The set of values is ordered, and each value is atomic. By **atomic** we mean that each element is distinct and cannot be subdivided into parts. Data types that have these two properties are called **scalar data types.**

Scalar Data Type

A set of distinct values (constants) that are ordered.

For example, values of type CHAR have an order that makes 'A' < 'B' < 'C' < 'D' . . . true. Values of type INTEGER are ordered so that 1 < 2 < 3 < 4 . . . is true.

Both subrange types and enumerated types are scalar types. Subrange types inherit their order from the host type; the order in which the constants are listed in an enumerated-type definition determines their order.

Ordinal Data Types

All of the scalar data types except type REAL are **ordinal data types.** This means that each value (except the first) has a unique predecessor and each value (except the last) has a unique successor. (Type REAL is not ordinal because its values do not have clearly defined predecessors or successors. If we add one more digit of precision, we change both predecessors and successors.)

Ordinal Data Type

A data type in which every value except the first has a unique predecessor and every value except the last has a unique successor.

Our definition of subrange type was not quite accurate. We said that a subrange type is a subrange of an already defined type. That type must be an ordinal type.

Operations on Ordinal Types

PRED and SUCC

There are two predeclared functions in Pascal, PRED and SUCC, that return the unique predecessor and unique successor of an ordinal expression.

PRED('B') returns 'A'.
SUCC(4) returns 5.
PRED(Item) returns 9 if Item is 10.
SUCC(Item) returns 11 if Item is 10.

You cannot use PRED(Item) where Item is the first value in the order or SUCC(Item) where Item is the last value in the order. Because PRED and SUCC are undefined here, you would end up with an error.

Remember that the order of enumerated types is defined by the order in which the constants are listed in the type definition. Using our sample declarations on page 271, PRED(Cat) returns Mouse and SUCC(Nissan) returns Toyota.

ORD

There is an additional predefined function for use with ordinal types. ORD takes an ordinal value as a parameter and returns an INTEGER value that represents the parameter's place in the ordering. For example:

ORD(Mouse) returns 0.
ORD(Cat) returns 1.
ORD(Elephant) returns 4.
ORD(Jaguar) returns 3.

The ORD of the first element in most types is zero. The ORD of an INTEGER type, however, is the expression itself. For example:

ORD(3) returns 3.
ORD(0) returns 0.
ORD(-5) returns -5.

The ORD function can be used to determine the order of the character set of any particular machine. That is, all the characters (letters, digits, special symbols) recognized by a machine (the *character set* of that machine) are ordered, but the order varies from machine to machine. The only thing we can count on is that the letters are in order and the digits are in order. However, letters come before digits in some machines and after digits in others.

In some character sets the letters are not contiguous; unprintable "control characters" are embedded in their order (see Appendix I). To simplify the examples in this text, we assume the character set **ASCII** (American Standard Code for Information Interchange), in which the letters are contiguous.

The following program prints the ordinal values of lowercase and upper-case letters:

```
PROGRAM OrdValues(INPUT, OUTPUT);
(* Ordinal values of lowercase and uppercase  *)
(* characters are printed.                     *)

VAR
   Character : CHAR;

BEGIN    (* OrdValues *)
   (* print lowercase letters and ordinal values *)
   FOR Character := 'a' TO 'z' DO
      WRITELN('Character', Character:2, ' ordinal position :',
              ORD(Character):3)

   (* print uppercase letters and ordinal values *)
   FOR Character := 'A' TO 'Z' DO
      WRITELN('Character', Character:2, ' ordinal position :',
              ORD(Character):3)

END.     (* OrdValues *)
```

Digits are contiguously ordered in all character sets. This means that the ORD of any digit minus the ORD of '0' gives the digit in numeric form!

ORD('0') − ORD('0') = 0
ORD('1') − ORD('0') = 1

.

.

ORD('9') − ORD('0') = 9

We use the ORD function in Chapter 12 to read integer numbers in character form and convert them to numeric form.

CHR

For type CHAR only, there is a function CHR that takes an INTEGER value and returns the corresponding character if it exists. Function CHR is useful in converting between uppercase and lowercase letters in the ASCII character set. The following function takes as input an ASCII character. If the character is an uppercase letter, the lowercase letter is returned. If the character is not an uppercase letter, the character is returned unchanged. The program converts from uppercase by taking the ORD of the uppercase letter, adding 32, and then taking the CHR of the result. (Each uppercase letter is 32 less than its lowercase equivalent in the ASCII character set.)

```
FUNCTION LowerCase(Character : CHAR) : CHAR;
(* Uppercase letters are converted to lowercase. *)
(* All other characters are unchanged.           *)

BEGIN   (* LowerCase *)
  IF (Character >= 'A') AND (Character <= 'Z')
     THEN
        LowerCase := CHR(ORD(Character) + 32)
     ELSE
        LowerCase := Character
END;    (* LowerCase *)
```

Structured Data Types

We have been talking about scalar data types, in which the set of values is ordered and each value is atomic. Sometimes it is necessary to show a relationship among variables or to store and reference variables as a group. Here we use **structured data types**, complex data types made up of organized collections of one or more scalar types. Each element in a structured data type is called a **component**. We characterize structured data types by how we access individual components.

Structured Data Type

A data type made up of an organized collection of one or more scalar data types, characterized by how individual components are accessed.

There are three built-in structured data types in Pascal: ARRAY, RECORD, SET, and FILE. We have already used FILE: TEXT is a file of CHAR.

Remember that Pascal is a strongly typed language. Assignment between two variables, whether they are simple scalar variables or structured variables, is allowed if they are both of the same type. Variables of type FILE are the exception; they can't be assigned to each other because *files are external to memory*. We can access (store or retrieve) only one component of a file at a time. On the other hand, all other data structures, just like simple variables, are stored in memory. They can be assigned to one another and are destroyed when a program terminates.

We discuss RECORD data types in Chapter 11. We introduce ARRAY data types in this chapter and continue discussing them in Chapters 9 and 10.

One-Dimensional Array

A **one-dimensional array** is a structured group of like elements given a common name. Each element is accessed by an **index** (or **subscript**) that gives the element's position within the group. So there are two types associated with each array: the component type and the index type. The **component type** is the type of the elements in the group; the **index type** is the type of the expression used to access the different elements in the group. The range of the index type specifies the number of elements in the group.

> **One-Dimensional Array**
> A structured group made up of a fixed number of components of the same type, with each component directly accessed by an index.

Here is the syntax diagram of a one-dimensional array:

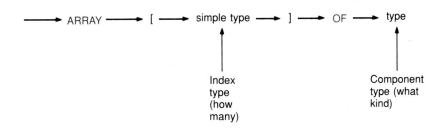

This is the syntax diagram for a simple type (notice that each type is *ordinal*):

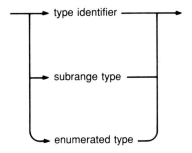

An ARRAY type should be defined in the TYPE section of the program block. For example,

```
TYPE
  Column = ARRAY[1..4] OF INTEGER;
```

defines the following type:

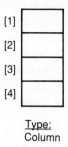

Type:
Column

Type Column is a pattern for a group of four INTEGER variables. Each of these four variables can be accessed by an index that gives its position within the group (that is, first, second, third, or fourth). No ARRAY variable of this pattern exists yet. In the TYPE section we only define patterns; in the VAR section we create variables based on those patterns.

```
TYPE
   Column = ARRAY[1..4] OF INTEGER;

VAR
   Numbers : Column;
   Index : INTEGER;
```

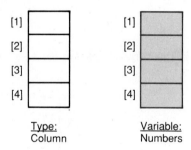

Type: Variable:
Column   Numbers

To access a particular component (cell) in the array, we use this syntax:

⟶ array identifier ⟶ [⟶ expression ⟶]

We access the four elements of type INTEGER in the group of components named Numbers like this:

Numbers[1] accesses the first component in the group.
Numbers[2] accesses the second component in the group.
Numbers[3] accesses the third component in the group.
Numbers[4] accesses the fourth component in the group.

Here the index (the expression in brackets) must be an INTEGER value within the subrange 1..4. If it's not, you will get a run-time error (INDEX OUT OF RANGE).

The following code fragment sets all the values in Numbers to zero:

```
FOR Index := 1 TO 4 DO
   Numbers[Index] := 0;
```

The number of items in the index type determines the number of components in the one-dimensional array. The index type can be any ordinal type except INTEGER. The index type can be (and often is) a subrange of type INTEGER; it just can't be type INTEGER itself because the array would be too large.

Let's look at some different ARRAY types and variables. In the first example, we define an array to hold the letter grades for the students in a class. We need as many components in the array as there are students in the class. For flexibility, we set the class size as a named constant and the index type as a subrange from one to the class size. The component type of the array is CHAR. The following declarations create this structure:

```
CONST
   ClassSize = 25;

TYPE
   IndexRange = 1..ClassSize;
   GradeType = ARRAY[IndexRange] OF CHAR;

VAR
   Grades : GradeType;
   GoodStudents, PoorStudents : INTEGER;
   Counter : IndexRange;
```

GradeType is a pattern for a structure that can contain 25 CHAR components.

Type:
GradeType

Variable:
Grades

Grades[25] is a CHAR variable.

Grades is an ARRAY variable that contains 25 CHAR elements.

This code fragment counts the number of students making good grades ('A', 'B', or 'C') and the number of students making poor grades ('D' or 'F'):

```
GoodStudents := 0;
PoorStudents := 0;
FOR Counter := 1 TO 25 DO
  CASE Grades[Counter] OF
     'A', 'B', 'C' : GoodStudents := GoodStudents + 1;
           'D', 'F' : PoorStudents := PoorStudents + 1
  END;     (* CASE *)
```

When Counter is one, the case selector expression is the contents of Grades[1] (an 'A' in this case), so the counter for good students (GoodStudents) gets incremented. At the second iteration, Grades[2] is used as the case selector; at the third, Grades[3], and so on. The loop executes twenty-five times, and each grade is tallied.

In this example, we use an enumerated type as the index type for an ARRAY variable with REAL components:

```
TYPE
  Drinks = (Coke, Pepsi, Sprite);
  SalesType = ARRAY[Drinks] OF REAL;

VAR
  SalesFigures : SalesType;
  SalesSum : REAL;
  Index : Drinks;
```

Type:
SalesType

Variable:
SalesFigures

SalesFigures[Coke] is the first component, SalesFigures[Pepsi] is the second component, and SalesFigures[Sprite] is the third component. This code fragment sums all the values in the ARRAY variable SalesFigures.

```
SalesSum := 0.0;
FOR Index := Coke TO Sprite DO
  SalesSum := SalesSum + SalesFigures[Index];
```

Yes, the variable identifier in the FOR loop can be a user-defined type. In fact the variable identifier in a FOR loop can be any ordinal type. Of course, the starting expression and the ending expression must be of the same type as the variable identifier.

Here we create an array of 350 components representing rooms in a hotel. The content of each component is a number between 0 and 5 representing the number of people registered in the room.

```
TYPE
    Occupant = 0..5;
    Rooms = ARRAY[1..350] OF Occupant;

VAR
    Hotel : Rooms;
    Room, NumVacant : INTEGER;
```

[1]		
[2]		
⋮	⋮	
[350]		

Type:
Rooms

[1]	0	← Hotel[Room] can contain the constants 0, 1, 2, 3, 4 or 5. Room must be between 1 and 350.
[2]	5	
⋮	⋮	
[350]	3	

Variable:
Hotel

If a zero represents a vacant room, the following code fragment counts the number of vacant rooms in the hotel:

```
NumVacant := 0;
FOR Room := 1 TO 350 DO
    IF Hotel[Room] = 0
        THEN
            NumVacant := NumVacant + 1;
```

When working with arrays we use a variable to help us find the element we are looking for.

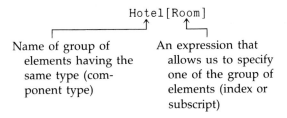

Hotel[Room]

Name of group of elements having the same type (component type)

An expression that allows us to specify one of the group of elements (index or subscript)

SAMPLE PROBLEM

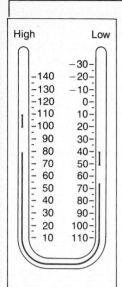

Problem: Read an unknown number of temperature readings from File TempData (one per line) and print the average temperature, the high temperature, the low temperature, the number of readings in which the temperature is above the average, and the number of readings in which the temperature is below the average. The readings can be hourly readings for a day or daily readings for a month or a year.

Discussion: This problem sounds like one we have solved before. Program TemperatureStatistics (see page 157) prints the average temperature, the high temperature, and the low temperature for a twenty-four-hour period. Let's see how much of that solution we can use here.

The temperature data in the original problem was examined just once. We were able to sum the values as they were being read. The task of printing the number of readings above and below the average requires that each temperature reading be examined more than once. So we read the temperatures into an array, then process them.

We have to go through the array of temperatures once to sum them in order to calculate the average and once to compare each temperature to the average. We have to examine each temperature twice because we don't have the average until each temperature has been examined once.

Input: Temperature readings (INTEGER values), one per line

Output: Echo-print the temperature readings.
Print the average, high, and low readings.
Print the number of readings above the average.
Print the number of readings below the average.

Assumptions: There will be no more than 365 temperatures.

Data Structures: Simple variables
A one-dimensional array of INTEGER values

The size of the array must be set at compile-time; that is, the index type of the array that determines the number of locations set aside for the group is not data dependent. In this problem, we don't know the number of temperature readings to be input; we will have to count them as we read them. We solve this dilemma by setting the index type to the maximum, the value given in the assumption. We assume there will be no more than 365 readings. The size of the array is 365.

MAIN MODULE   Level 0

```
Get data
Calculate Average, High, and Low
Count number above and below Average
Print results
```

GET DATA   Level 1

```
NumberOfReadings ← 0
Write 'Temperature Readings:'
WHILE more temperatures DO
    NumberOfReadings ← NumberOfReadings + 1
    Read Temperature
    Write Temperature
    Readings [NumberOfReadings] ← Temperature
```

CALCULATE AVERAGE, HIGH, AND LOW

```
Sum ← Readings[1]
HighSoFar ← Readings[1]
LowSoFar ← Readings[1]
FOR Counter from 2 TO NumberOfReadings DO
    Sum ← Sum + Readings[Counter]
    IF Readings[Counter] < LowSoFar
        THEN
            LowSoFar ← Readings[Counter]
    ELSE IF Readings[Counter] > HighSoFar
        THEN
            HighSoFar ← Readings[Counter]
Average ← Round(Sum / NumberOfReadings)
```

Notice that Sum, HighSoFar, and LowSoFar can all be initialized to the first temperature reading. The loop that processes the rest of the temperature readings goes from the second reading to the end of the temperatures.

COUNT NUMBER ABOVE AND BELOW AVERAGE

```
NumberAbove ← 0
NumberBelow ← 0
FOR Counter from 1 TO NumberOfReadings DO
   IF Readings[Counter] < Average
       THEN
           NumberBelow ← NumberBelow + 1
   ELSE IF Readings[Counter] > Average
       THEN
           NumberAbove ← NumberAbove + 1
```

Notice that we don't count the temperature readings that are equal to the average.

PRINT RESULTS

```
Write 'Average temperature was ' Average
Write 'High temperature was ' High
Write 'Low temperature was ' Low
Write 'Number above average was ' NumberAbove
Write 'Number below average was ' NumberBelow
```

Module Structure Chart:

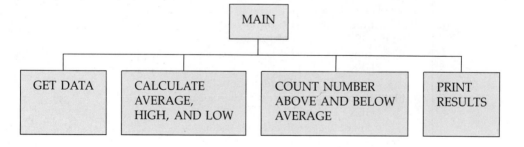

Interface Design Chart:

Program Variables

Identifiers	Type	Role
Readings	ARRAY	List of temperature readings
NumberOfReadings	INTEGER	Number of temperature readings
NumberAbove	INTEGER	Number of readings above the average
NumberBelow	INTEGER	Number of readings below the average
TempData	TEXT	Data file of temperature readings
High	INTEGER	Highest temperature reading
Low	INTEGER	Lowest temperature reading
Average	INTEGER	Average temperature

Procedures

Identifiers	Needs	Returns
GetData	TempData	Readings, NumberOfReadings
Calculate	Readings, NumberOfReadings	Average, High, Low
Count	Readings, NumberOfReadings, Average	NumberAbove, NumberBelow
PrintResults	Average, High, Low, NumberAbove, NumberBelow	Nothing

SAMPLE PROBLEM, CONTINUED

```
PROGRAM TempReadings(OUTPUT, TempData);
(* Statistical analysis of temperature readings *)

CONST
  Max = 365;

TYPE
  ListType = ARRAY[1..Max] OF INTEGER;

VAR
  Readings : ListType;      (* list of temperature readings      *)
  NumberOfReadings,         (* number of temperatures readings   *)
  NumberAbove,              (* number of readings above average  *)
  NumberBelow : INTEGER;    (* number of readings below average  *)
  TempData : TEXT;          (* input data file                   *)
  High,                     (* high reading                      *)
  Low,                      (* low reading                       *)
  Average : INTEGER;        (* average reading                   *)

(*****************************************************************)

PROCEDURE GetData(VAR TempData : TEXT; VAR Readings : ListType;
                  VAR NumberOfReadings : INTEGER);
(* Data values are read and stored until EOF(TempData). *)
(* Assumptions:  Data values are one per line.          *)
(*               Maximum of 365 data values.            *)

VAR
  Temperature : INTEGER;     (* local variable used for input *)

BEGIN    (* GetData *)
  NumberOfReadings := 0;
  WRITELN('Temperature Readings: ');
  WHILE NOT EOF(TempData) DO
    BEGIN
      NumberOfReadings := NumberOfReadings + 1;
      READLN(TempData, Temperature);
      WRITELN(Temperature);
      Readings[NumberOfReadings] := Temperature
    END
END;     (* GetData *)

(*****************************************************************)

PROCEDURE Calculate(Readings : ListType; NumberOfReadings: INTEGER;
                    VAR Average, HighSoFar, LowSoFar : INTEGER);
(* Average, high, and low temperature readings are calculated. *)
```

```
VAR
  Counter,               (* local loop control variable *)
  Sum : INTEGER;         (* sum of temperatures        *)

BEGIN   (* Calculate *)
  Sum := Readings[1];
  HighSoFar := Readings[1];
  LowSoFar := Readings[1];
  FOR Counter := 2 TO NumberOfReadings DO
    BEGIN
      Sum := Sum + Readings[Counter];
      IF Readings[Counter] < LowSoFar
          THEN
            LowSoFar := Readings[Counter]
      ELSE IF Readings[Counter] > HighSoFar
          THEN
            HighSoFar := Readings[Counter]
  END;
  Average := ROUND(Sum / NumberOfReadings)
END;    (* Calculate *)

(****************************************************************)

PROCEDURE Count(Readings : ListType; NumberOfReadings : INTEGER;
          Average : INTEGER; VAR NumberAbove, NumberBelow : INTEGER);
(* NumberAbove is the number of readings above Average.   *)
(* NumberBelow is the number of readings below Average.   *)
(* Assumption:  Readings equal to Average are not counted.*)

VAR
  Counter : INTEGER;     (* local loop control variable *)

BEGIN   (* Count *)
  NumberAbove := 0;
  NumberBelow := 0;
  FOR Counter := 1 TO NumberOfReadings DO
    IF Readings[Counter] < Average
        THEN
          NumberBelow := NumberBelow + 1
    ELSE If Readings[Counter] > Average
        THEN
          NumberAbove := NumberAbove + 1
END;    (* Count *)

(****************************************************************)

PROCEDURE PrintResults(Average, High, Low : REAL;
                    NumberAbove, NumberBelow : INTEGER);
```

SAMPLE PROBLEM, CONTINUED

```
BEGIN   (* PrintResults *)
  WRITELN('Average temperature was ', Average:7);
  WRITELN('High temperature was ', High:10);
  WRITELN('Low temperature was ', Low:11);
  WRITELN('Number above average was ', NumberAbove:6);
  WRITELN('Number below average was ', NumberBelow:6)
END;    (* PrintResults *)

(****************************************************************)

BEGIN   (* TempReadings *)
  RESET(TempData);
  GetData(TempData, Readings, NumberOfReadings);
  Calculate(Readings, NumberOfReadings, Average, High, Low);
  Count(Readings, NumberOfReadings, Average, NumberAbove, NumberBelow);
  PrintResults(Average, High, Low, NumberAbove, NumberBelow)
END.    (* TempReadings *)
```

Type Compatibility

Because Pascal is a strongly typed language, every variable must be declared in a VAR section with its type explicitly stated. When an assignment statement is compiled in your program, the type of the value to be computed is checked against the type of the variable into which it is to be stored. If the types do not match, there is a compile-time error. There is one exception: An INTEGER value can be stored into a REAL variable. At execution time the INTEGER value is converted into REAL form before the value is stored.

When a procedure or function call is compiled, the types of the actual parameters are compared with the types of the formal parameters. If they do not agree, an error message is printed. Now that we can define new types, the question arises, "Just when are two types **compatible**?"

1. Two types are compatible when they have the *same type identifier*.
2. Two types are compatible when they have the *same type definition*.
3. Two types are compatible when they are subranges of the *same host type* or when *one is a subrange of the other*.

Formal and actual VAR parameters must have the same type identifier. This makes sense because formal and actual VAR parameters refer to the same address in memory. In fact there is an additional constraint on type identifiers used on formal parameter lists: The type definitions must be globally defined.

A further check called *assignment compatibility* is required on values of subrange types. If the variable name on the left of an assignment statement is a subrange type, before a value is put in that location during execution the value is checked to be sure it is within the proper range. If it is not, an error occurs. Because value parameters are passed by putting a copy of their value on the message board, actual parameters must be assignment compatible with their formal parameters.

Assignment compatibility is particularly useful with arrays. Because the index type of an array is usually a subrange type, you cannot access places that do not exist. If you try to access the twenty-first element of an array whose index type is 1 . . 20, you get the error message INDEX OUT OF RANGE.

Pascal allows an ARRAY variable to be defined by putting the ARRAY definition next to the variable identifier in the VAR section of the program. This is called an **anonymous type** because the type does not have a name. An ARRAY variable declared in this way cannot be passed as a parameter to a procedure or function. Although anonymous typing is legal, don't do it. It's very bad style.

The 4-Cs Corner

Conciseness

Being concise means wasting nothing. A concise program is a program that runs efficiently, that does not waste machine time. A concise program also does not waste the programmer's time; if a solution already exists, use it.

Efficient Code

In Program TempReadings the array Readings was passed as a value parameter to Procedures Calculate and Count. An ARRAY variable, like any simple variable, is copied onto the message board if it's being passed by value. In the case of ARRAY variable Readings, 365 elements had to be copied onto the message board twice, once for each procedure call.

There are two competing issues here. All communication between program parts should be through parameter lists where "needs" variables are passed by value. Copying 365 values each time that ARRAY variable Readings is passed as a value parameter is not efficient. Which is more important?

When an ARRAY variable is small, little time is spent copying it onto the message board, so the variable should be passed by value. When an ARRAY variable is large and is passed many times, the parameter should be a VAR parameter. You have to determine "small" and "large" in light of the size of the machine you're using and its load.

Reusability

One of the reasons we use procedures and functions is that they allow us to save the solution to a task in a standard format that can be used in other programs. This means that the formal parameter list must be as general as possible.

For example, in Program TempReadings, Procedure Calculate finds the average, high, and low values in an INTEGER array. This set of tasks comes up often in different contexts. Could we rewrite our procedure so that it works on values of any numeric type? Yes, using a technique called *type aliasing*. Here's Procedure Calculate recoded:

```
PROCEDURE Calculate(List : ListType; Length : INTEGER;
                    VAR Average : REAL;
                    VAR HighSoFar, LowSoFar : ItemType);
(* Average, high, and low values in List are calculated. *)

VAR
   Counter : INTEGER;    (* local loop control variable *)
   Sum : ItemType;       (* sum of list                 *)

BEGIN    (* Calculate *)
  Sum := List[1];
  HighSoFar := List[1];
  LowSoFar := List[1];
  FOR Counter := 2 TO Length DO
    BEGIN
      Sum := Sum + List[Counter];
      IF List[Counter] < LowSoFar
         THEN
            LowSoFar := List[Counter]
      ELSE IF List[Counter] > HighSoFar
         THEN
            HighSoFar := List[Counter]
    END;
  Average := Sum / Length
END;    (* Calculate *)
```

To use our revised version of Procedure Calculate to find the average, high, and low of a list of INTEGER data values, we make the following declarations:

```
CONST
   Limit = (* whatever the maximum size is *)

TYPE
   IndexRange = 1..Limit;
   ItemType = INTEGER;
   ListType = ARRAY[IndexRange] OF ItemType;
```

To use Procedure Calculate to find the average, high, and low values of any other numeric type, ItemType would be defined to be the other numeric type. Setting a type equal to another type is what we mean by type aliasing.

Notice that we have made the identifiers on the formal parameter lists more general. Of course the variable identifiers don't change the meaning of the program, but it would be misleading to take a procedure in which the formal parameter lists use identifiers like Readings and NumberOfReadings and use it to find the average, high, and low values in a set of test grades. Our task is to find the average, high, and low in a list of values, and the formal parameters should reflect this general view.

In our original problem we calculate the average temperature. Because we only think of temperatures as whole numbers, the average was rounded to the nearest integer. In the general Procedure Calculate, Average is of type REAL. If the average is logically an integer, the application that uses Procedure Calculate should convert it.

Completeness

The interface design chart for a program is part of the program's documentation. It should be consistent with the code of the program. The identifiers listed under the needs and returns sections should reflect the specific application; they are the identifiers used in the actual parameter list. If the identifiers on the actual parameter list and the formal parameter list are not the same, you should note this in your documentation. This happens when you use one of your own general procedures or functions or when you recode a procedure or function in a general form.

Correctness

In our programs, a one-dimensional array is the structured data type used to represent a list of elements. There are three distinct viewpoints from which to consider this structure: the pattern for the structure (type), the ARRAY variable made from the pattern, and the semantics of the ARRAY variable within the program. Keeping these three viewpoints in mind can help to minimize the errors associated with using arrays.

For example, in Program TempReadings we defined the array to be 365 elements long because that was the maximum number of elements we might need. However, the loops that process the information in the array only look at those locations in the array into which values have been stored—locations 1 to NumberOfReadings. In other words, the program processes the list of temperature readings that is stored in part of the ARRAY variable Readings (see figure at the top of page 292).

Program TempReadings defines an ARRAY type and declares an ARRAY variable Readings. Procedure GetData takes this ARRAY variable and reads values into it, creating a list of temperature readings. An ARRAY variable has a fixed length, but a list does not; therefore, the length of the list is part of its definition.

The list (Readings) and its length (NumberOfReadings) is passed to Procedure Calculate. Procedure Calculate is performing a very general task that

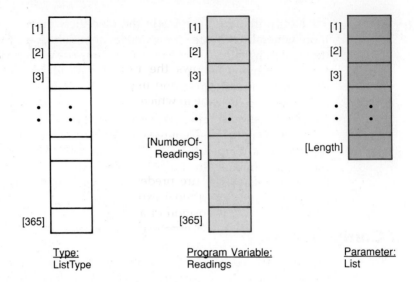

can be applied to any list of numeric values. Procedure Calculate knows nothing about the ARRAY variable Readings; Procedure Calculate is working with a list of values of ItemType. Procedure Calculate can be given any list of values of ItemType as long as it is stored in a variable of type ListType, and will calculate the average, maximum, and minimum values.

This separation of general tasks from the semantics of a particular problem can help you write correct reusable subprograms. The process is one of abstracting from the particulars of a specific problem to the general case: from the average, high, and low temperatures to the process of calculating statistics for any list of numeric values. Having done this abstraction, you'll be much more likely to recognize this situation within the context of another specific problem. Remember, don't rebuild the wheel.

Correctness Hints

1. Use a subrange type if you know the bounds or the values of a variable.
2. Use enumerated types to make your programs more readable.
3. Variables cannot be used in the declaration part of a type. Information in the CONST, TYPE, and VAR sections is used by the computer at compile-time. Variables do not get values until the program is executed. So declaring a subrange type 1 . . Length makes no sense unless Length is defined in the CONST section.
4. Use the same type identifier for *formal* and *actual* parameters if possible. Formal and actual value parameters must have compatible type definitions. Formal and actual VAR parameters must have the same type identifier.
5. Don't apply PRED to the first element of a type or SUCC to the last.

Summary

Pascal has four built-in scalar types: INTEGER, REAL, CHAR, and BOOL-EAN. Pascal also allows the user to define new types: types that are subranges of other types and user-defined types.

A scalar type is one in which the set of values is ordered and each value is atomic. An ordinal type is a scalar type in which each value except the first has a unique predecessor and each value except the last has a unique successor. INTEGER, REAL, CHAR, BOOLEAN, subrange types, and enumerated types are scalar; all except REAL are also ordinal.

PRED and SUCC are predefined functions that return the predecessor and successor of an ordinal expression. ORD is a predefined function that returns the ordinal position of an expression. CHR is a predefined function that takes an INTEGER expression within the range of zero to the number of characters in the character set less 1, and returns the corresponding character.

Pascal has a built-in structured data type ARRAY. An array is a pattern for a structured (ordered) group of like elements. Each individual element can be accessed by its position within the group. An ARRAY variable is a variable declared to be of an ARRAY type. Each element is accessed by giving the name of the ARRAY variable followed by an index (in brackets) that specifies the element's position.

Two types are compatabile if they have the same type identifier, the same type definition, are subranges of the same host type, or one is a subrange of the other.

EXERCISES

1. Define an enumerated type for each of the following:
   a. Area high schools
   b. Positions on a baseball team
   c. Members of your immediate family

2. Define a subrange type for each of the following:
   a. Numerals '0' to '9'
   b. Integers between −4 and 24 (inclusive)
   c. A subrange of Exercise 1b

3. Declare ARRAY variables for each of the following:
   a. A twenty-four-element REAL array in which the index goes from 1 to 24
   b. A twenty-six-element INTEGER array in which the index goes from 'A' to 'Z'
   c. A ten-element CHAR array in which the index goes from −5 to 4

4. Write a program fragment that does the following processing for the corresponding array in Exercise 3.
   a. Initializes each value to 0.0
   b. Initializes each value to zero
   c. Reads two characters into the array with the first character going into the component whose index is −5

5. Given the following declarations, write a program fragment that reverses the order of elements of ARRAY variable List.

```
TYPE
  (* Thing is any named type. *)
  ListType : ARRAY[1..10] OF Thing;

VAR
  List : ListType;
```

6. Given the following declarations, write a program fragment that finds the number of vehicles in service.

```
TYPE
  ServiceType = ARRAY[1..83] OF BOOLEAN;

VAR
  InService : ServiceType;
```

7. Scalar data types are ordered so that every variable must be less than, equal to, or greater than any other variable of that type. True or false?

8. INTEGER, CHAR, and enumerated types are ordinal types, so it's possible to declare a subrange type based on them. True or false?

9. Given the following type declaration:

```
TYPE
  Members = (Smith, Jones, Grant, White);
```

Is the expression Grant < Smith true or false?

10. Is the following TYPE declaration segment legal?

```
TYPE
  Family = (John, Joe, Evelyn, Burt);
  Friends = (Bill, Alice, Evelyn, John);
```

11. Does the following declaration section contain any errors?

```
TYPE
  RainTotals = ARRAY[1..NumberCounties] OF INTEGER;

VAR
  Rainfall : RainTotals;
  NumberCounties : INTEGER;
```

12. The predeclared function CHR receives a nonnegative integer as a parameter and returns the character that corresponds to it in the character set. True or false?

13. Every element in an array must be of the same type, which is fixed at declaration, and must match the type of its subscript. True or false?

14. What values result from the following function calls?
    a. ORD(Sunday), where Sunday is an element of type Days, and Days = (Monday, Tuesday, Wednesday, Thursday, Friday, Saturday, Sunday)
    b. CHR(3), where ORD('A') = 1

    c. ORD('D'), where CHR(1) = 'A'

    d. SUCC('Z'), where the entire character set is 'A'..'Z'

    e. PRED(0)

15. Write a function, Zero, that receives an ARRAY variable name as a parameter and returns TRUE if any of the elements of the array are zero. Assume these declarations in the main program:

```
TYPE
    ArrayType = ARRAY[1..50] OF INTEGER;

VAR
    List : ArrayType;
```

PRETEST

1. Type INTEGER is a scalar type, but a subrange type is not. True or false?

2. The type of function ORD must be INTEGER because it returns the internal integer representation of a character. True or false?

3. The range of subscripts for an array is fixed at declaration, and every element of the array must have the same fixed type. But during execution an array of fifty elements might only contain ten meaningful data items, leaving the other forty elements with undefined values. True or false?

4. What values result from the following function calls?
    a. PRED(12)
    b. SUCC('B')
    c. SUCC(Monday), where Monday is an element of type Days, and Days = (Monday, Tuesday, Wednesday, Thursday, Friday)
    d. ORD('C') where CHR(1) = 'A'
    e. CHR(5) where ORD('A') = 1

5. Define a subrange type or enumerated type (as appropriate) for each of the following:
    a. Crops consisting of rice, beans, corn, and peas
    b. All the days of the week
    c. Workdays Monday through Friday from the type in part b
    d. Range −10 to +200 inclusive
    e. Characters 'B' through 'K'
    f. A column counter of the range 1 to 72

6. Which of the following declaration segments are legal?
    a.
    ```
    TYPE
        Color = (Red, Yellow, Blue);
        Shade = (Light, Dark);
    ```
    b.
    ```
    TYPE
        Size = (Small, Medium, Large, Giant);
        Creatures = (Dwarf, Dragon, Giant, Knight);
    ```
    c.
    ```
    TYPE
        List = ARRAY[1..200] OF Code;
        Code = 1..10;
    ```

```
      VAR
        CodeList : List;
  d. TYPE
        Code = 1..5;
        List = ARRAY[Code] OF INTEGER;

      VAR
        CodeList : List;
  e. VAR
        CodeList : ARRAY[1..5] OF INTEGER;
  f. VAR
        Color : (Red, Yellow, Blue);
  g. TYPE
        Code = (Fixed, Varying, Mixed);
        RunType = ARRAY[1..15] OF Code;

      VAR
        List : RunType;
        Mixed : INTEGER;
```

7. Declare ARRAY variables for each of the following:
   a. A ten-element BOOLEAN array in which the index goes from 'A' to 'J'
   b. A REAL array in which the index goes from −10 to 10. (How many REAL variables are there in this array?)
   c. A thirty-six-element CHAR array in which the index goes from 1 to 36

8. Write a program fragment that does the following processing for the corresponding array in Problem 7:
   a. Initializes each value to TRUE
   b. Initializes each value to 0.0
   c. Reads twenty characters into the array with the first character going into the component whose index is 1

9. Write a function, PositiveArray, that receives an ARRAY variable name as a parameter and returns FALSE if any of the elements of the array are negative. Assume this declaration in the main program:

```
TYPE
  ArrayType = ARRAY[1..50] OF INTEGER;
```

Note: Other declarations would have to be made before this function can be called, but that's not part of the problem.

10. Write a procedure, SumArray, that receives an ARRAY variable name as a parameter, sums the values in that array, and returns the total to the calling program. Assume these declarations in the main program:

```
CONST
  TotalLimit = 200;

TYPE
  Totals = ARRAY[1..TotalLimit] OF INTEGER;
```

Note: Other declarations would have to be made before this procedure can be called, but that's not part of the problem.

PROGRAMMING ASSIGNMENTS

1. A company wants to know the percentage of its sales from each salesperson. Each salesperson has a data line that lists an identification number and the dollar value of his or her sales.

   Input: A record for each salesperson
   Output: Total sales and each salesperson's ID, sales, and percentage of total sales

2. The local baseball team is computerizing its records. You are to write a program that computes batting averages. There are twenty players on the team, identified by the numbers 1 through 20. Their batting records are coded on a file. Each line in the file contains four numbers: the player's identification number and the number of hits, walks, and outs in a particular game. For example,

       3 2 1 1

   means player number 3 was at bat 4 times, made 2 hits, 1 walk, and 1 out during one game. For each player there are several records on the file. To compute each player's batting average, add the total number of hits and divide by the total number of times at bat. A walk does not count as either a hit or a time at bat in calculating a batting average.

   Print ID, batting average, and number of walks for each player in descending order by batting average, labeled appropriately. (Remember to echo-print the input.)

3. You've been asked to do a simple analysis of the exam scores for a freshman class. Write and test a computer program that does the following:

   (1) Reads the test grades
   (2) Calculates the smallest and largest scores and the mode (the most frequent score)
   (3) Prints a single-page summary showing the smallest score, the largest score, the mode, and a list of grades with the frequency of appearance of each grade

   Input:
   (1) First data line: the number of exams to be analyzed (not to exceed 100) and an alphanumeric title for the report
   (2) Remaining data lines: a four-digit student ID number followed by a number grade between zero and 100

   Output:
   (1) Echo-print the input data.
   (2) Print the title beginning on a new sheet of output paper.
   (3) Print the minimum, maximum, and mode, all properly labeled.
   (4) Print the unique grades and the frequency of occurrence of each.

4. A local bank is gearing up for a big advertising campaign and would like to see how long its customers are waiting for service at drive-in windows. The bank has asked several employees to keep accurate records of the twenty-four-hour drive-in service. The collected information will be read from a file and will consist of the time of day in hours, minutes, and seconds that the customer arrived, the time the customer was actually served, and the ID number of the teller.

Write a program that executes the following steps:

(1) Reads in the wait data
(2) Computes the wait time in seconds
(3) Calculates the mean, standard deviation, and range
(4) Prints a single-page summary showing the values calculated in Step 3

Input:
(1) The first data line contains a title.
(2) The remaining lines each contain a teller ID, an arrival time, and a start time. The times are broken up into hours, minutes, and seconds according to the twenty-four-hour clock.

Processing:
(1) Calculate the mean and the standard deviation.
(2) Locate the shortest wait time and the longest wait time.
(3) The program should work for any number of records up to 100.

Output:
(1) Echo-print the input data.
(2) Print the title beginning on a new page.
(3) Print the following values, all properly labeled:
    (a) Number of records
    (b) Mean
    (c) Standard deviation
    (d) Range (minimum and maximum wait)

5. The final exam in your psychology class is thirty multiple-choice questions. Your instructor says that if you write a program to grade the finals you won't have to take it. You, of course, accept.

Input:
(1) The key to the exam. The correct answers are the first thirty characters followed by an integer number that says how many students took the exam (call it N).
(2) The next N lines contain a student's answer in the first thirty character positions followed by the student's name in the next ten character positions.

Output: For each student, print his or her name followed by the number of correct answers. If the number correct is 60 percent or better, print *PASS*; otherwise print *FAIL*.

9 Typical Problems Using Arrays

- To be able to follow the development of the top-down design of a problem that includes one of the following types of ARRAY variable processing (list processing):

    Searching
    Using parallel arrays
    Using indexes with meaning
    Sorting
    Merging

- To be able to read the code that implements each of these top-down designs.

- To be able to define, declare, and use string variables.

In Chapter 8 we introduced the concept of a one-dimensional array: a structured data type made up of a group of locations given a common name. Each individual location is accessed by its position (index) in the group. There are two types associated with each one-dimensional array: the type of what can be stored in each location (the component type) and the type of the variable, constant, or expression that specifies a particular location within the group (the index type).

This chapter is designed to give you more experience using one-dimensional arrays. We look at five kinds of processing—searching, using parallel arrays, using indexes with meaning, sorting, and merging—that are done again and again in programs using one-dimensional arrays, demonstrating these typical processes in the context of specific problems.

Finally, we introduce one new concept in this chapter: the string. We have been using literal strings in our programs from the very first. Here we show you how to read in characters and store and retrieve them as a group.

Searching

Looking systematically through the elements of an array for a specific value is called *searching*. There are two forms of searching. We use one when we want to know if the value is in the array; we use the other when we want to know its position in the array (if it's there).

SAMPLE PROBLEM

Problem: A suit manufacturing company wants a printed list of designs that were ordered during a particular week. The firm is not interested in how many of a particular design were ordered—only in which designs were ordered. To prepare this list you are provided with a week's worth of sales receipts on File SuitSales. Each sales receipt (line of data) contains the design number, the quantity of that design ordered, the unit cost, and the total cost of the order.

Discussion: How would you tackle this job if you were doing it by hand? You probably would go through the stack of orders one by one. If you have not seen a design number before, you would write it down. If you have seen it before, you would go on to the next order. How would you determine if you had seen a design before? By scanning (searching) the list of those you've written down. If it isn't there, you would write it down. The list you've written down is the list of designs sold that week.

This sounds promising. Writing the design number on a piece of paper can be translated into putting the value in the next open location in an array. Scanning the list can be translated into comparing each value already in the array with the design number on the order. If a value in the array matches the design number, you have seen this design number before. Now we understand the problem well enough to begin the top-down design.

Input: A sales file containing sets of the following:

> Design number (INTEGER)
> Quantity ordered (INTEGER)
> Unit cost (REAL)
> Total sale (REAL)

Output: A list of the designs that were ordered (on File Designs)

Data Structures: A one-dimensional ARRAY variable, DesignList, to hold a list of the design numbers

Assumption: The company has one thousand current designs.

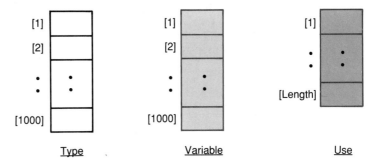

MAIN MODULE   Level 0

```
Get design list
Print design list
```

GET DESIGN LIST   Level 1

Design is the only value we're interested in. Why bother to input the other values simply because they are there? How do we bypass them? By using a READLN.

```
WHILE more Designs DO
    Readln Design
    IF Design NOT on DesignList
        THEN
            Put on DesignList
```

PRINT DESIGN LIST

> WHILE more Designs DO
>   Write Design

ON DESIGN LIST   Level 2

We have to compare the new design with each one already on the list until we either find a match or we reach the end of the list. We need a count-controlled loop, but we cannot use a FOR loop because we have two alternative ending conditions.

> Counter ← 0
> Found ← FALSE
> WHILE Counter < Length AND NOT Found DO
>   Counter ← Counter + 1
>   IF Design = DesignList[Counter]
>   THEN
>   Found ← TRUE
> OnDesignList ← Found

PUT ON DESIGN LIST

> Length ← Length + 1
> DesignList[Length] ← Design

Module Design Chart:

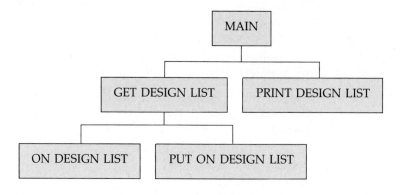

Module PUT ON DESIGN LIST is only two lines long and has no meaning outside of GET DESIGN LIST, so we code it in-line. Module PRINT DESIGN LIST is also short, but it is quite general. We change its name to PrintList and code it to print any list of type ListType on File Data. ON DESIGN LIST is coded as a BOOLEAN function; its name goes in the returns column of the interface design chart.

Interface Design Chart:

Program Variables

Identifiers	Type	Role
DesignList	ARRAY	List of suit design numbers
Length	INTEGER	Length of design list
SuitSales	TEXT	File of sales receipts
Designs	TEXT	File of unique designs

Subprograms

Identifiers	Needs	Returns
GetDesignList	SuitSales	DesignList, Length
OnDesignList	DesignList, Length, Design	OnDesignList (BOOLEAN)
PrintList	Designs, DesignList, Length	Nothing

```
PROGRAM DesignCount(OUTPUT, SuitSales, Designs);
(* A list of the suit designs appearing     *)
(* on a file of sales receipts is printed. *)

CONST
  Limit = 1000;

TYPE
  IndexRange = 1..Limit;
  IndexType = 0..Limit;
  ListType = ARRAY[IndexRange] OF INTEGER;

VAR
  DesignList : ListType;
  Length : IndexType;
  SuitSales,              (* input file  *)
  Designs : TEXT;         (* output file *)

(***********************************************************)
```

SAMPLE PROBLEM, CONTINUED

```
FUNCTION OnDesignList(DesignList : ListType; Length : IndexType;
                      Design : INTEGER) : BOOLEAN;

VAR
  Counter : IndexType;   (* loop control variable            *)
  Found : BOOLEAN;       (* set to TRUE if design is on list *)

BEGIN    (* OnDesignList *)
  Counter := 0;
  Found := FALSE;
  WHILE (Counter < Length) AND NOT Found DO
    BEGIN
      Counter := Counter + 1;
      IF Design = DesignList[Counter]
        THEN
          Found := TRUE
    END;
  OnDesignList := Found

END;    (* OnDesignList *)

(************************************************************)

PROCEDURE GetDesignList(VAR SuitSales : TEXT;
                        VAR DesignList : ListType;
                        VAR Length : IndexType);
(* Designs are read from File SuitSales. *)
(* Each new design is put on DesignList. *)

VAR
  Design : INTEGER;

BEGIN    (* GetDesignList *)
  Length := 0;
  WHILE NOT EOF(SuitSales) DO
    BEGIN
      READLN(SuitSales, Design);
      IF NOT OnDesignList(DesignList, Length, Design)
        THEN
          BEGIN
            Length := Length + 1;
            DesignList[Length] := Design
          END
    END
END;    (* GetDesignList *)

(************************************************************)
```

```
PROCEDURE PrintList(VAR Data : TEXT; List : ListType;
                          Length : IndexType);
(* Values in Data[1] to Data[Length] are printed. *)

VAR
   Counter : IndexType;      (* loop control variable *)

BEGIN    (* PrintList *)
   FOR Counter := 1 TO Length DO
      WRITELN(Data, List[Counter])
END;     (* PrintList *)

(************************************************************)

BEGIN    (* DesignCount *)
   RESET(SuitSales);
   REWRITE(Designs);
   GetDesignList(SuitSales, DesignList, Length);
   WRITELN(Designs, 'The following designs were ordered:');
   PrintList(Designs, DesignList, Length)
END.     (* DesignCount *)
```

In this example the search routine is coded as a BOOLEAN function because all we need to know is if the design number is in the list, not where it is. Let's recode this as a procedure and send back the location in the array where the value is found, if it is. To make it more general, we replace the problem-dependent variable names with general ones.

Let's call the array being searched List and the item being searched for Item. Length can remain the same. We need two VAR parameters: Found, which returns the result of the search, and Index, which contains the content of the loop control variable Counter if there is a match or Length + 1 if there isn't a match. Yes, the two output parameters are redundant. Index would be sufficient because the calling routine could check Index > Length rather than checking Found. For clarity, however, let's be redundant.

```
PROCEDURE Search(List : ListType;       (* array to be searched   *)
              Length : IndexType;        (* length of list         *)
              Item : ItemType;           (* item being looked for  *)
          VAR Found : BOOLEAN;           (* result of search       *)
          VAR Index : IndexType);        (* where found (if found) *)
```

```
BEGIN   (* Search *)
  Found := False;
  Index := 0;
  WHILE (Index < Length) AND NOT Found DO
    BEGIN
      Index := Index + 1;
      IF Item = List[Index]
        THEN
          Found := TRUE
    END
END;    (* Search *)
```

Notice that Item is not of type INTEGER but some globally defined type ItemType (the type of the components in the list). We assume that the following type definitions are in the main program:

```
CONST
  MaxLength = (* maximum possible number of items *);

TYPE
  IndexRange = 1..MaxLength;
  IndexType  = 0..MaxLength;
  ItemType = (* any type *);
  ListType = ARRAY[IndexRange] OF ItemType;
```

This procedure can now search an array of any type (ItemType) for a value of that type. We can use this generalized procedure in any program that requires a list search.

Using Parallel Arrays

In many problems there are several pieces of information that go together. For example, you might have student identification numbers and grades. You set up one INTEGER array for the student identification numbers and one CHAR array for the grades. A particular student identification number goes with a particular grade because they have the same position in their respective arrays (that is, they have the same index).

SAMPLE PROBLEM

Problem: Count the frequency of occurrence of certain characters in a sample of text.

Discussion: If you were doing this by hand, you would probably make a list of the characters you want to count. Then you would start processing the text, character by character. You would take each character and look for it in your list. If it's there, you would make a hash mark beside it.

We can use this algorithm directly. The list of characters whose frequency we want to count can be read into a CHAR array. This is analogous to making a list of the characters. To look for a character in the list, we can use our generalized search routine.

To simulate making a hash mark, we use a second array that is the same size as the one containing the characters. This second array should be of type INTEGER. Because the search routine returns the place in the array where the character is found, we use that position as an index into the second array and add a 1 at that position (make a hash mark). For example, if the first character in our list is 'A', each time we find 'A' the first slot in the INTEGER array is incremented by 1. Two (or more) separate arrays that contain related information in corresponding positions are called *parallel arrays*.

Input: A list of the characters to be counted (interactive input)
File Data, which contains the text to be processed

Output: The characters looked for and their frequency of occurrence

Data Structures: A one-dimensional ARRAY variable of type CHAR to hold the characters being counted
A one-dimensional ARRAY variable of type INTEGER to hold the frequencies

MAIN MODULE   Level 0

```
Get list of characters
Zero frequencies
WHILE NOT EOF(DATA) DO
   Read Character
   Search
   IF Found
       THEN
           Increment Frequencies[Index]
Print results
```

GET LIST OF CHARACTERS   Level 1

```
Writeln 'Input characters to be counted, one per line.'
Writeln 'Press < eof > to end input.'
Lenth ← 0
WHILE NOT EOF DO
   Readln Character
   Length ← Length + 1
   ListOfCharacters[Length] ← Character
```

SAMPLE PROBLEM, CONTINUED

ZERO FREQUENCIES

```
FOR Index from 1 TO Length DO
    Frequencies[Index] ← 0
```

SEARCH

We use the generalized search procedure.

PRINT RESULTS

```
Writeln 'Character Frequency'
FOR Index from 1 TO Length DO
    Writeln ListOfCharacters[Index]:7, Frequencies[Index]:12
```

Module Design Chart:

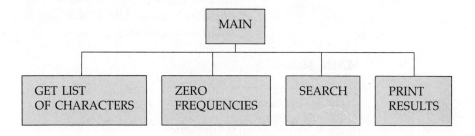

Remember that any variables in the returns column must be VAR parameters. Those listed in the needs column should be value parameters, except when files are passed as parameters or when you have a *large* data structure that is an input parameter only. In that case, the amount of extra storage needed to copy the data structure may take up more memory space than is available. In this case we pass the ARRAY variables as value parameters.

Interface Design Chart:

Program Variables

Identifiers	Type	Role
ListOfCharacters	ARRAY	List of characters to be counted
Frequencies	ARRAY	Frequencies of characters
Length	IndexType	Number of characters to be counted
Index	IndexType	Where in the array a character is found
Found	BOOLEAN	TRUE if the character is found
Data	TEXT	File containing characters to count
Character	CHAR	Used for reading characters on File Data

Subprograms

Identifiers	Needs	Returns
GetList	Data	ListOfCharacters, Length
ZeroFrequencies	Length	Frequencies
Search	ListOfCharacters, Length, Character	Found, Index
PrintResults	ListOfCharacters, Frequencies, Length	Nothing

```
PROGRAM CharacterCount(INPUT, OUTPUT, Data);
(* Frequency of occurrence of certain characters *)
(* are counted in File Data.                     *)

CONST
  MaxLength = (* number of characters in character set *)
```

SAMPLE PROBLEM, CONTINUED

```
TYPE
  IndexRange = 1..MaxLength;
  IndexType = 0..MaxLength;
  ItemType = CHAR;
  ListType = ARRAY[IndexRange] OF ItemType;
  ListOfCounts = ARRAY[IndexRange] OF INTEGER;

VAR
  ListOfCharacters : ListType;
  Frequencies : ListOfCounts;
  Length, Index : IndexType;
  Found : BOOLEAN;
  Data : TEXT;
  Character : CHAR;

(***************************************************************)

PROCEDURE GetList(VAR ListOfCharacters : ListType;
                  VAR Length : IndexType);
(* User is prompted to input characters to count. *)

VAR
  Character : CHAR;          (* used for input *)

BEGIN    (* GetList *)
  WRITELN('Input characters to be counted one per line.');
  WRITELN('Press End-of-File character to end input');
  Length := 0;
  WHILE NOT EOF DO
    BEGIN
      READLN(Character);
      Length := Length + 1;
      ListOfCharacters[Length] := Character
    END
END;     (* GetList *)


(***************************************************************)

PROCEDURE ZeroFrequencies(VAR Frequencies : ListOfCounts;
                              Length : IndexType);
(* Frequencies from 1 to Length is set to zero *)

VAR
  Counter : IndexType;     (* loop control variable *)

BEGIN    (* ZeroFrequencies *)
  FOR Counter := 1 TO Length DO
    Frequencies[Counter] := 0
END;     (* ZeroFrequencies *)
```

```
(*****************************************************************)

PROCEDURE Search(List : ListType;        (* array to be searched  *)
                 Length : IndexType;      (* length of list        *)
                 Item : ItemType;         (* item being looked for  *)
             VAR Found : BOOLEAN;         (* result of search      *)
             VAR Index : IndexType);      (* where found (if found) *)

BEGIN   (* Search *)
  Found := FALSE;
  Index := 0;
  WHILE (Index < Length) AND NOT Found DO
    BEGIN
      Index := Index + 1;
      IF Item = List[Index]
          THEN
            Found := TRUE
  END
END;    (* Search *)


(******************************************************************)

PROCEDURE PrintResults(ListOfCharacters : ListType;
                       Frequencies : ListOfCounts;
                       Length : IndexType);
(* Characters and their frequencies are printed. *)

VAR
  Counter : IndexType;   (* loop control variable *)

BEGIN   (* PrintResults *)
  WRITELN('Character    Frequency');
  FOR Counter := 1 TO Length DO
    WRITELN(ListOfCharacters[Counter]:7, Frequencies[Counter]:12)
END;   (* PrintResults *)


(******************************************************************)

BEGIN   (* CharacterCount *)
  RESET(Data);
  GetList(ListOfCharacters, Length);
  ZeroFrequencies(Frequencies, Length);
  WHILE NOT EOF(Data) DO
    BEGIN
      READ(Data, Character);
      Search(ListOfCharacters, Length, Character, Found, Index);
```

SAMPLE PROBLEM, CONTINUED

```
      IF Found
        THEN
           Frequencies[Index] := Frequencies[Index] + 1
      END;
   PrintResults(ListOfCharacters, Frequencies, Length)
END.    (* CharacterCount *)
```

Let's do a partial code walk-through of this program. Suppose the characters we want to count are

A E I O U

and the text is

PASCAL IS A STRUCTURED LANGUAGE,
AS STRUCTURED AS CAN BE.
I USED IT TO STRUCTURE MY PROGRAM,
AND NOW IT'S STRUCTURING ME!

The contents of ListOfCharacters and Frequencies just before the WHILE loop is executed are shown below.

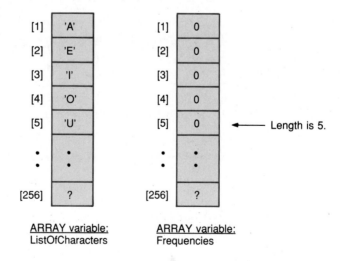

ARRAY variable: ARRAY variable:
ListOfCharacters   Frequencies

We assume Procedures GetList and ZeroFrequencies are correct. So we look at the three inner statements:

1. READ(Data, Character);

```
2. Search(ListOfCharacters,Length,Character,Found,Index);
3. IF Found
      THEN
          Frequencies[Index] := Frequencies[Index] + 1
```

Here's a partial code walk-through table. A dash means that the variable has not changed; a question mark means that the variable has not yet been given a value.

Statement	Character	Index	Found	Frequencies
1.1	P	?	?	All 0
2.1	—	6	FALSE	—
3.1	—	—	—	—
1.2	A	—	—	—
2.2	—	1	TRUE	—
3.2	—	—	—	[1] is 1
1.3	S	—	—	—
2.3	—	6	FALSE	—
3.3	—	—	—	—
1.4	C	—	—	—
2.4	—	6	FALSE	—
3.4	—	—	—	—
1.5	A	—	—	—
2.5	—	1	TRUE	—
3.5	—	—	—	[1] is 2

Notice that when Found is FALSE, Index is Length + 1. Here's the output from the program using our data:

```
Character     Frequency
    A             10
    E              7
    I              5
    O              3
    U             10
```

Using Indexes with Meaning

An index can have meaning beyond simple position: It can have semantic content. For example, suppose the employees in a company are assigned identification numbers ranging from 100 to 500. If we define a one-dimensional ARRAY variable of hourly pay rates,

```
TYPE
   PayRateType = ARRAY[100..500] OF REAL;

VAR
   HourlyRate : PayRateType;
```

then each employee's identification number would be the index into the employee's hourly rate.

Program CharacterCount is the implementation of an algorithm that both uses parallel arrays and parallels the way we would do the problem by hand. There is nothing wrong with this solution except that we are not taking advantage of all the information we have. Let's change the problem statement slightly and approach the solution from another angle, this time keeping in mind the features of Pascal.

SAMPLE PROBLEM

A	⧣⧣
B	//
⋮	
Z	/
a	⧣ /
b	///
⋮	
3	//
1	///
⋮	
9	//

Pascal was designed to take full advantage of the concepts of structured programming.

Problem: Count the frequency of occurrence of all the printable characters in a sample of ASCII text.

Discussion: Pascal already has a built-in list of all the characters it recognizes. They are the values in type CHAR. Pascal also allows us to use any ordinal type as an index type. So instead of searching a list of characters for a value and counting the frequency in a parallel array, let's let Pascal do all that for us. How? By using the characters themselves as the indexes into the frequency list.

We have simplified the problem somewhat by stating that the file is ASCII. We assume that the machine on which the program is being written is an ASCII machine. So we know that the character set contains 256 characters. There are nonprinting control characters in ASCII, but the problem statement says to ignore them. In ASCII the printing characters are contiguous; the first is the blank (' ') and the last is the tilde (~). We set these as named constants First and Last.

Input: File Data

Output: Each printable character in the character set followed by the number of times it occurs in File Data.

Data Structures: An ARRAY variable of frequencies (Frequencies) indexed by the subrange First . . Last

MAIN MODULE   Level 0

```
Zero Frequencies
WHILE NOT EOF(Data) DO
    Read Character
    Increment Frequencies[Character]
Print characters and Frequencies
```

ZERO FREQUENCIES

```
FOR Index from First to Last DO
    Frequencies[Index] ← 0
```

PRINT CHARACTERS AND FREQUENCIES

```
FOR Index from First TO Last DO
    Write Index 'OCCURRED' Frequencies[Index] ' TIMES'
```

Module Design Chart:

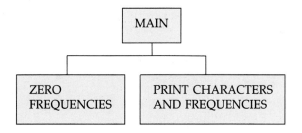

SAMPLE PROBLEM, CONTINUED

Interface Design Chart:

Program Constants and Variables

Identifiers	Type	Role
First*	CHAR	First printable character (blank)
Last*	CHAR	Last printable character (tilde)
Frequencies	ARRAY	Frequency counts of printable characters
Data	TEXT	File of characters to count
Character	CHAR	Variable for reading characters

Subprograms

Identifiers	Needs	Returns
ZeroFrequencies	Nothing	Frequencies
PrintResults	Frequencies	Nothing

*The constants First and Last are accessed globally.

```
PROGRAM CountAll(OUTPUT, Data);
(* The frequencies of all the printable *)
(* characters on File Data are printed. *)

CONST
  First = ' ';
  Last  = '~';

TYPE
  IndexRange = First..Last;
  ListOfCounts = ARRAY[IndexRange] OF INTEGER;

VAR
  Frequencies : ListOfCounts;
  Data : TEXT;
  Character : CHAR;    (* for reading input *)

(************************************************************)

PROCEDURE ZeroFrequencies(VAR Frequencies : ListOfCounts);
(* All the frequencies are set to zero. *)

VAR
  Index : IndexRange;
```

```
BEGIN    (* ZeroFrequencies *)
  FOR Index := First TO Last DO
    Frequencies[Index] := 0
END;      (* ZeroFrequencies *)


(*************************************************************)


PROCEDURE PrintResults(Frequencies : ListOfCounts);
(* Characters and Frequencies are printed. *)

VAR
  Index : IndexRange;

BEGIN    (* PrintResults *)
  WRITELN('Character   Frequency');
  FOR Index := First TO Last DO
    WRITELN(Index, ' OCCURRED', Frequencies[Index]:5, ' TIMES')
END;      (* PrintResults *)


(*************************************************************)


BEGIN    (* CountAll *)
  RESET(Data);
  ZeroFrequencies(Frequencies);
  WHILE NOT EOF(Data) DO
    BEGIN
      READ(Data, Character);
      Frequencies[Character] := Frequencies[Character] + 1;
    END;
  PrintResults(Frequencies)
END.      (* CountAll *)
```

The structured ARRAY type and variable look like this:

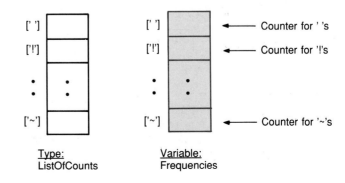

Type:
ListOfCounts

Variable:
Frequencies

SAMPLE PROBLEM, CONTINUED

By taking advantage of the fact that an index can have meaning in itself, we have simplified this program considerably. (Exercise 6 at the end of this chapter asks you to modify Program CountAll to produce the same output as Program CharacterCount.)

Using the same input file as the previous problem,

PASCAL IS A STRUCTURED LANGUAGE,
AS STRUCTURED AS CAN BE.
I USED IT TO STRUCTURE MY PROGRAM,
AND NOW IT'S STRUCTURING ME!

the output from Program CountAll is

```
A OCCURRED      10 TIMES
B OCCURRED       1 TIMES
C OCCURRED       6 TIMES
D OCCURRED       4 TIMES
E OCCURRED       7 TIMES
G OCCURRED       4 TIMES
I OCCURRED       5 TIMES
L OCCURRED       2 TIMES
M OCCURRED       3 TIMES
N OCCURRED       5 TIMES
O OCCURRED       3 TIMES
P OCCURRED       2 TIMES
R OCCURRED      10 TIMES
S OCCURRED      10 TIMES
T OCCURRED      11 TIMES
U OCCURRED      10 TIMES
W OCCURRED       1 TIMES
Y OCCURRED       1 TIMES
  OCCURRED      22 TIMES
, OCCURRED       2 TIMES
. OCCURRED       1 TIMES
' OCCURRED       1 TIMES
! OCCURRED       1 TIMES
```

Notice that <eoln> is read as a blank.

Sorting

Sorting means taking a list of values and rearranging them so that they are in order. There are many algorithms for rearranging values. We look at one here and at several others in later chapters. Sorting is the most common of all processing tasks.

SAMPLE PROBLEM

Problem: Read a file of test grades (one per line on File Numbers) and write them back out on the same file in ascending order. Because there was a question where each part was worth half a point, the test grades are real numbers.

Discussion: Arranging values in order is known as sorting. In Chapter 8 we discussed the order inherent in any scalar type. This order allows us to compare and sort, in ascending or descending order, values of any scalar type. There are many sorting algorithms available. One of the simplest is the *insertion sort*. As data is read in, it is inserted in its correct place in the data structure.

Suppose you have a stack of tests and want to put them in order with the highest grade on the bottom. One way to do this is to take the first test off the stack. It's the only one, so it's in order. Then take the next test off the stack. If the grade is higher than the one you're holding, put the second one behind the first. If it's lower than the first test grade, make the new test the first and move the other one to the second slot.

The process continues. You find the place where each new test should be inserted by looking at the test scores from the top of the stack. When you find a score that is higher than the one you're inserting, you have found where it should go, right before the one that's higher.

Remember, when you insert a test between two other tests, the ones to the rear move down one position in the stack of sorted tests.

You can program this algorithm very easily. The original stack of test grades is the file of grades. The stack that you're arranging one by one is a list implemented in an ARRAY variable. Whenever you insert a score between two other scores, all the values in the list that are greater than or equal to the one being inserted are moved down one position in the ARRAY variable. Then the new value (test score) is inserted in its proper place. The length of the list increases by 1 each time a new score is inserted.

Input: A file of real numbers (File Numbers), one per line

Output: The same numbers written on File Numbers in ascending order

Data Structure: An ARRAY variable in which to store the numbers in order as they are read

Assumption: The maximum number of tests is 150.

SAMPLE PROBLEM, CONTINUED

MAIN MODULE   Level 0

```
Length ← 0
WHILE NOT EOF(Numbers) DO
   Readln Score
   Insert in ListOfScores
REWRITE(Numbers)
Print list of scores
```

INSERT   Level 1

```
Find Place
Shift down
ListOfScores[Place] ← Score
Length ← Length + 1
```

PRINT LIST OF SCORES

We can use the module for Procedure PrintList from Program DesignCount.

FIND PLACE   Level 2

```
PlaceFound ← FALSE
Place ← 0
WHILE (Place < Length) AND NOT PlaceFound DO
   Place ← Place + 1
   IF Score < ListOfScores[Place]
       THEN
           PlaceFound ← TRUE
```

SHIFT DOWN

```
FOR Index from Length DOWNTO Place DO
   ListOfScores[Index + 1] ← ListOfScores[Index]
```

Module Design Chart:

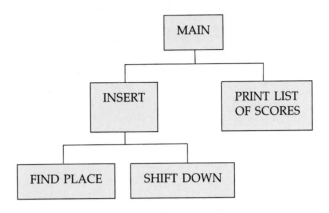

Interface Design Chart:

Program Variables

Identifiers	Type	Role
ListOfScores	ARRAY	List of sorted scores
Score	REAL	A score
Length	INTEGER	Length of list
Numbers	TEXT	File of scores to be sorted

Subprograms

Identifiers	Needs	Returns
Insert	Score	ListOfScores, Length
FindPlace	ListOfScores, Length, Score	Place
ShiftDown	Place	ListOfScores
PrintList	Numbers, ListOfScores, Length	Nothing

FindPlace and ShiftDown have no meaning outside of Insert. For a change, we'll embed them within Insert. FindPlace and ShiftDown access their parameters nonlocally within Insert. Because the task of inserting a value into an ordered list is so common, we code Insert with the generic identifiers List, Length, and Item.

SAMPLE PROBLEM, CONTINUED

```
PROGRAM SortScores(Numbers, OUTPUT);
(* File Numbers is sorted and rewritten. *)

CONST
  MaxTests = 150;

TYPE
  IndexRange = 1..MaxTests;
  IndexType = 0..MaxTests;
  ItemType = REAL;
  ListType = ARRAY[IndexRange] OF ItemType;

VAR
  ListOfScores : ListType;
  Score : ItemType;
  Length : IndexType;
  Numbers : TEXT;

(*************************************************************)

PROCEDURE Insert(VAR List : ListType;
                 VAR Length : IndexType;
                     Item : ItemType);
(* Item is inserted into its proper place in List. *)
(* Assumption:  Order is ascending.                *)

VAR
  Place : IndexType;
  (* --------------------------- *)

  PROCEDURE FindPlace;
  (* Find where Item belongs in List. *)

  VAR
    PlaceFound : BOOLEAN;

  BEGIN   (* FindPlace *)
    PlaceFound := FALSE;
    Place := 0;
    WHILE (Place < Length) AND NOT PlaceFound DO
      BEGIN
        Place <- Place + 1;
        IF Item < List[Place]
            THEN
              PlaceFound := TRUE
      END;     (* FindPlace *)

  (* --------------------------- *)
```

```
   PROCEDURE ShiftDown;
   (* Shift the items from Place to Length down one. *)

   VAR
      Index : IndexRange;

   BEGIN    (* ShiftDown *)
      FOR Index := Length DOWNTO Place DO
         List[Index + 1] := List[Index]
   END;     (* ShiftDown *)

   (* ------------------------- *)

BEGIN    (* Insert *)
   FindPlace;
   ShiftDown;
   List[Place] := Item;
   Length := Length + 1
END;     (* Insert *)

(*************************************************************)

PROCEDURE PrintList(VAR Data : TEXT; List : ListType;
                         Length : IndexType);
(* Values in Data[1] to Data[Length] are printed. *)

VAR
   Counter : IndexType;     (* loop control variable *)

BEGIN    (* PrintList *)
   FOR Counter := 1 TO Length DO
      WRITELN(Data, List[Counter])
END;     (* PrintList *)

(*************************************************************)

BEGIN    (* SortScores *)
   Length := 0;
   RESET(Numbers);
   WHILE NOT EOF(Numbers) DO
      BEGIN
         READLN(Numbers, Score);
         Insert(ListOfScores, Length, Score)
      END;
   REWRITE(Numbers);
   PrintList(Numbers, ListOfScores, Length)
END.     (* SortScores *)
```

Merging

Taking two arrays where the values are ordered in some fashion and producing a third array (or a listing) that contains the elements of both arrays ordered in the same fashion is called *merging*.

SAMPLE PROBLEM

Problem: Instead of a full-fledged problem, let's look at this algorithm within the context of a subproblem. Suppose we have two ARRAY variables each containing scalar values sorted in ascending order. These two arrays need to be merged onto one output file, DataOut.

The interface for our subproblem is specified in this procedure heading:

```
PROCEDURE Merge(VAR DataOut : TEXT;
                VAR List1, List2 : ListType;
                Length1, Length2 : IndexType);
(* Merge merges the scalar values in ARRAY variables List1   *)
(* (of Length1) and List2 (of Length2) onto File DataOut.    *)
(* Duplicates appear only once on File DataOut.              *)
(* Assumption:  List1 and List2 are in ascending order.     *)
```

Merging is the process of combining two ordered lists into one list, maintaining the order. What we do with duplicates depends on the application. In this case, a duplicate appears only once on the merged list.

Discussion: How would you tackle this process if you had two lists of numbers and had to do it by hand? You would probably look at the top item on each list and compare them. If they are the same, you would write the value in a new list and cross off each value from the original lists. If they are not the same, you would write the smaller value on the new list and cross it off the list it was on.

You would repeat this process until you have crossed off all the values on one list, then you would move the rest of the other list to the new one. Of course the lists may both end at the same time with a duplicate value.

As so often is the case, we can use this by-hand algorithm directly. Each list is stored in an ARRAY variable. Each list has an index variable that indicates the top of the list (the next value on the list to be examined). Crossing off a value is logically equivalent to incrementing an index.

Input: As specified on the formal parameter list

Output: As specified on the formal parameter list

Data Structures: List1 and List2, ordered ARRAY variables of some ordinal type

MERGE   Level 0

```
Index1 ← 1
Index2 ← 1
WHILE (Index1 <= Length1) AND (Index2 <= Length2) DO
   Which has smaller value
   CASE Smaller OF
     ListOne : Process List1
     ListTwo : Process List2
     Equal : Process List1
             Adjust List2
Write leftovers
```

WHICH HAS SMALLER VALUE   Level 1

```
IF List1[Index] < List2[Index2]
     THEN
         Smaller ← ListOne
ELSE IF List2[Index2] < List1[Index1]
     THEN
         Smaller ← ListTwo
ELSE
         Smaller ← Equal
```

PROCESS LIST1 AND PROCESS LIST2

We do not need two separate modules. We just make the list and the associated index parameters to module PROCESS LIST.

```
Write DataOut List[Index]
Index ← Index + 1
```

ADJUST LIST2

```
Index2 ← Index2 + 1
```

SAMPLE PROBLEM, CONTINUED

WRITE LEFTOVERS

```
IF Index1 <= Length1
    THEN
        Write rest of List1
ELSE IF Index2 <= Length2
    THEN
        Write rest of List2
```

WRITE REST OF LIST1 AND WRITE REST OF LIST2   Level 2

Again, we can use a module WRITE REST OF LIST and pass the appropriate
List, Length, and Index as parameters.

```
FOR Count from Index TO Length DO
    Write DataOut List[Count]
```

Module Design Chart:

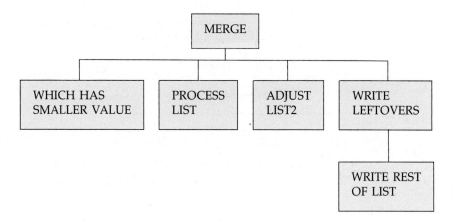

Module ADJUST LIST2 is only one line and should be coded in-line. Module WHICH HAS SMALLER VALUE should be coded as Function Smaller of a
user-defined type made up of constants ListOne, ListTwo, and Equal.

All of the parameters for the subprograms are either formal parameters of
Procedure Merge or local variables of Procedure Merge. Function Smaller and
Procedure WriteLeftOvers access their parameters nonlocally within Proce-
dure Merge.

Interface Design Chart:

Procedure Parameters and Variables

Identifiers	Type	Role
DataOut	TEXT	File on which List1 and List2 are merged
List1	ARRAY	List of scalar items in ascending order
List2	ARRAY	List of scalar items in ascending order
Length1	INTEGER	Length of List1
Length2	INTEGER	Length of List2
Index1	INTEGER	Loop counter for List1
Index2	INTEGER	Loop counter for List2

Subprograms

Identifiers	Needs	Returns
Smaller	List1, List2, Index1, Index2	ListOne, ListTwo, or Equal
ProcessList	List, Index	Nothing
WriteLeftOvers	List, Index, Length	Nothing
WriteRestOfList	List, Index, Length	Nothing

```
PROCEDURE Merge(VAR DataOut : TEXT;
                VAR List1, List2 : ListType;
                Length1, Length2 : IndexType);
(* Merge merges the scalar values in ARRAY variables List1  *)
(* (of Length1) and List2 (of Length2) onto File DataOut.   *)
(* Duplicates appear only once on File DataOut.             *)
(* Assumption:  List1 and List2 are in ascending order.     *)

TYPE
  SmallerType = (ListOne, ListTwo, Equal);

VAR
  Index1, Index2 : IndexType;   (* indexes for List1 and List2 *)

(* -------------------------------------------------------- *)
```

SAMPLE PROBLEM, CONTINUED

```
FUNCTION Smaller : SmallerType;
(* Determines the relationship of two scalar values. *)

BEGIN   (* Smaller *)
  IF List1[Index1] < List2[Index2]
    THEN
      Smaller := ListOne
  ELSE IF List2[Index2] < List1[Index1]
    THEN
      Smaller := ListTwo
  ELSE
    Smaller := Equal
END;    (* Smaller *)

(* ------------------------------------------------------------ *)

PROCEDURE ProcessList(VAR List : ListType;
                      VAR Index : IndexType);
(* Writes out List[Index] and increments Index. *)

BEGIN   (* ProcessList *)
  WRITELN(DataOut, List[Index]);
    Index := Index + 1
END;    (* ProcessList *)

(* ------------------------------------------------------------ *)

PROCEDURE WriteLeftOvers;
(* Any items remaining in a list are written out. *)

  (* ++++++++++++++++++++++++++++++++++++++++++++++++++++++ *)

  PROCEDURE WriteRestOfList(VAR List : ListType;
                           Index, Length: IndexType);
  (* List[Index] to List[Length] are written on File DataOut. *)

  VAR
    Counter : IndexType;

  BEGIN   (* WriteRestOfList *)
    FOR Counter := Index TO Length DO
      WRITELN(DataOut, List[Counter])
  END;    (* WriteRestOfList *)

  (* ++++++++++++++++++++++++++++++++++++++++++++++++++++++ *)
```

```
BEGIN   (* WriteLeftOvers *)
  IF Index1 <= Length1
     THEN
        WriteRestOfList(List1, Index1, Length1)
  ELSE IF Index2 <= Length2
     THEN
        WriteRestOfList(List2, Index2, Length2)
END;    (* WriteLeftOvers *)

(* ----------------------------------------------------- *)

BEGIN   (* Merge *)
  REWRITE(DataOut);
  Index1 := 1;
  Index2 := 1;
  WHILE (Index1 <= Length1) AND (Index2 <= Length2) DO
    BEGIN
      CASE Smaller OF
        ListOne : ProcessList(List1, Index1);
        ListTwo : ProcessList(List2, Index2);
        Equal : BEGIN
                  ProcessList(List1, Index1);
                  Index2 := Index2 + 1
                END
      END;   (* CASE *)
  WriteLeftOvers
END;      (* Merge *)
```

Strings: Packed Array of Char

A **packed array** is an array that takes up as little space in memory as possible by packing as many components as possible into each location in memory. A PACKED ARRAY OF CHAR is a special ARRAY type called a **string.** For example,

```
TYPE
   StringType = PACKED ARRAY[1..10] OF CHAR;

VAR
   Word : StringType;
```

defines Word as a string variable with ten character positions. String variables are special one-dimensional ARRAY variables with two very useful properties: They can be compared with relational operators, and they do not have to be printed character by character. Unfortunately, they must be read character by character.

String

A collection of characters that is interpreted as a single data item; a PACKED ARRAY OF CHAR.

Because a string variable is an ARRAY variable, its length is fixed by its type definition. You cannot store more characters in a string than its length allows. If the number of characters to be stored is shorter than the length of the string variable, you may have to pad the remaining character positions with blanks.

Compatible string variables and constants can be assigned to one another and can be compared using the relational operators. Strings are ordered by the order of the character set. The characters of the two strings are compared character by character from left to right. The first unequal pair of characters determines the order.

Compatible string variables and constants are strings that have the same type identifier or type definition. The type of a string constant is inherent in its definition. For example,

```
CONST
   AllBlanks = '
```

defines a type that is a PACKED ARRAY[1..10] OF CHAR.

```
Wordl = 'Cat';
```

defines a type which is a PACKED ARRAY[1..3] OF CHAR. We could not assign Word1 to a string variable of type StringType; one is ten characters long, the other is three characters long. They are not compatible.

Let's write a code fragment that reads characters from File Data and stores them in Word, a string variable of length 10, until either a blank is found or we have stored ten characters:

```
Word := AllBlanks;            ←   The string constant can be
Index := 0;                        stored directly to set
READ(Data, Character);             Word to all blanks.

WHILE (Character <> ' ') AND (Index < 10) DO
   BEGIN
      Index := Index + 1;
      Word[Index] := Character;   ←   Each character position
      READ(Data, Character)            is accessed separately.
   END;
WRITELN('Word is ', Word);     ←   The string is written
                                   as a whole.
```

The 4-Cs Corner
Completeness and Conciseness

In the problems throughout this chapter, we have applied common algorithms to lists of values stored in a one-dimensional ARRAY variable. We have

- created arrays, reading values from a file and storing them as a list in a one-dimensional ARRAY variable.
- printed the values in a list.
- searched for a specific value in a list.
- sorted the items in a list, arranging them in order.
- merged two ordered lists into one ordered list.

We have applied these algorithms to lists of scalar items. The lists have been of type ListType, the Items have been of type ItemType, and the indexes have been of type IndexType. Because of the special properties of strings, each of these algorithms can be applied to lists of strings.

Now, let's incorporate the code fragment that reads strings into a general procedure, GetData. We assume the following definitions are in the main program:

```
CONST
  WordSize = 10;
  AllBlanks = '            (* WordSize blanks *)
  Blank = ' ';               (* one blank        *)

TYPE
  ItemType = PACKED ARRAY[1..WordSize] OF CHAR;
```

Here is the procedure:

```
PROCEDURE GetData(VAR Data : TEXT; VAR Word : ItemType);
(* Leading blanks are skipped.                     *)
(* Characters are read into Word until a blank      *)
(* is encountered or WordSize characters have       *)
(* been read.  Word is padded with blanks.          *)
(* File Data is left positioned after the word.     *)
(* ASSUMPTION : <eof> is NOT TRUE on entry.         *)

VAR
  Index : 0..WordSize;      (* index into Word *)
  Character : CHAR;

(***************************************************************)
```

```
      PROCEDURE SkipBlanks(VAR DataFile : TEXT; VAR Character : CHAR);
      (*  Blanks are skipped.  Character is the first nonblank. *)

      BEGIN    (* SkipBlanks *)
        REPEAT
          READ(DataFile, Character)
        UNTIL (Character <> Blank) OR EOF(DataFile)
      END;     (* SkipBlanks *)
   (************************************************************)

BEGIN    (* GetData *)
  Word := AllBlanks;
  Index := 0;
  SkipBlanks(Data, Character);
  IF NOT EOF(Data)
     THEN
       WHILE (Character <> ' ') AND (Index < WordSize) DO
         BEGIN
           Index := Index + 1;
           Word[Index] := Character;
           READ(Data, Character)
         END;
   (* Read past any nonblank characters in case of a long word. *)
   WHILE Character <> ' ' DO
     READ(Data, Character)
END;     (* GetData *)
```

Using this procedure, we could convert Program DesignCount to count the designs where the design numbers contain special characters; that is, the designs can be considered strings instead of numbers. The CONST and TYPE definitions would have to be changed, and the READLN would have to be replaced with a call to Procedure GetData.

We can convert Program CharacterCount in the same way to count the occurrence of certain words in a file of text. Program CountAll *cannot* be converted to use strings. Strings cannot be used as an index type. Index types must be ordinal values. Program SortScores can be converted to sort words, and Procedure Merge can be converted to merge two lists of words.

Correctness

Let's go back over each of the five problems we have programmed in this chapter, look at difficulties that might arise, and determine what would constitute adequate testing. Although we discuss each in the context of the original data type, the same discussion would apply to strings.

Program DesignCount

In the suit design problem, we created a list of all the suit designs ordered over a week. The algorithm was to search the list for each design number read. If the design number was not there, it was added at the end of the list.

The design number (called Design in the program) is the only input. There are no constraints on the size of the number. A logical assumption might be that a design number should be positive. Before putting in a test for this on the data, however, you should go back to the customer for whom you are writing the program and make sure. If design numbers should be positive, find out what the customer wants to do in the case of bad data.

In Program DesignCount, we set MaxLength, the maximum number of designs possible, to 1,000. Because MaxLength is used to set the size of the array DesignList, which holds the designs ordered, it should be equal to the total number of designs possible. Although it is unlikely that all of the designs would be ordered during a week, it is possible. If you set the size to 250 and 251 designs are ordered, the attempt to store the 251st design would cause the run-time error SUBSCRIPT OUT OF RANGE.

What about testing the program? How do you know how many times the program must be run with different data values? You begin by listing all the possible cases, including data sets that might cause trouble:

- There were no orders.
- Every design was ordered.
- There were no duplicate designs ordered.
- Only one design was ordered many times.
- Some designs were ordered only once, some many times, and some not at all.

Here, then, you would need to run five data sets, one to test each of these cases.

Program CharacterCount

Our second problem was to count the frequency of occurrence of certain characters in a sample of text. To do this, we defined parallel arrays: ListOfCharacters holds the characters to be counted, and Frequencies holds the corresponding frequency counts. The characters to be counted come from the standard input device, and the text comes from File Data. The only possible error in the data would be a character that your particular machine doesn't recognize, which would result in a run-time error ILLEGAL CHARACTER IN TEXT. There is no way to test for this, because the error occurs when you are trying to read a character.

There is data coming in from the standard input device and File Data. Here, then, are the combinations that must be tested:

- No characters to be counted
- No text to count
- Input data in both files
- All the characters to be counted are on the file at least once.
- Some of the characters to be counted are on the file once, some are not on the file at all, and some are on the file more than once.

Program CountAll

This problem expanded our count of characters to every printable character in the ASCII character set. Instead of using an array to hold the characters and an array to hold the frequencies, we made the characters themselves the index into the frequency array.

To adequately test this program, we should create a data file that contains all of the printable ASCII characters at least once and some of the characters more than once. There should also be some nonprintable characters on the file.

A test with nonprintable characters (such as page eject) would determine that there is an error in Program CountAll. Did you notice it? The statement

```
Frequencies[Character] := Frequencies[Character] + 1;
```

where Character is a nonprintable character causes an OUT-OF-RANGE error. This statement should be embedded within the following test:

```
IF (Character >= First) AND (Character <= Last)
   THEN ..
```

Program SortScores

Program SortScores reads REAL values from File Numbers and places them in order in a list of ordered scores. The result is written back onto File Numbers. What are the possible cases that must be tested?

- The file is empty.
- The file has exactly one value.
- The file has duplicates.
- The file has no duplicates.
- The lowest (and highest) value is the first value on the file, the last value on the file, or somewhere in the middle.

Procedure Merge

The last problem was different because it called for a procedure, not a complete program. In order to test this procedure, we have to write a **driver program**, a program whose only purpose is to test a subprogram. The driver program sets up the actual parameters and calls the procedure or function.

> **Driver Program**
> A program that is designed to test a subprogram.

In this case, the subprogram must be called with the following conditions:

- List1 is empty and List2 is not.
- List2 is empty and List1 is not.
- Both are empty.
- Neither is empty.

In addition, there are other data-dependent conditions that should be tested:

- List1 has the smallest value.
- List2 has the smallest value.
- The first value in both lists is the same.
- The last value in both lists is the same.

Correctness Hints

1. If your program seems to execute but there is no output, check your data file. Most programs are written assuming that there is some data in the input file. If an EOF is encountered immediately, there is no data. What happens? If the data is to go into an array with a counter keeping track of the length of the array, that length will be zero. Most likely all subsequent processing will be skipped. You can test for this with

```
IF EOF(file)
   THEN write error message
   ELSE continue processing
```

2. Plan your testing in advance. While you're doing your top-down design, make notes to yourself about where you might want to put in debug WRITE statements for testing purposes.
3. Be sure your index is initialized and incremented correctly. Look at what happens in this simple reading loop when the incrementation is incorrect.

```
VAR
   List : ARRAY[1..10] OF INTEGER;

     .
     .
     .
   Index := 0;
   WHILE NOT EOF DO
     BEGIN
       READLN (List[Index]);
       Index := Index + 1
     END;
```

The first time the loop is executed, a SUBSCRIPT-OUT-OF-RANGE error occurs. If you correct the problem by initializing Index to 1, your count is off by 1. That is, Index points not to the last value stored but to that location plus 1. How do we fix this? Initialize the Index to zero and increment Index before the READ. Now it comes out right.

4. If you run out of memory space, check your ARRAY parameters. Using an

ARRAY variable as a VAR parameter uses the array structure already in memory. Using an ARRAY variable as a value parameter creates another copy of the array structure, thus using more memory (possibly too much). Notice that the array parameters for Procedure Merge are VAR parameters, even though the values in the lists are not changed.

5. Make sure your arrays are large enough for your processing. Trying to read and store more data than your array can hold causes a subscript range error. Stop reading when the limit of your array is reached and print out an appropriate message.

Declare the largest array you might need, and use a variable to keep track of the length of the subarray you actually use.

Summary

We designed Chapter 9 to make you feel more comfortable using one-dimensional ARRAY variables. Each of the five sample problems uses one-dimensional ARRAY variables in different ways. Although these problems have been couched in concrete terms for teaching purposes, the basic techniques will come up again and again in your programming career.

Much of the art of programming is being able to recognize general processes in the description of a specific problem. The problems in this chapter give you a set of routines to use in future problems.

Our discussion of arrays continues in Chapter 10, where we look at two-dimensional and multidimensional arrays. If you thoroughly understand how to use one-dimensional arrays, these extensions will seem both easy to use and very logical.

EXERCISES

1. Write a function, Index, that searches INTEGER array List for INTEGER value Value. The place in the array where Value is found is returned. There are Length values in List. If Value is not in the array, set Index to zero.

2. Write a procedure, Merge, that merges two ordered files, One and Two, into ordered array Combination. Remove duplicates. Combination is the only array you should use. The data in One and Two should be processed as it's read. One and Two are input parameters, and Combination and Length (number of elements in Combination) are output parameters. Assume the data is of type INTEGER.

3. Design a data structure for each of the following problems.
   a. A record store sells classical records (A), jazz records (B), rock records (C), and others (D). Sales receipts are kept in the following format:

      Code (A, B, C, or D)
      Amount (amount of sale)

      The owner of the store wants to total the amount of sales for each record category.
   b. A payroll master file is made up the following data:

ID (five-digit identification number for each employee)
Dependents (number of dependents)
Rate (hourly salary)

A transaction file is made up each month of the following data:

ID (five-digit number)
Hours (number of hours worked)

The payroll file is ordered; the transaction file is not. There are one hundred employees.

4. Describe the algorithms you would use with the data structures in Exercise 3. (Your answers should be like the discussion sections in the chapter. You are not being asked for top-down designs.)

5. Write a procedure, Add, that takes as input two parallel arrays A and B of length N. The procedure should return as output the sum of those elements of B where the corresponding elements of A are greater than 2. For example:

```
A:   0   5   0   3   0   2   5
B:   2   7   4   6   3   8   3
Sum: is 16.
```

6. Change Program CountAll (page 316) so that it produces the same output as Program CharacterCount (page 309).

7. Write a program that reads words from file WordFile (one word per line ended by <eoln>) and writes them back on WordFile in ordered form. Use these type definitions:

```
CONST
   WordSize = 10;
   NumberOfWords = 100;
```

8. Write a BOOLEAN function that returns TRUE if the contents of two packed arrays passed as parameters are equal. Assume this type declaration in the main program:

```
TYPE
   Word = PACKED ARRAY[1..10] OF CHAR;
```

PRETEST

1. Write a function, Found, that searches REAL array List for a REAL value greater than the value Value. If a larger value is found, the function returns TRUE; otherwise it returns FALSE. List is of type ArrayType. The number of elements in List should be a parameter.

2. Write a procedure, Parallel, that takes as input two parallel arrays A and B of length N. The procedure should return as output the product of those elements of B where the corresponding elements of A are negative.

3. Write a program, Merge, that merges two ordered files, Uno and Dos, onto an output file, Tres. Remove duplicates. Do not use arrays. EndData is a flag value that ends each file.

4. Design a data structure for each of the following problems.

a. A library lends books (1), equipment (2), records (3), magazines (4), tapes (5), and videos (6). Daily circulation is recorded in the following format:

> Category (1, 2, 3, 4, 5, or 6)
> Number (count of items loaned in the category)

The librarian wants to total the number of items loaned in each category for the year.

b. A university registrar's master file is made up of the following data:

> ID (four-digit identification number for each student)
> Hours (number of credit hours so far)
> Average (grade-point average so far, REAL)

A semester grades file is made up each semester of the following data for each course taken:

> ID (four-digit number)
> Hours (number of credit hours for the course)
> Grade (grade for the course, REAL)

The master file is ordered; the semester file is not. There are two thousand students.

5. Describe the algorithms you would use with the data structures in Problem 4. (Your answers should be like the discussion sections in the chapter. You are not being asked for top-down designs.)

6. Declare a string variable, Name, consisting of twenty-five characters.

7. Write a procedure that accepts any TEXT file as a parameter, reads a line, and returns the line in a packed array. No line is longer than eighty characters. Pad the array with blanks if the line is shorter than eighty characters. Assume these declarations in the main program:

```
TYPE
    Line = PACKED ARRAY[1..80] OF CHAR;
```

8. Write a BOOLEAN function that returns TRUE if a packed array contains the word *indigenous*. Assume these declarations in the main program:

```
TYPE
    Word = PACKED ARRAY[1..10] OF CHAR;
```

PROGRAMMING ASSIGNMENTS

1. The local bank in Programming Assignment 4 in Chapter 8 (page 297) was so successful with its advertising campaign that the parent bank decided to run a contest and collect data from banks all over the state. However, the bank has decided to add several elements.

Frustration levels have been assigned to wait times as follows:

Wait ≤ (Mean − SD)	→ 'Amazed'
(mean − SD) < Wait ≤ Mean	→ 'Pleased'
Mean < Wait ≤ (Mean + SD)	→ 'Calm'

(Mean + SD) < Wait ≤ (Mean + 2 × SD)   → 'Irritated'
(Mean + 2 × SD) < Wait   → 'Berserk'

where Mean is the mean waiting time, SD is the standard deviation, and Wait is the wait time. You've been asked to calculate frustration levels for each recorded wait.

Input: Same as the earlier assignment, except that the first two digits of the teller ID actually correspond to a bank ID

Output: Same as the earlier assignment, plus
(1) a bar graph (histogram) showing frustration-level distribution
(2) a table sorted by combination ID showing
    (a) ID number
    (b) wait time
    (c) frustration level

The table sorted by ID allows you to examine the performance of particular banks and tellers to see if any of them are particularly better or worse than the others.

2. The company you are working for has just taken over a smaller company. The accounting department would like to have a combined list of employees' social security numbers and department codes for the two groups. It wants the list in ascending order by social security number. Your job is to write a program that prints this list. A fifty-entry file is on Data1; a file of unknown length is on Data2.

    Input:
    (1) Data1: Fifty lines (in ascending order by social security number): social security number (nine characters) and department code (six characters) with a blank between, one pair per line.
    (2) Data2: An unspecified number of lines (in ascending order by social security number): social security number and department code, one pair per line. This is the current file of the larger firm.

    Output: An ordered list of social security numbers and department codes, one pair per line

    Note: You are not required to sort this information. The two lists are already sorted. You're required to merge them.

3. Your history professor has so many students in her class that she has trouble knowing how well the class is doing on exams. She's found out that you're a computer whiz and has asked you to write a program to do some simple statistical analyses on exam scores. In return, she will not flunk you even though you flashed on the first quiz. You, of course, cheerfully agree. Write and test a computer program that performs the following steps:

    (1) Reads the test grades from a data file.
    (2) Calculates the class mean, standard deviation, and percentage of test scores falling in ranges < 10, 10–19, 20–29, 30–39, . . . 80–89, and ≥ 90.
    (3) Prints a single-page summary showing the mean and standard deviation and a histogram of test score distribution. This page should be formatted so that it can be torn off as a complete one-page report.

    Input: The data lines are as follows:
    (1) The first line contains the number of exams to be analyzed (0 . . 100) and an alphanumeric title for the report.

(2) The remaining lines have ten test scores on each line until the last, which has one to ten scores. The scores are all integers.

Output:

(1) Print the input data as it is read.

(2) Print an analysis report, beginning on a new page. Your report should consist of the title read from data, the number of scores, mean and standard deviation (labeled), and a histogram showing the percentage distribution of scores.

4. A small postal system ships packages within your state. Parcels are subject to the following constraints:

- A weight limit of 50 pounds.
- No more than 3 feet in length, width, or depth, with the combined length and girth not to exceed 6 feet. The girth of a package is the circumference of the package around its two smallest sides. The formula is

$$\text{Girth} = 2 \times (\text{Side1} + \text{Side2} + \text{Side3} - \text{LargestSide})$$

where LargestSide is the largest of the three parcel dimensions, Side1, Side2, and Side3.

Your program should process a transaction file containing one entry for each box mailed during the week. Each entry contains a transaction number, followed by the weight of the box, followed by its dimensions (in no particular order). The program should print the transaction number, weight, and postal charge for all accepted packages, and the transaction number and weight for all rejected packages. At the end of the report, print the number of packages processed and the number rejected.

Input:

(1) *Parcel post table:* Weight and cost (show twenty-five values). This table should be sorted in two one-dimensional arrays. The postal cost of each parcel then can be determined by searching the weight array and using the corresponding element in the cost array. If a package weight falls between two weight categories in the table, the program should use the cost for the higher weight.

(2) *Transaction file:* Transaction number, weight, and three dimensions for an arbitrary number of transactions. Assume that all weights are whole numbers and that all dimensions are given to the nearest inch.

Output:

(1) First line: Appropriate headings

(2) Next N records: Transaction number, whether accepted or rejected, weight, and cost

(3) Last line: Number of packages processed and number of packages rejected

5. You work for a local business that has two stores in your town. Both stores maintain inventories of the products sold. A list of the total inventory for both stores is printed weekly by your department and sent to the general manager. Your program must take a list supplied by each store and print a unique list of the total inventory.

Input: Each store list contains the product ID, the number of items currently in the store, and the cost per item (a real number).

Note: The ID numbers on each list are sorted in ascending order. ID numbers do not necessarily appear on both lists.

Output: A labeled report containing the following information:
(1) Item ID, total items, cost per item, and the value of the total items
(2) A final line that gives the total value of the combined inventory

6. The students in a particular high school class have their names and school identification numbers recorded in a file. For example:

DALE   14
BROWN 23

(*Note:* No one in the school is allowed to have a name longer than ten characters.) The file is arranged alphabetically. Another file contains the names of new students for the same class; these names are also arranged alphabetically. Your program should read the two files and print all the names alphabetically along with each student's ID number. The smaller file (new students) has no more than fifty entries. *Note:* Your program should read the smaller file first and store its names in an array. Then the alphabetized list should be printed at the same time the larger file is read. (Why is it better to read the smaller file first? What is the advantage of printing the list while the second file is being read, instead of waiting until both files are read?)

10 Multidimensional Arrays

In Chapter 8 we introduced the structured data type ARRAY, the structure used to represent items in a list. In Chapter 9 we looked at five problems that dealt with manipulating items in a list and at the string data type (PACKED ARRAY OF CHAR), which allows us to compare items of compatible string types.

In this chapter we extend the concept of an array from one dimension to two or more dimensions; that is, we define a group of items and access each by its position on two or more dimensions. These structured data types—two-dimensional and multidimensional arrays—are used to represent data in table form.

Data Structures

Let's review the basic elements involved in programming:

- Problem solving and algorithm design (top-down design methodology)
- Statement structures (sequence, selection, repetition, procedure)
- Data structures (scalar data types, structured data types)
- A programming language (Pascal)

There is much more to programming than simply knowing the syntax and semantics of a programming language. A structured design methodology, proper use of programming language structures, and the choice of an appropriate structure in which to store data are all important parts of the process.

The structured data type we have been discussing is the one-dimensional array. This and other data structures play an important role in the design process. How we structure our data affects the algorithms we use to process that data. Our choice of a data structure also has an impact on the performance (efficiency) of our programs. We talk about the role of data structures in the design process later in this chapter.

Two-Dimensional Arrays

A **two-dimensional array** is a data type structured in two dimensions, in which each component (or element) is accessed by its position within the two dimensions. The component type of a two-dimensional array can be any built-in or user-defined data type. The index type of either dimension can be any simple type (remember, simple types are ordinal types). For obvious reasons the indexes are often called Row and Column.

> **Two-Dimensional Array**
> A structured data type made up of a fixed number of components of the same type structured in two dimensions. Each component is accessed directly by a pair of indexes.

Here's the syntax diagram for a two-dimensional array:

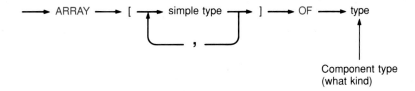

Component type
(what kind)

This is the syntax diagram for a simple type:

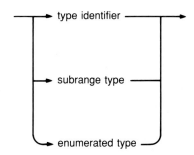

Notice that simple types are ordinal, but not all ordinal types are simple. For example, type INTEGER is ordinal, but it is not simple and cannot be used as an index type. A *subrange* of type INTEGER, however, is a simple type and can be used as an index type.

For example, this declaration section

```
CONST
  RowLimit = 4;
  ColumnLimit = 3;

TYPE
  RowRange = 1..RowLimit;
  ColumnRange = 1..ColumnLimit;
  TableType = ARRAY[RowRange, ColumnRange] OF INTEGER;

VAR
  Table : TableType;
  Row : RowRange;
  Column : ColumnRange;
```

translates into this ARRAY type and variable (page 346):

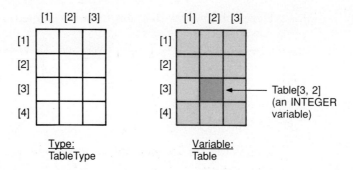

TableType is a pattern for a two-dimensional array with four rows and three columns. A one-dimensional array has one simple type listed in brackets following the word ARRAY. A two-dimensional array has two simple types listed in brackets with a comma between them. The first simple type tells how many rows the array has, and the second simple type tells how many columns the array has. The number of elements in the array is the number of rows times the number of columns.

Table is an ARRAY variable of type TableType. Each individual element is accessed by the name of the array and a pair of indexes or subscripts in brackets. The first index designates row; the second index designates column. There are two acceptable ways to write these indexes:

```
ArrayVariable[Index1, Index2]   ←   Preferred
```

First dimension   Second dimension
(usually called Row)   (usually called Column)

```
ArrayVariable[Index1] [Index2]      (alternate)
```

The first, in one bracket, is preferred.

The following code fragment stores zero in each element in Table:

```
FOR Row := 1 TO RowLimit DO
   FOR Column := 1 TO ColumnLimit DO
      Table[Row, Column] := 0;
```

There is a pattern to the two indexes in these nested FOR loops. Row is set to 1, and Column varies from 1 to 3. Row is incremented to 2, and Column varies from 1 to 3. Row is incremented to 3, and Column varies from 1 to 3. Row is incremented to 4, and Column varies from 1 to 3. The elements are processed (or visited) in this order: Table[1, 1], Table[1, 2], Table[1, 3], Table[2, 1], Table[2, 2], Table[2, 3], Table[3, 1], Table[3, 2], Table[3, 3], Table[4, 1], Table[4, 2] and Table[4, 3]. This is called *row processing*; the table is processed one row at a time.

The index type can be different for each dimension. Just be sure that the value of an expression referencing a dimension is of the index type for that dimension. Let's look at another example:

```
TYPE
   Drinks = (Coke, Pepsi, Sprite);
   SalesArray = ARRAY[1..7, Drinks] OF REAL;

VAR
   Sales : SalesArray;
   Week : INTEGER;
   SaleSum : REAL;
```

Type:
SalesArray

Variable:
Sales

Sales[5, Pepsi]
(a REAL
variable)

The following code fragment sums the sales of Coke for the week:

```
SaleSum := 0.0;
FOR Week := 1 TO 7 DO
   SaleSum := Sales[Week, Coke] + SaleSum;
```

Here's an example where both index types are enumerated types:

```
TYPE
   JobType = (Sales, Clerical, Managerial)
   SexType = (Male, Female);
   EmployeeType = ARRAY[JobType, SexType] OF INTEGER;

VAR
   Employees : EmployeeType;
   Job : JobType;
   Sex : SexType;
```

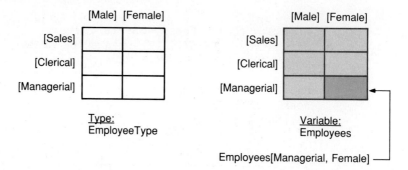

The following code fragment prints whether there are more men or women in each job category.

```
FOR Job := Sales TO Managerial DO
  BEGIN
    IF Employees[Job, Male] > Employees[Job, Female]
        THEN
          WRITE('There are more men in ')
        ELSE
          WRITE('There are more women in ');
    CASE Job OF
        Sales : WRITELN('sales jobs.');
        Clerical : WRITELN('clerical jobs.');
        Managerial : WRITELN('managerial jobs. ')
    END  (* CASE *)
  END;
```

SAMPLE PROBLEM

Problem: A real estate company with offices in Houston, Dallas, Austin, and El Paso is having a sales contest as an incentive for its sales force. The contest will be in effect for the month of February. A prize will be given to the office with the highest sales volume in each of three categories: single-family residential, multifamily residential, and commercial. The office staff in the city with the overall highest volume will get a weekend in Mexico. If you write a program to calculate the winners, you get to go to Mexico with them!

Discussion: The information you need is available on the sales contracts. If you were doing this by hand, you might take a sheet of paper and rule off a table with three rows and four columns. The rows would stand for the three categories, and the columns would stand for the four offices. When you receive a sales contract, you would add the sale to the appropriate place in the table. When the last contract for the month had been processed, the maximum in each row would be the winner in that category. To determine the grand prize winner, you would have to add up each column. The maximum of these totals would be the big winner.

Input: Sales contracts summarized as follows on File Contracts (one contract per line):

Category (A: Single-family, B: Multifamily, C: Commercial)
City Code (1: Houston, 2: Dallas, 3: Austin, 4: El Paso)
Dollar value of sale (REAL)

Output: Echo-print the input.
Print the sales totals by category by city, the winner in each category, and the grand prize winner.

Data Structures: A two-dimensional ARRAY variable (Sales). The first dimension is Category ('A' . . 'C'); the second dimension is City (1 . . 4).
A one-dimensional ARRAY variable for totals for each city (CitySums).

	[1]	[2]	[3]	[4]
['A']				
['B']				
['C']				

<u>Type:</u>
SalesType

	[1]	[2]	[3]	[4]
['A']				
['B']				
['C']				

<u>Variable:</u>
Sales

Legend: Category   City
['A'] Single-family [1] Houston
['B'] Multifamily   [2] Dallas
['C'] Commercial   [3] Austin
                      [4] El Paso

[1]	
[2]	
[3]	
[4]	

<u>Type:</u>
SumsType

[1]	
[2]	
[3]	
[4]	

<u>Variable:</u>
CitySums

SAMPLE PROBLEM, CONTINUED

MAIN MODULE   Level 0

```
Zero Sales
WHILE more Sales DO
    Readln Category, City, Amount
    Tally Sales
Print Sales
Print category winners
Print grand prize winner
```

ZERO SALES   Level 1

```
FOR Category from 'A' to 'C' DO
    FOR City from 1 TO 4 DO
        Sales[Category, City] ← 0.0
```

TALLY SALES

```
Sales[Category, City] ← Amount + Sales[Category, City]
```

PRINT SALES

To print the two-dimensional ARRAY variable Sales, we print each row on a line.

```
FOR Category from 'A' to 'C' DO
    FOR City from 1 TO 4 DO
        Write Sales[Category, City]
    Writeln
```

PRINT CATEGORY WINNERS

To find the winner for each category, we must find the maximum value in each row.

```
FOR Category from 'A' to 'C' DO
    MaxCity ← 1
    FOR City from 2 TO 4 DO
        IF Sales [Category, City] > Sales[Category, MaxCity]
            THEN
                MaxCity ← City
    Write MaxCity ' wins in category ' Category
```

PRINT GRAND PRIZE WINNER

To find the maximum sales volume, we must total each column. One-dimensional ARRAY variable CitySums holds the total for each city—it's a list of the totals for each city.

```
FOR City from 1 to 4 DO
    CitySums[City] ← 0.0
    FOR Category from 'A' to 'C' DO
        CitySums[City] ← Sales[Category, City] + CitySums[City]
Find city with maximum
Write 'City ' MaxCity ' wins the contest!'
```

FIND CITY WITH MAXIMUM   Level 2

To find the city with the highest sales volume, we must look for the maximum value in CitySums.

```
MaxCity ← 1
FOR City from 2 to 4 DO
    IF CitySums[City] > CitySums[MaxCity]
        THEN
            MaxCity ← City
```

Module Design Chart:

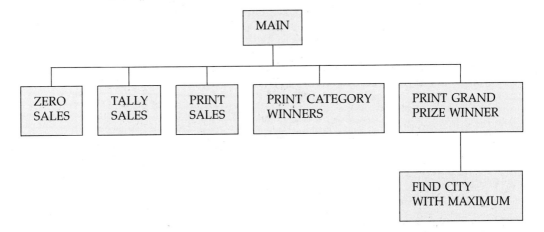

Module TALLY SALES should be coded in-line. The other modules should be coded as procedures.

SAMPLE PROBLEM, CONTINUED

Interface Design Chart:

Program Variables

Identifiers	Type	Role
Amount	REAL	Dollar amount of a sales contract
Sales	ARRAY	Table of sales totals for each city by category
Contracts	TEXT	File containing sales contracts
City	INTEGER	Code for a city
Category	CHAR	Code for a category

Subprograms

Identifiers	Needs	Returns
ZeroSales	Nothing	Sales
PrintSales	Sales	Nothing
PrintWinners	Sales	Nothing
PrintGrandWinner	Sales	Nothing
FindMaxCity	CitySums*	MaxCity

*CitySums is a local variable to Procedure PrintGrandWinner.

```
PROGRAM SalesContest(Contracts, OUTPUT);
(* Category winners and a grand prize winner are *)
(* calculated from sales figures.                *)

TYPE
  CategoryRange = 'A'..'C';
  CityRange = 1..4;
  SalesType = ARRAY[CategoryRange, CityRange] OF REAL;
  SumsType = ARRAY[CityRange] OF REAL;

VAR
  Amount : REAL;
  Sales : SalesType;
  Contracts : TEXT;
  City : CityRange;
  Category : CategoryRange;


(**************************************************************)

PROCEDURE ZeroSales(VAR Sales : SalesType);
(* All the components are set to zero. *)
```

```
VAR
  City : CityRange;
  Category : CategoryRange;

BEGIN    (* ZeroSales *)
  FOR Category := 'A' TO 'C' DO
    FOR City := 1 TO 4 DO
      Sales[Category, City] := 0
END;     (* ZeroSales *)

(*************************************************************)

PROCEDURE PrintSales(Sales : SalesType);
(* Sales figures are printed. *)

VAR
  City : CityRange;
  Category : CategoryRange;

BEGIN    (* PrintSales *)
  FOR Category := 'A' TO 'C' DO
    BEGIN
      FOR City := 1 TO 4 DO
        WRITE(Sales[Category, City]:10:2);
      WRITELN
    END
END;     (* PrintSales *)

(*************************************************************)

PROCEDURE PrintWinners(Sales : SalesType);
(* Winners are printed. *)

VAR
  City, MaxCity : CityRange;
  Category : CategoryRange;

BEGIN    (* PrintWinners *)
  FOR Category := 'A' TO 'C' DO
    BEGIN
      MaxCity := 1;
      FOR City := 2 TO 4 DO
        IF Sales[Category, City] > Sales[Category, MaxCity]
          THEN
            MaxCity := City;
      WRITELN(MaxCity, ' wins in category ', Category)
    END
END;     (* PrintWinners *)

(*************************************************************)
```

SAMPLE PROBLEM, CONTINUED

```
PROCEDURE FindMaxCity(CitySums : SumsType;
                          VAR MaxCity : CityRange);
(* Find index of maximum value in CitySums. *)

VAR
  City : CityRange;

BEGIN   (* FindMaxCity *)
  MaxCity := 1;
  FOR City := 2 TO 4 DO
    IF CitySums[City] > CitySums[MaxCity]
        THEN
          MaxCity := City
END;      (* FindMaxCity *)


(***************************************************************)


PROCEDURE PrintGrandWinner(Sales : SalesType);
(* Sales figures are summed for each city. *)
(* Winning city is calculated and printed. *)

VAR
  City, MaxCity : CityRange;
  Category : CategoryRange;
  CitySums : SumsType;

BEGIN   (* PrintGrandWinner *)
  FOR City := 1 TO 4 DO
    BEGIN
      CitySums[City] := 0.0;
      FOR Category := 'A' TO 'C' DO
        CitySums[City] := Sales[Category, City] + CitySums[City]
    END;
  FindMaxCity(CitySums, MaxCity);
  WRITELN('City ', MaxCity, ' wins the contest!')
END;      (* PrintGrandWinner *)


(***************************************************************)


BEGIN   (* SalesContest *)
  RESET(Contracts);
  ZeroSales(Sales);
  WHILE NOT EOF(Contracts) DO
    BEGIN
      READLN(Contracts, Category, City, Amount);
      Sales[Category, City] := Amount + Sales[Category, City]
    END;
  PrintSales(Sales);
```

```
   PrintWinners(Sales);
   PrintGrandWinner(Sales)
END.    (* SalesContest *)
```

Common Patterns for Tables

In Program SalesContest, Procedures ZeroSales and PrintSales process the ARRAY variable Sales by row; that is, the row index (Category) is the outer loop. Procedure PrintGrandWinner processes the ARRAY variable Sales by column; the column index (City) is the outer loop. These patterns are repeated over and over again whenever your data is represented in a two-dimensional ARRAY variable. The patterns are so common that it makes sense to look at them in general terms, outside of the context of any particular problem.

Let's look at these patterns in abstract terms, using these definitions and declarations:

```
CONST
   RowFirst = (* first value in row range *);
   RowLast = (* last value in row range *);
   ColumnFirst = (* first value in column range *);
   ColumnLast = (* last value in column range *);

TYPE
   RowRange = RowFirst..RowLast;
   ColumnRange = ColumnFirst..ColumnLast;
   ItemType = (* type of components in the structure *);
   TableType = ARRAY[RowRange, ColumnRange] OF ItemType;

VAR
   RowMin, RowMax : RowRange;
   ColumnMin, ColumnMax : ColumnRange;
   Table : TableType;
```

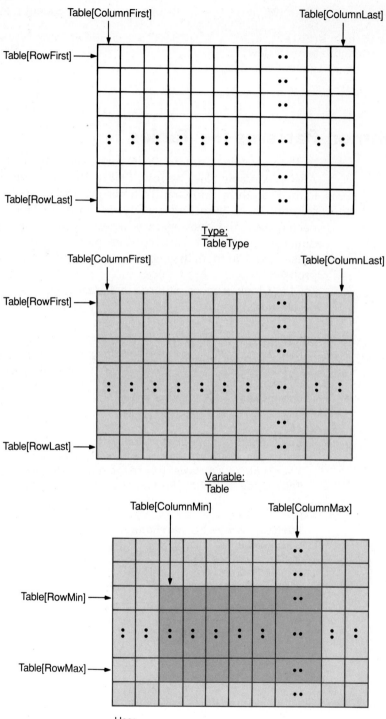

Access by Row

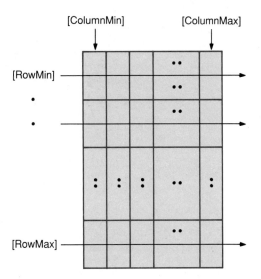

To access each element by row, the row index must vary more slowly than the column index. This means that the row must be the outer loop. The following procedure is a general one that takes as a parameter each variable that it needs. Notice that the loop control variables are local to the procedure. If they are used in a FOR loop, they must be local.

```
PROCEDURE AccessByRow(Table : TableType;
                      RowMin, RowMax : RowRange;
                      ColumnMin, ColumnMax : ColumnRange;
                      .. (* any other parameters needed *));
(* Components in Table are processed by row. *)

VAR
  Row : RowRange;
  Column : ColumnRange;

BEGIN    (* AccessByRow *)
  FOR Row := RowMin TO RowMax DO
    BEGIN  (* processing a row *)
      FOR Column := ColumnMin TO ColumnMax DO
        BEGIN  (* accessing elements of the row *)
          .
          .
          (* process Table[Row, Column] *)
          .
          .
        END   (* accessing elements of the row *)
    END     (* processing a row *)
END;      (* AccessByRow *)
```

Access by Column

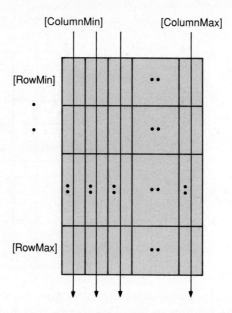

To process each element by column, the column index must move more slowly than the row index; it must be the outer loop.

```
PROCEDURE AccessByColumn(Table : TableType;
                         RowMin, RowMax : RowRange;
                         ColumnMin, ColumnMax : ColumnRange;
                         .. (* any other parameters needed *));
(* Components of Table are processed by column. *)

VAR
  Row : RowRange;
  Column : ColumnRange;

BEGIN   (* AccessByColumn *)
  FOR Column := ColumnMin TO ColumnMax DO
    BEGIN  (* processing a column *)
      FOR Row := RowMin TO RowMax DO
        BEGIN  (* accessing elements of the column *)
          .

          (* process Table[Row, Column] *)
          .

        END   (* accessing elements of the column *)
    END    (* processing a column *)
END;    (* AccessingByColumn *)
```

The difference between these two procedures is that the loops are reversed. The outer loop determines the major order of access (row or column), and the inner loop controls the access to individual elements of that row or column.

Notice that in many of our examples we use Row and Column as subscript identifiers. When working with arrays, it's helpful to choose subscript identifiers that have meaning. Make it a habit. If you have a math background, you might want to follow the subscript convention of using I for the row designator and J for the column designator.

A word of caution. Row and Column or I and J, as row and column designators, mean something to you but not to the compiler. The identifier in the first index position is the designator for the first dimension; the identifier in the second index position is the designator for the second dimension. If you said

```
Table[Column, Row]
```

Column would refer to the first dimension and Row would refer to the second dimension.

Another Way of Defining a Two-Dimensional Array

Look again at the syntax diagram of a two-dimensional array:

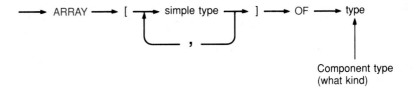

It says that the component type is a *type*. It does not say that the component type must be a *simple type*. The implication is that a two-dimensional array can be defined as a one-dimensional array where the component type is a one-dimensional array. In Program SalesContest we could have defined Sales like this:

```
TYPE
    CategoryRange = 'A'..'C';
    CityRange = 1..4;
    CityType = ARRAY[CityRange] OF REAL;
    SalesType = ARRAY[CategoryRange] OF CityType;
    SumsType = ARRAY[CityRange] OF REAL;
```

```
VAR
   Sales : SalesType;
```

We can treat Sales like a list of arrays. However, each individual element in Sales can still be accessed by a pair of indexes. The first of the pair accesses the proper component in the list (an array), and the second of the pair indexes the proper element in that array. Alternately, we can access each row of the array as a unit: Sales['A'] accesses the first row, Sales['B'] accesses the second row, and Sales['C'] accesses the third row.

The fact that CityType and SumsType are the same gives us a clue as to why we might want to define Sales this way. In Procedure PrintWinners, the maximum value in each row is found and printed. In Procedure FindMaxCity, the maximum value is found and returned. The same task is done four times: The location of the maximum value is found in a list of four elements. Let's code a generic procedure that finds the index of the maximum value in a list of elements.

```
PROCEDURE FindMaxIndex(List : ListType;
                       VAR MaxIndex : ListIndexType;
                       IndexMin, IndexMax : ListIndexType);
(* The index of the maximum value in List[IndexMin]    *)
(* to List[IndexMax] is returned in MaxIndex.          *)

VAR
   Index : ListIndexType;

BEGIN    (* FindMaxIndex *)
   MaxIndex := IndexMin;
   FOR Index := SUCC(IndexMin) TO IndexMax DO
      IF List[Index] > List[MaxIndex]
         THEN
            MaxIndex := Index
END;      (* FindMaxIndex *)
```

If ListIndexType is aliased to CityRange, we would use this statement in Procedure PrintWinners to invoke FindMaxIndex to find the index (City) with the maximum value for each category:

```
BEGIN    (* PrintWinners *)
   FOR Category := 'A' TO 'C' DO
      BEGIN
         FindMaxIndex(Sales[Category], MaxCity,         ← Procedure call
                 1 (* IndexMin *), 4 (* IndexMax *));
         WRITELN(MaxCity, ' wins in category ', Category)
      END
END;      (* PrintWinners *)
```

Procedure FindMaxCity would go away. The call to it would be replaced with this call to FindMaxIndex in the body of PrintGrandWinner:

```
BEGIN    (* PrintGrandWinner *)
   .
   .
   FindMaxIndex(CitySums, MaxCity, 1, 4);              ← Procedure call
   WRITELN('City ', MaxCity, ' wins the contest!')
END;     (* PrintGrandWinner *)
```

The only advantage of defining a two-dimensional array in this fashion is that a row (or column) can be passed to a procedure that operates on a one-dimensional ARRAY variable (that is, a list).

Multidimensional Arrays

Pascal places no limit on the dimensions of an array, so arrays with any number of dimensions are allowed. The number of dimensions of an array is the same as the number of indexes needed to reference a particular cell. A **multidimensional array** is a structured data type made up of a fixed number of components of the same type ordered on N dimensions, where N is greater than 1. A two-dimensional array is a multidimensional array where N is 2.

> **Multidimensional Array**
> A structured data type composed of a fixed number of components of the same type ordered on N dimensions (N > 1). Each component is directly accessed by N indexes, representing the component's position within each dimension.

For example, the following definitions and declarations define a three-dimensional array that represents the sales volume recorded by region by store by month.

```
CONST
   MaxRegions = (* number of regions *);
   MaxStores  = (* number of stores *);

TYPE
   Regions = 1..MaxRegions;
   Stores = 1..MaxStores;
   Months = 1..12;
   SalesType = ARRAY[Regions, Stores, Months] OF REAL;
```

```
VAR
  Sales : SalesType;
  Region: Regions;
  Store : Stores;
  Month : Months;
```

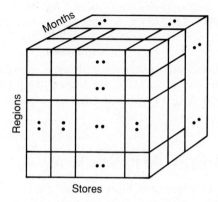

The following code fragment prints out the total sales by region by store by month. Region must be the outer loop, Store the middle loop, and Month the inner loop.

```
FOR Region := 1 TO MaxRegions DO
  BEGIN
    WRITELN('Region: ', Region);
    FOR Store := 1 TO MaxStores DO
      BEGIN
        WRITELN('Store: ', Store);
        FOR Month := 1 TO 12 DO
          WRITE(Sales[Region, Store, Month]:10:2);
        WRITELN
      END
  END;
```

To print the sum of each region for each month, Month must be the outer loop, Region the middle loop, and Store the inner loop.

```
FOR Month := 1 TO 12 DO
  BEGIN
    WRITELN('Month: ', Month);
    FOR Region := 1 TO MaxRegions DO
      BEGIN
        Sum := 0.0;
```

```
      FOR Store := 1 TO MaxStores DO
        Sum := Sum + Sales[Region, Store, Month];
      WRITELN('Region ', Region, ' sales: ', Sum:10:2)
    END
  END;
```

A slight variation in this algorithm would allow us to print totals by month or by store. The key point is that processing an ARRAY variable usually requires one loop for each index. (The exception to this rule is processing the diagonal of a two-dimensional array. Do you know why? See Exercise 5 on page 372.)

Compatibility Revisited

ARRAY variables (or any variables—simple or structured) of the same type can be assigned to each other. This is useful for storing values in a component of a multidimensional array. Using the definitions for Program SalesContest,

```
TYPE
  CategoryRange = 'A'..'C';
  CityRange = 1..4;
  CityType = ARRAY[CityRange] OF REAL;
  SalesType = ARRAY[CategoryRange] OF CityType;
  SumsType = ARRAY[CityRange] OF REAL;

VAR
  Sales : SalesType;
  CitySums : CityType;
  CityMinimums : CityType;
  Category : CategoryRange;
  City : CityRange;
```

the following are valid assignments:

```
Sales[Category] := CitySums;
```
← Assigns a one-dimensional ARRAY variable to a row of a table

```
CitySums := CityMinimums;
```
← Assigns a one-dimensional ARRAY variable to another one-dimensional ARRAY variable

```
CityMinimums := Sales[Category];
```
← Assigns a row of a table to a one-dimensional ARRAY variable

Be careful, though, when you *compare* arrays. Comparison here must be done item by item. For example, the following code sets Equal to TRUE if CitySums and CityMinimums are equal.

```
City := 0;
Equal := TRUE;
REPEAT
   City := City + 1;
   IF CitySums[City] <> CityMinimums[City]
      THEN
         Equal := FALSE
UNTIL NOT Equal OR (City = 4);
```

The 4-Cs Corner
Correctness

Program SalesContest: An Error

The algorithm for finding the maximum value (which was executed four times in Program SalesContest) contains a design flaw: It ignores the possibility of a tie. In the case of a tie, the first city with the maximum value would be declared the winner. Clearly, this would not go over very well with the troops! The problem occurs because we are not really looking for the maximum value but for the *index belonging to the maximum value.* That is, the index has meaning within this problem; the index is directly related to a specific city.

The solution is to separate the search for the maximum value from the index position in which it occurs. Procedure FindMaxIndex should be replaced with Procedure FindMaxValue, which returns the maximum value. A second pass through the totals finds and prints all the places where this maximum value occurs.

Procedure FindMaxIndex is still useful in a situation where no duplicate values can occur. An assumption should be added to the documentation stating that if a tie does occur, the first index where the maximum value is found is returned.

Choosing a Structured Data Type

To decide on an appropriate structured data type, you have to know the algorithms you're going to apply to the data. In the same way, to choose your algorithms, you have to know the way in which the data is logically structured. You choose your structured data types and develop your top-down design in one process; they cannot be separated.

Programs operate on data: They transform input data into output. The form of the data plays an important role in the process. It is the framework on which the program's operations are based.

As you develop a design, you assume that lower-level modules can perform the necessary operations on the data that you're specifying. Your main module, then, reflects your general solution by calling these lower-level modules.

At some point you have to choose the data types, structured or scalar, that you will use in your program. Your choice of data types limits your choice of algorithms to operate on the data. A poor choice here can affect the efficiency of a program. Don't be afraid to backtrack, to go up the design structure and change your choice of data types or algorithms.

In the outlines we have been using for our top-down designs, we describe the section on data structures before we break down the problem into modules. This implies that we choose the structured data types first, then our algorithms. This is not necessarily the case. These outlines are templates that show the data structures and decomposition for *final programs*. We may have considered many other structured data types before we made our final choice.

Variables of structured data types are called *data structures*. Simple scalar variables are data structures in the sense that they are places to store data. They are not, however, structured data types and are not included in the data structures section. If the data structures section of the top-down design is missing, it means that there are no structured data types in the program.

A one-dimensional ARRAY variable is an appropriate structure for a *list* of items; a two-dimensional ARRAY variable is an appropriate structure for a *table* of items. Sometimes, however, it is not clear whether we're working conceptually with parallel arrays or a table.

To use a two-dimensional array, the content of each location must be of the same type. In Program SalesContest, each location in the array Sales contains a REAL value representing the dollar volume for a sales category for a given city. We could have represented this data as four parallel arrays of REAL. However, for this problem we're interested in two aspects of each sale: its category and the office that closed the contract. Here, then, a two-dimensional array is appropriate.

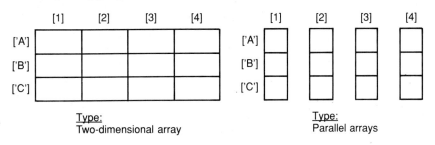

Type:
Two-dimensional array

Type:
Parallel arrays

Suppose we have a problem where we're processing paychecks, using the following data:

ID   (five-digit number, INTEGER)
Rate   (hourly salary, REAL)
Hours   (hours worked, REAL)

Here we can't use a two-dimensional ARRAY variable because the three items of data are not all the same type; we have to use three parallel one-dimensional arrays. What if we convert Rate to cents and Hours to minutes so that all three items are of type INTEGER? Now would a two-dimensional array be a better representation? No. It would be legal, but it wouldn't make much sense. One column would represent an identification number, one column would represent an hourly rate, and one column would represent hours worked. Row processing would have no meaning. If all we really want to do is process columns, then parallel arrays are a better data structure.

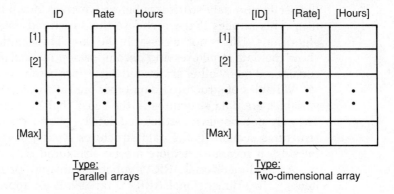

Type:
Parallel arrays

Type:
Two-dimensional array

Correctness Hints

We find the same errors with multidimensional arrays that we find with one-dimensional arrays. Subscript range errors are most common. Trying to access undefined (uninitialized) items can cause an undefined value error.

Nested loop structures are more complex and can lead to subtle errors in logic that don't generate run-time errors. The syntax may be valid, but what you intended to happen is not exactly what you coded.

1. Initialize all locations in an ARRAY variable if there is any chance that you will attempt to access the entire array. If you will be using only part of an ARRAY variable, keep track of which part you are using with indexes that mark the appropriate upper and lower bounds. This guarantees that you are accessing only valid data.
2. Use subrange types for index variables. If the only looping structure you will be using is a FOR loop, the type for the loop control variable can be the same as the index range used in defining the ARRAY type.

   If you may need to use a WHILE or REPEAT loop when referencing an array, the data type for the loop control variable must have one more value than the index range used to define the array, in order to accommodate the test when the entire array is used. That is, the loop control variable must exceed the range in one direction or the other in order for the loop to start or terminate when the entire array is being processed.

For example, this code fragment ends in a run-time error if there are ten data values, even though the ARRAY variable is designed to hold ten data values:

```
CONST
   Limit = 10;

TYPE
   IndexRange = 1..Limit;
   ListType = ARRAY[IndexRange] OF INTEGER;

VAR
   Index : IndexRange;
   List : ListType;

BEGIN
   Index := 1;
   WHILE  NOT EOF AND (Index <= Limit) DO
     BEGIN
        READLN(List[Index]);
        Index := Index + 1                  ← Index becomes Limit + 1
     END
END;
```

3. Follow some systematic order in processing array subscripts in nested loops.
4. Define data types globally to prevent type mismatches when passing arrays as parameters.
5. Use the proper number of subscripts with array names when referencing a cell in an array.
6. Row and Column are good index identifiers, but they have no meaning in Pascal. Remember, the first subscript applies to the first dimension, the second subscript applies to the second dimension.

Conciseness

Arrays are nice to have, but you shouldn't use them just because they're there. Ask yourself "Can I process as I read, or must all the data be read in before I can process it?" For example, to find the average of a list of temperature readings, each temperature can be added into the sum as it's read. All you need are simple variables—no structured data types are needed. What if you want to compare each temperature to the average? Because the average is not calculated until all the temperatures have been read, the list of temperatures must be kept in memory (or the file of temperatures must be read twice, which is very time consuming). Therefore, the temperatures should be stored in an array (Figure 10–1).

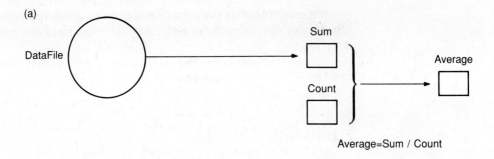

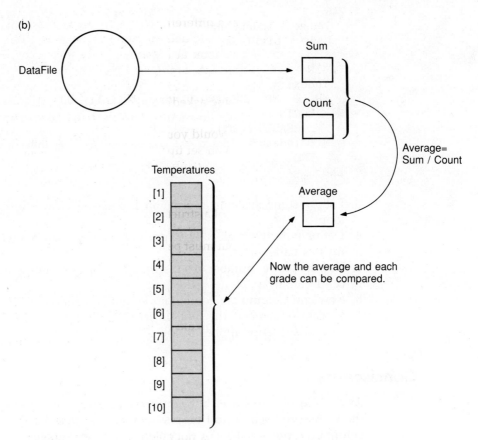

FIGURE 10–1 Processing temperature data: (a) find the average (array not necessary) and (b) find the average and compare to each grade (array necessary)

In Chapter 9 we developed a procedure that merges two one-dimensional arrays. If the lists of items to be merged are on files, we don't have to store each list in an array before we merge them. We only need one value from each file at a time. We can merge the lists directly from the two files by comparing only one number from each file and storing the smaller number in a third file (Figure 10–2). Using an array when it's not necessary is expensive in two ways: More storage is used, and accessing an element in an array takes more time than accessing a simple variable.

Clarity

We use clarity here in a different way than we have before. Our suggestions for choosing an appropriate data structure presuppose that you know where to begin. What if you look at a problem and don't even know what your choices for structuring data are? What if *nothing* is clear?

You must go back and carefully examine the problem statement. Do you understand what's being asked? Could you do the task by hand? If so, what sort of forms would you use? Would you just jot down a few values on the back of an envelope? Would you set up a table on a sheet of paper with rows and columns? Would you set up a column and make hash marks? More than likely the correct data structure will resemble the forms you would create to do the job by hand.

If you can't do the job by hand, your problem raises more fundamental issues than the choice of a structured data type. You need to clarify the problem. Try writing down everything you know about the problem. Then write down what your output must be. Now try writing down what you must have as input to produce that output.

Go back and reread the material on top-down design and problem-solving strategies. Try to integrate these ideas with the discussion about structured data types and your own programming experience. But most important, don't panic. Take a break: Go for a walk, to a concert, or to a movie. The problem will still be there when you get back, but it's amazing how much simpler it will seem.

Completeness

Our examples using arrays have been nonmathematical because we believe that formal mathematics is not a prerequisite for learning to program. However, our discussion would not be complete if we did not mention that one of the most useful applications of arrays is in matrix algebra.

In mathematics a one-dimensional array is called a *vector*; a two-dimensional array is called a *matrix*. Matrix algebra deals with vectors and matrices as data types and applies operations to data objects of their type. If you are familiar with matrix algebra (or just curious), look at Programming Assignment 5 on page 378.

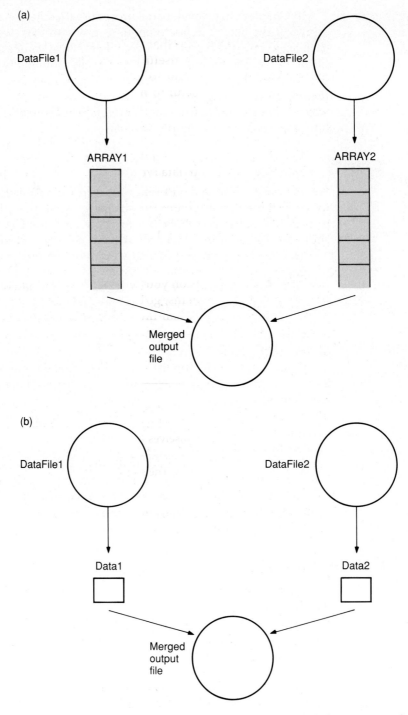

FIGURE 10–2 Two ways to merge data: (a) using arrays and (b) using simple variables

Summary

The number of dimensions that an ARRAY data type can have is unlimited. A one-dimensional array is useful to hold data that is a list of items. A two-dimensional array is useful to hold data that is a table of items. A three-dimensional array is useful to hold data in which each data item has three properties. Each dimension in an array reflects a relationship among the data items.

Nested FOR loops are handy for processing multidimensional arrays, but use WHILE or REPEAT loops if the loop is not a simple count-controlled loop.

Choosing structured data types and designing algorithms are a part of the same process. To choose appropriate data types, you must carefully analyze the problem and understand the algorithms that are applicable to each data structure. So far, our choices have been between simple variables and arrays, and between one-dimensional arrays and multidimensional arrays. Appropriate structured data types often resemble the forms we would create to do the job by hand.

When a design decision you've made results in an inefficient algorithm or in implementation problems, go back and change it. It is much easier to alter a design than to change a half-finished program.

EXERCISES

1. An array is a collection of identical-type elements referenced by a single name and a subscript. A multidimensional array is not a different data type; it's simply an array whose elements are themselves arrays. True or false?

2. An array is a collection of elements of the same type referenced by a single name and one or more subscripts. The subscripts must be of the same type. True or false?

3. Given these declarations:

```
PROGRAM VoteCount(INPUT,OUTPUT);

CONST
    CanLimit = 4;
    PreLimit = 47;

TYPE
    CRange = 1..CanLimit;
    PRange = 1..PreLimit;
    VoteTally=ARRAY[CRange, PRange] OF INTEGER;

VAR
    Primary, Election : VoteTally;
    PreTotal, Total : INTEGER;
    Precinct : PRange;
    Candidate : CRange;
```

Are the following statements true or false?

a. This code would find the winner of the election:

```
Total := 0;
FOR Candidate := 1 TO CanLimit DO
  FOR Precinct := 1 TO PreLimit DO
    Total := Total + Election[Candidate, Precinct];
IF Candidate > Total
  THEN
    WRITELN('The winner is Candidate ', Candidate:1);
```

b. This code would sum the number of votes cast for all candidates in the Third Precinct:

```
Precinct := 3;
PreTotal := 0;
FOR Candidate := 1 TO CanLimit DO
  PreTotal := Pretotal + Election[Precinct, Candidate];
```

c. This code would sum the votes for Candidate 1 across all precincts:

```
Candidate := 1;
Total := 0;
FOR Precinct := 1 TO PreLImit DO
  Total := Total + Election[Candidate, Precinct];
```

4. Write a program segment that initializes the elements of array Table to zero given the following declarations:

```
TYPE
   Range1 = 0..60;
   Range2 = 1..36;
   TableType = ARRAY[Range1, Range2] OF INTEGER;

VAR
   Table : TableType;
   A : Range1;
   B : Range2;
```

5. Write a procedure that initializes the diagonals of an N × N array to the character stored in input parameter Character. The ARRAY variable, N, and CHAR variable should be passed as parameters. Assume a global ARRAY type TableType.

6. Write a procedure that finds the maximum value in an M × N INTEGER array. Assume a global ARRAY type Table.

7. Write a procedure that initializes the elements of one specific column of an array to the value Waiting. The column to be set to Waiting should be passed as a parameter. Assume the following declarations in the main program:

```
CONST
   ColumnLimit = 50;
   RowLimit = 40;

TYPE
   RowRange = 1 .. RowLimit;
   ColumnRange = 1 .. ColumnLimit;
   ValueType = (Waiting, Stalled, IO);
   List = ARRAY[RowRange, ColumnRange] OF ValueType;

VAR
   Table : List;
   Column, Row : INTEGER;
```

Do not reference global variables directly in your procedure.

8. Write a function that returns TRUE if all the elements of an array passed as a parameter equal Stalled. Use the same declarations in the main program as in Exercise 7.

PRETEST

1. The elements of an array can themselves be arrays, and the elements of those arrays can be arrays. True or false?

2. A logging operation keeps records of thirty-seven loggers' monthly production using the following data structure:

```
CONST
   NumberLoggers = 37;

TYPE
   Months = 1..12;
   CutDataType = ARRAY[1..NumberLoggers, Months] OF INTEGER;
   LoggerIndex = 1..NumberLoggers;

VAR
   CutData : CutDataType;
   MonthlyHigh, MonthlyTotal,
   YearlyTotal, High : INTEGER;
   Month, BestMonth : Months;
   Logger, BestLogger : LoggerIndex;
```

Given these declarations, are the following statements true or false?

a. This statement would assign the January log total for Logger 7 to MonthlyTotal:

```
MonthlyTotal := CutData[7, 1];
```

b. This code would compute the yearly total for Logger 11:

```
YearlyTotal := 0;
FOR Month := 1 TO 12 DO
   YearlyTotal := YearlyTotal + CutData[Month, 11];
```

c. This code would find BestLogger (most logs cut) in March:

```
MonthlyHigh := 0;
FOR Logger := 1 TO NumberLoggers DO
   IF CutData[Logger, 3] > MonthlyHigh
      THEN
         BEGIN
            BestLogger := Logger;
            MonthlyHigh := CutData[Logger, 3]
         END;
```

d. This code would find the logger with the highest monthly production and his best month:

```
High := 0;
FOR Month := 1 TO 12 DO
   FOR Logger := 1 TO NumberLoggers DO
      IF CutData[Logger, Month] > High
         THEN
            BEGIN
               High := CutData[Logger, Month];
               BestLogger := Logger;
               BestMonth := Month
            END;
```

3. Write a procedure that initializes the elements of one specific row of an array to the value 1. The row to be set to 1 should be passed as a parameter. Assume the following declarations in the main program:

```
CONST
   ColumnLimit = 50;
   RowLimit = 40;

TYPE
   RowRange = 0..RowLimit;
   ColumnRange = 0..ColumnLimit;
   List = ARRAY[RowRange, ColumnRange] OF INTEGER;

VAR
   Table : List;
   Column, Row : INTEGER;
```

Do not reference global variables directly in your procedure.

4. Write a function that returns TRUE if all the elements of an array passed as a parameter are positive. Use the same declarations in the main program as in Problem 3.

5. A cookbook author keeps records of the required ingredients for thirteen recipes using the following array structure:

```
CONST
   NumberRecipes = 13;
```

```
TYPE
  RecipeIndex = 1..NumberRecipes;
  Ingredients = (Flour, Sugar, BrownSugar, Nuts, ChoChips);
  RecipesType =  ARRAY[RecipeIndex, Ingredients] OF REAL;

VAR
  Recipes : RecipesType;      (* amount in cups *)
  BigItem, ChipAverage, FlourAmount, SugarHigh : REAL;
  Item, ItemID : Ingredients;
  Recipe, RecipeID, Sweetest : RecipeIndex;
```

Given these declarations, are the following statements true or false?

a. This statement would assign the number of cups of flour for Recipe 3 to FlourAmount:

```
FlourAmount := Recipes[3, Flour];
```

b. This code would compute the average amount of chocolate chips used in the recipes:

```
ChipAverage := 0.0;
FOR Recipe := 1 TO NumberRecipes DO
   ChipAverage := ChipAverage + Recipes[ChoChips, Recipe];
ChipAverage := ChipAverage / NumberRecipes;
```

c. This code would find the sweetest (most sugar and brown sugar) of all the recipes:

```
SugarHigh := 0.0;
FOR Recipe := 1 TO NumberRecipes DO
IF Recipes[Recipe, Sugar] + Recipes[Recipe,
   BrownSugar] > SugarHigh
   THEN
     BEGIN
       Sweetest := Recipe;
       SugarHigh := Recipes[Recipe, Sugar] + Recipes
                      [Recipe, BrownSugar]
     END;
```

d. This code would find the recipe with the largest amount of any one ingredient and that ingredient's identity:

```
BigItem := 0.0;
FOR Recipe := 1 TO NumberRecipes DO
   FOR Item := Flour TO ChoChips DO
     IF Recipes[Recipe, Item] > BigItem
        THEN
          BEGIN
            BigItem := Recipes[Recipe, Item];
            ItemID := Item;
            RecipeID := Recipe
          END;
```

6. Define and declare a data structure that would allow a box company to keep track of its inventory of boxes with heights varying from 4 to 24 inches, widths varying from 6 to 24 inches, and lengths varying from 12 to 36 inches.

7. Write a program fragment that initializes all the elements of the data stucture in Problem 6 to zero.

PROGRAMMING ASSIGNMENTS

1. Photos taken in space by the Voyager spacecraft are sent back to Earth as a stream of numbers. Your job is to take a matrix of numbers and print it as a picture.

   If the numbers received represent levels of brightness, then one approach to generating a picture is to print a dark character (like a $) when the brightness level is low and print a light character (like a blank or a period) when the level is high. Unfortunately, errors in transmission sometimes occur. Your program should find and correct these errors, then print a corrected picture on a new page.

   Assume a value is in error if it differs by more than 1 from each of its four neighboring values. Correct the bad value by giving it the average of its neighboring values, rounding the average to the nearest integer. For example:

   ```
     5
   4 2 5
     5
   ```

   Here, the 2 is an error; its corrected value is 5.

   Notice that values on the corners or boundaries of the matrix must be processed differently from values on the interior.

   Print, on a new page, a negative image of the corrected picture.

2. The diagram below represents an island surrounded by water (shaded area). Two bridges lead off the island. A mouse is on the black square. Write a program that makes the mouse walk through the island. The mouse is allowed to travel one square at a time either horizontally or vertically. A random number between 1 and 4 should be used to decide which direction the mouse should take. The mouse drowns if it hits the water and escapes by crossing a bridge. What are the mouse's chances? You may generate a random number up to one hundred times. If the mouse does not find its way by the hundredth try, it will die of starvation. Start the mouse in a new array and repeat the whole process. Count the number of times it escapes, drowns, or starves.

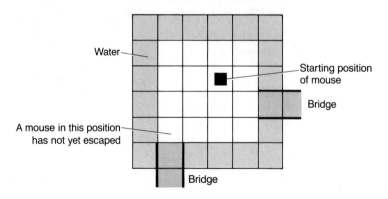

Input:

(1) First line: The size of the array, including the border of water and bridges (not larger than 20 × 20).

(2) Next N lines: The rows of the two-dimensional array. The positions containing negative numbers represent the water. The positions on the edge containing a zero represent the bridges. The position containing a 1 represents the starting position of the mouse. All others contain zeroes.

Output: For each trip by the mouse you should print the following (double-space between trips):

(1) A line stating whether the mouse escaped, drowned, or starved

(2) A line showing the mouse's starting position and the position of the bridges

(3) A map showing the frequency of the visits of the mouse to each position

3. In a diving competition, each diver makes three dives of varying degrees of difficulty. Nine judges score the dives from 1 to 10 in steps of 0.5. The total score is obtained by discarding the lowest and highest of the judges' scores, adding the remaining scores, then multiplying the scores by the degree of difficulty. The divers take turns; when a rotation is finished, they are ranked according to score. Write a program to do all this, using the following input and output specifications.

Input:

(1) Number of divers

(2) Diver's name (ten characters), degree of difficulty (REAL), and judges' ratings (REAL)

This data is input for each diver for each dive. All of the lines for Dive 1 are grouped together, as are the lines for Dive 2 and Dive 3.

Output:

(1) Echo-print in tabular form with appropriate headings.

(2) A table that contains the following information sorted by final total in descending order (highest diver first):

NAME	DIVE 1	DIVE 2	DIVE 3	TOTAL

NAME is the diver's name; DIVE 1, DIVE 2, and DIVE 3 are the total points received for a single dive. TOTAL is the diver's overall total.

4. You work for the Jet Propulsion Laboratory. Your boss wants you to write a program that takes an array containing the digitized representation of a picture of the night sky and locates the stars on it. Each element of the array represents the amount of light hitting that portion of the image when the picture was taken. Intensities range from zero to 20. Here's a sample of the input:

0	3	4	0	0	0	6	8
5	13	6	0	0	0	2	3
2	6	2	7	3	0	10	0
0	0	4	15	4	1	6	0
0	0	7	12	6	9	10	4
5	0	6	10	6	4	8	0

A star is probably located in the area covered by array element [I, J] if the following is the case:

$$(A[I, J] + \text{Sum of the 4 surrounding intensities}) / 5 > 6.0$$

Ignore possible stars along the edges of the array. The output is a star map containing asterisks where you've found a star and blanks elsewhere. For example:

```
-------------------------------------------
:
:      *
:
:             *
:             *      **
:
:
```

Input:
(1) A title
(2) An array of intensities

Output: A star map. Print two blanks where no star is found; print a blank followed by an asterisk where there is a star. The chart should have a border and be labeled with the title.

5. Many mathematical problems require the addition, subtraction, and multiplication of two matrices. Write a set of procedures to perform these operations. You are to use the following procedure headings as your interface. Write a program to test your procedures.

```
PROCEDURE Add(VAR A, B, Result : MatrixType;
                  RLength, CLength : INTEGER);
(* Result = A + B where + is matrix addition. *)

PROCEDURE Sub(VAR A, B, Result : MatrixType;
                  RLength, CLength : INTEGER);
(* Result = A - B where - is matrix subtraction. *)

PROCEDURE Mult(VAR A : Matrix1Type; VAR B : Matrix2Type;
               VAR Result : Matrix3Type;
               R1, C1, C2 : INTEGER);
(* Result = A * B where * is matrix multiplication. *)
(* Assumption:  A is R1 × C1        *)
(*              B is C1 × C2        *)
(*              Result is R1 × C2 *)
```

Records

- To be able to define a RECORD data type.

- To be able to declare a RECORD variable.

- To be able to access, compare, and assign values to the individual components of a RECORD variable.

- To be able to define data types that include hierarchical records and arrays of records.

- To be able to access, compare, and assign values to the individual components of hierarchical records and arrays of records.

- To be able to access individual components of a RECORD variable using the WITH statement.

In Chapter 8 we listed the built-in structured data types available in Pascal: ARRAY, RECORD, and FILE. We have examined arrays in detail. In this chapter we examine records. In the next chapter we look at files.

Arrays are homogeneous structures: Each element in an array must be of the same data type. Records are like arrays in that they both can represent a group of elements or components with a common name. Records, however, are not homogeneous structures: Each element in a record does not have to be of the same data type.

We access each element in an array with an index that specifies the element's place in the array. Each element in a record is given a name (called a *field identifier*) and is accessed by that name.

RECORD Data Type

RECORD is a very versatile data type. It is a grouping of elements of any data type in which the elements are given names. The components of a record are called **fields.** Each field has its own **field identifier** and type.

> **RECORD**
> A structured data type with a fixed number of components (not necessarily of the same type), which are accessed by name (not index).

> **Field Identifier**
> The name of a component (field) in a record.

This is the syntax diagram for a record:

$$\longrightarrow \text{RECORD} \longrightarrow \text{field list} \longrightarrow \text{END}$$

And this is the syntax diagram for a field list:

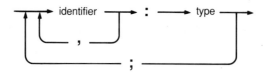

As with any type, we define the pattern in the TYPE section and declare variables of that type in the VAR section.

```
TYPE
   CarType = RECORD
                  Price  : REAL;
                  Weight : INTEGER;
                  Year : INTEGER;
                  MPG : REAL
              END;    (* RECORD *)
VAR
   MyCar : CarType;
```

CarType is a pattern for a group of four variables. MyCar is a RECORD variable with four fields. Price, Weight, Year, and MPG are the field identifiers, the names of the fields. The expression used to access each field of a RECORD variable is called a **field selector.**

Field Selector

The expression used to access components of a RECORD variable, composed of the RECORD variable name and the field identifier, separated by a period.

MyCar.Price is a REAL variable.
MyCar.Weight is an INTEGER variable.
MyCar.Year is an INTEGER variable.
MyCar.MPG is a REAL variable.

The following code fragment reads values into the RECORD variable MyCar. Notice that each field has to be read separately.

```
READLN(MyCar.Price, MyCar.Weight, MyCar.Year, MyCar.MPG);
```

Let's look at a more complex RECORD type:

```
CONST
   StringLimit = (* maximum string size *)
```

```
TYPE
   IndexRange = 1..StringLimit;
   IndexType = 0..StringLimit;
   StringType = PACKED ARRAY[IndexRange] OF CHAR;
   StudentType = RECORD
                    FirstName : StringType;
                    LastName : Stringtype;
                    Sex : (Male, Female);
                    Status : (Married, Single);
                    Class : (Fresh, Soph, Junior, Senior, Graduate)
                 END;   (* RECORD *)

VAR
   Student : StudentType;
```

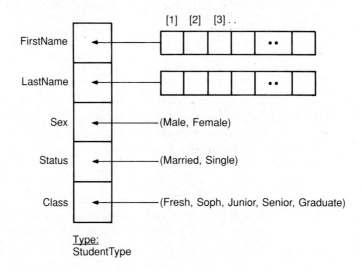

Type:
StudentType

FirstName, LastName, Sex, Status, and Class are the field identifiers in RECORD type StudentType. These field identifiers are used to access the different components of variable Student declared to be of type StudentType. Let's look at this record definition in detail.

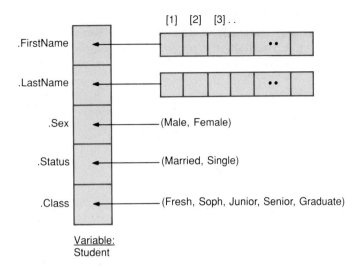

Variable:
Student

Student.FirstName accesses a string.
Student.LastName accesses a string.
Student.Sex accesses a user-defined data type (Male, Female).
Student.Status accesses a user-defined data type (Married, Single).
Student.Class accesses a user-defined data type (Fresh, Soph, Junior, Senior, Graduate).

Because the fields FirstName and LastName are one-dimensional arrays, the individual character positions can be accessed just like any ARRAY variable:

Student.FirstName[1] accesses the first character.
Student.FirstName[Index] accesses the character in the Index position.

The following code fragment writes out the content of Student:

```
WRITELN(Student.LastName, ', ', Student.FirstName, ': ');
CASE Student.Sex OF
  Male : WRITE('Male, ');
  Female : WRITE('Female, ')
END;   (* CASE *)
CASE Student.Status OF
  Married : WRITE('Married, ');
  Single : WRITE('Single, ')
END;   (* CASE *)
CASE Student.Class OF
  Fresh : WRITELN('Freshman');

    .

    .
  Graduate : WRITELN('Graduate student')
END;   (* CASE *)
```

Because we are discussing records, not how to represent data items, we have shown how these items are represented by looking at the type definition. Actually the process goes the other way: You decide how you want the data items to be represented, then write the type definitions.

Let's look at an example using the RECORD data type. Suppose a parts wholesaler wants to computerize his operation. Until now he has kept his inventory on handwritten 8 × 10 cards. A typical inventory card contains the following data:

Part number: 1A3321
Description: cotter pin
Cost: 0.012
Quantity on hand: 2100

A record would be a natural choice for this kind of data. Each item on the inventory card could be a field of the record. The part number would have to be a string because it contains both digits and letters. The size of the string would depend on the number of characters in the longest part number and whether or not the inventory might be expanding.

The description of the part would also be a string type. It might or might not be the same length as the part number. Even if the two could be the same type, they are really two different things: The part number is an identifier, and the description is text. It's better style to have them be two different string types.

The cost would be REAL, and the quantity on hand would be INTEGER. The only problem here would be if the quantity on hand is ever larger than MaxInt.

Before we go on, let's review the syntax of a record definition. The reserved words RECORD and END bracket the field declarations:

```
TYPE
  RecordType = RECORD
    Fieldl : FieldTypel;
    Field2 : FieldType2;
         .
         .
    FieldN : FieldTypeN
  END;   (* RECORD *)
```

Notice that the field identifiers are followed by a colon and a type, *just like the declaration of any variable.* The field selectors of a RECORD variable are actually treated and used just like any other declared variable. The field selector is the variable name for each field. It must be complete: the RECORD variable name followed by a period followed by the field identifier.

Hierarchical Records

Just as the components of an array can be of any type, so can the components of a record. We have already seen cases where the type of a field identifier is an array. A component of a record also can be another record. Records whose fields are themselves records are called **hierarchical records.**

Hierarchical Record
A record that contains a field that is a RECORD data type.

Let's look at an example where this kind of structure is appropriate. The owner of a small machine shop has asked us to write a Pascal program to keep information about the machines in her shop. She wants to keep static descriptive information (identification number, purchase date, cost, depreciated value) and statistical information (number of down days, fail rate, date of last service).

What's a reasonable representation for this information? We can divide the data into two groups: one that changes and one that does not. In addition there are two dates to be kept: the date of purchase and the date of last service. It seems, then, that we can use a record to describe a date, a record to describe the statistical data, and an overall record containing the other two as components. Our type definition reflects this structure:

```
TYPE
   DateType = RECORD
                 Month : 1..12;
                 Day : 1..31;
                 Year: 1800..2050
              END;   (* RECORD *)
   Statistics = RECORD
                  FailRate : REAL;
                  LastServiced : DateType;
                  DownDays : INTEGER
               END;   (* RECORD *)
   MachineRecord = RECORD
                     ID : INTEGER;
                     Purchased : DateType;
                     ServiceHistory : Statistics;
                     Cost : REAL;
                     DepreciatedValue : REAL
                  END;   (* RECORD *)

VAR
   Machine : MachineRecord;
```

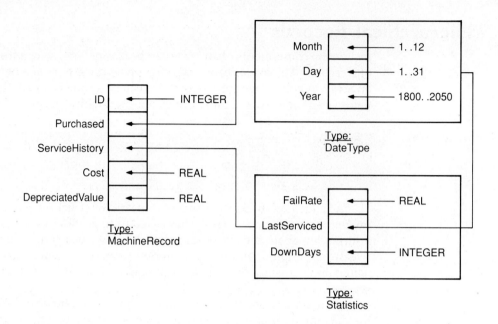

Two of the components of RECORD data type MachineRecord are themselves records: Purchased is of RECORD type DateType and ServiceHistory is
of RECORD type Statistics. Notice also that one of the components of REC-
ORD type Statistics is a RECORD type: LastServiced is of RECORD type
DateType.

Here are some examples of how the components of Machine can be manipulated. Assuming that Machine already contains valid values, the following statements would print out certain parts of the variable:

```
WRITELN('Machine # ', Machine.ID:1);
WRITELN;
WRITELN('Purchase date: ', Machine.Purchased.Month:1,
        '/', Machine.Purchased.Day:1, '/',
        Machine.Purchased.Year:1);
WRITELN('Total down days since purchased: ',
    Machine.ServiceHistory.DownDays:1);
WRITELN('Last serviced during ',
    Machine.ServiceHistory.LastServiced.Month:1, '/',
    Machine.ServiceHistory.LastServiced.Year:1);
```

The output from these statements might look like this:

```
Machine # 24

Purchase date: 2/10/1977
Total down days since purchased: 12
Last serviced during 1/1990
```

Notice that we used a fieldwidth specification of 1 (:1) for all integers. This ensures that the numbers are printed just where we want them. The alphabetic strings, describing what the values are that are being printed, all have an ending blank. Because Pascal expands the fieldwidth so that all the digits of a number are printed, using a fieldwidth of 1 guarantees that there will be just one blank between the label and the number.

We can use this statement to check for excessive downtime:

```
IF Machine.ServiceHistory.FailRate > 0.10
    THEN
      WRITELN('Excessive downtime')
```

If another date variable representing the current date is declared

```
VAR
   CurrentDate : DateType;
```

and the machine has just been serviced, we can change the last service date with these statements.

```
Machine.ServiceHistory.LastServiced.Month := CurrentDate.Month;
Machine.ServiceHistory.LastServiced.Day := CurrentDate.Day;
Machine.ServiceHistory.LastServiced.Year := CurrentDate.Year;
```

Because Pascal allows us to assign one data structure to another of the same type, there's a simpler way of setting the date:

```
Machine.ServiceHistory.LastServiced := CurrentDate;
```

Arrays of Records

Although single records can be useful, many applications require a collection of records. For example, a business needs a list of parts records, a school needs a list of student records. Arrays are ideal for this. We simply define an array whose components are records!

Here's an example of a list of CarType records:

```
CONST
   MaxCars = (* maximum number of cars in stock *);

TYPE
   CarType = RECORD
                Price : REAL;
                Weight : INTEGER;
                Year : INTEGER;
                MPG : REAL
             END;   (* RECORD *)
   InventoryType = ARRAY[1..MaxCars] OF CarType;
```

```
VAR
   Cars : InventoryType;
```

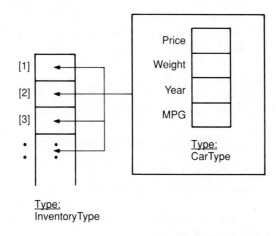

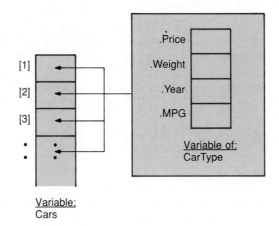

Cars[1].Price accesses the Price field of the first car.
Cars[1].Weight accesses the Weight field of the first car.
Cars[1].Year accesses the Year field of the first car.
Cars[1].MPG accesses the MPG field of the first car.

The index (in brackets) following the variable identifier tells us which car; the field selector tells us which field:

```
Cars[Index].Price
```
‿‿‿‿‿‿‿‿‿ ‿‿‿‿‿‿

    Which car   Which field

    In our machine shop example, we declared a RECORD variable Machine. We probably will need a list of all the machines in the machine shop. Here's how we do it:

```
CONST
  MaxMachines = (* maximum number of machines *)

TYPE
  MachineRange = 1..MaxMachines;
  IndexRange = 0..MaxMachines;
  DateType = RECORD
               Month : 1..12;
               Day : 1..31;
               Year: 1800..2050
             END;  (* RECORD *)
  Statistics = RECORD
                 FailRate : REAL;
                 LastServiced : DateType;
                 DownDays : INTEGER
               END;  (* RECORD *)
  MachineRecord = RECORD
                    ID : INTEGER;
                    Purchased : DateType;
                    ServiceHistory : Statistics;
                    Cost : REAL;
                    DepreciatedValue : REAL
                  END;  (* RECORD *)

  MachineList = ARRAY[MachineRange] OF MachineRecord;

VAR
  ListOfMachines : MachineList;
  Length : IndexRange;
```

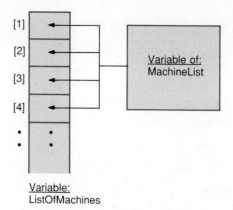

Variable:
ListOfMachines

The following code fragment prints information about all the machines in the inventory. Look carefully at how each element is accessed. Remember that the lowest-level component in any structured data type is a scalar type.

```
FOR Index := 1 TO Length DO
  BEGIN
    WRITELN('Machine # ', ListOfMachines[Index].ID:1);
    WRITELN;
    WRITELN('Purchase date: ',
            ListOfMachines[Index].Purchased.Month:1,
            '/', ListOfMachines[Index].Purchased.Day:1, '/',
            ListOfMachines[Index].Purchased.Year:1);
    WRITELN('Total down days since purchased: ',
            ListOfMachines[Index].ServiceHistory.DownDays:1);
    WRITELN('Last serviced during ',
ListOfMachines[Index].ServiceHistory.LastServiced.Month:1, '/',
    ListOfMachines[Index].ServiceHistory.LastServiced.Year:1);
  END;
```

Identifiers in a Pascal program must be unique in order to avoid ambiguity. However, identifiers can be used again and again as field identifiers of *different* records. For example, these declarations are valid even though the identifier Name is used in several places.

```
CONST
  StringLength = (* maximum length of string *)
  MaxPeople    = (* maximum number of people in list *)

TYPE
  NameString = PACKED ARRAY[1..StringLength] OF CHAR;
  PersonRecord = RECORD
                    Name : NameString;
                    Age  : 0..110;
```

```
                        Sex  : (Female, Male)
                  END;    (* RECORD *)
      CityRecord = RECORD
                    Name : NameString;
                    Population : (Small, Medium, Large)
                  END;    (* RECORD *)
      PeopleType = ARRAY[1..MaxPeople] OF PersonRecord;

VAR
   Name : NameString;
   APerson : PersonRecord;
   People : PeopleType;
   City : CityRecord;
```

There's no ambiguity here because the variables Name, APerson.Name, People[Index].Name, and City.Name are all unique. Still, it's not a good idea to repeat identifiers in different record field lists. The compiler won't get confused, but the person reading or maintaining the program may get very confused.

SAMPLE PROBLEM

Problem: Each month when your bank statement arrives, you get a lump of ice in the pit of your stomach. No matter how careful you are about recording each check and deposit, you never seem to agree with the bank. You know that the bank uses a computer and that computers never make mistakes, so you spend hours trying to figure out where you went wrong. You decide that if you can't beat 'em, join 'em: you'll computerize your own checkbook.

There are four tasks here: recording a check, recording a deposit, reconciling your checkbook, and printing the outstanding checks. You decide to use interactive input, with five items in the menu:

C	Record check
D	Record deposit
R	Reconcile checkbook
P	Print outstanding checks
Q	Quit processing

The rest of the data to be read depends on the processing:

C:	A check number (INTEGER)
	A payee (string)
	An amount (REAL)
D:	The amount deposited (REAL)

SAMPLE PROBLEM, CONTINUED

R:	The ending balance (REAL)
	The service charge (REAL)
	The number of checks cashed (INTEGER)
	The check numbers (INTEGER)
P and Q:	No further data needed

Discussion: You have all the forms you use to balance your checkbook by hand. In fact, the task is to automate that process. Each check can be represented as a record with three fields: the check number, the payee, and the amount. The checkbook can be represented as an array of checks (Check-Book).

Recording a check involves reading the proper values into a RECORD variable that is the next open place in the ARRAY variable CheckBook. The amount of the check must be deducted from the current balance. A deposit only requires adding the deposited amount to the current balance.

Reconciling the checkbook involves just what you do by hand: looking at the check numbers and marking off those that have been returned. When you've marked off all the ones returned, the sum of the checks not returned plus the current balance minus the service charge should equal the ending balance of the statement. In your program, you also have to remove the checks that have been returned from CheckBook (from the array of checks).

Clearly, you'll be using this program many times each month. You'll record checks and deposits at various times and reconcile your checkbook once a month. This means that the ARRAY variable CheckBook must be saved on a file and read each time you run the program. Although we have not written a file before that's output from one run to be used as input to the next run, it's a very common task. You need the current balance (CurrentBalance), the number of outstanding checks (Length), and the checks (CheckBook).

To start the process, you must write a program to create the array of checks (CheckBook) and write it on a file. That is, the file containing Check-Book must be initialized. CurrentBalance would be 0.0, Length would be zero, and there would be no checks.

Data Structures: An ARRAY variable CheckBook, in which the components are RECORD variables of CheckType

MAIN MODULE   Level 0

```
Get CheckBook
REPEAT
  Get Code
  CASE Code OF
    'c' : RecordCheck;
    'd' : RecordDeposit;
    'p' : PrintCheckBook;
    'r' : ReconcileCheckBook;
    'q' : ;
  END
UNTIL Code = 'q'
Write File Checks
```

GET CHECKBOOK   Level 1

```
Reset File Checks
Readln CurrentBalance
Readln Length
FOR Index from 1 TO Length DO
  Get a check (CheckBook[Index])
```

GET A CHECK   Level 2

```
Read CheckNumber
FOR Index from 1 TO StringLength DO
  Read Payee[Index]
Readln Amount
```

GET CODE   Level 1

```
REPEAT
  Print menu
  Readln Code
  Change Code to lowercase
UNTIL Code = 'c', 'd', 'p', 'r', or 'q'
```

PRINT MENU

Level 2

```
Writeln '**************************************************':50
Writeln '***      C: Record a check              ***':50
Writeln '***      D: Record a deposit            ***':50
Writeln '***      P: Print outstanding checks    ***':50
Writeln '***      R: Reconcile checkbook         ***':50
Writeln '***      Q: Quit processing and save    ***':50
Writeln '***         checkbook on File Checks    ***':50
Writeln '**************************************************':50
Writeln '***      You will be prompted for       ***':50
Writeln '***      further input. Always          ***':50
Writeln '***      press return after each value. ***':50
Writeln '**************************************************':50
```

LOWERCASE

You can use Function LowerCase (see page 276) to change Code to lowercase.

RECORD CHECK

Level 1

```
Length ← Length + 1
Writeln 'Check number (INTEGER): '
Readln CheckBook[Length].CheckNumber
Writeln 'Payee is (up to 10 characters) : '
Get Payee for CheckBook[Length]
Writeln 'Amount of check (REAL): '
Readln CheckBook[Length].Amount
CurrentBalance ← CurrentBalance − CheckBook[Length].Amount
```

GET PAYEE

Level 2

When you read CheckBook in from the file, you assume that there are exactly StringLength characters in Payee because that's how you will write it. When reading from the keyboard, you cannot trust the user to input exactly StringLength characters, so you have to read until there is an <eoln> or until you have read StringLength characters. There's a code fragment on page 330 that you can adapt and use here.

```
Index ← 0
WHILE NOT EOLN AND (Index < StringLength)
    Index ← Index + 1
    Read Character
    Payee[Index] ← Character
(* fill rest of Payee with blanks *)
FOR Index from INDEX + 1 TO StringLength DO
    Payee[Index] ← ' '
```

RECORD DEPOSIT

Level 1

```
Writeln 'Amount of deposit (REAL): '
Readln Amount
CurrentBalance ← CurrentBalance + Amount
```

PRINT CHECKBOOK

```
Writeln 'Current Balance is :', CurrentBalance :10:2
Writeln 'Outstanding checks are listed below. '
FOR Index from 1 TO Length DO
    Writeln CheckBook[Index].CheckNumber:4,
        CheckBook[Index].Payee,
        CheckBook[Index].Amount:10:2
```

RECONCILE CHECKBOOK

```
Writeln 'Ending balance (REAL): '
Readln EndingBalance
Writeln 'Service charge (REAL): '
Readln ServiceCharge
Writeln 'Number of canceled checks (INTEGER): '
Readln NumberCanceled
Writeln 'The ', NumberCanceled:1, ' check numbers are: '
Writeln '(Please enter them)'
FOR Counter from 1 TO NumberCanceled DO
    Read CheckNumber
    Process CheckNumber
Check balances
```

PROCESS CHECK NUMBER   Level 2

This takes a little thought. You don't physically remove a canceled check from your records, you just mark that it's been returned. In the program, however, you want to physically remove the canceled check from your list of outstanding checks. What you're calling CheckBook is actually the list of all *outstanding* checks.

So you have to search for each canceled check and remove it. You can use Procedure Search (see page 305) with a minor modification. In Procedure Search, we were looking for a value in a list of values. Here you are looking for a value in a *field of a record in a list of records*. You have to change the expression that does the comparison. All the parameters were made general enough to handle this change.

Once you have found the index of the returned check, you can decrement Length and shift all the other checks up one position in the list.

```
Search(Checkbook, Length, CheckNumber, Found, Index)
IF Found
    THEN
        Length ← Length − 1
        FOR Count from Index TO Length DO
            CheckBook[Index] ← CheckBook[Index + 1]
    ELSE
        Writeln 'There is no outstanding check ', CheckNumber
```

SEARCH   Level 3

You can use Procedure Search (see page 305) with the comparison expression changed to search for a field in a record.

CHECK BALANCES   Level 2

The ending balance of the statement should be the current balance minus the service charge plus all the checks that remain outstanding after the reconciliation.

```
SumOutstanding ← 0.0
FOR Index from 1 TO Length DO
    SumOutstanding ← SumOutstanding + CheckBook[Index].Amount
CurrentBalance ← CurrentBalance − ServiceCharge
IF EndingBalance = CurrentBalance + SumOutstanding
    THEN
        Writeln 'Congratulations. You and the bank agree.'
    ELSE
        Writeln 'Sorry. You and the bank do not agree.'
```

WRITE FILE CHECKS   Level 1

> Rewrite Checks
> Writeln CurrentBalance, Length
> FOR Index from 1 TO Length DO
>   Writeln CheckNumber, Payee, Amount

Module Design Chart:

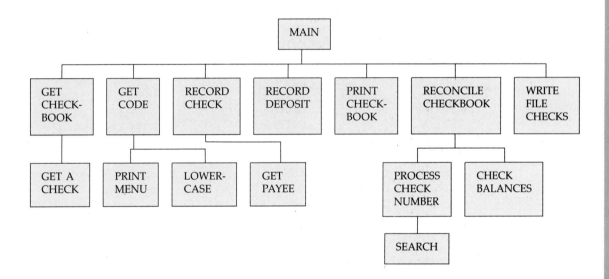

As you look at the number of modules in the module design chart, you feel better about having trouble balancing your checkbook. The task is nontrivial! Fortunately, Modules LOWERCASE and SEARCH already exist in function and procedure form. They can be adapted and used directly.

As your programs get more complex, the decision whether to make a module a separate procedure or function gets more complicated. For example, Module CHECK BALANCES is several lines long, but it is integrally tied to Module RECONCILE CHECKBOOK. Because it has no meaning outside of reconciling a checkbook, you should code it in-line. Although it's a judgment call, we would code all the other modules as procedures.

There are a lot of subprograms here, but the structure of the algorithm is not very complicated. There are four main tasks: recording a check, recording a deposit, printing the checkbook, and reconciling the checkbook. There are several utility modules that implement tasks like reading CheckBook and writing it back out again. In fact, most of the process is involved with writing prompts and reading in values. In addition there are several modules that do subtasks for other modules.

As the number of subprograms increases, the interface design gets more and more complex. The modules in this design have distinct roles, so we list them in the interface design chart according to those roles.

Interface Design Chart:

Program Constants and Variables

Identifiers	Type	Role
MaxChecks	INTEGER	Constant used to set size of CheckBook
StringLength	INTEGER	Constant used to set length of Payee
Checks	TEXT	File containing Check-Book
CheckBook	ARRAY	List of checks
Length	INTEGER	Number of checks
Code	CHAR	Character that determines processing
CurrentBalance	REAL	Difference between deposits and checks
Index	INTEGER	Loop control variable

Subprograms

Identifiers	Needs	Returns
GetCode	Nothing	Code
Called to do main tasks and utilities:		
GetCheckBook	Checks	CheckBook, Length, CurrentBalance
RecordCheck	Nothing	CheckBook, Length, CurrentBalance
RecordDeposit	Nothing	CurrentBalance
PrintCheckBook	CheckBook, Length, CurrentBalance	Nothing
Reconcile	Nothing	CheckBook, Length, CurrentBalance
WriteFile	Checks, CheckBook, Length, CurrentBalance	Nothing

continued

Subprograms, Continued

Identifiers	Needs	Returns
Called to do specific tasks for other subprograms:		
GetACheck	Checks	Check (CheckBook [Index])
PrintMenu	Nothing	Nothing
LowerCase	Character	Character (in lower-case)
GetPayee	Nothing	Payee (type NameString)
Search	CheckBook, Length, CheckNumber	Found, Index
ProcessCheckNumber	CheckNumber	CheckBook, Length
CheckBalances	ServiceCharge, CheckBook, Length	CurrentBalance

Because this program is so long, we do not reproduce all of it here. With one or two exceptions, we show only the procedure headings with an occasional short discussion of what is passed as a parameter.

```
PROGRAM CheckRegister(INPUT, OUTPUT, Checks);
(* This program records checks and deposits *)
(* and reconciles the checks.              *)

CONST
  MaxChecks = 100;       (* maximum number of checks   *)
                         (* currently in CheckBook     *)
  StringLength = 10;     (* maximum number of characters *)
                         (* in Payee                   *)

TYPE
  NameString = PACKED ARRAY[1..StringLength] OF CHAR;
  CheckType = RECORD
                CheckNumber : INTEGER;
                Payee : NameString;
                Amount : REAL
              END;  (* RECORD *)
  CheckBookType = ARRAY[1..MaxChecks] OF CheckType;
  IndexType = 0..NumberOfChecks;
  ItemType = INTEGER;
  ListType = CheckBookType;
```

SAMPLE PROBLEM, CONTINUED

```
VAR
  Checks : TEXT;
  CheckBook : CheckBookType;
  Code : CHAR;
  CurrentBalance : REAL;
  Index, Length : IndexType;


(************************************************************)


PROCEDURE GetACheck(VAR Checks : TEXT; VAR Check : CheckType);
(* A row of the ARRAY variable CheckBook is the *)
(* actual parameter.                            *)

VAR
  Index : 1..StringLength;

BEGIN    (* GetACheck *)
  READ(Checks, Check.CheckNumber);
  FOR Index := 1 TO StringLength DO
    READ(Checks, Check.Payee[Index]);
  READLN(Checks, Check.Amount)
END;     (* GetACheck *)


(************************************************************)


PROCEDURE GetCheckBook(VAR Checks : TEXT;
                       VAR CheckBook : CheckBookType;
                       VAR Length : IndexType;
                       VAR CurrentBalance : REAL);
  .
  .


(************************************************************)


PROCEDURE PrintMenu;
  .
  .


(************************************************************)


FUNCTION LowerCase(Character : CHAR) : CHAR;
  .
  .


(************************************************************)
```

```
PROCEDURE GetCode(VAR Code : CHAR);
(* User is prompted to enter a code indicating what *)
(* processing is to be done.                        *)

BEGIN    (* GetCode *)
  REPEAT
    PrintMenu;
    READLN(Code);
    Code := LowerCase(Code)
  UNTIL (Code = 'c') OR (Code = 'd') OR (Code = 'p') OR
        (Code = 'r') OR (Code = 'q')
END;         (* GetCode *)

(*****************************************************************)


PROCEDURE GetPayee(VAR Name : NameString);
 .
 .


(*****************************************************************)


PROCEDURE RecordCheck (VAR CheckBook : CheckBookType;
                       VAR Length : IndexType;
                       VAR CurrentBalance : REAL);
 .
 .


(*****************************************************************)


PROCEDURE  RecordDeposit(VAR CurrentBalance);
 .
 .


(*****************************************************************)


PROCEDURE PrintCheckBook(CheckBook : CheckBookType;
                         Length : IndexType;
                         CurrentBalance : REAL);
 .
 .


(*****************************************************************)


PROCEDURE Search(List : ListType;       (* array to be searched  *)
             Length : IndexType;         (* length of list        *)
             Item : ItemType;            (* item being looked for  *)
         VAR Found : BOOLEAN;            (* result of search      *)
         VAR Index : IndexType);        (* where found (if found) *)
```

SAMPLE PROBLEM, CONTINUED

```
BEGIN    (* Search *)
   .
   .
      BEGIN
        Index := Index + 1;
        IF Item = List[Index].CheckNumber         ← Notice the change.
           THEN
             Found := TRUE
      END
END;    (* Search *)
```

```
(*************************************************************)
```

```
PROCEDURE ProcessCheckNumber(CheckNumber : INTEGER;
                             VAR CheckBook : CheckBookType;
                             VAR Length : IndexType);
   .
   .


Search(CheckBook, Length, CheckNumber, Found, Index);  ←  Calls general purpose
                                                           search procedure
(*************************************************************)
```

```
PROCEDURE CheckBalances(CheckBook : CheckBookType;
                        Length : IndexType;
                        VAR CurrentBalance : REAL;
                        ServiceCharge : REAL);
   .
   .


(*************************************************************)
```

```
PROCEDURE Reconcile(VAR CheckBook : CheckBookType;
                    VAR Length : IndexType;
                    VAR CurrentBalance : REAL);
   .
   .


(*************************************************************)
```

```
PROCEDURE WriteFile(VAR Checks : TEXT;
                    CheckBook : CheckBookType;
                    Length : IndexType;
                    CurrentBalance : REAL);

VAR
  Index : IndexType;
```

```
BEGIN    (* WriteFile *)
  REWRITE(Checks);                                        We look at a
  WRITELN(Checks, CurrentBalance, Length);          ←    better way in
  FOR Index := 1 TO Length DO                            Chapter 12.
    WRITELN(Checks, CheckBook[Index].CheckNumber,
                    CheckBook[Index].Payee,
                    CheckBook[Index].Amount)
END;     (* WriteFile *)

(*************************************************************)

BEGIN (* CheckRegister *)
  .
  .
  .
END.  (* CheckRegister *)
```

WITH Statement

When using RECORD variables, we may access one or more fields of a REC-
ORD variable again and again in a small section of code. As you have seen,
field selectors can get long and cumbersome. The WITH statement allows us
to abbreviate the notation by specifying the RECORD variable name once and
then using just the field identifiers to select the record components.

This is the form of the WITH statement:

```
WITH RECORD variable DO
  Statement;
```

Within the scope of the WITH statement, field identifiers are treated as
variable identifiers; that is, the fields of the RECORD variable can be selected
by the field identifier alone (the full field selector is not necessary). For example, in Program CheckRegister, Procedure GetACheck could be rewritten like
this:

```
PROCEDURE GetACheck(VAR Checks : TEXT; VAR Check : CheckType);

VAR
  Index : 1..StringLength;

BEGIN    (* GetACheck *)
  WITH Check DO
    BEGIN
      READ(Checks, CheckNumber);
```

```
         FOR Index := 1 TO StringLength DO
             READ(Checks, Payee[Index]);
         READLN(Checks, Amount)
      END
END;     (* GetACheck *)
```

The entire procedure body is within the scope of the WITH, so CheckNumber refers to Check.CheckNumber, Payee[Index] refers to Check.Payee[Index], and Amount refers to Check.Amount.

WITH statements can be nested just like any other statements. For example, the statement

```
WITH RECORD variable1 DO
  WITH RECORD variable2 DO
    Statement;
```

is allowed. This can be abbreviated to

```
WITH RECORD variable1, RECORD variable2 DO
  Statement
```

Subrecords of records can also be referenced using the WITH statement. Let's go back to our machine shop example. If we want to find those machines with fail rates greater than 8 percent, we could use this statement:

```
IF Machine.ServiceHistory.FailRate > 0.08
    THEN
      WRITELN('Failure rate for machine ', Machine.ID:1,
              'is: ', Machine.ServiceHistory.FailRate:5:2);
```

Using a WITH statement, the code can also be written

```
WITH Machine.ServiceHistory DO
  IF FailRate > 0.08
    THEN
      WRITELN('Failure rate for machine ', ID:1,
              'is: ', FailRate:5:2);
```

Machine.ServiceHistory is both a field selector and a RECORD variable (a subrecord of Machine).

When we use arrays of records, the RECORD variable is an array element selected by a subscript. The body of Procedure WriteFile can be rewritten like this:

```
REWRITE(Checks);
WRITELN(Checks, CurrentBalance, Length);
FOR Index := 1 TO Length DO
```

```
WITH CheckBook[Index] DO
   WRITELN(Checks, CheckNumber, Payee, Amount);
```

The subscript of the RECORD variable cannot be changed within the body of a WITH statement. This fragment

```
WITH CheckBook[Index] DO
   FOR Index := 1 TO Length DO
      WRITELN(Checks, CheckNumber, Payee, Amount);
```

is incorrect. This code may or may not generate an error message, but it does not do what you want it to do. The expression CheckBook[Index] is evaluated outside the loop. If Index does not have a value within IndexRange at that point, a run-time error is generated. If Index happens to have a legal value, the same output line is generated Length times. The RECORD variable is CheckBook[Index] as it was outside the loop. Index may be changing, but the RECORD variable in the WITH statement is not.

The 4-Cs Corner
Clarity

Records generally are very descriptive. Record names and field identifiers reflect the meaning of the variables and the relationships among them. Records are easy to handle conceptually because we usually think in terms of related data items (not necessarily of the same types) that are attributes of a single object. Programs are easier to read, write, and debug if the structure of the program variables accurately reflects the logical relationships among the items in the real world.

The WITH statement makes a program clearer and more readable if you need a long, involved expression to access a record. However, you may be paying a price for this clarity because ambiguities can arise when using the WITH statement. The moral here is simple: Use WITH statements, but use them carefully.

Completeness

Program CheckRegister is a classic *data-processing problem*. There is a file of current information about some organization or process. This information is read, updated, and written out again. This process of reading, updating, and saving is repeated over and over again. The repetition can be on a regular basis (like reconciling your checkbook) or on a random basis (like recording checks and deposits).

The pattern is always the same:

1. Input the current state of the system (read the master file, Checks in our example).

2. Change the current state of the system.
3. Save the revised state of the system.

The changes or updates can be on a file themselves or read from the terminal. In our sample problem, we take input from the terminal, so the program has to prompt the user for the relevant data.

In many data-processing applications, the update data is also on a file. If the data on the update file is organized in the same way as the data on the master file, the two files can be read and processed in parallel. A payroll application operates like this. The information that is necessary to write checks is kept in order by either name or social security number. The information on the update file is ordered in the same way. The information about a person's salary is read from the master file, and the information about the hours worked is read from the update file. The program calculates one person's salary and writes that person's check before going on to the next person.

In our sample problem all the information must be available before any processing can be done. The information on all the checks that have been written must be in memory before the checkbook can be updated. This means the master file (Checks) must be read into memory in its entirety before we start any updating.

We commented earlier that there were a lot of modules in the solution to this problem but that the structure is not complex. This is one of the properties of data-processing problems. We also commented that there are a lot of input/output statements and prompts. This is also typical of a data-processing application.

Conciseness

Processing Efficiency

In Program CheckRegister, we delete a returned check by physically removing it from the list of checks. We could save machine time if we *logically* remove each check from the list of checks and only physically remove them as they are being written out to be saved for the next run.

How do you *logically* remove something? You can set a flag to indicate that the item is no longer active. The flag can be an explicit field in a record that is set to either active or inactive, or it can be one of the regular fields that is set to some special value. In the checkbook problem, you can set the amount of each returned check to zero. Because you do not write a check for zero dollars, the check is logically removed. The section of code that sums the amount of each outstanding check is still correct because the zeros do not change the total.

Isn't it inefficient to add those zero values? Yes, but shifting records in an array to physically remove each check is far more inefficient.

The canceled checks could be physically removed in Procedure WriteFile. The procedure would have to count the number of checks still outstanding (those with a nonzero amount) and write that value out for Length. The loop that writes each check would test Amount and would not write the check where Amount is zero.

Storage Efficiency

We introduced the PACKED ARRAY OF CHAR in Chapter 9. The relational operators can be applied to variables of this type, and variables of this type can be printed directly. What the PACKED option actually does is to instruct the compiler to pack as many characters into one word in memory as possible. On machines with a small word size, the PACKED option doesn't save much memory if any, but on machines with a large word size, it saves a lot.

The PACKED option may be applied to records as well. The compiler is instructed to pack as many fields as possible into one word in memory. A PACKED RECORD variable is accessed and manipulated exactly like a nonpacked RECORD variable. There are no special features associated with a PACKED record.

There is always a tradeoff when using the PACKED option. Memory space is saved at the cost of execution time. It takes longer to access a field or a character when it is packed into a word with another field or character.

Correctness

Choosing a Structured Data Type

In Chapter 10 we discussed how to go about choosing a structured data type when our choices were simple variables, one-dimensional arrays, parallel arrays, and two-dimensional arrays. Now we have added records to our set of choices. For many problems where we could use parallel arrays or even multi-dimensional arrays, a record or an array of records may be more appropriate. We no longer are restricted by all elements in the structure having to be of the same type.

Let's look again at the example where we are processing paychecks with the following data (see page 365):

ID (five-digit number)
Rate (hourly salary)
Hours (hours worked)

We said that even if all the values could be made integers, a two-dimensional array would not be appropriate. Clearly, the choice for information of this type is a record. If you ever use a language that does not have records, you will have to use parallel arrays.

Although our data structures and program designs should be as simple and straightforward as possible, the decision of which structure to use may not be clear-cut. Take, for example, the concept of elapsed time, which is characterized conventionally in terms of hours, minutes, and seconds. A data type ElapsedTime could be implemented as a record with three fields or as a single integer representing seconds. Let's examine both of these implementations and look at the pros and cons of each. We use two procedures, PrintTime and SumTime, to compare the implementations.*

First, let's look at ElapsedTime as a RECORD data type.

```
TYPE
   ElapsedTimeType = RECORD
                        Seconds : 0..60;
                        Minutes : 0..60;
                        Hours : 0..24
                     END;      (* RECORD *)
```

Procedure PrintTime is very simple using this implementation. We just have to print the value in each field.

```
PROCEDURE PrintTime(ElapsedTime : ElapsedTimeType);
(* Elapsed time is printed in hours, minutes, and seconds. *)

BEGIN    (* PrintTime *)
   WITH ElapsedTime DO
      WRITELN(Hours:2, ':', Minutes:2, ':', Seconds:2)
END;      (* PrintTime *)
```

Procedure SumTime, which takes two values of ElapsedTimeType and returns a third value that is the sum of the first two, is more complicated. We have to sum Seconds first and carry over to Minutes if the sum of Seconds is greater than 60. We immediately have a problem: The Seconds field is defined as a subrange. We either have to change the subrange or add the fields in a variable that is not a subrange field. We'll do the latter.

We also have to account for a possible carryover from Minutes to Hours. Let's just assume that Hours does not overflow. Of course, we must remember to state this assumption in a comment.

```
PROCEDURE SumTime(First, Second : ElapsedTimeType;
                  VAR Result : ElapsedTimeType);
(* Result is First plus Second.           *)
(* Assumption: Hours do not exceed 24. *)

VAR
   TempValue : INTEGER;
```

*This example is drawn from a problem on the free response section of the 1988 Advanced Placement Exam in Computer Science.

```
BEGIN    (* SumTime *)
  TempValue := First.Seconds + Second.Seconds;
  Result.Seconds := TempValue MOD 60;
  TempValue := TempValue DIV 60;    (* get carry *)
  TempValue := First.Minutes + Second.Minutes + TempValue;
  Result.Minutes := TempValue MOD 60;
  TempValue := TempValue DIV 60;    (* get carry *)
  Result.Hours := TempValue + First.Hours + Second.Hours
END;      (* SumTime *)
```

What happens when ElapsedTime is an INTEGER?

```
TYPE
  ElapsedTimeType = INTEGER;      ← Aliasing
```

Printing time in a standard format (hh:mm:ss) is more difficult in this implementation. First we have to take the INTEGER value and find the number of hours. ElapsedTime DIV 3600 gives us the number of hours; ElapsedTime MOD 60, the number of seconds. The problem is getting the number of minutes. We have to take ElapsedTime, remove the hours, and DIV the result.

```
PROCEDURE PrintTime(ElapsedTime : ElapsedTimeType);
(* Elapsed time is printed in hours, minutes, and seconds. *)

BEGIN    (* PrintTime *)
  WRITELN((ElapsedTime DIV 3600):2, ':',
          ((ElapsedTime MOD 3600) DIV 60):2, ':',
          (ElapsedTime MOD 60):2)
END;      (* PrintTime *)
```

Procedure SumTime, in contrast, is very simple with this implementation.

```
PROCEDURE SumTime(First, Second : ElapsedTimeType;
                  VAR Result : ElapsedTimeType);
(* Result is First plus Second.          *)
(* Assumption: Hours do not exceed 24. *)

BEGIN    (* SumTime *)
  Result := First + Second
END;      (* SumTime *)
```

How do these two implementations compare? In the record implementation, printing is easy, but the addition of two elapsed times is complicated. We have to carry over from seconds to minutes and from minutes to hours. If we don't use a temporary variable to store the result of each sum, there's the possibility of a value out of range.

In the integer implementation, summing is easy but printing is not. Although the printing is done in just one statement, the logic involved in calculating the expressions is complicated. (Anything involving DIVs and MODs is prone to error!)

There is an additional problem with the integer representation. The number of seconds in a minute is 60; the number of seconds in an hour is 3600; the number of seconds in 24 hours is 86,400—too big to be held in an INTEGER variable in most microcomputers.

Which is the *best* implementation? We can't answer that. We can only point out the questions that you should ask. What operations are going to be performed on the data type? Are there limitations on the values? Is one operation going to be performed more than the others? After you answer these kinds of questions, you can choose the best implementation for a specific problem.

This example brings up one of the most important principles in software engineering: *abstraction*. **Abstraction** is the separation of logical properties from the implementation details. The program unit that uses ElapsedTimeType really doesn't care how the type is implemented as long as it's implemented correctly (prints properly and sums properly). In fact, if the implementation is changed at some later time and the interface is the same, the invoking unit doesn't even need to know about the change.

Abstraction
The separation of logical properties from implementation details.

We defined a data type as a set of values and a set of allowable operations on those values. We could define a data type ElapsedTimeType and a set of procedures and functions that implement the allowable operations on values of ElapsedTimeType. If the only access to values of ElapsedTimeType is through the procedures and functions provided, we have what's called an *abstract data type*.

We have talked about making procedures as general as possible so that they can be used over and over again. Creating abstract data types is the mirror image of what we have been talking about. We can start with a procedure and make it general to use later, or we can decide that we need a data type and a set of operations on values of that type and provide them as a group. The result is the same—code that is both reusable and reliable.

Running Out of Memory Space

There's a fixed amount of space in memory. If your program needs more space than is available, you get a run-time error. If you can't increase your memory space, you may have to decrease the size of your data structure (for example, reduce a 2,000-element array to a 500-element array). If you can't do this, you may have to change your approach to the problem, changing both data structure and algorithm.

The problem of running out of memory space can be caused by something as simple as passing a large data structure as a value parameter instead of a VAR parameter. Remember that when you pass a data structure as a value parameter, another copy of the data structure is created. You may not have enough memory space for the copy.

Recursion (a procedure or function calling itself) also uses a lot of memory space. Each call to the procedure or function takes up space on the message board for actual parameters, local variables, and other information that the run-time system needs.

Correctness Hints

1. Be sure to specify the full field selector when you reference a component of a RECORD variable. The only exception is when you're using a WITH statement, which specifies the RECORD variable.
2. When using arrays in records or arrays of records, be sure to include the subscript with the array name when you access individual components.
3. Process each field of a record separately, except when you're assigning one RECORD variable to another (of the same type) or passing the record as a parameter.
4. Beware of confusion or ambiguity when you use the WITH statement.
5. Avoid using the same field identifiers in different record types.
6. If the RECORD variable in a WITH statement is a record from an array of records, do not change the subscript of the specified RECORD variable within the WITH statement.

Summary

RECORD is a very useful structured data type for grouping data of different types that relates to a single object. Often, a record is more descriptive of the data than another structured data type. In fact, the form of the data often indicates a record as the best choice.

You can use a RECORD variable to refer to the record as a whole, or a field selector to access any individual field (component) of the record. Records of the same type can be assigned directly to each other, but comparison of records must be done field by field. Reading and writing records also is done field by field.

Because the components of arrays and records can be of any type, you can use records with array components and arrays of records.

The WITH statement lets you abbreviate the field selector. It can save writing time and make a program easier to read, but it also can be confusing. If you're using a WITH statement, be sure your references are clear.

EXERCISES

1. Write a record declaration that contains the following information about a textbook:

   Title (string of one hundred characters)
   Number of authors
   Author name(s) (string of one hundred characters)
   Publisher (string of forty characters)
   Year of publication

2. Write a procedure to initialize the fields of a RECORD variable of the type in Exercise 1. Set character string fields to blanks, numeric fields to zero.

3. a. Write a record declaration that contains the following information about a student:

   Name (string of twenty characters)
   Social security number (string of eleven characters)
   Class (freshman, sophomore, junior, senior)
   Grade-point average
   Sex (M, F)

   b. Declare a RECORD variable of the type in part a, and write a program segment that prints the information in each field.
   c. Declare Roll to be an ARRAY variable of three thousand records of the type in part a.

4. Write a program segment that reads in a set of part numbers and associated unit costs. Keep the data sorted by part number as you read it in. Use an array of records with two fields, Number and Price, to represent each pair of input values. Assume one pair of input values per line of data.

5. a. Declare a RECORD type called Class that keeps track of grades in a university. Include the following fields:

   Title (up to twenty characters)
   UniqueNum (INTEGER)
   Date (up to eight characters)
   Grade (REAL)

   b. Declare Transcript to be an ARRAY variable of up to one hundred records of type Class.
   c. Write a procedure that reads values into the fields of a variable of type Class. (The record is passed as a parameter.) The data should be read in the same order as the items in the record. Assume that character data is padded with blanks to the maximum length.

6. Write a hierarchical record description for the following:

   Name (up to thirty characters)
   Student ID number
   Credit hours to date
   Number of courses taken
   Course grades (a list of up to fifty elements containing the course number and a letter grade)
   Date first enrolled (month and year)
   Class (Fresh, Soph, Jr, Sr, Grad)

Grade-point average

Each record and user-defined ordinal type should have a separate type defini-tion.

7. Given the following declarations:

```
TYPE
    Code = PACKED ARRAY[1..25] OF CHAR;
    Ref = RECORD
              Token : ARRAY[1..2000] OF Code;
              Symbol : ARRAY[1..20] OF Code
          END;  (* RECORD *)
    Map = RECORD
              MapCode : Code;
              Style : (Formal, Brief);
              Chart : Ref
          END;  (* RECORD *)
    GuideType = ARRAY[1..200] OF Map;

VAR
    Guide : GuideType;
    AMap : Map;
    ARef : Ref;
    I, Count : INTEGER;
    ACode : Code;
```

Which of the following would be valid statements in the main program? (Assume valid variables have defined values.)

a. IF Map.Style = Brief
       THEN
           Count := Count + 1;

b. Guide[1].Chart.Token[2] := AMap;

c. Guide[6].Chart := ARef;

d. AMap.MapCode[1] := ARef.Token[1];

e. Guide[100].Chart.Token[1, 2] := ACode[2];

f. Guide[20].Token[1] := ACode;

g. IF Guide[20].Style = Formal
       THEN Guide[20].Chart.Token[1, 1] := 'A';

h. AMap := Guide[5];

i. AMap.Chart := ARef;

8. Using the declarations in Exercise 7, write statements to do the following:
   a. Assign the value in the Chart field of AMap to ARef.
   b. Assign AMap to the fourth element of Guide.
   c. Assign ACode to the MapCode field of the tenth element of Guide.
   d. Compare the first characters in ACode and in the MapCode field of the second

element of Guide. If they are equal, then output the MapCode field and the Style field of the second element of Guide.

e. Compare AMap.Chart and ARef. Show which elements (if any) are not equal by outputting the subscripts indicating the appropriate Token fields or Symbol fields. For example, if the second Token field of both records is not equal, you would output the number 2.

PRETEST

1. a. Declare a RECORD type called Apartment for an apartment locator service. Include the following information:

    Landlord (up to twenty characters)
    Address (up to twenty characters)
    Bedrooms (INTEGER)
    Price (REAL)

    b. Declare Available to be an ARRAY variable of up to 200 records of type Apartment.

    c. Write a procedure that reads values into the fields of a variable of type Apartment. (The RECORD variable is passed as a parameter.) The data should be read in the same order as the items in the record.

2. a. Declare a RECORD type called Animal for a record-keeping system aboard Noah's ark. Include the following fields:

    Name (up to thirty characters)
    FavoriteFood (up to twenty characters)
    Gestation (INTEGER)
    AvgWeight (REAL)

    b. Declare Ark to be an ARRAY variable of up to a thousand records of type Animal.

    c. Write a procedure to initialize the fields of a variable of type Animal. (The record is passed as a parameter.) Set character string fields to blanks, numeric fields to zero.

3. Given the following declarations:

```
TYPE
   Name = ARRAY[1..25] OF CHAR;
   Map = RECORD
            Street : ARRAY[1..2000] OF Name;
            Park : ARRAY[1..20] OF Name
         END;    (* RECORD *)
   City = RECORD
            CityName : Name;
            Population : INTEGER;
            Location : (NE, NW, SE, SW, NC, SC);
            List : Map
          END;    (* RECORD *)
   ListType = ARRAY[1..200] OF City;
   Box = RECORD
```

```
          Length, Width, Height : INTEGER;
          Cube : BOOLEAN
        END;    (* RECORD *)
    PackingType = ARRAY[1..80] OF Box;

VAR
  CityList : ListType;
  Carton : Box;
  Packing : PackingType;
  ACity : City;
  AMap : Map;
  I, Count : INTEGER;
  Handle : Name;
```

Which of the following would be valid statements in the main program? (Assume valid variables have defined values.)

a. ACity := CityList[5];

b. Carton := Count;

c. CityList[6].List := AMap;

d. Packing.Width := I;

e. ACity.CityName[1] := AMap.Street[1];

f. CityList[100].List.Street[1, 2] := Handle[2];

g. IF Packing[3].Cube
      THEN Count := Count + 1;

h. IF CityList[20].Location = SW
      THEN CityList[20].List.Street[1, 1] := 'D';

i. ACity.Population := I;

j. IF Cube
      THEN Count := Count + 1;

k. I := City.Population;

l. ACity.List := AMap;

m. IF City.Location = NW
      THEN Count := Count + 1;

n. CityList[1].List.Street[2] := Handle;

o. Packing[100].Length := I;

p. CityList[20].Street[1] := Handle;

PROGRAMMING ASSIGNMENTS

1. Write a program that simulates the game Bingo. Each player uses a Bingo card like this one:

| | | | | |
| B | I | N | G | O |

B	I	N	G	O
14	20	33	47	71
3	18	40	51	68
11	21	FREE	50	70
1	16	37	52	63
7	29	31	55	74

The card is broken up into five columns and five rows. The center position is a free space. Numbers in the other positions are random within a certain range for each column:

B: 1–15
I: 16–30
N: 31–45
G: 46–60
O: 61–75

Tokens numbered 1 to 75 are drawn at random and announced. Numbers called are covered by a marker on the player's card. Play continues until a player or players have a winning combination of markers. These are the winning combinations:

A horizontal row of five numbers
A vertical row of five numbers
A diagonal row of five numbers

Your program should read three Bingo cards for three players. Generate numbers between 1 and 75 using a random-number generator. Each number should be identified by its column letter, and both letter and number should be printed. No number should be printed more than once. Play continues until there's a winner (or winners). Output should include the players' original cards, the letters and numbers generated, the players' cards at the end of the game with positions covered by markers (displayed as zeroes), and the winning player's number (1, 2, or 3).

2. The local police department keeps a file of city residents who have marked their belongings with a unique seven-character code (digits and letters). Write a program to match items recovered by the department with codes in the file.

The program should begin by reading the file that contains the residents' codes, names, and phone numbers. For example:

A123456   JOHN SMITH   4527836

John Smith, whose phone number is 4527836, has the unique code A123456.

Then a file of items recovered has to be read. This file contains a code and item description (up to fifteen characters). If the code of a found item matches the code of a person in the first file, print the code, the person's name and phone number, and the item description. If the code is not found, print the code number, *NO MATCH*, and the item description.

3. Write a program that maintains a service for the owners of lost pets. The program should read a file that describes the pets and lists the finders' names and phone numbers. For example,

SIAM CAT   MABEL DAVIS   7143261

Mabel Davis, whose phone number is 7143261, found a Siamese cat. A similar file for those who've lost pets should be processed. If a lost pet matches a found pet, then the program should print the name of the pet as well as the finder, the loser, and their phone numbers. If the pet is not found, print *NOT FOUND* under the finder column. Process each lost-pet record as it's read.

4. Your cousin—the noisy one—has been sitting in the corner for hours, quietly absorbed with a new game. You're a little bored (and curious), so you ask if you can play. The game is played with a black box with numbers on all sides.

Five obstructions, called baffles, are placed in the box. You can't see them. The object of the game is to find the baffles. You choose a number between zero and 39, which activates a laser beam originating at that location. Then you're told where the beam leaves the box. If the beam does not encounter a baffle, it exits directly opposite the number where it entered. If the beam encounters a baffle, it's deflected at right angles, either right or left, depending on the direction of the baffle. You can locate the baffles by shooting beams into the box, using the deflections of the beams to guess the placement and direction of the baffles.

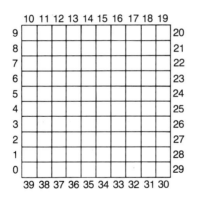
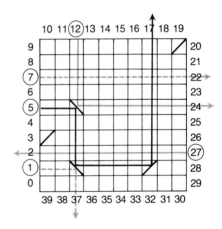

A beam shot from 7 comes out at 22. A beam shot from 1 is deflected once; it exits at 37. A beam shot from 27 exits at 2 without being deflected. A beam shot from 5 comes out at 17 after three deflections. A beam shot from 12 is deflected once, exiting at 24.

The player scores 1 point for each laser shot and 2 points for each guess. The lower the score, the better the player.

When your cousin demands his game back, you decide to write a computer program to simulate the game. (*Note*: Your program is not supposed to *solve* the problem; it's supposed to simulate the game.) Clearly this should be an interactive program. The baffles should be set by a random-number generator, with a player either firing a laser beam or making a guess about the position of a baffle. You decide to write the program and test it first. You can add the prompts for interactive play later.

Input/Output:

(1) In the game, the baffles are set by a random-number generator. To test the program, however, you read in the coordinates from an input file. The information for each baffle is one line of input in the format

                              X   Y   DIR

where X is an integer between zero and 9, Y is an integer between 10 and 19, and DIR (direction) is either R (right) or L (left). X, Y, and DIR are separated by at least one blank, maybe more.

Here's an example:

    5   12   L   sets   5

    9   19   R   sets   9

Error checking: You can't be sure that each line of input is unique (just as the random-number generator may coincidentally come up with the same coordinates for two baffles). You can only place a baffle in a "free" position—one that has not been previously set. You need to set a total of 5 *unique* baffles.

When you've set five unique baffles, skip all input until you encounter an asterisk (*).

(2) Input for playing the game follows the *. Each command to the game is on a separate line in the input file. Echo-print each command before the specified output. Use this format for the command input:

Column 1	Columns 2–80	Meaning
P		Print the box, showing the locations and directions of all the baffles that already have been found.
L	Integer (0–39)	Laser shot. Shoot the laser, with the beam entering the box at the designated location. Your output should be

                    LASER SHOT #____ EXITED THE BOX AT
                    ____

G	X	Y	DIR*	Guess the location of one baffle. X, Y, and DIR refer to the coordinates and direction of the baffle. Output:

THIS IS GUESS NUMBER ___ .

If the guess is correct, print

CONGRATULATIONS, YOU HAVE FOUND ___ BAFFLE(S).

If the guess is correct, but the baffle was found on a previous guess, print

YOU HAVE ALREADY
FOUND THIS BAFFLE.

If the guess is incorrect, print

SORRY, BETTER LUCK NEXT TIME.

S   Score. Output:

NUMBER OF SHOTS: ___
NUMBER OF GUESSES: ___
CURRENT SCORE: ___

*The same format used in part (1).

Continue processing until all five baffles are found. Output a message of congratulations and the final score. Print the box showing the location and direction of all the baffles.

Error checking: In addition to the specific error checking mentioned above, you must check all input. If an error is found in any line, that line is not used and an appropriate warning should be printed (use your imagination). You can assume that the number of items on a line and their respective types are correct.

For example, if the input is

L   40

you might print out

*** LASER SHOT OUT OF BOUNDS - - TRY AGAIN ***

If the input is

B   5   12   R

you might print out

*** ILLEGAL COMMAND - - TRY AGAIN ***

Here's a sample game:

Input file:

```
5      12     L
9      19     R
2      17     J
3      10     R
9      19     L
14      3     R
1          12        L
 1     17          R
  3       13     R
 9                    11      L
*
L8
L12
G 5 12 L
P
L 30
G      30   20    R
G      9    19              R
G      17
L      17
G             5    12           L
S
:
:
G      1    10    R
L 1
G      1    12          L
```

Output:

```
***   SET BAFFLES   ***
5      12   L        BAFFLE 1 SET
9      19   R        BAFFLE 2 SET
2      17   J        *** error message ***
3      10   R        BAFFLE 3 SET
9      19   L        *** error message ***
14      3   R        *** error message ***
1      12   L        BAFFLE 4 SET
1      17   R        BAFFLE 5 SET
```

Ignore rest of input until * is encountered.

```
*** PLAY GAME ***

L    3
        LASER SHOT #1 EXITED THE BOX AT 21.
```

```
L       12
        LASER SHOT #2 EXITED THE BOX AT 24.

G       5    12    L
        THIS IS GUESS #1.
        CONGRATULATIONS, YOU HAVE NOW FOUND 1 BAFFLE(S).

P
```

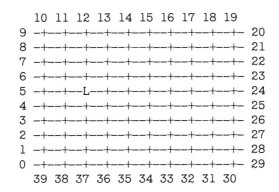

```
        10 11 12 13 14 15 16 17 18 19
    9  -+--+--+--+--+--+--+--+--+--+- 20
    8  -+--+--+--+--+--+--+--+--+--+- 21
    7  -+--+--+--+--+--+--+--+--+--+- 22
    6  -+--+--+--+--+--+--+--+--+--+- 23
    5  -+--+--L--+--+--+--+--+--+--+- 24
    4  -+--+--+--+--+--+--+--+--+--+- 25
    3  -+--+--+--+--+--+--+--+--+--+- 26
    2  -+--+--+--+--+--+--+--+--+--+- 27
    1  -+--+--+--+--+--+--+--+--+--+- 28
    0  -+--+--+--+--+--+--+--+--+--+- 29
        39 38 37 36 35 34 33 32 31 30
```

```
L       30
        LASER SHOT #3 EXITED THE BOX AT 20.

G       30   20    R
        *** OPERANDS OUT OF BOUNDS -- TRY AGAIN ***

G       9    19    R
        THIS IS GUESS #2.
        CONGRATULATIONS, YOU HAVE NOW FOUND 2 BAFFLE(S).

K       17
        *** ILLEGAL COMMAND -- TRY AGAIN ***

L       17
        LASER SHOT #4 EXITED THE BOX AT 5.

G       5    12    L
        THIS IS GUESS #3.
        YOU HAVE ALREADY FOUND THIS BAFFLE.

S
        NUMBER OF SHOTS:  4
        NUMBER OF GUESSES:  3
        CURRENT SCORE:  10
    .

    .

G       1    10    R
        THIS IS GUESS #15.
        SORRY, BETTER LUCK NEXT TIME.
```

```
L     1
                  LASER SHOT #26 EXITED THE BOX AT 37.
G     1     12    L
            THIS IS GUESS #16.
            CONGRATULATIONS, YOU HAVE NOW FOUND 5 BAFFLE(S)

*************** YOU FOUND ALL THE BAFFLES ***************

NUMBER OF SHOTS:   26
NUMBER OF GUESSES:   16
CURRENT SCORE:   58

    10 11 12 13 14 15 16 17 18 19
9 -+--+--+--+--+--+--+--+--+--R- 20
8 -+--+--+--+--+ -+--+--+--+--+- 21
7 -+--+--+--+--+--+--+--+--+--+- 22
6 -+--+--+--+--+--+--+--+--+--+- 23
5 -+--+--L--+--+--+--+--+--+--+- 24
4 -+--+--+--+--+--+--+--+--+--+- 25
3 -R--+--+--+--+--+--+--+--+--+- 26
2 -+--+--+--+--+--+--+--+--+--+- 27
1 -+--+--L--+--+--+--+--R--+--+- 28
0 -+--+--+--+--+--+--+--+--+--+- 29
    39 38 37 36 35 34 33 32 31 30
```

Your output may differ in minor details from this example because of different error messages and slight format differences.

12 Files and Sets

In this chapter we finish our discussion of the built-in structured data types in Pascal. We have talked about ARRAY and RECORD. Here we look at FILE. You are already familiar with one form of file—the TEXT file. There are other forms too. In Pascal the components of a file can be of any type except another file.

SET is the only unstructured composite data type; that is, it is made up of a group of unstructured components. The set is not available in many programming languages. We discuss its usefulness and how to work with it.

Files

Programs communicate with the outside world and with each other through files. Results that a person should see are written to a file that goes to a printer or a terminal. Data that needs to be saved from one run of a program to the next must be written to a file to be saved on a peripheral storage device. Data cannot stay in memory after a program has finished executing because that memory space is needed by other programs. Files for people to see or programs to read are called **external files**. These files have meaning outside of the executing program that creates them.

External File
A file that is used to communicate with people or programs.

Input data can come from a terminal, a tape drive, a disk drive, or another computer. Output can go to a terminal, a printer, a tape drive, a disk drive, or another computer. All of these physical devices look different and operate differently. However, Pascal makes them all appear to be the same to the programmer. In other words, input, output, and storage devices vary physically, but Pascal makes no distinction among them in the READ and WRITE statements in a program.

Data on different peripheral devices is represented differently. For example, data on a disk is physically different from data displayed on a terminal. However, we do not have to worry about these differences. When our programs access these files, the file components are changed from their physical representation into a standard logical representation (Figure 12–1). Who or what makes this change? The Pascal run-time support system. That system, working with the operating system of the particular machine you are using, translates from the physical file to the logical file or from the logical file to the physical file.

Files are not fixed in length because they are not stored in memory. A file is like an array in that it represents a list of components. Unlike an array, however, only one component of a file is accessible to a program at a time. The **FILE data type** is a homogeneous sequence of components, accessed sequentially.

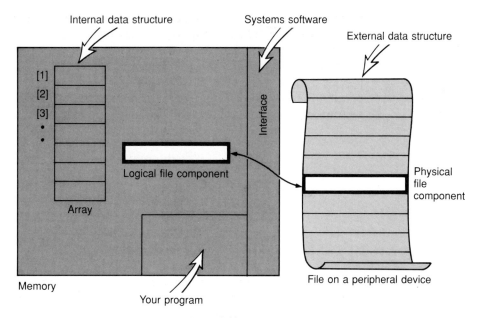

FIGURE 12–1 Physical versus logical file component

FILE Data Type

A structured data type consisting of a sequence of like components accessed sequentially.

Pascal files are sequential files; they are made up of a sequence of components that must be accessed in a fixed order. Because files are stored externally, it takes more time to access each component than to access a component of a data structure in memory. Once a component of a file has been accessed, all the components that come before it on the file are inaccessible (unless they have been stored in an internal data structure). Of course, the file can be RESET and read again, but this is a time-consuming process.

We have seen that a file can be used for both input and output at different points in a program. File Checks in Program CheckRegister was both an input and output file. The current balance, the number of outstanding checks, and a list of all outstanding checks were saved as output from the program to be read in as input at the beginning of the next run.

We tell the compiler that we are going to use external files by listing the file identifiers in the program heading as program parameters. For example,

```
PROGRAM Example(INPUT, OUTPUT, File1, File2);
```

states that four external files are going to be used: the standard input and output devices and File1 and File2.

A file can also be used strictly as a data structure *internal* to the program. For example, a procedure or program may need more memory space for temporary data storage than is available. Here we declare a FILE variable as a local variable of the procedure or program. We use REWRITE to prepare the file for output. When we need to read the data back in, we use RESET to prepare the file for reading. **Internal files** are not listed in the program heading and are destroyed when the program terminates.

Internal File

A file that is created and used while a program is running, but that is destroyed when the program ends.

Notice that *internal* and *external* here refer to the file's role in the program. All files are external in the sense that they reside on external storage.

Files can be passed as parameters to procedures. They must be passed as VAR parameters, not value parameters, because a copy of the file can't be written on the message board—files are external to memory. We have to access one file component at a time, so we have to know where to go to get the next component.

Standard Files

The standard files INPUT and OUTPUT are predeclared for use as FILE variables of type TEXT. The variable declarations are automatic, and the files are "opened" for input and output automatically. All other FILE variables *must* be declared, and the procedures RESET and REWRITE must be used to prepare them for input or output. File INPUT is defined to be the standard input device, which is usually the terminal. File OUTPUT may be defined on your system as the terminal or the printer.

The standard procedure RESET prepares a file to be an input file; that is, the reading pointer is placed at the beginning of the file. The standard procedure REWRITE prepares a file to be an output file. The first value written to the file is placed at the beginning of the file. The previous content of the file (if any) is lost.

TEXT Files

Although you have been using TEXT files for almost a semester, let's review some of their important features. Files of type TEXT are files of type CHAR that are broken up into lines. There are two special symbols recognized in

TEXT files: <eoln>, which represents the end of a line, and <eof>, which represents the end of the file.

The standard procedures READLN and WRITELN and the function EOLN are used only with TEXT files. READLN and WRITELN recognize and generate this file structure. EOLN is TRUE at the end of a line when the last character is read and the next character is <eoln>. If we issue a character read when the reading pointer is at <eoln>, READ returns a blank. If this extra blank affects your processing, test for EOLN and move the reading pointer to the beginning of the next line with a READLN.

TEXT files are input character by character. When we do an INTEGER or REAL read, the READ looks at every character to see where a number begins and ends on the line and then converts the character representation of the number to a numeric value. Numeric reads ignore blanks to find the start of a numeric value and continue until the next blank is found (but not read). In character reads, the next character is read no matter what it is.

Reading numeric data character by character and converting it ourselves give us more control over the validity of our data. If you are doing an INTEGER read using READ and there is an invalid character in the file, you will get a run-time error. You can avoid this by doing character reads and your own numeric conversions. Invalid characters can be detected and reported, and processing can continue if the situation calls for it.

Let's write a procedure, ReadInteger, to read and convert unsigned INTEGER values from a TEXT file. This procedure is similar to the READ procedure in Pascal, but it reads and returns only one INTEGER value at a time and continues until any nonnumeric character is read. If that nonnumeric character is a blank, ReadFlag is set to Blank; otherwise, ReadFlag is set to NonBlank. If a nonnumeric character or <eof> is read before a numeric character is found, ReadFlag is set to Error.

```
PROCEDURE ReadInteger(VAR DataFile : TEXT;
                      VAR Number : INTEGER;
                      VAR ReadFlag : FlagType);
(* An integer number is read in character form on    *)
(* DataFile and converted to numeric form. ReadFlag  *)
(* is Blank if a blank ends the number, NonBlank if  *)
(* some other character ends the number, and Error if *)
(* no number is found or <eof> is encountered.       *)

VAR
  Character : CHAR;
```

```
BEGIN   (* ReadInteger *)
  Number := 0;
  IF EOF(DataFile)
    THEN
      ReadFlag := Error
    ELSE
      REPEAT   (* skip blanks *)
        READ(DataFile, Character)
      UNTIL (Character <> ' ') OR EOF(DataFile);
  IF EOF(DataFile) OR NOT (Character IN ['0'..'9'])
    THEN
      ReadFlag := Error
    ELSE
      (* convert character representation to numeric value *)
      REPEAT
        Number:= Number * 10 + ORD(Character) - ORD('0') ;
        READ(DataFile, Character)
      UNTIL NOT (Character IN ['0'..'9']);
  IF ReadFlag <> Error
    THEN
      IF Character = ' '
        THEN
          ReadFlag := Blank
        ELSE
          ReadFlag := NonBlank
END;    (* ReadInteger *)
```

Procedure ReadInteger uses the Pascal set notation and the reserved word IN (used to test set membership). The expression

```
NOT (Character IN ['0'..'9'])
```

is equivalent to

```
(Character < '0') OR (Character > '9')
```

We explain this construct in detail later in the chapter.

Figure 12–2 shows the execution of Procedure ReadInteger with four different lines of data. (Each example is independent.)

Data line: □□□□□□□□□□54□□□□□□□□□□
(□ is a blank)
   First loop   Second loop reads to here
   reads to here.   after doing the following:

         1. Number = 0 * 10 + 5 (5)
         2. Number = 5 * 10 + 4 (54)

       Number is 54. Character is a blank, so ReadFlag
       is set to Blank.

Data line: □□□□□□□□□A□54
   First loop   Character is not a digit,
   reads to here.   so ReadFlag is set to Error.

Data line: □□□□□□234A□

   First loop   Second loop reads to here
   reads to here.   after doing the following:

         1. Number = 0 * 10 + 2 (2)
         2. Number = 2 * 10 + 3 (23)
         3. Number = 23 * 10 + 4 (234)

       Number is 234. Character is an A, so ReadFlag is
       set to NonBlank.

Data line: <eof>

   First EOF   ReadFlag is set to Error.
   is TRUE.

FIGURE 12–2

SAMPLE PROBLEM

Problem: Our publisher has asked us to produce an index for this text. The first step in the process is to decide which words should go into the index; the second is to produce a list of the pages on which each word occurs.

Instead of trying to choose the words out of thin air, we decide to let the computer produce a list of all the words used in the manuscript and their frequency of occurrence. We can go over that list and choose the words we want in the index. In good top-down fashion, let's write the program to create the list of words. We can worry about making the index later.

SAMPLE PROBLEM, CONTINUED

Discussion: Because we need to create a list of words and their frequency of occurrence, the first thing we must do is to define *word*. Once we do that, we can develop an algorithm to create a list of words.

Looking back at the last paragraph, how would you define *word* in this context? How about "something between two blanks"? This definition works for most of the words, but what about the words followed by commas and periods? We don't want to end up with punctuation marks in our list of words.

Let's try another definition:

Word: A string of characters between markers, where markers are blanks and all punctuation marks.

Does this work? Yes, if <eoln> is returned as a blank, which it is.

On to our algorithm. What we want to do is find the beginning of a word and collect letters into an array until an end-of-word marker is found. After we have a word, we need to check to see if it's one we have had before. If it is, we increment the frequency count and continue looking for the next word. If it's a new word, we have to add it to our list of words.

Does this sound familiar? It should. Look at Program DesignCount in Chapter 9. At the end of that chapter, we said the program would work with strings as well as integers. We are not going to use that algorithm directly, but take this problem as a way of introducing you to some other algorithms.

Because an ordered list would be much simpler to work with in developing our index, we use the insertion sort (again, from Chapter 9) every time we get a new word. The insertion sort uses a linear search to find a position in a list. Here we introduce a faster method, called a *binary search*. Like the linear search, the binary search finds the item if it is there and tells us where it should be if it is not there.

A binary search is based on the principle of divide and conquer. In this problem, it involves dividing the list in half (dividing by 2—that's why it's called a *binary* search) and determining if the word is in the upper or lower half. We keep doing this until the search finds the word (or at least the place where it goes if it's not in the list).

This method is much like the way we look up words in a dictionary. We open the dictionary and compare the word we're looking for with the word on the top of the left-hand page. If the word we're looking for comes alphabetically before that word, we continue our search with the left-hand section of the dictionary. Otherwise, we continue with the right-hand section. We keep doing this until we find the word. If it's not there, either we have misspelled it or our dictionary isn't complete.

If the list of values is called List and the value we're looking for is called Item, this is the algorithm for a binary search:

1. Middle ← (first index + last index) DIV 2
   Compare Item to List[Middle]
   - If Item = List[Middle], then you've found it.
   - If Item < List[Middle], then Item is in the first half of List if it's in List at all.
   - If Item > List[Middle], then Item is in the second half of List if it's in List at all.
2. Redefine List to be that half of List that Item is in (if it's there at all) and repeat Step 1.
3. Stop when you've found Item or know it isn't there. (You know that Item isn't there when there is nowhere else to look and you still have not found it.)

This algorithm makes intuitive sense. With each comparison, at best you find the value for which you're searching; at worst you eliminate half of the list from consideration.

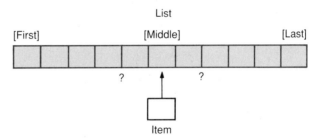

We can express this algorithm in terms of Item and List and through the indexes First, Middle, and Last.

```
First ← 1
Last ← Length
Found ← FALSE
WHILE (Last >= First) AND NOT Found DO
      Middle ← (First + Last) DIV 2;
      IF Item < List[Middle]
            THEN
                  Last ← Middle − 1
            ELSE
                  If Item > List[Middle]
                        THEN
                              First ← Middle + 1
                        ELSE
                              Found ← TRUE
```

SAMPLE PROBLEM, CONTINUED

Let's do a code walk-through, searching for the values 24, 106, and 406. We assume that array List contains these values:

	[1]	[2]	[3]	[4]	[5]	[6]	[7]	[8]	[9]	[10]	[11]
	12	64	72	86	92	103	106	125	200	300	400

	INDEXES				
Number	**First**	**Last**	**Middle**	**List[Middle]**	**Terminating Condition**
24	1	11	6	103	
	1	5	3	72	
	1	2	1	12	
	2	2	2	64	
	2	1			Last < First
106	1	11	6	103	
	7	11	9	200	
	7	8	7	106	Found is TRUE
406	1	11	6	103	
	7	11	9	200	
	10	11	10	300	
	11	11	11	400	
	12	11			Last < First

Sorry for the detour, but a binary search is an important algorithm that you will use again and again. Now let's return to our problem, where we use a binary search in a specific context.

Input: Book (a TEXT file)

Output: Ordered list of words with the frequency of occurrence (on File Words)

Data Structures: A packed array (Word) to hold a word
An array (List) of records containing words and their frequency of occurrence

MAIN MODULE   Level 0

There are often problems associated with using EOF on a TEXT file. To avoid these problems, we will use a flag to indicate the end of the file. Because this is our manuscript, inserting a special flag does not cause any problems. The flag must be something that does not appear in the manuscript. We use a word of five percent signs. This flag is the named constant EndOfText.

```
Rest Book
Rewrite Words
Length ← 0
WHILE NOT Finished AND List NOT full
  Get a Word
  IF Word = EndOfText
      THEN
          Finished ← TRUE
      ELSE
          Update List
IF List Full AND NOT Finished
      THEN
          Writeln 'Only partial list'
Print List
```

GET A WORD   Level 1

This module is somewhat like Module GET PAYEE in Program CheckRegister (see page 394), but the control structure is slightly different. Here we continue reading and collecting characters until either we find a character that is in the set of punctuation marks or the word is too long. We also change each upper-case letter to lowercase so that a word that begins a sentence is not considered a different word from the same word used elsewhere in a sentence. Finally, we define a global constant AllBlanks, which is a word of all blanks. This allows us to set Word to AllBlanks to begin with instead of having to pad the remainder of the word with blanks.

SAMPLE PROBLEM, CONTINUED

```
Word ← AllBlanks
Index ← 0
(* skip over extra punctuation *)
REPEAT
   Read (Book, Character)
UNTIL NOT Character IN [' ', ' ', '.', '!', '?'])
WHILE NOT Character IN [' ', ',', '.',  '!', '?'])
         AND Index < StringLength DO
   Index ← Index + 1
   Word[Index] ← LowerCase(Character)
   Read (Book, Character)
(* skip over extra letters *)
WHILE NOT Character IN [' ', ',', '.',  '?', '!'])
   Read (Book, Character)
IF EOLN(Book)
     THEN
        Readln(Book)
```

LOWERCASE   Level 2

We can pick up Function LowerCase (page 276) and use it here.

UPDATE LIST   Level 1

```
Search using binary search algorithm
IF Found
     THEN
        List[Index].Frequency ← List[Index].Frequency + 1
     ELSE
        Item.Frequency ← 1
        Item.Word ← Word
        Shift down
        Length ← Length + 1
        List[Index] ← Item
```

BINARY SEARCH   Level 2

The algorithm that we developed on page 431 can be coded directly. We use the same parameters as Procedure Search, which we have used several times. Our assumption about this procedure is that the list of items is in ascending order (either alphabetic or numeric).

SHIFT DOWN

```
For Count from Length DOWNTO Index DO
    List[Count + 1] ← List[Count]
```

PRINT LIST   Level 1

```
Writeln Words, 'Word' :StringLength + 1, 'Frequency' :10
FOR Index from 1 TO Length DO
    Writeln Words, List[Index].Word, List[Index].Frequency
```

Module Design Chart:

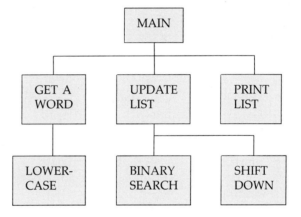

In Program SortScores (page 322) we choose to code Module SHIFT DOWN in-line in Procedure Insert. If we had not, we would have had the debugged procedure ready to use here. This time, we will make it a parameterized procedure.

SAMPLE PROBLEM, CONTINUED

Interface Design Chart:

Program Variables

Identifiers	Type	Role
StringLength	INTEGER	Maximum size of a word, balance skipped
MaxWords	INTEGER	Maximum size of word List
List	ARRAY	A list of words and associated frequencies
Word	String	A word of text
Book	TEXT	Input file with text of book
Words	TEXT	Output file of words and frequencies
Length	INTEGER	Number of words on List
Finished	BOOLEAN	Termination flag set to TRUE when word = EndOfText (%%%%)

Subprograms

Identifiers	Needs	Returns
Lowercase	Character	Character (lowercase)
GetAWord	Book	Word
BinarySearch	List, Length, Word	Found, Index
ShiftDown	Length, Index	List
UpdateList	Word	List, Length
PrintList	Words, List, Length	Nothing

```
PROGRAM WordList(OUTPUT, Book, Words);
(* The unique words along with their frequency of    *)
(* occurrence in File Book are written on File Words. *)

CONST
  StringLength = 10;
  MaxWords = 500;
  AllBlanks = '          ';
  Blank = ' ';
  EndOfText = '%%%%      ';
```

```
TYPE
  IndexRange = 1..MaxWords;
  WordString = PACKED ARRAY[1..StringLength] OF CHAR;
  WordRecord = RECORD
                  Word : WordString;
                  Frequency : INTEGER
               END;   (* RECORD *)
  ListType = ARRAY[IndexRange] OF WordRecord;
  ItemType = WordString;
  IndexType = 0..MaxWords;

VAR
  List : ListType;
  Word : WordString;
  Book,                  (* text of manuscript                    *)
  Words : TEXT;          (* output list of words and frequencies *)
  Length: IndexType;
  Finished : BOOLEAN;

(* **************************************************************** *)

FUNCTION LowerCase(Character : CHAR) : CHAR;
(* Uppercase letters are converted to lowercase. *)
(* All other characters are unchanged.           *)

BEGIN    (* LowerCase *)
  IF (Character >= 'A') AND (Character <= 'Z')
     THEN
        LowerCase := CHR(ORD(Character) + 32)
     ELSE
        LowerCase := Character
END;    (* LowerCase *)

(* **************************************************************** *)

PROCEDURE GetAWord(VAR DataFile : TEXT; VAR Word : WordString);
(* The next word is read on File DataFile. *)

VAR
  Index : 0..StringLength;
  Character : CHAR;

BEGIN    (* GetAWord *)
  Word := AllBlanks;
  Index := 0;
```

SAMPLE PROBLEM, CONTINUED

```
(* Skip all blanks and punctuation characters. *)
REPEAT
  READ(DataFile, Character)
UNTIL NOT (Character IN [' ',',','.', '!','?']);

(* Characters are collected into Word until a *)
(* blank or a punctuation character is read.  *)
WHILE NOT (Character IN [' ', ',', '.', '!', '?']) AND
      (Index < StringLength) DO
  BEGIN
    Index := Index + 1;
    Word[Index] := LowerCase(Character);
    READ(DataFile, Character)
  END;

(* Skip to next blank or punctuation mark. *)
WHILE NOT (Character IN [' ', ',', '.', '!', '?']) DO
    READ(DataFile, Character);
IF EOLN(DataFile)
    THEN
      READLN(DataFile)
END;   (* GetAWord *)


(*****************************************************************)


PROCEDURE BinarySearch(List : ListType;  Length : IndexType;
                       Item : ItemType;  VAR Found : BOOLEAN;
                       VAR Index : IndexType);
(* If Item is in the Word field of List, Found is TRUE *)
(* and Index is the place found.  If Found is FALSE,   *)
(* Index is where value should go.                     *)

VAR
  First, Last, Middle : IndexType;

BEGIN   (* BinarySearch *)
  First := 1;
  Last := Length;
  Found := FALSE;

  (* Search List. *)
  WHILE (Last >= First) AND NOT Found DO
    BEGIN
      Middle := (First + Last) DIV 2;
      IF Item < List[Middle].Word
          THEN
            Last := Middle - 1
          ELSE
            IF Item > List[Middle].Word
```

```
                    THEN
                      First := Middle + 1
                    ELSE
                      Found := TRUE
        END;

    IF Found
      THEN
        Index := Middle
      ELSE
        Index := First
END;    (* Binary Search *)


(***************************************************************)

PROCEDURE ShiftDown(VAR List : ListType;
                    Length, Index : IndexType);
(* Items in List[Index] to List[Length] are shifted down. *)

VAR
  Count : IndexType;

BEGIN    (* ShiftDown *)
  FOR Count := Length DOWNTO Index DO
    List[Count + 1] := List[Count]
END;    (* ShiftDown *)


(***************************************************************)

PROCEDURE UpdateList(Word : WordString; VAR List : ListType;
                     VAR Length : IndexType);
(* If Word is in List, its frequency is incremented.  If not, *)
(* Word is inserted into list with a frequency of 1.  List is *)
(* maintained in alphabetic order.                            *)

VAR
  Index : IndexType;
  Found : BOOLEAN;
  Item : WordRecord;

BEGIN    (* UpdateList *)
  BinarySearch(List, Length, Word, Found, Index);
  IF Found
    THEN
      List[Index].Frequency := List[Index].Frequency + 1
    ELSE
      BEGIN
        Item.Frequency := 1;
```

SAMPLE PROBLEM, CONTINUED

```
          Item.Word := Word;
          ShiftDown(List, Length, Index);
          Length := Length + 1;
          List[Index] := Item
       END
END;     (* UpdateList *)


(*************************************************************)

PROCEDURE PrintList(VAR Words : TEXT; List : ListType;
                    Length : IndexType);
(* Words and frequencies are printed. *)

VAR
  Index : IndexType;

BEGIN   (* PrintList *)
  WRITELN(Words, 'Word':StringLength + 1, 'Frequency':10);
  FOR Index := 1 TO Length DO
    WRITELN(Words, List[Index].Word:StringLength + 1,
            List[Index].Frequency:10)
END;     (* PrintList *)


(*************************************************************)

BEGIN   (* WordList *)
  RESET(Book);
  REWRITE(Words);
  Length := 0;
  Finished := FALSE

  WHILE (Length < MaxWords) AND NOT Finished DO
    BEGIN
      GetAWord(Book, Word);
      IF Word = EndOfText
        THEN
          Finished := TRUE
        ELSE
          UpdateList(Word, List, Length)
    END;

  IF (Length = MaxWords) AND NOT Finished
    THEN
      WRITELN('Only partial list');
  PrintList(Words, List, Length)
END.     (* WordList *)
```

Binary Files

In the beginning of this chapter we described the FILE as a structured data type consisting of a sequence of components and having no fixed length. Because sequential files are the only files in Pascal, they are known simply as files.

The predefined type associated with the standard input and output devices is type TEXT, in which the component of the file is a character. We can define a file in which the component can be of any type (except another file). Here's the syntax diagram:

$$\longrightarrow \text{identifier} \longrightarrow \texttt{=} \longrightarrow \text{FILE} \longrightarrow \text{OF} \longrightarrow \text{type}$$

The identifier defines a structured file of whatever type is listed. Let's look at some examples defined using some of the definitions and declarations we made in Program WordList:

```
CONST
   StringLength = 10;
   MaxWords = 500;
   AllBlanks = '
   Blank = ' ';

TYPE
   IndexRange = 1..MaxWords;
   WordString = PACKED ARRAY[1..StringLength] OF CHAR;
   WordRecord = RECORD
                   Word : WordString;
                   Frequency : INTEGER
                END;   (* RECORD *)
   ListType = ARRAY[IndexRange] OF WordRecord;
   ItemType = WordString;
   FileOfWords = FILE OF WordString;
   FileOfItems = FILE OF ItemsType;
   FileOfArrays = FILE OF ListType;

VAR
   WordFile : FileOfWords;
   ItemFile : FileOfItems;
   ListFile : FileOfArrays;
   Book : TEXT;
```

WordFile is a file in which the components are strings of length StringLength.
ItemFile is a file in which the components are records with two fields: Word and Frequency.
ListFile is a file in which the components are arrays of records.
Book is a garden variety TEXT file.

READ and WRITE, when applied to non-TEXT files, input or output one component of the file at a time. There can only be one parameter for either the READ or the WRITE for a non-TEXT file. READLN and WRITELN have no meaning with non-TEXT files because there are no <eoln>s in those files. There is, however, an <eof> at the end of every file. Using <eof> to control the reading of a non-TEXT file is much easier because there is not the problem of the intervening <eoln> before the <eof>.

READ(WordFile, Word) reads a string of length StringLength.
READ(ItemFile, Item) reads a record with two fields.
READ(ListFile, List) reads an array of records.

Non-TEXT files are called **binary files** because no conversion takes place between the internal representation of a component in memory and the external representation of the component on the file. Whatever is stored in that variable in memory is written on the file; conversely, whatever is written on the file is read directly into the variable.

Binary File

A file in which no conversion takes place as a component is written to or read from the file; a non-TEXT file.

Because the components in a binary file are just a pattern of bits with no interpretation, the file must be written by a Pascal program that uses the same type definition as the Pascal program that is going to read the file. *A binary file cannot be written by a word processor or text editor.* Word processors and text editors by definition process text: The files that are created on them are TEXT files.

This means that you cannot sit down at the terminal and create a binary data file to use to test a program. You have to create the file in TEXT form and write a utility program to read the file in TEXT form and write it in binary form.

File Buffer Variables

Whenever we declare a FILE variable, we automatically create another variable known as the **file buffer variable**. The file buffer variable is denoted by the file name followed by an up-arrow (↑). The type of this variable is the same as the component type of the file. For example, here are the buffer variables for Files WordFile, ItemFile, ListFile, and Book:

WordFile↑ (a variable of type WordString)
ItemFile↑ (a variable of type ItemType)
ListFile↑ (a variable of type ListType)
Book↑ (a variable of type CHAR)

> **File Buffer Variable**
>
> A variable of the same type as the component of a file, which is automatically created when a FILE variable is declared. It is accessed by the file identifier followed by an up-arrow (↑).

The buffer variable is the "window" through which we can inspect the next component to be read or the last component appended (written) to a file. Whenever we do a READ or WRITE, we are actually manipulating the file buffer variable. In fact, now we can more precisely define what RESET does. RESET moves the first component of the file into the file buffer variable.

Pascal provides standard procedures GET and PUT to manipulate the buffer variable directly. Provided that File DataIn has been reset and File DataOut has been rewritten,

GET(DataIn) advances the current position of the File DataIn to the next component and assigns the value of the component to the buffer variable DataIn↑.

PUT(DataOut) appends the value of the buffer variable DataOut↑ to the file DataOut.

In fact, these two procedures are the primitive operators out of which the procedures READ and WRITE are built. The statement

```
READ(DataIn, Item);
```

is equivalent to

```
Item := DataIn↑;
GET(DataIn);
```

And

```
WRITE(DataOut, Item);
```

is equivalent to

```
DataOut↑ := Item;
PUT(DataOut);
```

These equivalences hold for items of any type with the exception of numeric READs or WRITEs from a TEXT file. When numeric values are read from a file of type TEXT (or the standard input device), the values are converted from character form and collected as we did in Procedure ReadInteger. When numeric values are written to a file of type TEXT (or to the standard output device), the values are converted to character representation. Each of these conversions manipulates the file buffer variable as many times as is needed for the complete value to be read or written.

We can use GET, PUT, and the file buffer variable to copy information from one file to another.

Using READ and WRITE	**Using GET and PUT**
| ```
WHILE NOT EOF(DataIn) DO
  BEGIN
    READ(DataIn, Item);
    WRITE(DataOut, Item)
  END;
``` | ```
WHILE NOT EOF(DataIn) DO
  BEGIN
    DataOut↑ := DataIn↑;
    PUT(DataOut);
    GET(DataIn)
  END;
``` |

SAMPLE PROBLEM

Problem: Write a general purpose merge procedure that merges the records on two binary files. Here is the procedure interface:

```
PROCEDURE MergeFiles(VAR InFile1, InFile2, OutFile : ItemFileType);
(* The records on InFile1 and InFile2 are to be merged onto *)
(* OutFile using the Item field.  The relational operators  *)
(* may be applied to the values in field Item.              *)
```

Discussion: In Chapter 9 we wrote a merge procedure that merges the values in two arrays (see page 327). The merge algorithm we use here is the same except that we take values from files rather than from arrays. Our original discussion is still valid. Our control structures are quite different, but that doesn't change the algorithm. We look at a value from each file and write out the smaller one, replacing it with the next component from that file. The process stops when one (or both) of the files runs out of records. Any remaining records then are written.

Input: Binary Files InFile1 and InFile2

Output: Binary File OutFile

Data Structures: Three binary files

MERGE FILES

Level 0

Normally a top-down design is written in general terms that can be translated into any language. This is not the case here. We know that we are dealing with binary files in Pascal, so our design is more specific than usual.

```
Reset InFile1 and InFile2
Rewrite OutFile
WHILE NOT EOF(InFile1) AND NOT EOF(InFile2) DO
  IF InFile1↑.Item < InFile2↑.Item
      THEN
        OutFile↑ : = InFile1↑
        GET(InFile1)
      ELSE
        OutFile↑ : = InFile2↑
        GET(InFile2)
  PUT(OutFile)
IF NOT EOF(InFile1)
    THEN
      Write rest InFile1
IF NOT EOF(InFile 2)
    THEN
      Write rest InFile2
```

WRITE REST

```
WHILE NOT EOF(InFile) DO
  OutFile↑ : = InFile↑
  GET(InFile)
  PUT(OutFile)
```

Module Design Chart:

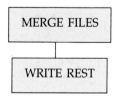

SAMPLE PROBLEM, CONTINUED

Interface Design Chart:

Procedure Parameters and Variables

Identifiers	Type	Role
InFile1	ItemFileType	Input file
InFile2	ItemFileType	Input file
Outfile	ItemFileType	Output file

Procedures

Identifiers	Needs	Returns
WriteRest	InFile	Nothing

Because the design is so specific, we have left the code for you to write. See Exercise 13 on page 462.*

Sets

SET is an unusual built-in data type: We do not find it in many commonly used programming languages. In mathematics, a set is a collection, group, or class of objects. A Pascal set is just the same, but the objects must all be of the same type. In mathematics a set can be of any size, but Pascal places an implementation-dependent limit on the size of a set.

> **Set**
> An unordered group of distinct components (members) chosen from the values of an ordinal type.

This is the syntax diagram of a set:

⟶ SET ⟶ OF ⟶ simple type

*You cannot implement this design in Turbo Pascal because the Turbo compiler does not support the file buffer variable. You have to use READ and WRITE.

To declare a SET type, we use the following syntax:

```
TYPE
   LetterRange = 'a'..'z';
   LetterSet = SET OF LetterRange;

VAR
   Vowels, Consonants : LetterSet;
```

Type LetterSet describes a SET type in which the component type is the lowercase letters of the alphabet. The declaration

```
VAR
   Vowels, Consonants : LetterSet;
```

creates two SET variables of this type. Vowels and Consonants are undefined (like all variables) until they are initialized in the program. Be careful: Each is a structure that can contain none, one, or a combination of alphabetic characters. They do not start out with the letters in them.

To put elements into a set, you must use an assignment statement.

```
Vowels  :=  ['a', 'e', 'i', 'o', 'u'];
```

puts the elements 'a', 'e', 'i', 'o', and 'u' into the SET variable Vowels. Notice that brackets are used here, not parentheses.

We cannot access the individual elements of a set, but we can ask if a particular element is a member of a SET variable. We can also apply three standard set operations: union, intersection, and difference. These operations are defined below.

Set Operation	Symbol	Description
Union	+	The union of two SET variables is a SET variable made up of the elements that are in either or both of the SET variables.
Intersection	*	The intersection of two SET variables is a SET variable made up of those elements occurring in both SET variables.
Difference	−	The difference between two SET variables is a SET variable made up of those elements in the first SET variable but not in the second.

The table below shows how the three set operations work. Let1 and Let2 are of type LetterSet.

Statement	Results
`Let1 := ['a', 'b', 'c'];`	['a', 'b', 'c']
`Let2 := Let1 + ['x', 'y', 'z'];`	['a', 'b', 'c', 'x', 'y', 'z']
`Let1 := Let1 - Let2`	[]
`Let1 := Let1 + ['x', 'w'];`	['x', 'w']
`Let1 := Let1 + ['x', 'z'];`	['x', 'w', 'z']
`Let2 := Let1 * Let2;`	['x', 'z']

If we want to add one element to a set, we use the union operator:

```
Vowels := Vowels + ['y'];
```

To delete an element from a set, we use the difference operator:

```
Vowels := Vowels - ['y']
```

If we add an element that is already in a set, nothing happens. If we delete an element that is not in a set, again nothing happens.

If we want to initialize Vowels and Consonants to the vowels and consonants respectively, we would use these statements:

```
Vowels := ['a', 'e', 'i', 'o', 'u'];
Consonants := ['a'..'z'];
Consonants := Consonants - Vowels;
```

This is a lot easier than listing every letter we want in Consonants.

The relational operators (= , <>, >=, <=, < , >) can all be applied to sets. In addition, there is a test for set membership:

Expression	Returns TRUE If
Set1 = Set2	Set1 and Set2 are identical.
Set1 <> Set2	There is at least one element in Set1 not in Set2 or there is at least one element in Set2 not in Set1.
Set1 <= Set2	All the elements in Set1 are in Set2.
Set1 < Set2	All the elements in Set1 are in Set2 and there is at least one element in Set2 not in Set1.
Set1 >= Set2	All the elements in Set2 are in Set1.
Set1 > Set2	All the elements in Set2 are in Set1 and there is at least one element in Set1 not in Set2.
Element IN Set1	Element is a member of Set1.

Let's look more closely at IN, a very useful operator.

```
IF Character IN ['a', 'e', 'i', 'o', 'u']
   THEN
      Statement;
```

is equivalent to

```
IF (Character = 'a') OR (Character = 'e') OR (Character = 'i')
                     OR (Character = 'o') OR (Character = 'u')
   THEN
      Statement;
```

We also could have used

```
IF Character IN Vowels
   THEN
      Statement;
```

if Vowels had been initialized to ['a', 'e', 'i', 'o', 'u']. Testing for set member-ship is a much faster operation than evaluating a long expression in an IF statement, and it certainly is easier to read.

Order has no meaning in sets. The assignment

```
Vowels := ['a', 'e', 'i', 'o', 'u'];
```

is the same as

```
Vowels := ['e', 'o', 'a', 'u', 'i'];
```

It doesn't matter how we list values within the set brackets.

We can use subranges to assign values to sets. Here order is important: The second value must be greater than the first. For example,

```
Let1 := ['c'..'a'];
```

actually makes Let1 the **empty set**, the set with no members at all. This is what we really want:

```
Let1 := ['a'..'c'];
```

Because ordering has no meaning, we could assign Let1 like this:

```
Let1 := ['p'..'t', 'a'..'c', 'z', 'k'..'m'];
```

It makes better sense, however, to list the values in alphabetical order because that's how we usually think of them.

Just like variables of other types, we need to initialize the value of a SET variable before we manipulate it. If we want a SET variable to be empty before we add elements to it, then we assign the empty set to it:

```
Let1  := [];
```

In Chapter 7 we noted that the result of executing a CASE statement in which the case selector does not match any of the constants in the case label list is undefined (see page 248). The SET data type can be used to determine if the case selector is in one of the case label lists (the set of labels). If it is not, you can decide what to do about it.

One of the examples we used in Chapter 7 was

```
CASE Grade OF
   'A', 'B' : WRITE('Good work');
   'C'      : WRITE('Average work');
   'D', 'F' : WRITE('Poor work')
END;  (* CASE *)
```

If Grade does not contain an 'A', 'B', 'C', 'D', or 'F', you might get a run-time error or the statement might be skipped, depending on your compiler. You can prevent this happening by checking to be sure Grade is one of the case labels, using the test for set membership:

```
IF Grade IN ['A', 'B', 'C', 'D', 'F']
   THEN
     CASE Grade OF
       'A', 'B' : WRITE('Good work');
       'C'      : WRITE('Average work');
       'D', 'F' : WRITE('Poor work')
     END   (* CASE *)
   ELSE
     WRITELN('Grade contains an illegal character.');
```

The general pattern for this test is

```
IF case selector IN [set of labels]
     THEN
        CASE statement
     ELSE
        whatever you want to do under this condition
```

Another obvious use for the SET construct is to check for correct input characters. For example, in Program CheckRegister (page 399), we prompt the user to input the letters 'c', 'd', 'p', 'r', or 'q'. The body of Procedure GetCode, which inputs the proper code, could be written like this:

```
REPEAT
  PrintMenu;
  READLN(Code);
  Code := LowerCase(Code)
UNTIL Code IN ProperCodes;
```

where ProperCodes is defined as the following SET variable:

```
ProperCodes := ['c','d','p','r','q'];
```

Another way to handle menu input is to print the menu outside the loop. You enter the loop only if there is an error. Within the loop you can write a message saying that the input is in error and new input is requested.

```
PrintMenu;
READLN(Code);
WHILE NOT Code IN ProperCodes DO
  BEGIN
    PrintErrorPrompt;
    READLN(Code)
  END;
```

Notice that the WHILE expression is NOT Code IN ProperCodes. If you say Code NOT IN ProperCodes, you will generate a compile-time error because of type mismatch. The correct construction of the IN is

```
identifier IN SET variable
```

where the type of the identifier is the same as the type of the components in the SET variable.

SAMPLE PROBLEM

Problem: Employee personnel records are kept on a master file. You have been asked to go through the records and make a copy of the record of every employee who is enrolled in either the company health plan or the company retirement plan. There are going to be some major changes in benefits, and the company wants to mail personal letters to those affected.

The employee records are kept on a binary file, in which each employee is represented by a record like this:

SAMPLE PROBLEM, CONTINUED

```
TYPE
   OptionsType = (Retirement, Health, ProfitSharing,
                      Bonds, UnitedWay);
          .
          .
   OptionsSet = SET OF OptionsType;
   EmployeeRecord = RECORD
                        LastName, FirstName : NameString;
                        Address, CityState : AddressString;
                        Options : OptionsSet
                    END;  (* RECORD *)
```

Discussion: If the list was on paper instead of a computer file, you would go through it with a pencil and check off those people whose options are Health or Retirement. That is exactly what we do in the program. We ask if Health is IN Options or Retirement is IN Options. All input is very simple because we are using binary files.

Input: Binary File Master

Output: Binary File Special

Data Structures: A record as described above for each employee, which contains four strings and a set

MAIN MODULE   Level 0

```
Reset Master
Rewrite Special
WHILE NOT EOF(Master) DO
    Read employee record
    IF Health IN Employee.Options OR
          Retirement IN Employee.Options
       THEN
          Write employee record
```

```
PROGRAM LetterInput(OUTPUT, Master, Special);
(* Employee records are written on binary File   *)
(* Special if the employee has the company health *)
(* plan or the retirement plan.                   *)

CONST
  NameLength = 15;
  AddressLength = 20;
```

```
TYPE
  OptionsType = (Retirement, Health, ProfitSharing, Bonds,
                 UnitedWay);
  NameRange = 1..NameLength;
  AddressRange = 1..AddressLength;
  NameString = PACKED ARRAY[NameRange] OF CHAR;
  AddressString = PACKED ARRAY[AddressRange] OF CHAR;
  OptionsSet = SET OF OptionsType;
  EmployeeRecord = RECORD
                     LastName, FirstName : NameString;
                     Address, CityState : AddressString;
                     Options : OptionsSet
                   END;  (* RECORD *)
  EmployeeFile = FILE OF EmployeeRecord;

VAR
  Employee : EmployeeRecord;
  Master, Special : EmployeeFile;

BEGIN   (* LetterInput *)
  RESET(Master);
  REWRITE(Special);
  WHILE NOT EOF(Master) DO
    BEGIN
      READ(Master, Employee);
      IF (Health IN Employee.Options) OR
         (Retirement IN Employee.Options)
           THEN
             WRITE(Special, Employee)
    END
END.   (* LetterInput *)
```

The 4-Cs Corner
Clarity

Look back at Procedure GetAWord (page 437). It looks pretty cluttered, doesn't it? The set constant [' ', ',', '.', '!', '?'] is repeated three times. Did you wonder why we didn't declare a named set constant instead of repeating the literal set constant three times? The problem is that named constants can only be constants of the data types REAL, INTEGER, CHAR, and BOOLEAN or character strings in single quotes.

Now that we have discussed sets in general, let's look at a better, clearer way to handle the situation. We begin by defining a SET type to contain any characters that might ever be word separators. Then we declare a SET variable of that type and assign to it the punctuation marks that we are interested in. This variable can be passed as a parameter to Procedure GetAWord. This way the procedure is clearer and more general. The following definitions and declarations would be added to Program WordList:

```
TYPE
  .
  .
  MarkerType =  ' '..'~';   (* ASCII printable characters *)
  MarkerSet = SET OF MarkerType;

VAR
  Punctuation : MarkerSet;
  .
  .
(****************************************************************)

PROCEDURE GetAWord(VAR DataFile : TEXT; VAR Word : WordString;
                   Punctuation : MarkerSet);
  .
  .
(****************************************************************)

BEGIN   (* WordList *)
  Punctuation := [' ', ',', '.', '!', '?'];
  .
  .
    GetAWord(Book, Word, Punctuation);
  .
  .
END.    (* WordList *)
```

Within Procedure GetAWord, the test would be

```
Character IN Punctuation
```

Conciseness

It is a wise decision to use a binary file anytime that the output from a program is going to be used as input to a program. Communication between the program and the outside world is very slow because it involves the physical movement of data. If the data has to be converted into a different form before it's stored, the process is even slower.

Program CheckRegister saves the current balance, the number of checks outstanding, and the checks from one run to another. The program would run much faster if we used a binary file. There is a problem, however. A binary file is made up of components that are all the same type. In Program

CheckRegister we have three different types of information: the current balance (REAL), the length (INTEGER), and the checks (RECORDS).

There are three ways that this information can be organized so that a binary file can be used. The first is to define a record with three fields: CurrentBalance, Length, and CheckBook (an array). This record could be written and read in its entirety. The problem here is that the complete ARRAY variable CheckBook would have to be written, even if we are only using a part of it.

Another option is to write a file of records of CheckType, calculating Length as the records are read. (We could have done this originally.) Where does that leave the current balance? We could have the user input it from the keyboard.

Finally, we can make RECORD type CheckType a *variant record*. One variant of the record has only one field: CurrentBalance. The second variant has three fields: CheckNumber, Payee, and Amount. Although this is not the classic reason for using a variant record, it allows us to use a binary file efficiently (and gives us a chance to talk about variant records).

Variant Records

Within a group of data objects described by a RECORD type, there may be variation in some of the attributes of those objects. Instead of declaring a RECORD variable large enough to contain all the variations, you can use the variant record. A variant record is a way of overlapping fields if you know they cannot occur in the same RECORD variable. All the possible variant fields are defined in the type definition, and the variant to be used for a particular RECORD variable is specified during execution. The compiler allocates only enough space for the RECORD variable to include the largest variant.

For example, take a RECORD type that describes a person's travel arrangements. If you're taking the train, you will need to know the date and time of departure. If you're taking a plane, you will need to know the date, time of departure, flight number, and seat assignment. If you are going by car, the only information you need is the date of departure.

The only information that is necessary in all three cases is the date of departure; this becomes the fixed part of the record. Each of the other fields is a variant. Records can contain a fixed and a variant part. If both are present, the fixed part must precede the variant part in the record definition. The variant part is introduced with the word CASE:

```
TYPE
     .
     .
  KindOfTrip = (Train, Plane, Car);
  TripInfo = RECORD
             Date : DateType;
```

```
      CASE Tag : KindOfTrip OF
        Train : (TimeT : TimeType);
        Plane : (TimeP : TimeType;
                    FltNumber : INTEGER;
                    SeatNumber : SeatType);
        Car   : ()
      END;   (* RECORD *)
```

The identifier next to CASE is called the tag field (Tag in this example).

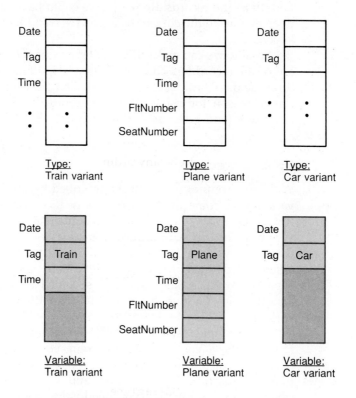

When you use a RECORD variable that has a variant part, you can specify which variant it is by setting the tag field. For a trip by train, Tag is set to Train; for a trip by plane, Tag is set to Plane; and for a trip by car, Tag is set to Car. When Tag is Train, the Time field exists in the RECORD variable. When Tag is Plane, the Time, the FltNumber, and SeatNumber fields exist in the RECORD variable. When Tag is Car, no variant fields exist.

If you do not explicitly assign a value to the tag field in a RECORD variable, the tag field is implicitly set by the first access to a variant field. If you store a value into the SeatNumber field of a RECORD variable, you specify that it is a Plane variant.

Here are some points you should bear in mind when using variant records:

- A record definition can contain only one variant part, although field lists in the variant part can contain a variant part (a nested variant).
- All field identifiers within a record definition must be unique.
- The CASE clause in the variant part is not the same as a CASE statement.
    There is no matching END for the CASE; the END of the record definition is used.
    The case selector is a *type* (KindOfItem). You can put an identifier and a colon before it, but it is not necessary. For example, we could have written the CASE expression like this:

```
CASE KindOfTrip OF
```

    If we had, we would not have had an explicit field (Tag) to tell us which variant we were working with. Here, the field names that we use specify the variant.
    Each variant is a field list labeled with a case label list. Each label is a constant of the tag type (KindOfItem).
    The field lists are in parentheses.
    The field list defines the fields and field types of the variant.
- The tag type can be any ordinal type, but it must be a type identifier. That is, you cannot say

```
CASE (Train, Plane, Car) OF . .
```

- A field list can be empty, which is denoted by (). The field list for the variant Car is empty.
- When the tag field of a RECORD variable is set (either explicitly or implicitly), you may access the fields associated with that tag field.

    Back to our checkbook problem. This definition would allow us to use binary files in Program CheckRegister:

```
TagType = (Balance, Regular);
CheckType = RECORD
               CASE TagType OF
                 Balance :(CurrentBalance : REAL);
                 Regular :(CheckNumber : INTEGER;
                            Payee : NameString;
                            Amount : REAL)
            END;   (* RECORD *)
```

The following code fragment would read the information from File Checks (assumes OneCheck has been defined to be of type CheckType):

```
READ(Checks, OneCheck);
CurrentBalance := OneCheck.CurrentBalance;
Length := 0;
```

```
WHILE NOT EOF(Checks) DO
  BEGIN
    Length := Length + 1;
    READ(Checks, OneCheck);
    CheckBook[Length] := OneCheck
  END;
```

By accessing OneCheck.CurrentBalance, you are stating that this is the variant that has the field CurrentBalance. That field is accessed. Because we have written the first record on the file to be of that variant, everything is fine. All the rest of the records are of the other variant (regular checks). When you access the fields of CheckBook[Index], you will get what you expect.

Correctness

In the real world, it is especially important to validate program input. At the beginning of this chapter, we talked about using a procedure to read and convert characters to INTEGER values. Procedure ReadInteger reports errors in the data, and the calling segment can decide whether or not to continue processing.

Actually, the nature of the program determines how error conditions are handled. In an interactive program, the user can be "told" about the error and prompted to reenter the data. In a **batch program**—a program that's executed without user interaction—it's generally best to write a detailed description of the error and stop processing.

Correctness Hints

1. All files (including binary files) passed as parameters to a procedure must be VAR parameters.
2. Like all variables, SET variables must be initialized before they are used.
3. Don't try to print sets directly—you can't. Test elements for set membership and print each element that is a member.
4. Always use brackets to denote sets. The statement

   ```
   Let1 := Let1 + 'a';
   ```

   is not valid. Both operands must be sets (and of the same set type). Using brackets around the 'a' makes it a set.

   ```
   Let1 := Let1 + ['a'];
   ```

   is a valid statement.
5. Remember that the arithmetic operators (+ , − , and *) have different meanings when they are used with SET variables.
6. Explicitly set the tag field in a variant record and use a CASE statement in your processing. If you use the field FltNumber in an expression, the

RECORD variable is assumed to be a Plane variant, and the value in the fourth field of the RECORD variable is returned. This value will be meaningless if the RECORD variable is not a Plane variant. Most run-time systems do not check for this error.

Summary

FILE is the data type that allows programs to communicate with people and with each other. Pascal programs can use multiple input and output files. EOLN is a standard function used in processing files of type TEXT; EOF is a standard function used in processing any type of file.

Files allow us to store data both before and after a program is executed. Because files are not limited in length, they can be used internally in a program where an array is too big for available memory space.

SET is another data type. Its declaration defines what the elements of the set can be. SET variables are then defined to be of that SET type. Union, intersection, and difference are the standard set operations. Relational operators also can be used with sets. The operator IN is used between an element of the component type and a SET variable to test for set membership.

SET variables are very useful for validating input from an interactive menu and guarding against an error with a CASE statement.

EXERCISES

1. Write a function that returns the length of a string passed as a parameter. Do not count padded blanks. Use this type definition:

```
TYPE
   String = PACKED ARRAY[1..20] OF CHAR;
```

2. Write a procedure that reads a data line from a TEXT file (passed as a parameter) and returns the line in reverse order in a packed array. Pad with blanks if necessary. Use this type definition:

```
TYPE
   Line = PACKED ARRAY[1..80] OF CHAR;
```

3. Write a procedure that reads a symbol from a TEXT file. Each symbol is made up of five characters enclosed in asterisks (*) beginning at the first character position on a line. Verify the beginning and ending asterisks for each symbol. Use this type definition:

```
TYPE
   Symbol = PACKED ARRAY[1..5] OF CHAR;
```

4. Write a procedure that accepts any TEXT file as a parameter, reads a word of text, and returns the word in a packed array. Assume that the next character to be read when the procedure is called is alphabetic, and that no word is longer than twenty-five characters. Pad the array with blanks for words shorter than twenty-five letters. Assume this declaration in the main program:

```
TYPE
   Word = PACKED ARRAY[1..25] OF CHAR;
```

5. Answer the following statements true or false.
   a. An external file is any file that resides on external storage.
   b. An internal file is one that's created in the computer's memory.
   c. Standard files include all files of type TEXT.
   d. The standard procedures READLN and WRITELN can be used with any file.
   e. A binary file cannot be written by a word processor or text editor.
   f. After a READ statement the file buffer variable contains the same component as the program variable used in the READ statement.
   g. A CASE in a variant record tests the tag variable to be sure it matches one of the case labels.
   h. Variant records must have at least one overlapping variable.
   i. Every field list used with a case selector in a variant record must contain at least one variable.
   j. The tag type of a variant record must be a type identifier.

6. Given the following declarations:

```
TYPE
   String20 = PACKED ARRAY[1..20] OF CHAR;
   String10 = PACKED ARRAY[1..10] OF CHAR;
   Man = RECORD
              Name : String20;
              Address : String20;
              Class : 1..6;
              Sex : (M, F)
         END;    (* RECORD *)
   ManFile : FILE OF Man;

VAR
   AString : String20;
   I : INTEGER;
   J : INTEGER;
   Word : String10;
   Person : Man;
   Data : ManFile;
```

Write a program segment that reads values from file Data and prints them until EOF.

7. Using the declarations in Exercise 6, which of the following statements are valid? (Assume valid variables have defined values.)

```
a. FOR I := 1 TO 10 DO;
      Person.Name[I] := Word[I];

b. WRITE(AString);

c. READ(Person);

d. WRITE(AString[J]);
```

```
   e. IF Word = 'Large'
         THEN
            I := J;

   f. READ(AString);

   g. Word := 'Tight';

   h. AString := Person.Name;

   i. Person.Name := Word;

   j. Word[1] := AString[1];

   k. READ(Data, Person)
```

8. Write a program segment that inputs values from a file of arrays and prints the average of each array. Process until the end of the file. Assume these declarations and initializations:

```
TYPE
   List = ARRAY[1..10] OF INTEGER;

VAR
   AList : List;
   Data : FILE OF List;
   I, Sum : INTEGER;
   Average : REAL;
   .
   .
   RESET(Data);
   Sum := 0;
```

9. Rewrite the following using set notation:
   a. (0 < I) AND (I < 25)
   b. (Ch = 'A') OR (Ch = 'J') OR (Ch = 'K')
   c. (X = 1) OR (X > 50) AND (X <=100)

10. Use the following definitions to answer the questions below.

```
TYPE
   Months = (January, February, March, April,
            May, June, July, August, September,
            October, November, December);
   MonthSet = SET OF Months;

VAR
   SummerMonths, WinterMonths, NewSet, SchoolMonths,
     JMonths : MonthSet;
```

   a. Assign the months June, July, and August to SummerMonths.
   b. Assign the months December, January, and February to WinterMonths.
   c. Assign the months September through May to SchoolMonths.
   d. Assign the months that begin with the letter *J* to JMonths.

11. Using the definitions and assignments in Exercise 10, show the content of NewSet after the following operations.
    a. NewSet : = SummerMonths + WinterMonths;
    b. NewSet : = SummerMonths * JMonths;
    c. NewSet : = SummerMonths * WinterMonths;
    d. NewSet : = SchoolMonths − JMonths;
    e. NewSet : = WinterMonths − SummerMonths;

12. Using the definitions and assignments in Exercise 10, give the value of each Boolean expression below.
    a. SummerMonths * WinterMonths = []
    b. SummerMonths <> SchoolMonths
    c. WinterMonths >= SchoolMonths
    d. WinterMonths − JMonths <= SchoolMonths

13. Write a procedure, MergeFiles, that merges the records from two binary files (In-File1 and InFile2) into a third binary file (OutFile) in ascending order using the Item field. (See pages 444–446.) Assume no duplicates.

PRETEST

1. Write a program segment that counts the number of characters in the first line of a data file. Use INPUT as the file, Character as the character variable, Count as an INTEGER variable. Assume there is more than one line of data in INPUT.

2. Write a program segment that reads an entire file (INPUT) and prints each line that starts with an asterisk. (Don't print the asterisk.)

3. Write a Boolean function that returns TRUE if a packed array passed as a parameter contains at least one nonblank character. Assume this declaration in the main program:

```
TYPE
   String = PACKED ARRAY[1..10] OF CHAR;
```

4. Answer the following statements true or false.
    a. A file that resides on external storage can be an external file or an internal file depending on how it's used.
    b. Internal files exist after the program that uses them is through running.
    c. INPUT and OUTPUT are the only standard files in Pascal.
    d. The standard procedures READLN and WRITELN cannot be used with every FILE type.
    e. A binary file can only be written by a Pascal program that uses the same type definition as the Pascal program that will read the file.
    f. With a non-TEXT file, READ and WRITE can input or output several different data structures from or to one file.
    g. After a RESET statement and before any READ statement, a file buffer variable is empty.
    h. Variant records cannot have overlapping fields.
    i. The case selector in a variant record must end with END.
    j. The tag type of a variant record must be a variable.

5. Given the following declarations:

```
TYPE
   Name = PACKED ARRAY[1..20] OF CHAR;
   Word = PACKED ARRAY[1..10] OF CHAR;
   Person = RECORD
               Name, Address : Name;
               Age : 1..200;
               Sex : (M, F)
            END;    (* RECORD *)
   NameFile = FILE OF Name;

VAR
   Handle : Name;
   Token : Word;
   Student : Person;
   I, J : INTEGER;
   Data : NameFile
```

Which of the following statements are valid? (Assume valid variables have defined values.)

a. READ(Handle);

b. WRITE(Handle);

c. READ(Token);

d. WRITE(Handle[J]);

e. IF Token = 'Big'
     THEN

        I := J;

f. Token := 'VERY LARGE';

g. Handle := Student.Name;

h. Student.Name := Token;

i. READ(Data, Handle)

j. FOR I:= 1 TO 10 DO
     Student.Name[I] := Token[I];

6. a. Define a SET type that contains all the uppercase letters of the alphabet.
   b. Declare three SET variables (SetA, SetB, SetC) of the type in part a.
   c. Assign 'A'..'N' to SetA.
   d. Assign 'K'..'Z' to SetB.

7. Using the definitions and assignments in Problem 6, show the content of SetC after the following operations.

   a. SetC := SetA + SetB;

   b. SetC := SetA − SetB;

c. SetC := SetA * SetB;

d. SetC := SetB - SetA;

8. Evaluate the following expressions.

a. SetA <> SetB

b. SetA <= SetB

c. SetA * SetB > SetA

d. SetA + SetB >= SetA

PROGRAMMING ASSIGNMENTS

1. The Emerging Manufacturing Company has just installed a computer and hired you as a junior programmer. Your first program is to read employee pay data and produce two reports: an error and control report and a payroll report.

   Input:
   Transaction file (TEXT):
   (1) Set of five job site number/name pairs
   (2) One line for each employee containing
       (a) ID number
       (b) job site number
       (c) number of hours worked
   This data has been presorted by ID number.
   Master file (file of records):
   (1) ID number
   (2) Name
   (3) Pay rate per hour
   (4) Number of dependents
   (5) Type of employee (union/management—zero is union, 1 is management)
   (6) Job site
   (7) Sex (M or F)
   This file also is ordered by ID number.

   Note: (1) Union members get time and a half for hours over forty; managers get nothing for hours over forty.
   (2) The formula to compute tax is as follows: If the number of dependents is 1, the tax rate is 15 percent; otherwise the tax rate is

   $$1 - \frac{\text{Number of dependents}}{\text{Number of dependents} + 6} \times 0.15$$

   Output:
   Error and control report:
   (1) List the input lines for which there is no corresponding master record, or where the job site numbers do not agree. Continue processing with the next line of data.
   (2) Give the total number of employee records that were processed correctly during each run.

Payroll report (labeled for management):

(1) A line for each employee containing name, ID number, job site name, gross pay, and net pay

(2) A total line showing the total amount of gross pay and total amount of net pay

2. The Emerging Manufacturing Company has decided to use its new computer for parts inventory control as well as payroll. You've been asked to write a program to run each night. It should take the stock tickets from the day's transactions, make a list of the parts that need ordering, and print an updated report that must be given to the five job site managers each morning. Notice that you are not being asked to update the file.

   Input:

   Transaction file (TEXT):

   (1) Set of five job site number/name pairs

   (2) One line for each stock transaction containing

   (a) part ID number

   (b) job site number

   (c) number of parts bought and sold (a negative number indicates that a part has been sold)

   This data has been presorted by site number within part number.

   Master file (file of records):

   (1) Part ID number

   (2) Part name (no embedded blanks)

   (3) Quantity on hand

   (4) Order point

   (5) Job site

   This file also is ordered by job site number within part ID number. If a part is not in the master file and the transaction is a sale, print an error message. If the transaction is a purchase, list it in the proper place in the out report.

   Note: There's a separate entry in the master file for parts at each job site.

   Output:

   (1) Error and control report that contains error messages and a list of the parts that need to be ordered (when quantity on hand is less than order point)

   (2) A report for *all* the parts in the master file containing

   (a) part number

   (b) part name

   (c) job site name

   (d) number on hand

   Remember, this report is for managers. Be sure it's written so they can read it.

3. You've taken a job with the Internal Revenue Service, hoping to learn how to save on your income tax. Your boss wants you to write a toy tax-computing program in order to gauge your programming abilities. The program should read in the names of members of families and each person's income, and compute the tax the family owes. You can assume that consecutive people in input with the same last name are in the same family. The number of deductions that a family can count is equal to the number of people listed in the family in the input data. Use these formulas to compute tax:

Adjusted income = Income − (500 × number of deductions)
Tax rate = Adjusted income/100,000 if income < 27,000

otherwise

Tax rate = 0.27
Tax = Tax rate × adjusted income

There are no refunds. So you must check for negative taxes and set them to zero.
Input: The data is on file Tax, which is a file of records of FileType:

```
TYPE
  Person = RECORD
              First, Last : PACKED ARRAY[1..20] OF CHAR;
              Income : REAL
           END;    (* RECORD *)
  FileType = FILE OF Person
```

Output: A table listing all of the families, one family per line, with each line containing the last name of the family, and the family's total income and computed tax

4. Your assignment is to write a program for a computer dating service. Clients give you their names, phone numbers, and a list of interests. It's your job to maintain lists of men and women using the service and to match up compatible couples.

   The problem requires you to maintain two lists, men and women. The lists must include the following information:
   (1) Name (twenty characters)
   (2) Phone number (eight characters including hyphen)
   (3) Number of interests (maximum is ten)
   (4) Interests (ten characters each, in alphabetical order)
   (5) A variable that gives the position of the client's current match (zero if not matched, 1 if matched)
   New clients should be added to the bottom of the appropriate list. (You do not have to keep the names of the clients in alphabetical order.)

   Input:
   (1) Number of current clients.
   (2) Sex (seven characters), name (twenty characters), phone number (eight characters), number of interests, and list of interests (ten characters for each one). Interests must be sorted; they are separated by commas with a period after the final interest. (*Note:* There should be a record like this for each of the current clients.)

   The rest of the file includes data lines that look like one of the following (all the lines start with a ten-character word):

   NEWCLIENT   sex (seven characters), name (twenty characters), number of interests, interests (ten characters for each one; see above for description)

   When the key word NEWCLIENT occurs, add the client to the appropriate list by storing the necessary information. Match the client with a member of the opposite sex. (A match occurs when three of the interests are the same. Use the fact that interests are sorted to make the match process easier.) Make sure you then designate both clients as matched. Print the name of the new client, his or her match, and both phone numbers. If no match is found, print an appropriate message.

OLDCLIENT name (twenty characters)

Unmatch this name with his (or her) current match by setting the match variables for this name and his (or her) match to zero.

PRINTMATCH

Print a list of all matched pairs.

PRINTNOT

Print the names and phone numbers of clients who are not currently matched.

STOPPROG

This is the last line in the file.

Output: Print the information described above, with appropriate titles.

Note: Use an insertion sort to sort the interests.

5. Although many people think of computers as large number-crunching devices, much of computing deals with alphanumeric processing. For example, the compiler reads your program as alphanumeric data.

   To give you a taste of this type of processing, the input data for this problem is a Pascal program. The assignment is to read the program and find all of the assignment statements. From each of these, extract the variable being assigned a value (the one before the assignment operator) and all of the variables in the expression on the right-hand side. Assume that no variable contains an embedded blank and that each statement is on a line by itself.

   Input: A Pascal program (Why not this one?)

   Output: Print out each assignment statement and next to it the variables you've extracted. Label the output. Here's an example:

```
ASSIGNMENT STATEMENTS                 LEFT    RIGHT
X := B;                               X       B
X := 5.6;                             X
Test := (X + 5.4) * 2 + Y / A;        Test    X       Y      A
X := Rec + Num * (Age - 10);          X       Rec     Num    Age
```

13 Pointers and Linked Lists

Here we are at the last chapter. We have only one Pascal construct left to cover: the pointer variable. The pointer variable is a variable that contains the address of (or pointer to) another variable. The pointer variable is defined just like any other variable. It is used to create other variables at run-time.

Dynamic Variables

All of the variables, both simple and structured, that we have worked with so far are **static variables.** Static variables have their size fixed at compile time.

A static variable is around as long as the part of the program (block) in which it is declared is executing. This means that the variables declared in the VAR section of the main program are always there while the program is running. The variables declared in the VAR sections of procedures and functions are around from the time they are called until control is passed back to the invoking routine.

Pascal also has a mechanism for creating **dynamic variables.** We can define a type at compile-time but not actually create any variables of that type until run-time. Dynamic variables can be created or destroyed at any time during execution of the program. They can be defined as being of any simple or structured type.

> **Dynamic Variable**
> A variable created at run-time and accessed, not by name, but through a pointer variable; a referenced variable.

We reference a dynamic variable, not by name, but through a pointer. A **pointer** is a variable that contains the address (location) in memory of the dynamic variable it references. Every new dynamic variable created has an associated pointer to reference (select) it.

We can use dynamic variables to overcome the problems of representing a list in an array where we must know the size at compile time. Dynamic variables allow us to create new components for our list only as they are needed. We don't have to know in advance how long the list will be. The only limitation here is the amount of available memory space. By having each component contain the link or pointer to the next component in the list, we can create a **dynamic data structure** to represent our list, a structure that can expand or contract as the list does.

Using dynamic variables makes it easy to change the order of the components of a list: We just change the pointer values. Inserting and deleting components are easier and faster, too. We don't have to shift each component of the list in one direction or the other; again, we simply have to change one or two pointer values (Figure 13–1).

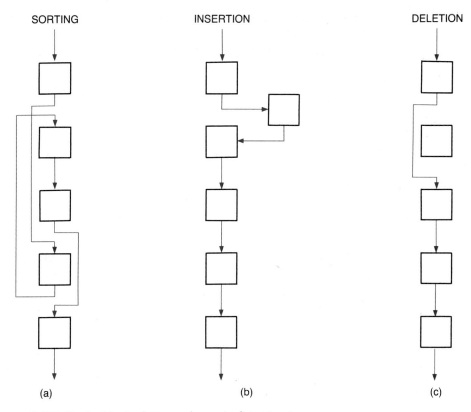

SORTING   INSERTION   DELETION

(a)   (b)   (c)

FIGURE 13–1 Manipulating a dynamic data structure

Dynamic data structures are extremely flexible. We discuss in later sections how they can be used. First, let's look at the pointer mechanism in more detail.

Pointer Data Type

Dynamic variables are referenced, not by name, but through a pointer. In fact, dynamic variables are often called **referenced variables**. The **pointer data type** is a predefined data type in Pascal.

> **Pointer Data Type**
> A simple data type that contains the address or otherwise indicates the location of a variable of a given type.

The syntax diagram for defining pointer types is

———→ type identifier ———→ **=** ———→ ↑ ———→ type identifier

Pointer is not a reserved word in Pascal; the word is not used in defining a pointer variable.

Here are definitions and declarations that show how pointer types are defined and pointer variables are declared:

```
TYPE
   Range = 1..25;
   RangePointer = ↑Range;
   Drink = (Coke, Sprite, DrPepper);
   DrinkPointer = ↑Drink;

VAR
   Pointer1 : RangePointer;
   Pointer2 : DrinkPointer;
   Pointer3 : ↑BOOLEAN;
```

Pointer1, Pointer2, and Pointer3 are pointer variables. Pointer1 is a pointer to a variable of Type Range. Pointer1 can point to an INTEGER variable whose value is in the subrange 1 to 25. The declaration causes the compiler to name a memory location Pointer1, the contents of which will be a memory address. However, as usual, the value of Pointer1 is not yet defined.

Pointer1

Even though Pointer1 exists, the dynamic (referenced) variable it is pointing to does not.

Pointer2 is a pointer to a variable of Type Drink; it can point to a variable that contains Coke, Sprite, or DrPepper. Pointer3 is a pointer to a BOOLEAN variable; it can point to a variable that contains TRUE or FALSE.

Creating a Dynamic Variable

To create a dynamic variable, the standard procedure **NEW** is used.

```
NEW(SomePtr);
```

creates a variable of the type referenced by pointer SomePtr and stores a pointer to the new variable in SomePtr. The statements

```
NEW(Pointer1);
NEW(Pointer2);
NEW(Pointer3);
```

leave the address in Pointer1, Pointer2, and Pointer3 of each of the newly created referenced variables.

> **NEW**
> The standard procedure that creates a dynamic variable.

Accessing a Dynamic Variable

How do we access the newly created dynamic variable? The pointer variable followed by an up-arrow (↑) gives us the variable pointed to. NEW(Pointer1) creates the dynamic variable Pointer1↑; NEW(Pointer2) creates the dynamic variable Pointer2↑; and NEW(Pointer3) creates the dynamic variable Pointer3↑. For the referenced variables we just created, these are valid assignments:

```
Pointer1↑ := 18;
Pointer2↑ := DrPepper;
Pointer3↑ := TRUE;
```

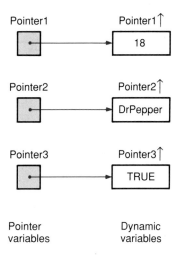

On most machines, the value of a pointer is an integer. (Memory locations have addresses ranging from zero to the size of memory.) However, a pointer type is *not* an INTEGER type. Remember, Pascal is a strongly typed language. We cannot assign an INTEGER value to a pointer. We can't even assign Pointer1, Pointer2, and Pointer3 to one another because they do not point to variables of the same type. (We can assign pointers of the same type to one another.) Nor can we print a pointer value.

The pointer contains the *address* of the dynamic variable, not its value. Here, for example, Pointer1 contains the memory location 402. In that memory location is the value of the referenced variable Pointer1↑, the integer 18.

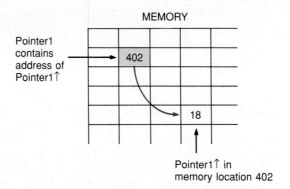

You actually have seen pointers used twice before. When a VAR parameter is left on the message board, what is really there is a pointer to the actual parameter; that is, the slot on the message board contains the address of the actual parameter. A file buffer variable also is a referenced variable. Although it is created when the file is declared, it has no name of its own; it is accessed through the file identifier followed by an up-arrow.

Operations on Dynamic Variables and Pointers

Any operation that is legal on a named variable of a certain type is legal on a dynamic variable of that type. However, assignment and a test for equality are the only legal operations on pointer variables. For example, given these declarations:

```
TYPE
   Range = 1 . .25;
   RangePointer = ↑Range;

VAR
   Pointerl, Pointer2 : RangePointer;
```

we can do the following:

```
NEW(Pointerl);
NEW(Pointer2);
READ(Pointerl↑, Pointer2↑);
WRITELN('The sum of ', Pointerl↑:1, ' and ', Pointer2↑:1,
        ' is ', Pointerl↑ + Pointer2↑:1);
```

Notice that the expression Pointer1↑ + Pointer2↑ is legal because we are adding the contents of the two dynamic variables of Type Range pointed to by Pointer1 and Pointer2. Pointer1 + Pointer2 is *not* legal because we cannot add pointer variables. We can only assign pointers of the same type or compare them for equality or inequality. In other words, we can make two pointers reference the same variable, or we can test whether or not two pointers point to the same variable.

Suppose we assign Pointer1↑ the value 18 and Pointer2↑ the value 21:

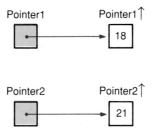

The following expressions are legal, and both evaluate to FALSE:

```
Pointer1 = Pointer2          ← Evaluates to FALSE
Pointer1↑ = Pointer2↑        ← Evaluates to FALSE
```

We can assign one pointer to another. For example,

```
Pointer1 := Pointer2;
```

makes both of the expressions above true.

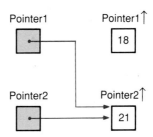

What happens to the value Pointer1 originally pointed to? It's floating free in memory. There is no pointer pointing to it; there is no way to access it. We cannot even dispose of it for reuse. Obviously, if we do this too much, we eventually can run out of memory space.

We use the assignment statements and tests for equality and inequality of pointers to implement and access linked data structures.

Using Dynamic Variables to Share Memory

Dynamic variables help us use memory more efficiently because we never have more storage space allocated than we need. When a dynamic variable is no longer needed, the storage location (or locations) it occupies can be returned to the run-time support system with the **DISPOSE** procedure.

```
DISPOSE(SomePtr);
```

destroys the variable referenced by pointer SomePointer. That is, the location (or locations) occupied by the variable is returned to be assigned to some other variable.

DISPOSE

The standard procedure that returns the memory location (or locations) used for a dynamic variable (when it is no longer needed) to the run-time support system.

If two large structures must be created for a program but do not need to be present at the same time, we can have them share the same memory space by making them dynamic variables. For example, look at the structures created by the following declarations:

```
TYPE
    CubeRange = 1..30;
    CubeType = ARRAY[CubeRange, CubeRange, CubeRange] OF INTEGER;
    CubePointer = ↑CubeType;
    RecordType = RECORD
                    First : ARRAY[CubeRange] OF REAL;
                    Second : ARRAY[CubeRange] OF CHAR
                 END;   (* RECORD *)
    ListType = ARRAY[1..10000] OF RecordType;
    ListPointer = ↑ListType;

VAR
    Cube : CubePointer;
    List : ListPointer;
```

NEW(Cube) is used to create a variable of CubeType. This variable (Cube↑) can be passed to the subprograms that process it. The subprograms do not need to know that Cube↑ is a dynamic variable. When Cube↑ is no longer needed, DISPOSE(Cube) returns the 27,000 memory locations to the run-time system. NEW(List) is used to create a variable of ListType (List↑), reusing the locations that were first used by Cube↑.

Using Dynamic Variables to Build Dynamic Structures
Dynamic Components

We can use pointers, like arrays, to create lists of items. We do this by making the components of the list dynamic variables and linking them together. Because we must have some way of linking each component to the next one in the structure, each component must contain a link or pointer that references the next component in the structure. The record is ideal as a component of a dynamic data structure. It can contain fields of different types with the pointer being one of them. For example:

```
TYPE
   PointerType = ↑Person;       ← Pointer to a person record
   Person = RECORD
               Name : PACKED ARRAY[1..20] OF CHAR;
               Next : PointerType       ← Pointer to the next
                                          element in the list

            END; (* RECORD *)

VAR
   Pointer : PointerType;
```

In the TYPE section, we describe what the dynamic variable can look like. In the VAR section, we declare a variable to be a *pointer* to a variable of that type. When we need one of the referenced variables, we use the procedure NEW, which has as its **argument** (actual parameter) a pointer declared in the VAR section. This procedure creates the variable, but instead of returning that variable itself, it returns a pointer to it. We use that pointer to access the variable itself.

Notice that the definition of PointerType includes the identifier Person before it is defined. We have to use a type identifier in the definition of a pointer type. This is an exception to the general rule that identifiers must be defined or declared before they are used. It allows us to define a pointer to an object (referenced variable) before defining the object itself.

When the program begins executing, no variables of type Person exist. To get a variable of type Person, we invoke the procedure

```
NEW(Pointer);
```

during run-time. This creates a RECORD variable of type Person. Information on where that variable is located is left in pointer variable Pointer. Notice that the two fields of this new variable (Name and Next) are undefined.

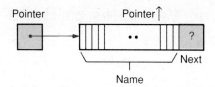

By using NEW repeatedly, we can generate additional variables of this type. Between the calls to NEW, we link the variable we have just created to the previous one, to form a linked (dynamic) data structure. Pointers always reference unnamed variables. Pointers themselves can be named or unnamed; that is, we can create a chain of unnamed pointers dynamically with each one pointing to the one that follows it. This kind of chain, however, must have at least one named pointer variable pointing to it or we would have no way at all of accessing it.

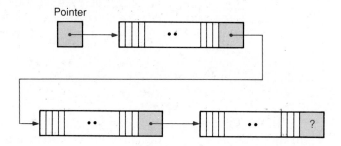

It's a little like a party game where you have to follow a chain of clues. Each clue tells you where to go to find the next clue and so on until you find the prize. Without the location of the first clue, there would be no way to start along the chain.

The pointer to the first component in a linked structure—the first clue—must be a named pointer. We call this named pointer the **external pointer** to the structure.

> **External Pointer**
>
> The named pointer variable that points to the first component in a linked structure.

We have used a specific RECORD type to illustrate the concept of dynamic components being linked together. Our example has the two parts that must be present in a dynamic chain: the information that makes up the component of the list and a pointer to the next component. These two parts (component and pointer) form what is called the **node** in a linked structure. For obvious reasons, the field that contains the pointer is often called Next or

Link. Neither of these identifiers has any special meaning in Pascal; they are just good, descriptive identifiers for a field containing a pointer.

Node in a linked structure

Linking Dynamic Components

To generate a list, we have to link the components into a chain. The process is simple. We get the first node and save its location in the external pointer to the list. (Again, for obvious reasons, the external pointer is often called List.) We then define the Component field of the node. The second step is to get another node, put its address into the Next field of the first node, and define its Component field. We repeat the second step until there are no more components in the list.

The following code fragment creates a linked list of personnel records from binary File Master.

```
TYPE
   NodePointer = ↑NodeType;
   PersonType = RECORD
                   (* Personnel information *)
                END;  (* RECORD *)
   NodeType = RECORD
                   Component : PersonType;
                   Next : NodePointer
                END;  (* RECORD *)
   FileType = FILE OF PersonType;

VAR
   List,                    (* external pointer to list          *)
   Current,                 (* pointer to last node in the list *)
   NodePtr : NodePointer;   (* new node being put on list        *)
   Master : FileType;       (* file of personnel records         *)

BEGIN
   .
   .
   NEW(List);
   READ(Master, List↑.Component);
   Current := List;
   WHILE NOT EOF(Master) DO
     BEGIN
        NEW(NodePtr);
        READ(Master, NodePtr↑.Component);
        Current↑.Next := NodePtr;
        Current := NodePtr
     END;
```

Let's do a code walk-through of this fragment:

Statement	Explanation
NEW(List);	Creates a variable of type NodeType
READ(Master, List↑.Component);	Reads data into the Component field of List
Current := List;	Sets Current to point to the first node in List
WHILE NOT EOF(Master) DO	Exits the loop if the last record has been read, leaving Current pointing to the last node in List
NEW(NodePtr);	Creates a variable of type NodeType
READ(Master, NodePtr↑.Component);	Reads data into the Component field of NodePtr
Current↑.Next := NodePtr;	Places the pointer to the newly created node in the Next field of the previous node
Current := NodePtr	Sets Current to point to newly created node

The process continues until the last record has been read. Current always points to the last node in the list.

This diagram shows the state of the structure before the loop is entered:

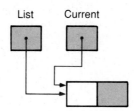

This is what the structure looks like after the loop has been executed:

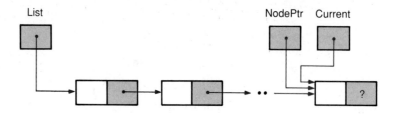

The list has been created, but the last node in the list has a Next field that is undefined. The reserved word **NIL** is the constant pointer that means "end of the list." After we exit the loop, we must set the Next field of Current to this special constant.

NIL can be assigned to a pointer variable of any type. It means that the pointer points to nothing. We can compare the Next field of each component in the list to NIL to see whether we have reached the end of the list. We use this technique when we need to access each of the components in the list in sequence, a process called *traversing the list*.

Algorithms on Linked Lists

In this section we look at several algorithms that allow us to manipulate lists implemented with linked structures. Throughout we use the following declarations:

```
TYPE
   ComponentType = (* whatever information we wish *);
   NodePointer = ↑NodeType;
   NodeType = RECORD
                 Component : ComponentType;
                 Next : NodePointer
              END;

VAR
   List : NodePointer;    (* external pointer to list *)
```

We assume that ComponentType is a simple type.

Printing a Linked List

To print (or access in sequential order) the elements in a linked list, we begin by printing (accessing) the value of the first element, then the second, then the third, and so on until we reach the end. This looks like a loop of some sort where the expression is "WHILE NOT end of list DO." What we have to do is use a pointer as a loop control variable. To increment it each time, we set it to the Next field of the current node. The end-of-loop condition is reached when the pointer (Current) equals NIL.

```
PROCEDURE PrintList(List : NodePointer);
(* Prints each Component field in List on a line. *)
(* One blank is printed between each value.       *)

VAR
   Current : NodePointer;

BEGIN    (* PrintList *)
   Current := List;       ← Initializes Current to first element
   WHILE Current <> NIL DO
      BEGIN
         WRITE(Current↑.Component:1, ' ');
         Current := Current↑.Next       ← Advances Current
      END
END;     (* PrintList *)
```

This procedure works even with an empty list (where List equals NIL).

If the linked list contains the values 49, 50, 48, and 45, the procedure would produce this output:

```
49 50 48 45
```

Notice the different values of Current (the local pointer) while the procedure is executing:

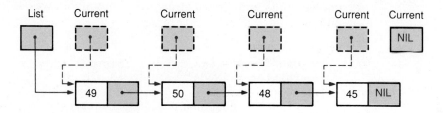

Inserting into a Linked List

A procedure for inserting into a linked list must have two parameters: the list and the element to be inserted. We also have to determine whether we want to insert an element at the beginning of the list or in some order (alphabetic or numeric) within the list.

Inserting an element as the first one in a linked list is a two-step process: creating the new element and making it the first.

```
PROCEDURE Push(VAR List : NodePointer; Item : ComponentType);
(* Inserts Item as the first component in List. *)

VAR
   NewNode : NodePointer;

BEGIN    (* Push *)
   NEW(NewNode);        ← Creates new node
   NewNode↑.Component := Item;     ← Stores component
   NewNode↑.Next := List;     ← Sets new node to point to
                                    previous first node
   List := NewNode        ← Sets external pointer to point to new node
END;      (* Push *)
```

Notice that before this procedure is called the first time, List must be initialized to NIL.

This is the structure when we enter Procedure Push:

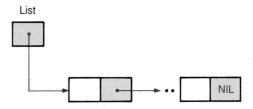

This is the structure during processing:

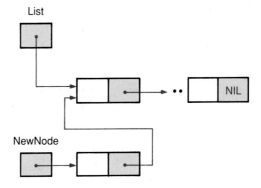

This is the structure when we exit from Push:

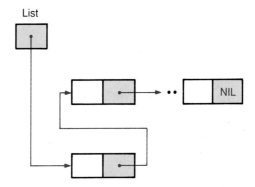

To insert an element into a specific place involves an additional step: finding that place. Suppose we want the list sorted in increasing order. We have to loop through all of the nodes until we find one whose Component field is *greater* than the value we want to insert. The following fragment does this search:

```
Current := List;
WHILE (Current↑.Component < Item) DO
    Current := Current↑.Next;
```

If the node referenced by Current is the one whose value is greater than the one to be inserted, then the new item should be inserted before that node. This causes a problem: We have to know the previous node in the list so we can change its pointer field to point to the new element. This means we have to keep track of two pointers as we go through the list: the pointer to the current node (Current) and the pointer to the previous node (Back). We use the following fragment:

```
Back := NIL;
Current := List;
WHILE (Current↑.Component < Item) DO
  BEGIN
    Back := Current;
    Current := Current↑.Next
  END;
```

This code takes care of the case where the element goes in the middle of the list. What happens with the two end cases, when the new item should be the first or the last? If the new item is the first, we can use the algorithm we've just written. If it's the last, we have trouble because the test

```
Current↑.Component < Item
```

causes an error at the end of the list. Trying to access Current↑ when Current is NIL gives a run-time error.

Our loop has to have two conditions. Our first thought would be to use

```
(Current <> NIL) AND (Current↑.Component < Item)
```

but this won't work. Most Pascal compilers evaluate both sides of the expression even if the first evaluates to FALSE. That is, Current being NIL does not stop Current↑.Component from being evaluated. We have to use a BOOLEAN variable Found. We initialize it to FALSE and change it to TRUE when we find the place to insert the element:

```
(Current <> NIL) AND NOT Found
```

When we exit the loop, we set the Next field of the new node (NewNode) to point to Current. If the new node is the first, we set List to NewNode; otherwise, we set the Next field of Back to point to NewNode. This takes care of the three cases: insertion at the front, middle, and end.

Here's our general insertion algorithm:

```
PROCEDURE InsertInPlace(VAR List : NodePointer;
                        Item : ComponentType);
(* Inserts an element in a list while maintaining *)
(* the sorted order (increasing).                 *)
```

```
VAR
   Found : BOOLEAN;
   Current, Back, NewNode : NodePointer;      ← Local pointers

BEGIN   (* InsertInPlace *)
   NEW(NewNode);
   NewNode↑.Component := Item;
   Back := NIL;              }  Initialize Back and Current
   Current := List;          }
   Found := FALSE;

   (* Loop until the insertion place is found. *)
   WHILE (Current <> NIL) AND NOT Found DO
     IF Current↑.Component < Item
         THEN
           BEGIN
             Back := Current;
             Current := Current↑.Next
           END
         ELSE
           Found := TRUE;
   NewNode↑.Next := Current;
   IF Back = NIL              ← If Back is NIL, the element must be
       THEN                              the first
         List := NewNode      ← Inserts as first
       ELSE
         Back↑.Next := NewNode
END;     (* InsertInPlace *)
```

Notice that List has to be a VAR parameter for the case where the new item is inserted as the first element.

Let's go through this code for each of the three cases. The original list is shown below. ComponentType is assumed to be INTEGER.

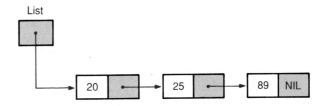

Let's insert the number 15 into the list. We get a new node (NewNode↑) and put 15 into the Component field. Our back pointer (Back) is set to NIL, our loop pointer (Current) is set to point to the first node, and Found is initialized to FALSE.

Current is not NIL and Found is FALSE, so the WHILE loop is executed. Current↑.Component (now 20) is greater than Item, so Found is set to TRUE.

The WHILE loop is not executed again, and NewNode↑.Next is set to Current. Back is NIL (indicating that the new item should be in the first node), so List is set to NewNode. The structure just before exiting the procedure is shown below. It includes the local variables.

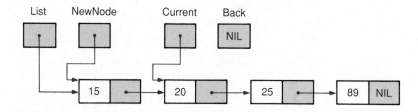

Now let's insert the number 17 into the new list. Our initialization is the same as above, except that NewNode↑.Component now contains 17. The expression in the IF statement in the WHILE loop is FALSE (15 < 17), so Back is set to Current and Current is advanced to Current↑.Next. The WHILE loop is executed again. Now the expression in the IF statement is TRUE, so Found is set to TRUE. The structure at this point looks like this:

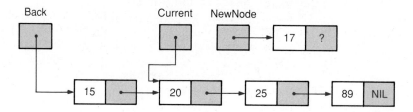

The WHILE loop is not executed because Found is now TRUE. NewNode↑.Next is set to Current. Back is not NIL, so Back↑.Next becomes NewNode.

In the third case, the element is inserted at the end of the list. Let's insert the number 100. Instead of going through all the iterations of the WHILE loop, we pick up where this diagram represents the structure:

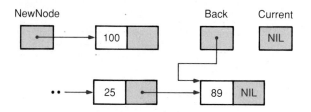

The WHILE loop is not executed because Current is NIL. NewNode↑.Next becomes Current (NIL in this case) and Back↑.Next becomes NewNode.

Deleting from a Linked List

To delete a node from a linked list, we again have two choices. We can delete the first node or we can delete a node with a specified value in the Component field.

Removing the first node is the mirror image of inserting an element as the first node. The value of the Component field of the first node (the one removed) is sent back as an output parameter.

```
PROCEDURE Pop(VAR List : NodePointer; VAR Item : ComponentType);
(* Removes the first node in a list and returns  *)
(* the component of the node that is removed.     *)

VAR
  Current : NodePointer;

BEGIN    (* Pop *)
  Current := List;      ← Saves first node to return to available space
  Item := List↑.Component;
  List := List↑.Next;
  DISPOSE(Current)      ← Sends Current↑ back to be used again
END;      (* Pop *)
```

The procedure we use to delete a node whose Component field is a certain value is very similar to Procedure InsertInPlace. The difference is that we are looking for a match here, not a Component field greater than the item.

```
PROCEDURE Delete(VAR List : NodePointer; Item : ComponentType);
(* Removes node that contains Item in its Component field. *)
(* If there is more than one node that contains Item, only *)
(* the first one is removed.                               *)
(* Assumption:  A node containing Item is in List.         *)

VAR
  Current, Copy : NodePointer;

BEGIN    (* Delete *)
  Copy := List;
  IF Item = List↑.Component
     THEN          (* Item is in the first node. *)
       List := List↑.Next
     ELSE          (* Search list for Item. *)
       BEGIN
         Current := List;
         WHILE Current↑.Next↑.Component <> Item DO
           Current := Current↑.Next;
         Copy := Current↑.Next
         Current↑.Next := Current↑.Next↑.Next
       END;
     DISPOSE(Copy)
END;    (* Delete *)
```

Notice that we avoid having to keep track of a back pointer in this procedure by using Current↑.Next↑.Component and Current↑.Next↑.Next. This works even if Current↑.Next↑.Next is NIL. However, if no match is found, there will be a run-time error when Current↑.Next is NIL.

Complex Pointer Expressions

Pointer expressions can be very complex. For example, look at this diagram:

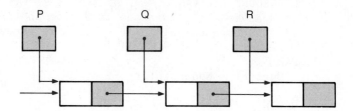

P, Q, and R point to nodes in a list. To access the fields of the nodes, you use P↑, Q↑, and R↑. Based on the diagram, the following expressions are TRUE:

```
P↑.Next = Q
P↑.Next↑ = Q↑
P↑.Next↑.Next = R
P↑.Next↑.Next↑ = R↑
Q↑.Next = R
Q↑.Next↑ = R↑
```

Remember the semantics of the assignment statement:

```
P := Q;
```

assigns the value of pointer Q to pointer P, and

```
P↑ := Q↑;
```

assigns the value of the variable referenced by pointer Q to the variable referenced by pointer P.

SAMPLE PROBLEM

Problem: A Fortune 500 company is having a stockholders' meeting. When people arrive for the meeting, their names are entered at a console. You are to write a program to keep a list of attendees. At the end of the meeting the list of attendees should be printed in alphabetical order.

SAMPLE PROBLEM, CONTINUED

Discussion: The total number of stockholders is 50,000; however, no more than 500 stockholders have ever attended any meeting. If you use an array to store their names, the index type must be 1..50000 because they might all come! If you use dynamic storage, you need only as much storage space as there are people.

Input: Last name ',' first name (a carriage return ends the first name)
A '/' entered after the last person has signed in ends the data

Output: First name followed by last name, in alphabetical order by last name.

Data Structures: Linked list of records containing names

MAIN MODULE   Level 0

```
List ← NIL
Get Name
WHILE NOT EndOfData DO
   Insert in List
   Get Name
Sort List
Print List
```

GET NAME   Level 1

```
Write Prompt for Name
Get Last Name
IF NOT EndOfData
   THEN
      Get First Name
```

INSERT IN LIST

We already have two insert routines. Which should we use? The one called Push inserts an item at the beginning of the list. The one called InsertInPlace inserts an element in its proper place. Push is much faster, but InsertInPlace creates the list in order. Either is acceptable. Let's use InsertInPlace here so that we won't have to sort the list before we print it. The algorithm is the same; only a few details need to be changed because the type of element to be inserted is different.

SORT LIST

This is no longer needed.

PRINT LIST

We can use Procedure PrintList on page 481 with a slight change in the WRITE statement.

GET LAST NAME   Level 2

We can use a simplified version of Procedure GetAWord from Program WordList (page 437). We need to read and collect characters until we get a comma. If the first character read is a '/', EndOfData is TRUE and the procedure returns.

```
LastName ← AllBlanks
EndOfData ← FALSE
Read Character
IF Character = '/'
     THEN
         EndOfData ← TRUE
IF NOT EndOfData
     THEN
         Index ← 0
         WHILE Character <> ',' DO
             Index ← Index + 1
             LastName[Index] ← Character
             Read Character
```

GET FIRST NAME

```
Index ← 0
WHILE NOT EOLN DO
   Read Character
   Index ← Index + 1
   FirstName[Index] ← Character
Readln
```

Although modules GET FIRST NAME and GET LAST NAME both input character strings, their logic is different enough to code them as separate procedures.

Module Design Chart:

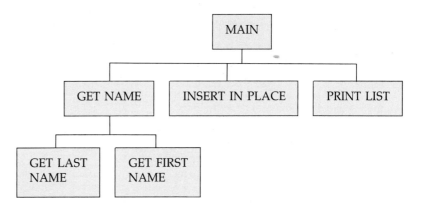

Interface Design Chart:

Program Constants and Variables

Identifiers	Type	Role
AllBlanks	CHAR	A name of all blanks
StringLength	INTEGER	Maximum number of characters in name fields
List	NodePointer	External pointer to list of names
Name	RECORD	Component in list with a first name and last name field
EndOfData	BOOLEAN	Signal to end input (first character in a line is a '/')

Procedures

Identifiers	Needs	Returns
GetLastName	Nothing	LastName, EndOfData
GetFirstName	Nothing	FirstName
GetName	Nothing	Name, EndOfData
InsertInPlace	Name	List
PrintList	List	Nothing

SAMPLE PROBLEM, CONTINUED

```
PROGRAM StockHolders(INPUT, OUTPUT);
(* A list of attendees at a stock holders meeting is *)
(* created and printed alphabetically by last name.  *)

CONST
  StringLength = 10;
  AllBlanks  = '          ';

TYPE
  NameStringType = PACKED ARRAY[1..StringLength] OF CHAR;
  NameType = RECORD
               FirstName : NameStringType;
               LastName  : NameStringType
             END;  (* RECORD *)
  ComponentType = NameType;
  NodePointer = ↑NodeType;
  NodeType = RECORD
               Component : ComponentType;
               Next : NodePointer
             END;  (* RECORD *)

VAR
  List : NodePointer;  (* external pointer to list *)
  Name : NameType;
  EndOfData : BOOLEAN;


(*********************************************************)

PROCEDURE GetLastName(VAR NameString : NameStringType;
                      VAR EndOfData : BOOLEAN);
(* Reads characters into NameString until a comma is found.  *)
(* EndOfData is TRUE if '/' is the first character.          *)
(* Assumption:  Number of characters does not exceed         *)
(*              StringLength.                                 *)

VAR
  Index : 0..StringLength;
  Character : CHAR;

BEGIN    (* GetLastName *)
  NameString := AllBlanks;
  EndOfData := FALSE;
  Index := 0;
  READ(Character);
  IF Character = '/'
     THEN
       EndOfData := TRUE;
```

```
    IF NOT EndOfData
      THEN
        WHILE (Character <> ',') DO
          BEGIN
            Index := Index + 1;
            NameString[Index] := Character;
            READ(Character)
          END;
END;     (* GetLastName *)

(************************************************************)

PROCEDURE GetFirstName(VAR NameString : NameStringType);
(* Reads characters into NameString until <eoln> is found. *)
(* Assumption:  Number of characters does not exceed        *)
(*              StringLength.                                *)

VAR
  Index : 0..StringLength;
  Character : CHAR;

BEGIN    (* GetFirstName *)
  Index := 0;
  Name := AllBlanks;
  WHILE NOT EOLN DO
    BEGIN
      READ(Character);
      Index := Index + 1;
      Name[Index] := Character
    END;
  READLN
END;     (* GetFirstName *)

(************************************************************)

PROCEDURE GetName(VAR Name : NameType; VAR EndOfData : BOOLEAN);
(* Reads in an attendee's name.  If there are no more names, *)
(* EndOfData is set to TRUE.                                 *)

BEGIN    (* GetName *)
  WRITELN('Enter your name in the following form:');
  WRITELN('(last name) (comma) (first name) (return)');
  GetLastName(Name.LastName, EndOfData);
  IF NOT EndOfData
    THEN
      GetFirstName(Name.FirstName)
END;     (* GetName *)
```

SAMPLE PROBLEM, CONTINUED

```
(***********************************************************)

PROCEDURE InsertInPlace(VAR List : NodePointer;
                            Item : ComponentType);
(* Inserts an element in a list while maintaining *)
(* the sorted order (increasing).                 *)

VAR
  Found : BOOLEAN;
  Current, Back, NewNode : NodePointer;

BEGIN    (* InsertInPlace *)
  NEW(NewNode);
  NewNode↑.Component := Item;
  Back := NIL;
  Current := List;
  Found := FALSE;

  (* Loop until the insertion place is found. *)
  WHILE (Current <> NIL) AND NOT Found DO
    IF Current↑.Component < Item
        THEN
          BEGIN
            Back := Current;
            Current := Current↑.Next
          END
        ELSE
          Found := TRUE;

  NewNode↑.Next := Current;
  IF Back = NIL
      THEN
        List := NewNode
      ELSE
        Back↑.Next := NewNode
END;       (* InsertInPlace *)

(***********************************************************)

PROCEDURE PrintList(List : NodePointer);
(* Prints the first name, a blank, and last name. *)

VAR
  Current : NodePointer;

BEGIN    (* PrintList *)
  Current := List;
  WHILE Current <> NIL DO
```

```
   BEGIN
     WRITELN(Current↑.Component.FirstName, ' ',
            Current↑.Component.LastName);
     Current := Current↑.Next
   END
END;    (* PrintList *)

(**********************************************************)

BEGIN    (* StockHolders *)
   List := NIL;
   GetName(Name, EndOfData);
   WHILE NOT EndOfData DO
     BEGIN
       InsertInPlace(List, Name);
       GetName(Name, EndOfData)
     END;
   PrintList(List)
END.     (* StockHolders *)
```

Other Linked Data Types

Dynamic components can be used to implement other structured data types. Three of these data types are the *stack*, the *queue*, and the *binary search tree*. We mention them briefly here as a preview of things to come if you continue to study computing.

Stack

Did you notice the funny procedure names Push and Pop above? The names come from terminology that relates to stacks. A **stack** is a structured data type in which elements are inserted and removed at just one end. The last element inserted (Push) is the first element removed (Pop).

> **Stack**
> A structured data type in which insertions and deletions are made from just one end.

A stack models many things in real life. Accountants call it *LIFO*, which stands for "*last in, first out.*" The plate holder in a cafeteria has this property. When you take the top plate, you're taking the last one put in. (The plate below it rises to the top.) Canned goods on your grocer's shelf also exhibit this property. When you take the front can, you are taking the last can put there.

Stacks are extremely useful in computing. The following code fragment, which uses Push and Pop, prints the characters on a line in reverse order.

```
Stack := NIL;        ← Initializes a linked list (stack),
WHILE NOT EOLN DO        whose external pointer is Stack
  BEGIN
    READ(Character);
    Push(Stack, Character)
  END;
WHILE Stack <> NIL DO
  BEGIN
    Pop(Stack, Character);
    WRITE(Character)
  END;
```

The last character read is the first one printed, and so on.

Queue

A **queue** (pronounced like the letter *Q*) is a structured data type in which elements are entered at one end and removed from the other. Accountants call this FIFO, for "*first in, first out.*" This sounds like a waiting line in a bank or supermarket. In fact, queues are used to simulate this type of situation.

Queue

A structured data type in which insertions are made at one end and deletions are made at the other.

The terminology we use to refer to the insert and remove operations on stacks is standard (*Push* and *Pop*); there are no standard terms with queues. The operation of inserting at the rear is called by many names in the literature: Insert, Enter, and Enq are three common ones. The operation of removing from the front is called Delete, Remove, and Deq. We call our procedures Enq and Deq. Because we are accessing both ends, we need two external pointers: Front and Rear.

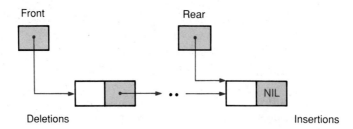

Front   Rear

NIL

Deletions   Insertions

To insert an element at the Rear we must take care of two cases: when the queue is empty and when it has at least one element. If the queue is empty (Rear = NIL) then we must set both Rear and Front to point to the element that is entering the queue. If there is at least one element in the queue already, we have to insert the new element after Rear↑ and redefine Rear to point to the new element. For Procedures Enq and Deq, we use the following declarations:

```
TYPE
   ComponentType =   (* what goes on the queue *);
   NodePointer = ↑NodeType;
   NodeType = RECORD
                 Component : ComponentType;
                 Next : NodePointer
              END;   (* RECORD *)
   QueueType = RECORD
                 Front, Rear : NodePointer
              END;   (* RECORD *)

PROCEDURE Enq(VAR Queue : QueueType; Item : ComponentType);
(* Insert Item as the last element in Queue. *)

VAR
   NewNode : NodePointer;

BEGIN    (* Enq *)
   NEW(NewNode);
   NewNode↑.Component := Item;
   NewNode↑.Next := NIL;
   IF Queue.Rear = NIL
      THEN
        BEGIN
           Queue.Rear := NewNode;
           Queue.Front := NewNode
        END
      ELSE
        BEGIN
           Queue.Rear↑.Next := NewNode;
           Queue.Rear := NewNode
        END
END;     (* Enq *)
```

To remove an element from the front is logically just like popping a stack. In fact, we can just call Pop (page 487) with Queue.Front as the actual parameter. However, we must remember to set Queue.Rear to NIL if Queue.Front is NIL on return from Pop.

```
PROCEDURE Deq(VAR Queue : QueueType; VAR Item : ItemType);
(* Remove the first element in Queue and return its   *)
(* Component field in Item.                           *)
```

```
BEGIN    (* Deq *)
  Pop(Queue.Front, Item);
  IF Queue.Front = NIL
     THEN
        Queue.Rear := NIL
END;      (* Deq *)
```

There are other ways to implement stacks and queues, but because these structures vary greatly in size during run-time, they are often implemented using linked lists, as we have described here.

Binary Search Tree

The concept of a linked list can be extended to structures containing nodes with more than one pointer field. One of these structures is a binary search tree. A **binary search tree** is a structure that is organized for fast searches, insertions, and deletions in an ordered list. Each node in a binary search tree has three fields—a component field and two pointer fields (usually called Left and Right). The list is ordered by the values in the component field (or by a field within the component field).

A binary search tree is referenced by an external pointer to the **root node**, the top or base node of the tree. The Left field of the root node points to the root's *left child* and the Right field points to its *right child*. The left child is the root of a tree (subtree) that contains all the values less than the value in the root, and the right child is the root of a tree (subtree) that contains all the values that are greater. Each child also has two pointers: one to its left child and one to its right child and each of these nodes has two pointers, and so on. If one of the pointers is NIL, the subtree is empty.

> ### Binary Search Tree
> A binary tree in which the information in any node is greater than the information in its left child and any of its children (left subtree) and less than the information in its right child and any of its children (right subtree).

Figure 13–2 shows a binary search tree with six nodes. The Root node has a left child and a right child. The left child of the root has both a left child and a right child. However, the right child of the root has only a left child; its right child is NIL (empty). A node in which both pointers are NIL is called a *leaf node*. Children of the same node are *siblings*.

The reason a binary search tree is so useful is that if you are looking for a certain value, you can tell which half of the tree it is in by one comparison. You then can tell which half of that half it is in by one comparison. This process continues until you either find the value or you determine that it is not there.

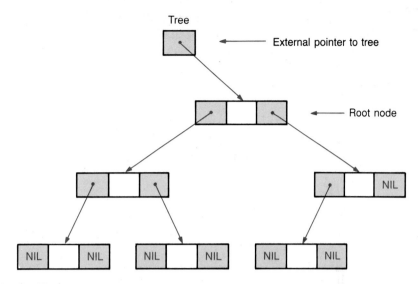

FIGURE 13–2 Binary search tree

Suppose we are searching for the number 50 in the binary search tree in Figure 13–3. The first comparison shows that 50 is in the right subtree of the root (if it's there). The second comparison shows that 50 is in the right subtree of the node whose value is 28 (if it's there). The third comparison finds the value 50 in the tree.

Suppose we are searching for a number that is not in the tree, say 18. The first comparison shows that 18 is in the left subtree of the root (if it's there). The second comparison shows that 18 is in the right subtree of the node whose value is 17 (if it's there). The third comparison shows that 18 is in the left subtree of the node whose value is 19 (if it's there). Here the left child is NIL, so 18 is not in the tree. We know it's not there; if we want to insert it, we're at the right place.

This algorithm is coded in the BOOLEAN Function IsThere using these definitions:

```
TYPE
  TreePointer = ↑TreeNode;
  TreeNode = RECORD
               Component : INTEGER;
               Right, Left : TreePointer
             END;  (* RECORD *)

FUNCTION IsThere(Tree : TreePointer; Item : INTEGER); BOOLEAN;
(* IsThere is TRUE if Item is in the tree; FALSE, otherwise. *)

VAR
  Pointer : TreePointer;
  Found : BOOLEAN;
```

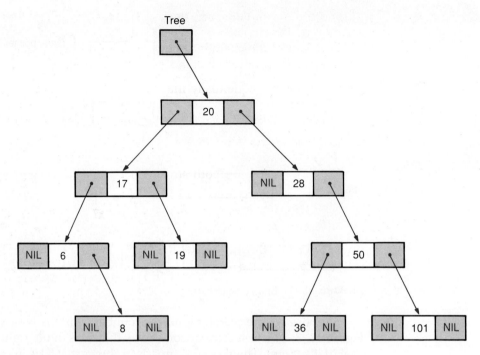

FIGURE 13–3 Binary search tree with integer components

```
BEGIN    (* IsThere *)
  Pointer := Tree;
  Found := FALSE;
  WHILE (Pointer <> NIL) AND NOT Found DO
    IF Pointer↑.Component = Item
        THEN
          Found := TRUE
        ELSE
          IF Pointer↑.Component > Item
              THEN    (* look in the left subtree *)
                Pointer := Pointer↑.Left
              ELSE    (* look in the right subtree *)
                Pointer := Pointer↑.Right

  IsThere := Found
END;     (* IsThere *)
```

The 4-Cs Corner

Correctness

Choosing a Structured Data Type

Deletions and insertions into a list are time consuming when an array is used
to represent the list; insertions and deletions in a linked list representation are

simpler and faster. However, there are operations on lists that work better in an array representation.

Let's look at the operations you might want to apply to a list and examine the advantages and disadvantages of each representation.

- Reading items sequentially into a list.
  This process is a little faster using an array representation because Procedure NEW doesn't have to be called for each item.

- Accessing all the items in a list in sequence.
  Accessing the items in sequence takes approximately the same amount of time for both structures.

- Inserting or deleting the first item in a list.
  Inserting or deleting the first item in a list is much faster using a linked representation.

- Inserting or deleting the last item in a list.
  Inserting or deleting the last item in a list can be done much more efficiently in an array representation because you have direct access to the last element (position Length) and no shifting is necessary. In a linked representation, you have to search through the entire list to find the last element.

- Inserting or deleting the nth item in a list.
  On the average, the time spent inserting or deleting the nth item from a list should be about equal. A linked representation is better for small values of n; and an array representation, for values of n near the end of the list.

- Accessing the nth item in a list.
  Accessing the nth element is *much* faster using an array representation. You can access the nth element directly by using n as the index into the array. In a linked representation, you have to access the first $n - 1$ items to reach the nth item.

- Sorting the items in a list.
  In sorting an existing linked list, you can remove the elements one by one and insert them in place into a second linked list. When you finish, you can set the external pointer of the original list to point to the first element of the new list. If you DISPOSE each node as you remove an item, you will not use any additional memory space for your sorted list. With a linked list, however, you are limited to this type of sorting algorithm. With an array, you can use much faster sorting algorithms.

- Searching the list for a specific item.
  Searching an ordered list for a specific item is much faster in general in an array representation because you can use a binary search. If the items in the list to be searched are not ordered, the two representations take about the same amount of time.

When you're trying to decide whether to use an array representation or a linked representation of a list, determine which of these operations you'll be applying most frequently. Then choose the representation that will work best in the context of your particular problem.

There are a couple of other points to consider: How accurately can you predict the maximum number of items in the list? Does the number of items in the list fluctuate widely? If you know the maximum and it remains fairly constant, an array representation is probably called for. Otherwise, it's better to choose a linked representation in order to use memory more efficiently.

Treating Pointers with Respect

Pointer variables contain memory addresses. We can't print out these values, and even if we could, they might not tell us what we need to know to debug a program. Programs using pointers, then, can be more difficult to debug than programs without them.

It is hard to tell whether or not pointer variables contain valid values. We can print out the values of the variable referenced by a pointer (by using a debug WRITE statement), which might help us in our debugging. This assumes, of course, that the pointer is pointing to something.

Programmers often make mistakes in referencing variables with pointers. Pay careful attention to complex pointer expressions, and be sure to distinguish between the pointer value itself and the thing the pointer is pointing to.

Correctness Hints

1. Be sure a pointer is not NIL before accessing its referenced variable. If Pointer is a pointer that is either NIL or undefined, accessing Pointer↑ will give you a run-time error.
2. Be careful with compound expressions in your WHILE loop. On most compilers, both sides of expressions with AND or OR are evaluated, regardless of how the first expression is evaluated. This is why

```
(Pointer <> NIL) AND (Item <> Pointer↑.Component)
```

causes an error when Item is not in the list.
3. Remember that DISPOSE(Current) leaves Current undefined. If you try to access Current↑, you'll cause a run-time error.
4. Return variables to available space when you are finished with them. When deleting an element from a linked list, use DISPOSE to return the memory cells for later use. If you don't, you might run out of memory.

   If you have DISPOSEd of unneeded variables and you still run out of memory, check to be sure you do not have an inadvertent recursive call or an infinite loop in which NEW is called.
5. Keep track of pointers. Changing pointer values prematurely may cause problems when you try to get back to a referenced variable.

6. Pointers must be of the same type in order to be compared or assigned to one another.

Completeness

For the sake of completeness, we talk here about three other features of Pascal: the unconditional branch (GOTO statement), the use of functions and procedures as parameters, and a mechanism for forward referencing procedures and functions. The GOTO statement should be used rarely if at all; the other two features are advanced but should be useful in future programming.

GOTO Statement

A GOTO statement, or unconditional branch, is provided in most common programming languages. Pascal is no exception, but because all the control structures already exist, you rarely need the GOTO. In more primitive languages, IF and GOTO are used to construct control structures. In Pascal, the IF, CASE, WHILE, FOR, and REPEAT control structures make programs more readable and the flow of control clearer.

The GOTO statement passes control directly from one point in a program to another. The GOTO specifies the label of a statement to which control is transferred. The label must be declared in the declaration section of the block.

Using GOTOs is considered bad style in all but a very few situations. One in which it might be acceptable is when bad input data has been found and the program logic has no way of handling that data. The GOTO allows us to print an error message and pass control directly to the end of the program.

For example, let's assume that Procedure ReadInteger (page 427) is being used to convert integers in character form. Procedure GetData is the procedure that calls ReadInteger. Procedure ReadInteger sets ReadFlag to Error if an error occurs during the reading process. Assume that in this example Procedure GetData has no way of recovering from the error, so it prints an error message and transfers control to the end of the program.

```
PROGRAM GoToExample(INPUT, OUTPUT, DataFile);

LABEL 1;
   .
   .


PROCEDURE ReadInteger(VAR DataFile : TEXT;
                      VAR Number : INTEGER;
                      VAR ReadFlag : FlagType);
   .
   .


PROCEDURE GetData(VAR DataFile : TEXT;
                  VAR Number : INTEGER);
```

```
TYPE
  FlagType = (Blank, NonBlank, Error);

VAR
  ReadFlag : FlagType;

BEGIN    (* GetData *)
  ReadInteger(DataFile, Number, ReadFlag);
  IF ReadFlag = Error
     THEN
       BEGIN
         WRITELN('Error on File DataFile.  Program halts.');
         GOTO 1
       END
END;     (* GetData *)

BEGIN    (* GoToExample *)
  .

  .

1:END.   (* GoToExample *)
```

The LABEL section must be the first section in the block. It is a list of unsigned integer constants. In our example, we use the label 1. This tells the compiler that there will be a statement with the label 1 somewhere in the block.

Within Procedure GetData, the statement

```
GOTO 1
```

says to unconditionally transfer control to the statement labeled 1. In this case, it is the END at the end of the program. The syntax has the label (followed by a colon) directly before the statement.

Some languages have a stop or halt statement that terminates the program at some position other than the last END in the main block. Pascal does not, but this kind of statement can be simulated by using GOTO in the way we've shown.

These are the rules for using the GOTO statement:

- All labels must be declared.
- Label declarations precede all others in the block.
- Labels are unsigned integers in the range 1 to 9999.
- Each label can be declared only once and can be used to label only one statement.
- A GOTO branch into a control structure or block (procedure or function) is not permitted. A GOTO branch out of a control structure or a block is allowed.

Structured programming is characterized by the use of control structures with just one entry and one exit. The GOTO leads to unstructured programming: multiple entries and exits from control structures. This makes programs harder to read, understand, modify, and debug. The GOTO should be avoided because of this. Use it only for exceptional circumstances and forward (not backward) jumps.

Functions and Procedures as Parameters

In addition to VAR and value parameters, Pascal allows procedure and function parameters, in which the actual parameter is a procedure or function identifier.* The only restriction is that procedures and functions used as parameters can only have value parameters themselves.

This is the complete syntax diagram for a formal parameter list:

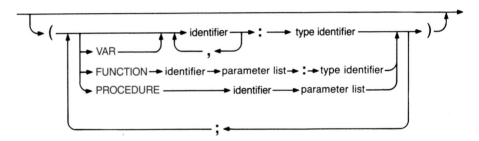

Suppose we want to sort a group of records first on one field and then on another field. So far the only way we can handle the situation is to include two sorting procedures, where the only difference between them is the fields in the RECORD variables that are being compared.

The ability to pass a procedure or function as a parameter gives us another way to handle this. We can write two comparison functions, one for each field. The sorting procedure can have the function that does the comparison as a parameter. For example, here's the heading for Procedure Insert (page 322), which implements the insertion sort, with an added function parameter:

```
PROCEDURE Insert(VAR List : ListType;
                 VAR Length : IndexType; Item : ItemType;
            FUNCTION GreaterThan(Item1, Item2: ItemType) : BOOLEAN);

(* Item is inserted into its proper place in List. *)
(* Assumption:  Order is ascending.                *)
```

---

*Turbo Pascal does not support this feature.

The section of code that does the comparison between two values in the original procedure is embedded in a local procedure, FindPlace. The loop in which the comparison is made is rewritten like this:

```
WHILE  (Place <= Length) AND NOT PlaceFound DO
   IF GreaterThan(Item, List[Place])
      THEN
         Place := Place + 1
      ELSE
         PlaceFound := TRUE
```

One function passed as an actual parameter might compare fields of packed arrays representing names. Another might compare fields of REAL values representing salary figures. Procedure Insert can be called any number of times with a different function identifier passed as the actual parameter corresponding to the formal parameter GreaterThan. You could use Procedure Insert to sort a list on every field of a record if you choose. Of course, you have to write as many functions as you have fields in the record.

Another important use of the procedure or function as a parameter is in mathematical programming. The same plotting routine can be used to plot any number of functions that are passed as parameters.

FORWARD Statement

Identifiers in Pascal must be defined before they are used (the type identifier in the pointer type definition is an exception). We described recursion as the ability of a procedure or function to call itself. There are recursive situations where one procedure or function calls another, which in turn calls the first. Clearly, they cannot physically both come first.

The solution is to tell the compiler that a procedure or function will be defined later. The FORWARD statement allows us to do this. For example, let's assume that Procedure One calls Procedure Two and Procedure Two calls Procedure One. We use the FORWARD statement to tell the compiler that Procedure Two will be defined later. Then we define Procedure One, then Procedure Two.

```
(************************************************************)

PROCEDURE Two(VAR SomeItem : SomeItemType); FORWARD;

(************************************************************)

PROCEDURE One(VAR AnotherItem : AnotherType);
```

```
    BEGIN
        .
        .
      Two(OneParameter);

    END;

    (*********************************************************)

    PROCEDURE Two;

    BEGIN
        .
        .
      One(AnotherParameter);
    END;
```

Notice that the parameter list is written only in the FORWARD reference; it is not repeated in the actual declaration of the procedure (or function). The compiler "remembers" the parameter declarations when it encounters the actual procedure definition.

Summary

Pascal has a predefined data type called a pointer. We declare a pointer in the TYPE section by putting ↑ before the type to which the pointer is to point. (A pointer type always points to a specific type.)

A dynamic variable is defined by the procedure NEW. Its argument is a pointer variable. NEW returns the pointer to the newly created variable. These variables have no names; their contents are referenced by the pointer variable followed by ↑.

Linked lists are created by defining records with two (or more) fields, where one field is a pointer to records of its own type. The pointer to the first node is saved in a place called the external pointer to the list; the pointer to each succeeding node is placed in the pointer field of the one before. NIL is put in the pointer field of the last node to indicate the end of the list.

Many interesting data structures can be built using pointers. Stacks, queues, and binary search trees are three you will use in real-life problems.

EXERCISES

Use these declarations to answer Exercises 1–3:

```
    TYPE
      Pointer = ↑Node;
      Node = RECORD
                Info : INTEGER;
                Next : Pointer
             END; (* RECORD *)
```

```
VAR
  P, Q, R : Pointer;
```

1. Show what the commands listed below do to this schematic diagram of a linked list.

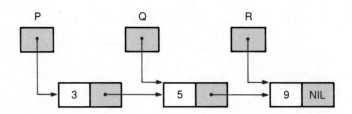

   a. P : = P↑.Next;
   b. Q : = P;
   c. R : = P↑.Next;
   d. P↑.Info : = Q↑.Info;
   e. P↑.Info : = Q↑.Next↑.Info;
   f. R↑.Next : = P;

2. Write one statement (using the ↑ notation) to effect the change indicated by the broken line in each of the following diagrams.

   a.

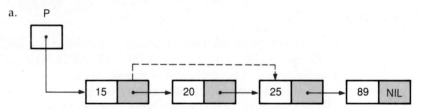

   b.

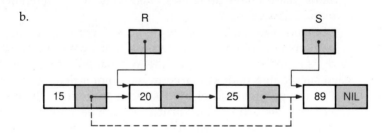

   c.

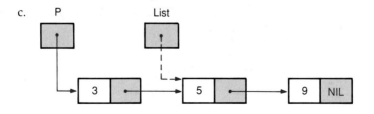

d.

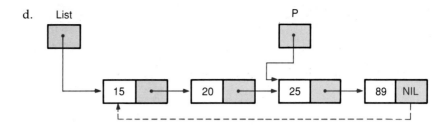

3. Show what is written by the following code fragments.
   a. ```
   New(P);
   New(Q);
   P↑.Info := 5;
   Q↑.Info := 6;
   P := Q;
   P↑.Info := 1;
   WRITELN(P↑.Info, Q↑.Info);
   ```

   b. ```
   New(P);
   P↑.Info := 3;
   New(Q);
   Q↑.Info := 2;
   New(P);
   P↑.Info := Q↑.Info;
   Q↑.Info := 0;
   WRITELN(P↑.Info, Q↑.Info);
   ```

   c. ```
   New(P);
   New(Q);
   P↑.Info := 0;
   P↑.Next := Q;
   Q↑.Next := NIL;
   Q↑.Info := 5;
   P↑.Next↑.Next := P;
   Q↑.Info := Q↑.Next↑.Info;
   P := Q;
   P↑.Next↑.Info := 2;
   WRITELN(P↑.Info, Q↑.Info);
   ```

4. The following type declaration is illegal because Pointer = ↑Node is a reference to an undefined type called Node.

   ```
   TYPE
      String = PACKED ARRAY[1..10] OF CHAR;
      Pointer = ↑Node;
      Node = RECORD
               Name : String;
               Next : Pointer
             END; (* RECORD *)
   ```

5. Given these declarations for a linked list of company employees:
   ```

```
TYPE
  Pointer = ↑Employee;
  Employee = RECORD
                Name : PACKED ARRAY[1..25] OF CHAR;
                Department : 1..20;
                EmpNumber : 0..1000;
                Salary : INTEGER;
                Next : Pointer
            END; (* RECORD *)

VAR
  P, Employees : Pointer;
```

a. Initialize Employees, a pointer to a company list, with a special dummy first node (header node) that contains a zero employee number. Assume that the list will be ordered by employee number.
b. Write a code fragment that reads in data about an employee and stores it in a node (to be inserted later into the linked list of employees). Assume that the data about each employee is located on a separate line of input in this format:

col.	1–25	27–28	30–33	35–40
	Name	Department	Emp Number	Salary

Feel free to use any additional variables you need.
c. Write a procedure that inserts a new employee node into the list you initialized in part a. The procedure should take Employees (pointer to the list) and Emp (pointer to the new employee's node). The list is ordered by employee number.

6. Given these global declarations:

```
TYPE
  NodePtr = ↑Node;
  Node = RECORD
            Info : INTEGER;
            Next : NodePtr
         END;
```

Debug the following codes:

a.
```
FUNCTION Even(P : ↑Node) : BOOLEAN;
  BEGIN    (* Even *)
    IF P↑.Info MOD 2 = 0
      THEN
        Even := TRUE
      ELSE
        Even := FALSE
  END;    (* Even *)
```

b.
```
PROCEDURE Successor(P : Pointer);
  BEGIN    (* Successor *)
    WHILE P <> NIL DO
      WRITELN(P↑.Info, ' is followed by ', P↑.Next↑.Info)
  END;    (* Successor *)
```

7. Answer the following statements true or false.
   a. Although pointers may exist at compile-time, the variables they are pointing to do not.
   b. The standard procedure DISPOSE returns the memory locations used for a dynamic variable and its pointer to the run-time support system to be used again.
   c. Pointer1 + Pointer2 is legal.
   d. Pointer1 : = Pointer2 is legal.
   e. After the assignment in part d, we cannot access Pointer1 unless we already have assigned Pointer1 to another pointer variable.
   f. NIL can be assigned to a variable of any type accessed by a pointer.
   g. A stack is a data structure that is accessed from just one end.
   h. A queue is a data structure characterized by the acronym LIFO (last in, first out).
   i. In a binary tree, the external pointer accesses the root; other nodes have two pointers each.
   j. The FORWARD statement tells the compiler that the procedure or function named will be defined later.

PRETEST

Use these declarations to answer Problems 1 and 2:

```
TYPE
    Pointer = ↑Node
    Node = RECORD
             Info : CHAR;
             Link : Pointer
           END; (* RECORD *)


VAR
    S, T, P : Pointer;
```

1. Show what the commands listed below do to this schematic diagram of a linked list.

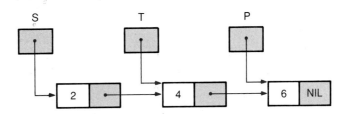

   a. S : = P↑.Link;
   b. S↑.Info : = P↑.Info;
   c. P↑.Link : = S;

2. Write one statement (using the ↑ notation) to effect the change indicated by the broken line in each of the following diagrams.

a.

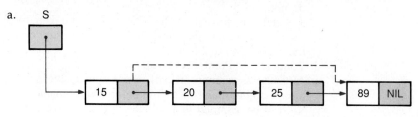

b.

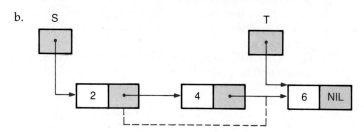

c.

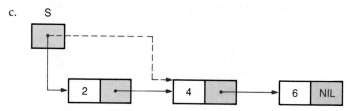

3. Write an INTEGER function, EvenSum, that sums the Info fields of all nodes whose Info fields are even.

4. Write a procedure, ReadAndStore, that reads in the integer numbers in a file and stores them in numerical order in a linked list pointed to by List. Use EOF to indicate the end of the data. Assume one value per line.

5. Write an INTEGER function, OddNodeSum, that sums the Info fields of the first node, the third node, the fifth node, and so on.

6. Answer the following statements true or false.
   a. The variables pointers point to are created at compile-time.
   b. The standard procedure NEW is used to create a new pointer.
   c. Pointer1 = Pointer2 is legal and evaluates to TRUE or FALSE.
   d. Pointer2 : = Pointer1 is invalid.
   e. After the assignment in part d, the value of Pointer2 is undefined.
   f. NIL can be assigned to a pointer variable of any type.
   g. A stack is a data structure characterized by the acronym FIFO (first in, first out).
   h. A queue is a data structure in which elements are entered at one end and removed from the other.
   i. In a binary tree, there are two pointers pointing to each child.
   j. The GOTO statement label is created by the GOTO statement.

PROGRAMMING ASSIGNMENTS ──────────────

1. Write a set of utility routines to manipulate a group of three stacks. The specifications for these routines are given in terms of preconditions and postconditions. The preconditions to each routine tell you what you can assume to be true on entry to the routine. The postconditions state what is true on exit from the routine. The notation is as follows:

   - Stack' is the specified stack on input to the operation.
   - Stack is the stack on exit from the operation.

   Stack operations:

   PROCEDURE Create(VAR Stack : StackType);
   Pre: True
   Post: Stack exists

   PROCEDURE Push(VAR Stack : StackType; Item : ItemType);
   Pre: NOT Full(Stack')
   Post: Stack is Stack' with Item inserted

   PROCEDURE Pop(VAR Stack : StackType; VAR Item : ItemType);
   Pre: NOT Empty(Stack')
   Post: Item is the item that has been in Stack the shortest time; Stack is Stack' with Item removed

   PROCEDURE Clear(VAR Stack : StackType);
   Pre: Stack' exists
   Post: Empty(Stack)

   FUNCTION Empty(Stack : StackType) : BOOLEAN;
   Pre: Stack' exists
   Post: Empty = (Stack'is empty) AND Stack = Stack'

   FUNCTION Full(Stack : StackType) : BOOLEAN;
   Pre: Stack' exists
   Post: Full = (Stack' is full) AND Stack = Stack'

   Testing: The input data consists of a series of commands to test your routines. There are an arbitrary number of blanks between commands. Be sure to echo-print each command before you execute it.

   Stacks are designated by the integers 1 through 3. Elements will be strings of up to twenty characters, including embedded blanks, delimited by a period. The commands are

   - CREATE StackNumber:
     Execute Procedure Create on StackNumber.
   - PUSH Element
     Execute Procedure Push, using Element as the value to be put on the designated stack.
   - POP StackNumber
     Execute Procedure Pop, using the designated stack, and print the value returned.

- CLEAR StackNumber
  Execute Procedure Clear, using the designated stack.
- EMPTY StackNumber
  Execute Function Empty, using the designated stack, and print the result.
- FULL StackNumber
  Execute Function Full, using the designated stack, and print the result.
- PRINT StackNumber
  Print the elements in the designated stack. The stack must be returned to its original state. (*Hint:* Use a temporary stack.)
- DUMP
  Print the elements in *all* the stacks.
- STOP
  Stop executing.

   Error conditions: You can assume that each stack is created before any operations are indicated for it.

   The preconditions must be *guaranteed*. This means that before any stack operation is called, the preconditions must be tested. If an error occurs, print an error message and do not execute the stack operation.

2. Given a starting point in a maze, you are to determine if there is a way out. The maze is represented by a 10×10 array of 1s and 0s. There is one exit from the maze. The door to the exit contains an asterisk (*). You can move vertically or horizontally in any direction that contains a 0; you may not move to a cell with a 1. If you move into the cell with the *, you have exited. If you are in a cell with 1s on three sides, you must go back the way you came and try another path. You cannot move diagonally.

   Input:
   1. A 10×10 array of characters (1, 0, *). Each data line consists of one row of the maze.
   2. Each succeeding line consists of pairs of values, representing starting points in the maze (row and column numbers). Process these entry points until EOF.

   Output: For each entry into the maze, print the maze with an E in the entry square, followed by the message 'I AM FREE' if a way out exists from that point or 'HELP, I AM TRAPPED' if a way out does not exist from that point.

   Processing: Begin at the entry point and continue moving until you find the way out or have no more moves to try. Remember, you can move into any cell with a 0, but cells with a 1 block you.

   Data structures: There are two distinct sets of data structures for this assignment: the stack utility routines written in Assignment 1 and the data structure used to represent the maze.

   Error handling: You can assume that your entry positions are within the maze. You also can assume that the starting position contains a 0.

3. Rewrite Assignment 2 in Chapter 11 using a linked structure to hold the list of residents who have had their belongings marked.

4. Rewrite Assignment 2 in Chapter 11 using a binary tree to hold the list of residents who have had their belongings marked.

5. Rewrite Assignment 3 in Chapter 11 using a linked structure to hold the list of found pets.

6. Rewrite Assignment 3 in Chapter 11 using a binary tree to hold the list of found pets.

7. Rewrite Assignment 4 in Chapter 12 using a linked structure to hold the lists of men and women.

8. Rewrite Assignment 4 in Chapter 12 using a binary tree to hold the lists of men and women.

Appendixes

Appendix A Reserved Words

AND	END	MOD	REPEAT
ARRAY	FILE	NIL	SET
BEGIN	FOR	NOT	THEN
CASE	FORWARD	OF	TO
CONST	FUNCTION	OR	TYPE
DIV	GOTO	PACKED	UNTIL
DO	IF	PROCEDURE	VAR
DOWNTO	IN	PROGRAM	WHILE
ELSE	LABEL	RECORD	WITH

EXTERN, FORTRAN, GLOBAL, LOCAL, OTHERWISE, VALUE, and other words can be reserved words in some implementations. FORWARD is technically not a reserved word—it is a special word called a *required directive*. However, in the context of this text it behaves exactly like a reserved word.

Appendix B Standard Identifiers

Standard Constants
FALSE   TRUE   MaxInt

Standard Types
INTEGER   BOOLEAN   REAL   CHAR   TEXT

Standard Files
INPUT   OUTPUT

Standard Functions

	Parameter Type	Result Type	Returns
ABS(X)	INTEGER or REAL	Same as parameter	Absolute value of X
ARCTAN(X)	INTEGER or REAL	REAL	Arctangent of X in radians
CHR(X)	INTEGER	CHAR	Character whose ordinal number is X
COS(X)	INTEGER or REAL	REAL	Cosine of X (X is in radians)
EOF(F)	FILE	BOOLEAN	End-of-file test of F
EOLN(F)	TEXT FILE	BOOLEAN	End-of-line test of F
EXP(X)	REAL or INTEGER	REAL	e to the X power
LN(X)	REAL or INTEGER	REAL	Natural logarithm of X
ODD(X)	INTEGER	BOOLEAN	Odd test of X
ORD(X)	Ordinal (scalar except REAL)	INTEGER	Ordinal number of X
PRED(X)	Ordinal (scalar except REAL)	Same as parameter	Unique predecessor of X (except where X is the first value)
ROUND(X)	REAL	INTEGER	X rounded
SIN(X)	REAL or INTEGER	REAL	Sine of X (X is in radians)
SQR(X)	REAL or INTEGER	Same as parameter	Square of X
SQRT(X)	REAL or INTEGER	REAL	Square root of X
SUCC(X)	Ordinal (scalar except REAL)	Same as parameter	Unique successor of X (except where X is the last value)
TRUNC(X)	REAL	INTEGER	X truncated

Standard Procedures

	Description
DISPOSE(P)	Destroys the dynamic variable referenced by pointer P by returning the variable to the available space list.
GET(F)	Advances the current position of File F to the next component and assigns the value of the component to F↑.
NEW(P)	Creates a variable of the type referenced by pointer P, and stores a pointer to the new variable in P.
PACK(U, I, P)	Copies the elements beginning at subscript position I of array U into packed array P beginning at the first subscript position of P.
PAGE(F)	Advances the printer to the top of a new page before printing the next line of TEXT File F.
PUT(F)	Appends the value of the buffer variable F↑ to File F.
READ(F, parameter list)	Reads data values from TEXT File F (if F is not specified, default is INPUT) and assigns these values to the variable(s) in the parameter list until the list is satisfied.
READLN (F, parameter list)	Same as READ except advances the file pointer to the beginning of the next line after satisfying the parameter list.
RESET(F)	Resets File F to its beginning for reading.
REWRITE(F)	Resets File F to its beginning for writing; old contents of F are lost.
UNPACK(P, U, I)	Copies the elements beginning at the first subscript position of packed array P into array U beginning at subscript position I.
WRITE(F, parameter list)	Writes the data in the order specified in the parameter list to TEXT File F (if F is not specified, default is OUTPUT).
WRITELN(F, parameter list)	Same as WRITE except generates an end-of-line marker after satisfying its parameter list.

Some compilers provide other types, files, functions, and procedures as well. Check the manual for your specific implementation to see what is available.

Appendix C Pascal Operators and Symbols

Symbol	Description
+	Plus or set union
−	Minus or set difference
*	Times or set intersection
/	Divide (REAL)
DIV	Divide (INTEGER)
MOD	Modulus (remainder from INTEGER division)
<	Is less than
<=	Is less than or equal to
=	Is equal to
<>	Is not equal to
>=	Is greater than or equal to
>	Is greater than
AND	Boolean conjunction
OR	Boolean inclusive disjunction
NOT	Boolean negation
IN	Tests set membership
:=	Becomes (separates sides in an assignment statement)
,	Separates items in a list
;	Separates statements
:	Separates variable name and type
	Separates case label list and statement
	Separates statement label and statement
,	Delimits CHAR and string literals
.	Decimal point
	Record selector
	Program terminator
. .	Subrange specifier
↑	File buffer variable indicator (alternate: @); pointer variable indicator (alternate: @)
(	Starts parameter list or nested expression
)	Ends parameter list or nested expression
[	Starts subscript list or set expression [alternate: (.]
]	Ends subscript list or set expression [alternate: .)]
(*	Starts a comment (alternate: {)
*)	Ends a comment (alternate: })

Appendix D   Precedence of Operators

Note

1. Parentheses can be used to change the order of precedence.
2. When operators of equal precedence are used, they are executed in order from left to right.

NOT	Highest precedence
* / DIV MOD AND	
+ − OR	
< <= = >= > <> IN	Lowest precedence

Appendix E   Syntax Diagrams

Program

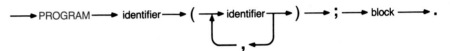

Identifier

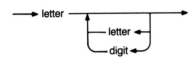

Block

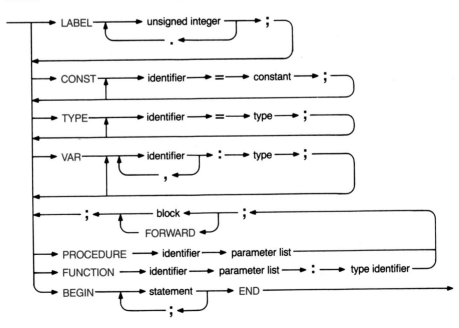

Constant

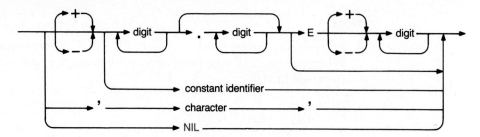

Type

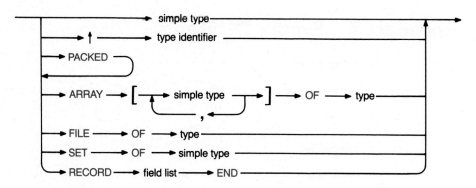

Simple Type

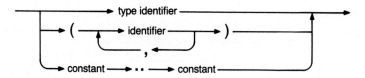

Field List

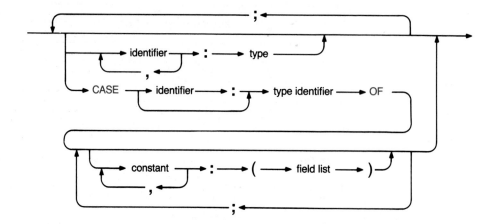

Parameter List

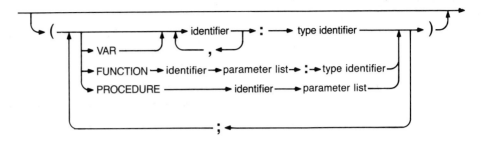

Statement

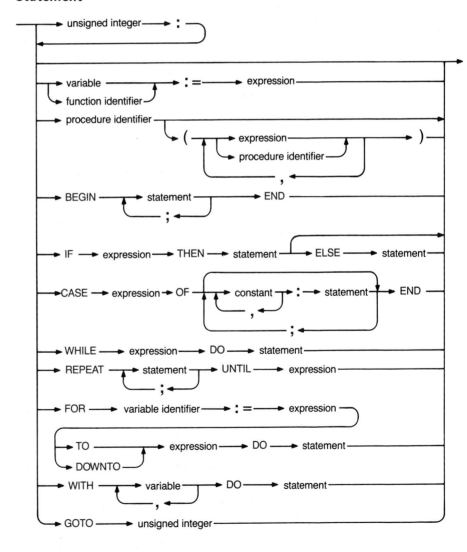

Variable

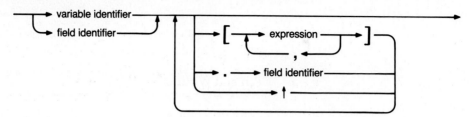

Expression

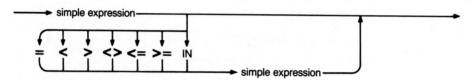

Simple Expression

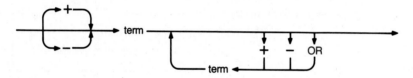

Term

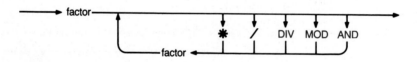

Factor

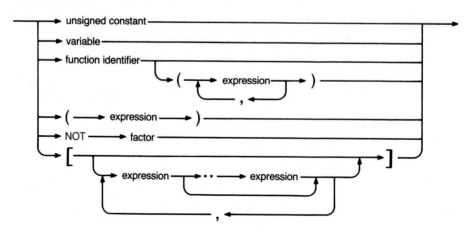

Appendix F   Compiler Error Messages

Error codes are produced by the compiler to inform the user of an error during the compilation phase. The following list is based on *Pascal User Manual and Report* by Jensen and Wirth. Many compilers do not use this notation for errors. You should consult the manual for your compiler to determine the exact meaning of any error message.

1:	Error in simple type
2:	Identifier expected
3:	'PROGRAM' expected
4:	')' expected
5:	':' expected
6:	Illegal symbol (possibly missing ';' on line above)
7:	Error in parameter list
8:	'OF' expected
9:	'(' expected
10:	Error in type
11:	'[' expected
12:	']' expected
13:	'END' expected
14:	';' expected (possibly on line above)
15:	Integer expected
16:	'=' expected
17:	'BEGIN' expected
18:	Error in declaration part
19:	Error in <field-list>
20:	',' expected
21:	'*' expected
50:	Error in constant
51:	':=' expected
52:	'THEN' expected
53:	'UNTIL' expected
54:	'DO' expected
55:	'TO' or 'DOWNTO' expected in FOR statement
56:	'IF' expected
57:	'FILE' expected
58:	Error in <factor> (bad expression)
59:	Error in variable
101:	Identifier declared twice
102:	Lower bound exceeds upper bound
103:	Identifier is not of the appropriate class

104:   Undeclared identifier
105:   Sign not allowed
106:   Number expected
107:   Incompatible subrange types
108:   File not allowed here
109:   Type must not be REAL

110:   \<tag field\> type must be scalar or subrange
111:   Incompatible with \<tag field\> type
112:   Index type must not be REAL
113:   Index type must be scalar or a subrange
114:   Base type must not be REAL
115:   Base type must be scalar or a subrange
116:   Error in type of standard procedure parameter
117:   Unsatisfied FORWARD reference
118:   FORWARD referenced type identifier in variable declaration
119:   Must not repeat parameter list for a FORWARD declared
          procedure

120:   Function result type must be scalar, a subrange, or a pointer
121:   File value parameter not allowed
122:   Must not repeat result type for a FORWARD declared function
123:   Missing result type in function declaration
124:   E-format for REALs only
125:   Error in type of standard function parameter
126:   Number of parameters does not agree with declaration
127:   Illegal parameter substitution
128:   Result type does not agree with declaration
129:   Type conflict of operands

130:   Expression is not of SET type
131:   Tests on equality allowed only
132:   Strict inclusion not allowed
133:   File comparison not allowed
134:   Illegal type of operand(s)
135:   Type of operand must be BOOLEAN
136:   SET element type must be scalar or subrange
137:   SET element types must be compatible
138:   Type of variable is not array
139:   Index type is not compatible with declaration

140:   Type of variable is not RECORD
141:   Type of variable must be FILE or pointer
142:   Illegal parameter substitution
143:   Illegal type of loop control variable
144:   Illegal type of expression
145:   Type conflict
146:   Assignment of files not allowed

147: Label type incompatible with selecting expression
148: Subrange bounds must be scalar
149: Index type must not be INTEGER

150: Assignment to standard function is not allowed
151: Assignment to formal function is not allowed
152: No such field in this record
153: Type error in READ
154: Actual parameter must be a variable
155: Control variable must be local and not a parameter
156: Multidefined case label
157: Too many cases in CASE statement
158: No such variant in this record
159: REAL or string tag fields not allowed

160: Previous declaration was not FORWARD
161: Previously declared as FORWARD
162: Parameter size must be constant
163: Missing variant in declaration
164: Substitution of standard procedure/function not allowed
165: Multidefined label
166: Multideclared label
167: Undeclared label
168: Undefined label
169: Base type of set exceeds implementation limit

170: Value parameter expected
171: Standard file was redeclared
172: Undeclared external file
173: FORTRAN procedure or function expected
174: Pascal procedure or function expected
175: Missing File INPUT in program heading
176: Missing File OUTPUT in program heading

201: Error in REAL constant—digit expected
202: String constant must not exceed source line
203: INTEGER constant exceeds range
204: Digit exceeds radix

250: Too many nested scopes of identifiers
251: Too many nested procedures/functions
252: Too many FORWARD references of procedure entries
253: Procedure too long
254: Too many long constants in this procedure
255: Too many errors on this source line
256: Too many external references
257: Too many externals
258: Too many local files
259: Expression too complicated

300:   Division by zero
301:   No case provided for this value
302:   Index expression out of bounds
303:   Value to be assigned is out of bounds
304:   Element expression out of range

398:   Implementation restriction
399:   Feature NOT implemented

Appendix G   Program Documentation

The rules below should be followed when you document your programs.

1. Use meaningful identifiers.
2. The first comments after the program heading should contain the following information:

```
(* Your name                        *)
(* The date                         *)
(* A brief description of the problem *)
(* and what the program does        *)
```

3. Your top-down design can be a separate document, or you can insert it as comments immediately following the items specified in Rule 2. Your top-down design should include the following information:

   Input (by form and type)
   Output (by form and type)
   Data structures (if any)
   Assumptions (if any)
   Main module
   Remaining modules by levels

   Every module must be expanded until each statement can be coded directly. Use English or pseudocode. Pascal code is not necessary here because your program shows the code. Your program must reflect your top-down design.
4. Repeat the names of your programs, procedures, and functions in comments at the main BEGIN-END pairs.

```
PROGRAM Example(INPUT, OUTPUT);
      .
      .
      .
BEGIN    (* Example *)
      .
      .
END.    (* Example *)
```

5. Comment the END of CASE statements and RECORD definitions.

```
CASE SelectFrom OF
      1: Statement;
   2, 3: Statement;
      4: Statement
END;  (* CASE *)
```

6. Comment procedures and functions immediately after their headings with a brief description of their purpose. Be sure to state any assumptions.
7. Comment code where necessary for clarity. Don't tell how or why something is done, but what is being done. Pseudocode from your top-down design is excellent for this.

Appendix H   Program Formatting

The following suggestions on formatting can make your programs more readable. They are based on rules presented in *Pascal with Style: Programming Proverbs* by Ledgard, Nagin, and Huares. (The author admits to putting in some of her own biases.)

1. Begin each statement on a separate line.
2. Put a space on both sides of the symbols ":=" and "=".
3. Put a space after the symbols ":", ",", and ";".
4. Separate procedures and functions by a blank line, a line of some special symbol enclosed as a comment, and another blank line.

```
<blank line>
(**************************************************)
<blank line>
```

5. Program, Procedure, and Function headings should begin at the left margin. However, nested procedures and functions should be indented. Separate nested procedures and functions by a line of a different special symbol. The symbol you use is not important; just be consistent.
6. The following reserved words should be on a line by themselves:

LABEL	VAR	THEN
CONST	BEGIN	ELSE
TYPE	END	REPEAT

7. The main BEGIN-END block for programs, procedures, and functions should be lined up with its corresponding heading.
8. Each statement within a BEGIN-END, REPEAT-UNTIL, or CASE statement should be aligned, either at the left or on the punctuation.
9. The bodies of CONST, TYPE, and VAR declarations; BEGIN-END blocks; and FOR, REPEAT, WHILE, CASE, and WITH statements should be indented from the corresponding header keywords. Indent consistently.

10. IF-THEN-ELSE statements should be displayed like this:

```
IF Expression
   THEN
      Statement
   ELSE
      Statement;
```

Of course, Statement can be a compound statement:

```
IF Expression
   THEN
      BEGIN
         Statements (compound statement)
      END
   ELSE
      BEGIN
         Statements (compound statement)
      END;
```

An exception is allowed for multiple nesting (a generalized case statement):

```
IF Expression
   THEN
      Statement
ELSE
   IF Expression
      THEN
         Statement

         .
         .

ELSE
   Statement
```

11. Be consistent with capitalization.

Appendix I   Character Sets

The following charts show the ordering of the most common character sets: ASCII (American Standard Code for Information Interchange), EBCDIC (Extended Binary Coded Decimal Interchange Code), and CDC Scientific. Only printable characters are shown. The ordinal number for each character is shown in decimal. The blank character is denoted by a "□".

Left Digit(s)	Right Digit	ASCII 0	1	2	3	4	5	6	7	8	9
3				□	!	"	#	$	%	&	'
4		(	)	*	+	,	−	.	/	0	1
5		2	3	4	5	6	7	8	9	:	;
6		<	=	>	?	@	A	B	C	D	E
7		F	G	H	I	J	K	L	M	N	O
8		P	Q	R	S	T	U	V	W	X	Y
9		Z	[	\	]	∧	—	`	a	b	c
10		d	e	f	g	h	i	j	k	l	m
11		n	o	p	q	r	s	t	u	v	w
12		x	y	z	{	|	}				

Codes 00–31 and 127 are nonprintable control characters.

Left Digit(s)	Right Digit	EBCDIC 0	1	2	3	4	5	6	7	8	9
6						□					
7						¢	.	<	(	+	|
8		&									
9		!	$	*	)	;	¬	‾	/		
10								,		%	—
11		>	?								
12				:	#	@	'	=	"		a
13		b	c	d	e	f	g	h	i		
14							j	k	l	m	n
15		o	p	q	r						
16				s	t	u	v	w	x	y	z
17									\	{	}
18		[	]								
19					A	B	C	D	E	F	G
20		H	I								J
21		K	L	M	N	O	P	Q	R		
22								S	T	U	V
23		W	X	Y	Z						
24		0	1	2	3	4	5	6	7	8	9

Codes 00–63 and 250–255 are nonprintable control characters.

Left Digit(s)	Right Digit	CDC									
		0	1	2	3	4	5	6	7	8	9
0		:	A	B	C	D	E	F	G	H	I
1		J	K	L	M	N	O	P	Q	R	S
2		T	U	V	W	X	Y	Z	0	1	2
3		3	4	5	6	7	8	9	+	−	*
4		/	(	)	$	=	□	,	.	≡	[
5		]	%	≠	↱	∨	∧	↑	↓	<	>
6		≤	≥	⌐	;						

Glossary

abstract data type See *data type.*

abstraction The separation of logical properties from implementation details.   (Ch. 11)

actual parameter An identifier listed in a procedure or function call.   (Ch. 6)

actual parameter list The list of actual parameters in a procedure or function call.   (Ch. 6)

address A label (name, number, or symbol) that designates a location in memory.   (Ch. 1)

algorithm A step-by-step procedure for solving a problem in a finite amount of time.   (Ch. 1)

alphanumeric character A general term for a human-readable alphabetic letter, numeric digit, or special character that can be processed by the machine.   (Ch. 2)

anonymous type A type defined in the VAR section of a program that does not have an identifier associated with it.   (Ch. 8)

argument The actual parameter that substitutes for a formal parameter.   (Ch. 13)

arithmetic logic unit (ALU) The computer component that performs arithmetic operations (addition, subtraction, multiplication, division) and logical operations (comparison of two values).   (Ch. 1)

arithmetic operator A symbol used in a numeric expression whose operation results in a numeric value; +, −, *, /, DIV, or MOD.   (Ch. 2)

ARRAY data type A structured collection of like components ordered on N dimensions (N >= 1), where each component is accessed by N indices, each of which represents the component's position within that dimension.   (Ch. 10)

ASCII American Standard Code for Information Interchange; widely used encoding scheme for a character set made up of printable and control characters.   (Ch. 8)

assembler A program that translates an assembly language program into machine language.   (Ch. 1)

assembly language A language, similar to machine language, that uses mnemonics to represent operations, and identifiers to represent addresses.   (Ch. 1)

assignment operator In Pascal, the symbol := used in an assignment statement.   (Ch. 2)

assignment statement A statement that takes the value of an expression on the right-hand side of the assignment operator and stores that value in the place named on the left-hand side of the assignment operator.   (Ch. 2)

atomic That each element in a data type is distinct and cannot be subdivided into parts.   (Ch. 8)

batch program A program that executes without intermediate user interaction.   (Ch. 12)

binary file A file in which no conversion takes place as a component is written to or read from the file; a non-TEXT file.   (Ch. 12)

binary number system A number system in which data is represented by patterns of 1s and 0s; also called *base 2 number system.*   (Ch. 1)

binary operator An operator requiring two operands. See *arithmetic operator* and *relational operator.*   (Ch. 4)

binary search A search algorithm for sorted lists that involves dividing the list in half and determining, by value comparison, whether the item would be in the upper or lower half; the process is performed repeatedly until either the item is found or it is determined that the item is not on the list.   (Ch. 12)

binary search tree A binary tree in which the information in any node is greater than the information in its left child and any of its children (left subtree) and less than the information in its right child and any of its children (right subtree).   (Ch. 13)

bit A *bi*nary dig*it* (1 or 0) used to represent information in a computer.   (Ch. 1)

block A program unit consisting of an optional declarations part and a compound statement; Pascal is a block-structured language.   (Ch. 2)

BOOLEAN data type A data type consisting of the values TRUE and FALSE.   (Ch. 2)

Boolean expression   A sequence of identifiers, separated by compatible operators, that evaluates to TRUE or FALSE.   (Ch. 4)

Boolean operator   An operator applied to values of type BOOLEAN; in Pascal, the symbols AND, OR, and NOT.   (Ch. 4)

bug   An error in a program that prevents compilation or execution, or causes incorrect results. (Ch. 4)

call   To transfer control from the portion of a program to a named subprogram (procedure or function) by using the subprogram identifier as a statement; also called *invoke*.   (Ch. 6)

cancellation error   A loss in accuracy during addition or subtraction of numbers of widely differing sizes, due to limits of precision. See *representational error*.   (Ch. 7)

case label list   A list of constants of the same type as the case selector, appearing in the body of the CASE statement.   (Ch. 7)

case selector   An ordinal expression whose value determines the case label list selected.   (Ch. 7)

central processing unit (CPU)   The "brain" of a computer; the element that interprets and executes instructions.   (Ch. 1)

CHAR data type   In Pascal, a built-in data type made up of alphanumeric characters.   (Ch. 2)

character set   The set of alphanumeric characters, encoded according to a specific coding system, that a machine can process.   (Ch. 2)

coding   Translating an algorithm into a programming language.   (Ch. 1)

collating sequence   The order of a computer's character set.   (Ch. 2)

comment   A note in a program intended for the human user that is ignored by the compiler. (Ch. 1)

compatible   Two types having the same type identifier or definition, being subranges of the same type, or one being a subrange of the other. (Ch. 8)

compile   To translate a program in a high-level language into machine language, using a compiler.   (Ch. 1)

compiler   A program that translates a high-level language (source code) into machine language (object code).   (Ch. 1)

compile-time   The phase in which the source program is translated.   (Ch. 3)

component   One of the elements that makes up a structured data type.   (Ch. 8)

component type   The type of the elements that make up a structured data type.   (Ch. 8)

compound statement   Any group of statements enclosed by the key words BEGIN and END. The executable statement section of a program (the part between the BEGIN-END pair).   (Ch. 2)

computer   A programmable electronic device that can store, retrieve, and process data.   (Ch. 1)

constants   All the specific instances of values that are legal for a data type.   (Ch. 2)

control structure   A construct that determines the order in which other parts of a program are executed; the basic types are selection, procedure, loop, and sequence.   (Ch. 1)

control unit   The computer component that controls the actions of the other components in order to execute instructions (the program) in sequence.   (Ch. 1)

count-controlled loop   A loop that executes a known number of times.   (Ch. 5)

data   Information in symbolic form that can be used by a computer.   (Ch. 1)

data structure   See *structured data type*.

data type   A description of a set of values and the operations that can be applied to those values.   (Ch. 8)

data validation   The process of verifying the accuracy of input data.   (Ch. 4)

debug   To correct errors in a program.   (Ch. 1)

declaration section   The part or parts of a program where identifiers are specified.   (Ch. 2)

default value   The value assumed by the compiler when no specific value is assigned by the program.   (Ch. 2)

DISPOSE   The standard procedure that returns the memory location used for a dynamic variable (when it is no longer needed) to the run-time support system.   (Ch. 13)

documentation   Written descriptions, specifications, design, code, and comments (internal and external to a program) that make a program readable, understandable, and easier to modify; also the user's manual for a program. See *self-documenting code*.   (Ch. 3)

driver program   A program that is designed to test a subprogram.   (Ch. 9)

dynamic data structure   A data structure that can expand and contract during run-time.   (Ch. 13)

dynamic variable   A variable created at run-time and accessed, not by name, but through a pointer variable; also called *referenced variable.* (Ch. 13)

editor   An interactive program that allows the user to enter, modify, and save TEXT files. (Ch. 1)

empty set   The set with no members at all.   (Ch. 12)

end-of-file marker (<eof>)   A mechanism for indicating the end of a file.   (Ch. 3, 12)

end-of-line marker (<eoln>)   A mechanism for indicating the end of a line; Pascal returns a blank when <eoln> is read.   (Ch. 3)

enumerated type   See *user-defined type.*

event-controlled loop   A loop that terminates when something happens inside the loop body to signal that the loop should not be repeated. (Ch. 5)

execute   To carry out the instructions in a statement or program; to run a program.   (Ch. 1)

expression   A sequence of identifiers (variables or constants) separated by compatible operators. (Ch. 2)

external file   A file that is used to communicate with the user or other programs.   (Ch. 12)

external pointer   The named pointer variable that points to the first component in a list.   (Ch. 13)

field   A component of a record.   (Ch. 11)

field identifier   The name of a component in a record.   (Ch. 11)

field selector   An expression used to access components of a RECORD variable, made up of the RECORD variable name and the field identifier, separated by a period.   (Ch. 11)

fieldwidth specification   A colon and integer value following a parameter in a WRITE or WRITELN statement, specifying the number of columns in which that parameter should be printed and right-justified.   (Ch. 2)

file   An area in secondary storage that has a name and is used to hold a collection of data; the data itself.   (Ch. 1)

file buffer variable   A variable of the same type as the component of the file with which it is associ-

ated; automatically created by the system when a FILE variable is declared; denoted by the file name followed by an up-arrow (↑). (Ch. 12)

FILE data type   A data structure consisting of a sequence of components that are all of the same type.   (Ch. 12)

flag   A special data value used to mark the end of a data file; also called *sentinel.*   (Ch. 5)

floating-point representation   The representation of a real number in which the number of significant digits is fixed and the decimal point floats. (Ch. 7)

flow of control   The order in which statements are executed in a program. See *control structure.* (Ch. 4)

formal parameter   An identifier defined in a procedure or function heading.   (Ch. 6)

formal parameter list   A list of formal parameters in a procedure or function heading.   (Ch. 6)

function   A subprogram called from within an expression that returns a value through the function name.   (Ch. 7)

global identifier   An identifier declared in the outermost block (the main program).   (Ch. 6)

hardware   The physical components of a computer.   (Ch. 1)

heading   The first part of a program or subprogram; in a program, the word PROGRAM followed by the program name (identifier) and a list of identifiers in parentheses.   (Ch. 2)

hierarchical record   A record in which at least one of the fields is itself a record.   (Ch. 11)

high-level language   A programming language that is closer to natural language than assembly language, and whose statements each translate into more than one machine language instruction.   (Ch. 1)

identifier   The name associated with a process or object and used to refer to that process or object; Pascal identifiers are made up of letters and numbers, and must begin with a letter. (Ch. 2)

implementation phase   The second stage of the programming process; involves identifying a specific solution (writing a program), then testing and using the solution. See *problem-solving phase.*   (Ch. 1)

index An ordinal value that identifies a particular component of a data structure; also called *subscript*. (Ch. 8)

index type The type of the expression used to index different elements in an array. (Ch. 8)

infinite loop A loop whose terminating condition is never reached. (Ch. 1)

information Any knowledge that can be communicated. (Ch. 1)

initialize To set an element to a starting value. (Ch. 5)

input The external data used by a program. (Ch. 3)

INPUT Standard input device. (Ch. 3)

input unit A device that accepts information to be stored in memory; the standard input device is the keyboard. (Ch. 1)

integer A positive or negative whole number (no fractional part). In Pascal, INTEGER is a built-in data type. (Ch. 2)

interactive program A program that requires direct communication with the user. (Ch. 3)

interface The shared boundary where independent systems meet and act on or communicate with each other. (Ch. 6)

interface design Using formal and actual parameters to establish communication between a procedure or function and an invoking program unit. (Ch. 6)

interface design chart A chart that describes program variables and the needs and returns of procedures and functions. (Ch. 6)

internal file A file that is created and used while a program is running but is not saved. (Ch. 12)

invoke See *call*.

literal constant A constant value written in a program; also called *literal*. (Ch. 2)

local identifier An identifier declared in the block where it is used. (Ch. 6)

loop A control structure that allows a statement or statements to be executed more than once (until a termination condition is reached). (Ch. 1)

loop control variable The counter that controls entry to a loop. (Ch. 5)

machine language A set of binary-coded instructions that is built into the hardware of the computer; the language used directly by the computer; also called *machine code*. (Ch. 1)

magnetic disk A secondary storage medium that provides a large amount of permanent storage; a rotating disk used to store and retrieve magnetically encoded data through a read/write head. (Ch. 1)

magnetic tape A secondary storage medium that provides a large amount of permanent storage; a thin plastic strip with a magnetic surface that is used to store and retrieve magnetically encoded data through a read/write head. (Ch. 1)

MaxInt The largest integer number that can be represented in a given computer; −MaxInt is the smallest. (Ch. 2)

memory The ordered sequence of storage cells (locations, words, places) in a computer, which are accessed by address and used to temporarily hold the instructions and variables of an executing program. (Ch. 1)

memory unit The internal storage device of a computer. (Ch. 1)

modular programming See *top-down design*.

module A logical part of a design or program; a task or subtask in a top-down design. (Ch. 3)

module design chart A hierarchical chart showing the relationship of modules in a top-down design. (Ch. 3)

multidimensional array A structured data type composed of a fixed number of components of the same type ordered on N dimensions, with each component directly accessed by N indexes, representing the component's position within each dimension. (Ch. 10)

named constant A location in memory where a data value that cannot be changed is stored. (Ch. 2)

name precedence The priority of a local identifier over a more global (nonlocal) identifier, where the identifiers have the same name. See *scope*. (Ch. 6)

nested logic A control structure contained within another control structure. (Ch. 5)

NEW The standard procedure that creates a dynamic variable. (Ch. 13)

NIL In Pascal, the constant that is assigned to the pointer variable at the end of a list, indicating that the pointer points to nothing. (Ch. 13)

node The two parts—component and pointer—of a linked structure. (Ch. 13)

nonlocal identifier A parameter or local variable that is accessible to embedded procedures or functions. (Ch. 6)

object program The machine language produced by a compiler or assembler from a source program; also called *object code*. (Ch. 1)

one-dimensional array A structured data type made up of a fixed number of components of the same type, with each component directly accessed by an index. (Ch. 8)

operating system A program that manages computer resources. (Ch. 1)

operator A symbol that indicates what operation should be performed. (Ch. 2)

ordinal data type A set of distinct values that are ordered so that each value except the first has a unique predecessor and each value except the last has a unique successor; any scalar data type except type REAL. (Ch. 8)

output The data produced by a program. (Ch. 3)

OUTPUT Standard output device, usually the screen. (Ch. 3)

output unit A device that prints or otherwise displays information stored in memory, or copies information stored in memory and stores it in another device. (Ch. 1)

overflow The condition where the results of a calculation are too large to represent in a given machine. (Ch. 7)

packed array An array that takes up as little space in memory as possible by having as many array components as possible packed into each memory word. A packed array whose elements are of type CHAR is called a string and has special properties in Pascal. (Ch. 9)

parallel arrays Two or more separate arrays that contain related information in corresponding positions. (Ch. 9)

parameter list A mechanism for communicating between two parts of a program. (Ch. 2)

peripheral device An input unit, output unit, or auxiliary storage device of a computer. (Ch. 1)

pointer A variable that indicates the address or location of the dynamic variable it references. (Ch. 13)

pointer data type A simple data type that contains or indicates the address or location of a variable of a given type. (Ch. 13)

posttest loop A loop that tests the condition at the end of the loop; will be executed at least once. (Ch. 7)

precedence The order in which operations are performed in an expression. (Ch. 2)

precision The maximum number of significant digits. (Ch. 7)

pretest loop A loop that tests the condition at the beginning of the loop; the loop may never be executed, or it may be executed one or more times. (Ch. 7)

problem-solving phase The first stage of the programming process; involves determining the task that needs doing by analyzing the problem, finding a general solution (algorithm), then testing that solution. See *implementation phase*. (Ch. 1)

procedure A subprogram that is executed when called. (Ch. 1)

procedure identifier The name of the action; when used as a statement, the procedure identifier invokes the procedure. (Ch. 6)

program A sequence of instructions written to perform a specific task. (Ch. 1)

programming The process of defining the sequence of instructions that makes up a program. (Ch. 1)

programming language A set of rules, symbols, and special words used to construct a program. (Ch. 1)

pseudocode A mixture of English and programming language control structures used in writing the modules for a top-down design. (Ch. 3)

queue A data structure in which elements are entered at one end and removed from the other; a first in, first out (FIFO) structure. (Ch. 13)

range From the smallest to the largest allowable values. (Ch. 7)

range checking The automatic detection of an out-of-range value having been assigned to a variable. (Ch. 8)

real number A number that has a whole and a fractional part; a decimal number. In Pascal, REAL is a built-in data type. (Ch. 2)

RECORD data type A structured data type with a fixed number of components (not necessarily of the same type) that are accessed by name (not by index). (Ch. 11)

recursion The ability of a procedure or function to call itself. (Ch. 7)

referenced variable See *dynamic variable.*

relational operator A symbol that forms an expression with two values of compatible types, and whose operation of comparing those values results in a BOOLEAN value. (Ch. 4)

representational error An arithmetic error that occurs when the precision of the result of an arithmetic operation is greater than the precision of a given machine. (Ch. 7)

reserved word An identifier that has a specific meaning in a programming language and cannot be used for any other purpose in a program. (Ch. 3)

root node The external pointer to a tree data structure; the top or base node of a tree. (Ch. 13)

round off To truncate (or make zero) one or more least significant digits of a number, and to increase the remaining least significant digit by 1 if the truncated value is more than half of the number base. (Ch. 7)

run-time The phase in which the object program is executed. (Ch. 3)

scalar data type A set of distinct values (constants) that are ordered; an unstructured data type; any of the Pascal types INTEGER, REAL, BOOLEAN, or CHAR, or any user-defined ordinal type. (Ch. 8)

scientific notation A method of representing a number as an expression consisting of a number between 1 and 10 multiplied by the appropriate power of 10. (Ch. 2)

scope The area within a program in which an identifier is known. (Ch. 6)

selection A control structure that selects one of two or more options or paths in the flow of control, based on the value of some expression. (Ch. 1)

self-documenting code A program containing meaningful identifiers, named constants, and judiciously used clarifying comments. (Ch. 3)

semantics The set of rules that gives the meaning of instructions in a language. (Ch. 1)

sentinel See *flag.*

SET data type An unordered group of distinct components (members) chosen from the values of an ordinal base type. (Ch. 12)

side effect A change within a procedure or function to a variable that is external to, but not passed to, the procedure or function. (Ch. 6)

significant digits Those digits that begin with the first nonzero digit on the left and end with the last nonzero digit on the right (or a zero digit that is exact). (Ch. 7)

simple data type A type identifier, a user-defined ordinal type, or a subrange type. (Ch. 8)

software Computer programs; the set of all programs available to a computer. (Ch. 1)

source program A program in its original form (in the language in which it was written), before it is compiled; also called *source code.* (Ch. 1)

stack A data structure in which elements are entered and removed from just one end; a last in, first out (LIFO) structure. (Ch. 13)

standard identifier A predefined identifier in Pascal (like MaxInt) that can be redefined in a program. (Ch. 3)

statement An instruction in a programming language. (Ch. 2)

statement separator A symbol used to tell the compiler where one instruction ends and another begins in a program; in Pascal, a semicolon. (Ch. 2)

static data structure A data structure whose size is fixed at compile-time. (Ch. 13)

stepwise refinement See *top-down design.*

string A collection of characters interpreted as a single data item; a PACKED ARRAY OF CHAR. (Ch. 9)

string constant A series of alphanumeric characters written within single quotes. (Ch. 2)

structured data type A data type made up of an organized collection of one or more scalar data types, characterized by how individual components are accessed. (Ch. 8)

structured program A program in which each logical unit has just one entry and one exit. (Ch. 1)

subprogram A named sequence of statements in a program that is treated as a distinct entity, performs a specific task, and can be called (invoked) from other points in the program; a procedure or function. (Ch. 2)

subrange type A data type made up of a specified range of any standard or user-defined ordinal type. (Ch. 8)

subscript See *index*.

syntax The formal rules governing the construction of valid statements in a language. (Ch. 1)

syntax diagram A schematic definition of the syntax rules of a programming language. (Ch. 2)

systems software The set of programs that improves the efficiency and convenience of using a computer; includes utility programs, the operating system, assemblers, and compilers. (Ch. 1)

testing Running a program with the intention of finding errors. (Ch. 1)

TEXT file A file of characters that is divided into lines. (Ch. 3)

time sharing A method of operation in which a computer is shared by several users simultaneously. (Ch. 1)

top-down design A design methodology that works from an abstract functional description of a problem (top) to a detailed solution (bottom); a hierarchical approach to problem solving that divides a problem into functional subproblems represented by modules; also called *stepwise refinement* and *modular programming*. (Ch. 3)

trace To follow the logical flow of a computer and determine the value of variables after each instruction; also called *code walk-through* and *playing computer*. (Ch. 2)

truncate To decrease the precision of a number by removing one or more least significant digits. (Ch. 7)

two-dimensional array A structured data type made up of a fixed number of components of the same type structured in two dimensions; each component is accessed directly by a pair of indexes. (Ch. 10)

type definition The definition of a data type in the TYPE section of a block, with the type identifier on the left side of an equal sign and the definition on the right. (Ch. 8)

unary operator An operator requiring only one operand; for example, the Boolean operator NOT. (Ch. 4)

underflow A condition that occurs when the results of a calculation are too small to represent in a given machine. (Ch. 7)

user-defined type The ordered set of distinct values (constants) defined as a data type in a program; also called *enumerated type*. (Ch. 8)

value parameter A formal parameter that is a local variable of a procedure or function but whose value is initialized to the value of an actual parameter in a call to the procedure or function; a copy of the content of the actual parameter is left on the message board. (Ch. 6)

variable A location in memory, referenced by a variable name (identifier), where a data value can be stored; a value that can be changed while a program is executing. (Ch. 2)

variable declaration A declaration in the VAR section of a block that specifies both the name of the variable (to the left of the colon) and its data type (to the right of the colon). (Ch. 2)

VAR parameter A formal parameter that is replaced by an actual parameter in a call to a procedure or function; the address of the actual parameter is left on the message board. (Ch. 6)

word A group of bits that is treated as a unit or location in memory. (Ch. 7)

Answers to Exercises

Chapter 2

1. **a.** Invalid **c.** Valid **e.** Valid **g.** Valid
    b. Valid **d.** Invalid **f.** Invalid **h.** Invalid

2. **a.** Invalid **c.** Valid **e.** Valid **g.** Valid
    b. Invalid **d.** Invalid **f.** Invalid **h.** Valid

3. **a.** 13.33, REAL **e.** −4, INTEGER
    b. 2, INTEGER **f.** 1.0, REAL
    c. 5, INTEGER **g.** Illegal; MOD operator is for
    d. 13.75, REAL INTEGER operands only.

4. **a.** 3 **c.** 37 **e.** 23
    b. 4 **d.** 22 **f.** 16

5. **a.** Invalid **c.** Valid **e.** Invalid
    b. Invalid **d.** Invalid (CONST is a reserved word)

6.  ```
    CONST
       InchesPerFoot = 12;
    ```

7.  ```
    VAR
       Rate, Weight : REAL;
    ```

8. 5

9.  ```
    VAR
       BirthYr : INTEGER;
       GdPt : REAL;
       Marked : BOOLEAN;
       Code : CHAR;
       ID : INTEGER;
    ```

10. ```
    WRITELN('***DANGER***');
    WRITELN('Overvoltage Condition');
    ```

11. True

12. **a.** A := B + C; or C := A + B; **d.** PROGRAM One(INPUT, OUTPUT);
    b. Y := Contents; **e.** CONST
    c. X := B;   X = 18;

13. True

14. ```
    WRITELN('Amount = ', Amount:6);
    ```
    Assumption: Amount requires 6 spaces.
    ```

15. Cost is
   300
   Price is 30Cost is 300
   Grade A costs   300

16. **a.** 15   **c.** 2   **e.** 5   **g.** 17   **i.** 18   **k.** 9
    b. 11   **d.** 8   **f.** 16   **h.** 4   **j.** 19

Chapter 3

1. True

2. **a.** READLN(Payroll, EmployeeNo, DeptNo);
     READLN(Payroll, DeductCode, RegHrs, OTHrs);
   b. READLN(GradeSheet, StudentID, Blank, ClassCode, Blank,
          Grade1, Blank, Grade2, Blank, Grade3, Blank, Grade4)
          (* Blank is of type CHAR. *)

3. **a.** U   **c.** R   **e.** U   **g.** U
    b. R   **d.** R   **f.** U   **h.** R

4. **a.** A =   5 B = 2
    b. Sum =   7
    c.   2
    d.   −3

5. **a.** 24   **c.** 46
    b. 72   **d.** 18

6.

X	Y	Z
25	20	2
47	20	2
1	20	2
1	20	10
1	11	10
−27	11	10
−27	11	10

7. **a.** A: 42
      B: 24
      C: 15
      D: 31
    b. A: 19
      B: 25
      C: 16
      D: 13
    c. A: 17
      B: 24
      C: 58

8. **a.** READLN(InventoryFile, StockNo, Cost, SalePrice);
    b. READLN(StationFile, IdentNumber);
      READLN(StationFile, Blank, Code, Quantity);

9. Meaningful identifier names, proper indention, comments, named constants, top-down design

10. **a.** $(A + B) / (C + D)$ **b.** $(A + B)$ DIV $(C + D)$

11. **Input:** Invoice number, quantity ordered, unit price (INTEGER)

    Output: Input data and total price

    Assumption: Data is correct.

    MAIN MODULE   Level 0

    ```
    Get data
    Get total
    Print data
    Print total
    ```

    GET DATA   Level 1

    ```
    Writeln prompt message
    Readln InvoiceNum, Quantity, UnitPrice
    ```

    GET TOTAL

    ```
    Total = Quantity * UnitPrice
    ```

    PRINT DATA

    ```
    Writeln 'Invoice number ', InvoiceNum
    Writeln 'Quantity ordered ', Quantity
    Writeln 'Unit price ', UnitPrice
    ```

    PRINT TOTAL

    ```
    Writeln 'Total price = ', Total
    ```

```
PROGRAM TotalPrice(INPUT, OUTPUT);

VAR
  InvoiceNum, Quantity, UnitPrice, Total : INTEGER;

BEGIN   (* TotalPrice *)
  WRITELN('Enter the invoice number, the quantity, and',
        ' the unit price on one line, with spaces between them.');
  WRITELN('Press return.');
  READLN(InvoiceNum, Quantity, UnitPrice);
  Total := Quantity * UnitPrice;
      WRITELN('Invoice number ', InvoiceNum);
      WRITELN('Quantity ordered ', Quantity);
      WRITELN('Unit price ', Unit Price);
      WRITELN('Total price = ', Total)
  END.    (* TotalPrice *)
```

12. False

13. **a.** ' ' (blank)   **c.** '2'
    b. 'A'   **d.** ' ' (blank)

14. PROGRAM ChangeIt(OUTPUT, FileA, FileB);

```
    VAR
       Item1, Item2 : INTEGER;
       FileA, FileB : TEXT;

    BEGIN   (* ChangeIt *)
      RESET(FileA);
      REWRITE(FileB);
      READLN(FileA, Item1, Item2);
      WRITELN(FileB, Item2, Item1)
    END.      (* ChangeIt *)
```

Chapter 4

1. **a.** Not legal   **b.** (MinimumAge <= Age) AND (Age < MaximumAge)

2. Available := NumberOrdered <= NumberOnHand - NumberReserved;

3. VAR
      Eligible : BOOLEAN;
      .
      .
      Eligible := TRUE

4. **a.** TRUE   **b.** TRUE   **c.** TRUE   **d.** FALSE

5. Candidate := (SATScore >= 1100) AND (GPA >= 2.5) AND (AGE > 15);

6. LeftPage := (PageNumber MOD 2) = 0;
    There are other ways too.

```
7.  IF Age > 64
        THEN
           WRITE('Social Security')
        ELSE
           IF Age < 18
               THEN
                  WRITE('Exempt')
               ELSE
                  WRITE('Taxable');
8.  IF A > B
        THEN
           IF A > C
               THEN
                  Largest := A
               ELSE
                  Largest := C
        ELSE
           IF B > C
               THEN
                  Largest := B
               ELSE
                  Largest := C;
```

or

```
IF A > B
   THEN
      Largest := A
   ELSE
      Largest := B;
IF C > Largest
   THEN
      Largest := C;
```

or

```
IF (A > B) AND (A > C)
   THEN
      Largest := A
   ELSE
      IF (B > A) and (B > C)
          THEN
             Largest := B
          ELSE
             Largest := C;
```

9. a. Eligible to serve.
   b. Nothing. The ELSE in the sixth line is part of the closest IF statement.

10. **Input:**   Birthday, birth month, birth year (INTEGER)
Current day, month, year (INTEGER)

Output: Birthday
Current age

Assumption: Data is correct.

MAIN MODULE   Level 0

```
Get data
Find age
Print birthdate
Print age
```

GET DATA   Level 1

```
Writeln prompt message
Read birthdate
Writeln prompt message
Read current date
```

FIND AGE

```
IF (current month > birth month) OR
   ((current month = birth month) AND
   (current day >= birthday))
   THEN
      Age = current year − birth year
   ELSE
      Age = current year − birth year − 1
```

PRINT BIRTHDATE

```
Writeln 'Birthdate is ', birth month, '/',
        birthday, '/' , birth year
```

PRINT AGE

```
Writeln 'Age in years = ', Age
```

```
PROGRAM ComputeAge(INPUT, OUTPUT);

VAR
  BDay, BMonth, BYear,
  CurDay, CurMonth, CurYear, Age : INTEGER;

BEGIN   (* ComputeAge *)
  WRITELN('Enter birth day, month, year separated by spaces only.   ',
          'Press return when through.');
  READLN(BDay, BMonth, BYear);
  WRITELN('Enter today''s date, day, month, year, separated by ',
          'spaces only. Press return when through.');
  READLN(CurDay, CurMonth, CurYear);
  IF (CurMonth > BMonth) OR
     ((CurMonth = BMonth) AND (CurDay >= BDay))
       THEN
         Age := CurYear - BYear
       ELSE
         Age := CurYear - BYear - 1;
  WRITELN('Birthdate is ', BMonth:1, '/', BDay:1,
          '/', BYear:2);
  WRITELN('Age in years = ', Age:1)
END.    (* ComputeAge *)
```

Note: Your program and design may not look exactly like this. Also notice the fieldwidth specifications for the dates in the WRITELN statements. The style here gets rid of extra blanks, so we see '10/2/1960' output for an input of '02 10 1960'. The ':2' after BYear takes care of input years of either 2 or 4 digits.

11.
```
PROGRAM Exercise(INPUT, OUTPUT);

CONST
  A = 10;
  B = 5;
  C = 6;

VAR
  D, E, F : INTEGER;

BEGIN   (* Exercise *)
  READ(D, E, F);
  IF (D > A)
     THEN
       D := A + D
     ELSE
       D := A;
  E := D + F;
  WRITE('This program does not make any sense ', E, F, D)
END.    (* Exercise *)
```

12. TRUE

13.

```
PROGRAM Weather(INPUT, OUTPUT);

CONST
  Cool = 75;
  Warm = 90;

VAR
  Day, Temp : INTEGER;

BEGIN    (* Weather *)
  WRITELN('Enter the day of the month and temperature ',
          'separated only by spaces.   Press return when through.');
  READ(Day, Temp);
  WRITE(Day, ' ');
  IF Temp < Cool
     THEN
        WRITELN('Cool.')
     ELSE
        IF Temp < Warm
           THEN
              WRITELN('Warm.')
           ELSE
              WRITELN('Hot.')
END.     (* Weather *)
```

14.

```
PROGRAM M4V3(INPUT, OUTPUT);

CONST
  A = 29;

VAR
  I, J, K : INTEGER;

BEGIN    (* M4V3 *)
  READ(K);
  I := 29 DIV A;
  J := 9;
  IF (K = I) OR (K = J)
     THEN
        K := 0
     ELSE
        WRITE('Nope');
  READ(I, J);
  IF I = J
     THEN
        WRITELN('Equal');
  J := I + K + J + A
END.     (* M4V3 *)
```

15. **a.** I: 7, J: 58, K: 12   **b.** Nope

Chapter 5

1.  ```
    PROGRAM Count(FileCount, OUTPUT);

    VAR
      Number, Positive, Negative : INTEGER;
      FileCount : TEXT;
    BEGIN    (* Count *)
      RESET(FileCount);
      Positive := 0;
      Negative := 0;
      WHILE NOT EOF(FileCount) DO
        BEGIN
          READLN(FileCount, Number);
          IF Number < 0
            THEN
              Negative := Negative + 1
            ELSE
              IF Number > 0
                THEN
                  Positive := Positive + 1
        END;
      WRITELN('Negative integers: ', Negative,
              '   Positive integers: ', Positive)
    END.    (* Count *)
    ```

2. **a.** Event-controlled loop   **b.** Counting events

3.  ```
    I := 16;
    Sum := 0;
    WHILE I <= 26 DO
      BEGIN
        Sum := Sum + I;
        I := I + 2
      END;
    ```

4.  ```
    I := 1;                    ← Initializes counter for
    WHILE I <= 6 DO                 number of lines
      BEGIN
        J := 1;                ← Initializes counter for
        Sum := 0;                   number of values
        WHILE J <= 5 DO
          BEGIN
            READ(DataFile, Data);
            Sum := Sum + Data;
            J := J + 1
          END;
        WRITELN( 'Line', I, ' sum = ', Sum);
        READLN;
        I := I + 1
      END;
    ```
    ```

5. **a.** Both loops are count-controlled loops.
   b. The outer loop initializes variables; the inner loop reads and sums values.

6.
```
Negative := FALSE;
Count := 1;
WHILE (Count <= 10) AND NOT Negative DO
  BEGIN
    READ(Data);
    IF Data < 0
        THEN
          Negative := TRUE
        ELSE
          Count := Count + 1
  END;
```

7. **Input:** Number of integers (N) followed by N integers
   Output: Average
   Assumption: Data is correct.

MAIN MODULE   Level 0

```
Initialize variables
Prompt user for input
Get number of data items
Get data (and find Sum)
Find Average
Print Average
```

INITIALIZE VARIABLES   Level 1

```
Sum ← 0
Counter ← 1
```

PROMPT USER FOR INPUT

```
Writeln 'Input number of data items
  followed by the data.'
```

GET NUMBER OF DATA ITEMS

```
Read N
```

GET DATA

```
WHILE more data DO
    Read Number
    Sum ← Sum + Number
    Counter ← Counter + 1
```

FIND AVERAGE

```
Average ← Sum / N
```

PRINT AVERAGE

```
Writeln 'Average  =  ' Average
```

```
PROGRAM GetAverage(INPUT, OUTPUT);

VAR
   N, I, Sum, Number : INTEGER;
   Average : REAL;

BEGIN    (* GetAverage *)
   Sum := 0;
   I := 1;
   WRITELN('Input number of data items followed by the data.');
   READ(N);
   WHILE I <= N DO
      BEGIN
         READ(Number);
         Sum := Sum + Number;
         I := I + 1
      END;
   Average := Sum / N;
   WRITELN('Average = ', Average)
END.      (* GetAverage *)
```

8. **a.** Count-controlled loop
    b. Reading and summing values.

9.
```
Overflow := FALSE;
WHILE NOT Overflow DO
  BEGIN
    READ(Level);
    IF Level > 200.0
       THEN
           Overflow := TRUE
  END;
```

10.
```
PROGRAM TemperatureStatistics(Tempdata, OUTPUT);

CONST
  HoursInDay = 24;

VAR
  Temperature, HighSoFar, LowSoFar, Sum, HourCounter :
  INTEGER; Average : REAL; TempData : TEXT;

BEGIN  (* TemperatureStatistics *)
  RESET(TempData);
  READ(TempData, Temperature);
  WRITELN(Temperature);
  Sum := Temperature;
  HighSoFar := Temperature;
  LowSoFar := Temperature;
  HourCounter := 1;
  WHILE HourCounter < HoursInDay DO
    BEGIN
      READ(TempData, Temperture);
      WRITELN(Temperature);
      Sum := Sum + Temperature;
      IF Temperature > HighSoFar
         THEN
             HighSoFar := Temperature;
      IF Temperature < LowSoFar
         THEN
             LowSoFar := Temperature;
      HourCounter := HourCounter + 1
    END;
  Average := Sum / HoursInDay;
  WRITELN('Average temperature is ', Average:6:1);
  WRITELN('High temperature is ', HighSoFar:9);
  WRITELN('Low temperature is ', LowSoFar:10)
END.  (* TemperatureStatistics *)
```

```
11.  WHILE NOT EOF (DataFile) DO
       BEGIN
         READLN(DataFile, First, Second);
         IF First < Second
            THEN
               WRITELN(First, Second)
            ELSE
               WRITELN(Second, First);
       END;
12.  a.  WRITELN('SALES':13);
         WRITELN('WEEK1    WEEK2    WEEK3');
     b.  WRITELN(Week1:5, Week2:8, Week3:8);
13.  Positive := TRUE;
     WHILE Positive DO
       BEGIN
         READ(Data);
         Positive := Data > 0
       END;
14.  WHILE NOT EOF(File1) AND ((Character <> 'A') AND
       (Character <> 'B') AND (Character <> 'C')) DO
       READ(File1, Character);
     IF EOF(File1)
        THEN
           WRITE('Alphanumeric')
        ELSE
           WRITE('Alphabetic');
```

15. **a.** 8 **b.** −2

    c. No. The data does not contain a 1, so the exit on Flag is not tested.

Chapter 6

1. **Input:** Integers

   Output: Number of negative integers
   Number of positive integers

   Assumption: Data is correct.

   MAIN MODULE   Level 0

   > Initialize variables
   > Process data
   > Print values

INITIALIZE VARIABLES   Level 1

Positive ← 0
Negative ← 0

PROCESS DATA

```
WHILE NOT EOF DO
    Readln Number
  IF Number < 0
    THEN
        Negative = Negative + 1
    ELSE IF Number > 0
      THEN
          Positive = Positive + 1
```

PRINT VALUES

Writeln 'Negative integers: ' Negative,   Positive integers: ' Positive

Interface Design Chart

Program Variables

Identifiers	Type	Role
Negative	INTEGER	Event counter for negative numbers
Positive	INTEGER	Event counter for positive numbers
FileCount	TEXT	File of Integers

Procedures

Identifiers	Needs	Returns
ProcessData	FileCount	Negative, Positive
PrintValues	Negative, Positive	Nothing

```
PROGRAM Count(FileCount, OUTPUT);

VAR
  Negative, Positive : INTEGER;
  FileCount : TEXT;
```

```
(**************************************************)

PROCEDURE Process Data(VAR FileCount : TEXT;
                       VAR Negative, Positive : INTEGER);

VAR
  Number : INTEGER;

BEGIN   (* ProcessData *)
  WHILE NOT EOF(FileCount) DO
    BEGIN
      READLN(FileCount, Number);
      IF Number < 0
        THEN
          Negative := Negative + 1
        ELSE IF Number > 0
             THEN
             Positive := Positive + 1;
  END
END;   (* ProcessData *)

(**************************************************)

PROCEDURE PrintValues(VAR Negative, Positive : INTEGER);

BEGIN   (* PrintValues *)
  WRITELN('Negative integers: ', Negative, '   Positive integers: ',
          Positive)
END;    (* PrintValues *)

(**************************************************)

BEGIN   (* Count *)
  RESET(FileCount);
  Positive := 0;
  Negative := 0;
  ProcessData(Negative, Positive);
  PrintValues(Negative, Positive)
END.    (* Count *)
```

2. a.
```
PROCEDURE Add(N, M : INTEGER; VAR, Answer : INTEGER);
(* Assumes N and M are even *)

VAR
  I : INTEGER;

BEGIN    (* Add *)
  Answer := 0;
  I := N;
  WHILE I <= M DO
    BEGIN
      Answer := Answer + I;
      I := I + 2
    END
END;    (* Add *)
```
b. `Add (16, 26, Answer);`

3. a.
```
PROCEDURE Sums(VAR Sum : INTEGER;
               VAR AllPositive : BOOLEAN);
(* Assumes no premature EOF in data *)

VAR
  Count, Data : INTEGER;

BEGIN    (* Sums *)
  Count := 1;
  Sum := 0;
  AllPositive := TRUE;
  WHILE AllPositive AND (Count <= 10) DO
    BEGIN
      READ(Data);
      IF Data >= 0
        THEN
          Sum := Sum + Data
        ELSE
          AllPositive := FALSE;
      Count := Count + 1
    END
END;  (* Sums *)
```
b. `Sums(Sum, AllPositive);`

4. a. A statement that transfers control from the main program (or a subprogram) to a procedure.
b. The mechanism for communicating between two parts of a program.
c. Formal and actual parameters are matched up by position.
d. An identifier defined in a procedure heading.
e. An identifier listed in a procedure call.
f. The type of parameter where the address of the actual parameter is left on the message board.
g. A variable that is declared in the block where it is used.

5. 2 4 6 12

6. True

7. True

8. True

9. True, if the identifier is not redeclared in an inner block

10. The compiler automatically looks for a local variable; only if it doesn't find one does it go to outside the block.

11.   a. True   c. True
     b. True   d. False

12.   a. False   f. True
     b. False   g. False
     c. False   h. True
     d. True   i. True
     e. False   j. True

13.

```
PROGRAM ScopeRules;
VAR
    A, B : INTEGER;

        PROCEDURE Block1;
        VAR
            A1, B1 : INTEGER;

                PROCEDURE Block2;
                VAR
                    A, A2, B2 : INTEGER;


        PROCEDURE Block3;
        VAR
            A3, B3 : INTEGER;
```

14.   a. A formal parameter that is a local variable of a procedure but whose value is initialized to the value of an actual parameter in the call to the procedure; a copy of the content of the actual parameter is left on the message board.

     b. A variable declared in the outermost block (the main program).

     c. The area within a program in which an identifier is known.

     d. The priority of a local identifier over a more global (nonlocal) identifier, where the identifiers have the same name.

     e. Changes within a procedure or function to a variable that is external to, but not passed to, the procedure or function.

     f. A parameter or local variable that is accessible to embedded procedures.

15. **a.** A: 10, B: 7
    b. X: 10, Y: 7, B: U
    c. A: 10, B: 17

16. **a.** A: 5, B: 4
    b. X: 5, Y: 4, B: U
    c. A: 9, B: 4

17. **a.** A: 7, B: 10
    b. X: 7, Y: 10, B: 10
    c. A: 7, B: 10

Chapter 7

1. ```
FUNCTION P5(Data : REAL) : REAL;

BEGIN   (* P5 *)
  P5 := Data * Data * Data * Data * Data
END;   (* P5 *)
```

2. ```
FUNCTION Minimum(A, B, C : INTEGER) : INTEGER;

BEGIN      (* Minimum *)
  IF (A < B) AND (A < C)
     THEN
       Minimum := A
     ELSE
       IF (B < A) AND (B < C)
          THEN
            Minimum := B
          ELSE
            Minimum := C
END;      (* Minimum *)
```

3. ```
FUNCTION Accept(GradePoint : REAL; SAT : INTEGER) : BOOLEAN;

BEGIN   (* Accept *)
  Accept := (GradePoint >= 3.4) OR (SAT >= 1300)
END;   (* Accept *)
```

4. False

5. True

6. False

7. False
```

8.
```
PROGRAM Count(FileCount, OUTPUT);
(* Assumption:  FileCount is not empty. *)

VAR
  Number, Positive, Negative : INTEGER;
  FileCount : TEXT;

BEGIN   (* Count *)
  RESET(FileCount);
  Positive := 0;
  Negative := 0;
  REPEAT
    READLN(FileCount, Number);
    IF Number < 0
      THEN
        Negative := Negative + 1
      ELSE
        IF Number > 0
          THEN
            Positive := Positive + 1
  UNTIL EOF(FileCount);
  WRITELN('Negative integers: ', Negative,
          '  Positive integers: ', Positive)
END.    (* Count *)
```

9.
```
Count := 1;
REPEAT
  READ(Data);
  Count := Count + 1
UNTIL (Data < 0) OR (Count > 10);
```

10.
```
CASE Storeys OF
      1, 2, 3, 4  : BEGIN
                      WRITELN('No restrictions');
                      Inspection := FALSE
                    END
5, 6, 7, 8, 9, 10 : WRITELN('Address restrictions')
END;  (* CASE *)
```

11.
```
CASE Grade OF
      'A' : Sum := Sum + 4;
      'B' : Sum := Sum + 3;
      'C' : Sum := Sum + 2;
      'D' : Sum := Sum + 1;
      'F' : WRITELN('Student is on probation.')
END;  (* CASE *)
```

12.
```
CASE Error OF
      1 : WRITELN('Invalid input');
      2 : WRITELN('Results out of range');
      3 : WRITELN('Error Type 3');
   4, 5 : WRITELN('Undefined error')
END;  (* CASE *)
```

13.
   a. Valid   **f.** Valid
   b. Valid   **g.** Valid
   c. Invalid   **h.** Invalid
   d. Invalid   **i.** Valid
   e. Invalid   **j.** Valid

14.
   a. `WRITE(Area);`   **c.** `WRITE(Area:11:7);`
   b. Can't be done; the exponent is wrong.   **d.** `WRITE(Area:6:2);`

15.
   a. False   **d.** False
   b. True   **e.** True
   c. False

16.
```
FUNCTION Factor(N : INTEGER) : INTEGER;

BEGIN     (* Factor *)
  IF N = 0
     THEN
        Factor := 1
     ELSE
        Factor := N * Factor (N - 1)
END;      (* Factor *)
```

17.
```
SumScore := 0;
FOR Number := 1 TO 10 DO
  BEGIN
    READ(Score);
    SumScore := SumScore + Score
  END;
Average := SumScore / 10;
```

18.
```
CheckTotal := 0;
READLN(BeginBalance, N);
FOR I := N DOWNTO 1 DO
  BEGIN
    READ(Amount);
    CheckTotal := CheckTotal + Amount
  END;
EndBalance := BeginBalance - CheckTotal;
```

Chapter 8

1. **a.**
```
TYPE
     School = (Lincoln, Jefferson, Adams, Washington);
```

b. TYPE
```
Team = (First, Second, Third, SS, LF, RF, CF,
        Catcher, Pitcher);
```
c. TYPE
```
Family = (Judy, Susy, Sarah, June, Bobby);
```

2. a. TYPE
```
Numerals = '0'..'9';
```
b. TYPE
```
Range = -4..24;
```
c. TYPE
```
SubTeam = First..SS;
```

3. a. TYPE
```
ListlType = ARRAY[1..24] OF REAL;

VAR
  List1 : List1Type:
```
b. TYPE
```
List2Type = ARRAY['A'..'Z'] OF INTEGER;

VAR
  List2 : List2Type;
```
c. TYPE
```
List3Type = ARRAY[-5..4] OF CHAR;

VAR
  List3 : List3Type;
```

4. a.
```
FOR I := 1 TO 24 DO
  List1[I] := 0.0;
```
b.
```
FOR Ch := 'A' TO 'Z' DO
  List2[Ch] := 0;
```
c.
```
READ(List3[-5], List3[-4]);
```

5. Assumptions: Temp is of type Thing, and I and J are INTEGER.

```
I := 1;
J := 10;
WHILE I < J DO
  BEGIN
    Temp := List[I];
    List[I] := List[J];
    List[J] := Temp;
    I := I + 1;
    J := J - 1
  END;
```

6.
```
Sum := 0;
FOR I := 1 TO 83 DO
  IF InService[I]
    THEN
      Sum := Sum + 1;
```

7. True

8. True

9. False

10. No. (John and Evelyn appear in both definitions.)

11. Yes. (Number Counties must be defined as a constant.)

12. True

13. False

14. **a.** 6   **b.** 'C'   **c.** 4   **d.** Undefined   **e.** −1

15.
```
FUNCTION Zero(List : ArrayType) : BOOLEAN;

   VAR
     I : INTEGER;
     Flag : BOOLEAN;

   BEGIN    (* Zero *)
     Flag := FALSE;
     I := 1;
     WHILE (I <= 50) AND NOT Flag DO
       BEGIN
         Flag := (List[I] = 0);
         I := I + 1
       END;
     Zero := Flag
   END;     (* Zero *)
```

Chapter 9

1.
```
FUNCTION Index(List : ArrayType;
               Value, Length : INTEGER) : INTEGER;

   VAR
     I : INTEGER;
     Found : BOOLEAN;

   BEGIN
     I := 1;
     Found := FALSE;
     WHILE (I <= Length) AND NOT Found DO
       IF Value = List[I]
          THEN
            Found := TRUE
          ELSE
            I := I + 1;
     IF Found
        THEN
          Index := I;
        ELSE
          Index := 0
   END;     (* Index *)
```

```
2.  PROCEDURE Merge(VAR One, Two : TEXT;
                      VAR Combination : ArrayType;
                      VAR Length : INTEGER);
    (* Global flag EndFlag ends data on files One and Two. *)
    VAR
      Value1, Value2 : INTEGER;

    BEGIN   (* Merge *)
      Length := 0;
      READ(One, Value1);
      READ(Two, Value2);
    WHILE(Value1 <> EndFlag) AND (Value2 <> EndFlag) DO
         BEGIN
           Length := Length + 1;
           IF Value1 > Value2
             THEN
               BEGIN
                 Combination[Length] := Value2;
                 READ(Two, Value2)
               END
             ELSE
               IF Value1 = Value2
                 THEN
                   BEGIN
                     Combination[Length] := Value1;
                     READ(One, Value1);
                     READ(Two, Value2)
                   END
                 ELSE
                   BEGIN
                     Combination[Length] := Value1;
                     READ(One, Value1)
                   END
         END;
    WHILE(Value1 <> EndFlag DO
      BEGIN
        Length := Length + 1;
        Combination[Length] := Value1;
        READ(One, Value1)
      END;
    WHILE(Value2 <> EndFlag DO
      BEGIN
        Length := Length + 1;
        Combination[Length] := Value2;
        READ(Two, Value2)
      END
    END;   (* Merge *)
```

3. **a.** TYPE
```
     Code = 'A'..'D';
     SalesType = ARRAY[Code] OF REAL;

VAR
     Sales : SalesType;
```
   b. CONST
```
     NumEmployees = 100;

TYPE
     IDType : ARRAY[1..NumEmployees] OF INTEGER;
     DependentType : ARRAY[1..NumEmployees] OF INTEGER;
     RateType : ARRAY[1..NumEmployees] OF REAL;

VAR
     ID : IDType;
     Dependents : DependentType;
     Rate : RateType;
     TransactionID : INTEGER;
     Hours : REAL;
```

4. **a.** The process involves getting a transaction code and amount, then incrementing Sales[Code] by Amount.
   b. This is a parallel-arrays problem. One of the files must be read into a set of arrays. The second file must be read one set of values at a time and the ID searched for in the ID array.

5.
```
PROCEDURE Add(A, B : ArrayType; N : INTEGER;
                  VAR Sum : INTEGER);

VAR
   I : INTEGER;

BEGIN     (* Add *)
   Sum := 0;
   FOR I := 1 TO N DO
     IF A[I] > 2
         THEN
            Sum := Sum + B[I]
END;      (* Add *)
```

6. Only Procedure PrintResults needs to be changed. It must read in the characters to be printed.

```
   PROCEDURE PrintResults(Frequencies : ListOfCounts);

   BEGIN   (* PrintResults *)
     WRITELN('Enter the characters to be counted.');
     WRITELN('Do not put spaces between them. Press return.');
     WHILE NOT EOLN DO
       BEGIN
         READ(Character);
         WRITELN('Character    ' occurred ',
                 Frequencies[Character]:3, ' times');
       END
   END;     (* PrintResults *)
```

7.
```
   PROGRAM SortWords(WordFile, OUTPUT);
   (* Words are read from WordFile and sorted.           *)
   (* Words are padded or truncated to WordSize characters. *)

   CONST
     WordSize = 10;
     NumberOfWords = 100;
     AllBlanks = '          ';

   TYPE
     ItemType = PACKED ARRAY[1..WordSize] OF CHAR;
     IndexRange = 1..NumberOfWords;
     IndexType = 0..NumberOfWords;
     ListType = ARRAY[IndexRange] OF ItemType;

   VAR
     WordFile : TEXT;
     List : ListType;
     Length : INTEGER;
     Word : ItemType;

   (************************************************************)

   PROCEDURE GetData(VAR Data : TEXT; VAR Word : ItemType);
   (* Characters are read into Word until EOLN   *)
   (* is encountered or WordSize characters have *)
   (* been read.  Word is padded with blanks.    *)
   (* File Data is left positioned at the        *)
   (* beginning of the next line of input.       *)

   VAR
     Index : 0..WordSize;      (* index into Word *)
     Character : CHAR;
```

```
BEGIN     (* GetData *)
  Word := AllBlanks;
  Index := 0;
  WHILE NOT EOLN(Data) AND (Index < WordSize) DO
    BEGIN
      READ(Data, Character);
      Index := Index + 1;
      Word[Index] := Character;
    END;
  READLN(Data);
  WRITELN(Character)
END;     (* GetData *)

(*************************************************************)


PROCEDURE Insert(VAR List : ListType; VAR Length : INTEGER;
          Item : ItemType);
(* Item is inserted into its proper place in List. *)
(* Assumption: Order is ascending.                 *)

(* Code is exactly as shown on page 324.           *)

(*************************************************************)


PROCEDURE PrintList (VAR Data : TEXT; List : ListType;
                     Length : IndexType);

(* Code is exactly as shown on page 325. *)

(*************************************************************)


BEGIN     (* SortWords *)
  Length : = 0;
  RESET(WordFile);
  WHILE NOT EOF(WordFile) DO
    BEGIN
      GetData(WordFile, Word);
      Insert(List, Length, Word)
    END;
  PrintList(WordFile, List, Length)
END.     (* SortWords *)
```

8. ```
   FUNCTION Equal(String1, String2 : Word) : BOOLEAN;

   BEGIN     (* Equal *)
     Equal := String1 = String2
   END;     (* Equal *)
   ```
   ```

Chapter 10

1. True. It can be viewed that way.

2. False

3. **a.** False
   b. False
   c. True

4.
```
FOR A := 0 TO 60 DO
   FOR B := 1 TO 36 DO
      Table[A, B] := 0;
```

5.
```
PROCEDURE Initialize(VAR Table : TableType; Character : CHAR;
                         N : INTEGER);

VAR
   I : INTEGER;

BEGIN    (* Initialize *)
   FOR I := 1 TO N DO
      BEGIN
         Table[I, I] := Character;
         Table[N - I + 1, I] := Character
      END
END;     (* Initialize *)
```

6.
```
PROCEDURE Maximum(Table1 : Table; VAR MaxValue : INTEGER;
                     M, N : INTEGER);

VAR
   I, J : INTEGER;

BEGIN    (* Maximum *)
   MaxValue := -MaxInt;
   FOR I := 1 TO M DO
      FOR J := 1 TO N DO
         IF Table1[I, J] > MaxValue
            THEN
               MaxValue := Table1[I, J]
END;     (* Maximum *)
```

7. PROCEDURE Initialize(VAR Table : List;
                         Column : ColumnRange);

    VAR
      Row : RowRange;

    BEGIN   (* Initialize *)
      FOR Row := 1 TO RowLimit DO
        Table[Row, Column] := Waiting
    END;   (* Initialize *)

8. FUNCTION AllStalled(Table : List;
                        Rows, Columns : INTEGER) : BOOLEAN;

    VAR
      Row, Column : INTEGER;
      Flag : BOOLEAN;

    BEGIN   (* AllStalled *)
      Row := 1;
      Flag := TRUE;
      WHILE Flag AND (Row <= RowLimit) DO
        BEGIN
          Column := 1;
          WHILE Flag AND (Column <= ColumnLimit) DO
            IF Table[Row, Column] = Stalled
              THEN
                Column := Column + 1
              ELSE
                Flag := FALSE;
          Row := Row + 1
        END;
      AllStalled := Flag
    END;   (* AllStalled *)

Chapter 11

1. TYPE
      LongType = PACKED ARRAY[1 . . 100] OF CHAR;
      PublisherType = PACKED ARRAY[1 . . 40] OF CHAR;
      Book = RECORD
              Title : LongType;
              NumAuthors : INTEGER;
              Authors : LongType;
              Publisher : PublisherType;
              PubDate : INTEGER
            END; (* RECORD *)

2.
```
PROCEDURE Initialize(VAR Tome : Book);

CONST
  Blank = ' ';

VAR
  I : INTEGER;

BEGIN    (* Initialize *)
  FOR I := 1 TO 100 DO
    BEGIN
      Tome.Title[I] := Blank;
      Tome.Authors[I] := Blank
    END;
  Tome.NumAuthors := 0;
  FOR I := 1 TO 40 DO
    Tome.Publisher[I] := Blank;
  Tome.PubDate := 0
END;    (* Initialize *)
```

3. a.
```
TYPE
    String20 = PACKED ARRAY[1..20] OF CHAR;
    String11 = PACKED ARRAY[1..11] OF CHAR;
    StudentType = RECORD
                    Name : String20;
                    SocSecNum : String11;
                    Class : (Freshman, Sophomore,
                          Junior, Senior);
                    GradePoint : REAL;
                    Sex : (M, F)
                  END;  (* RECORD *)
```

b. VAR
   Student : StudentType;
     .
     .
   WRITELN(' Name   SocSec#   Class   GdPt',
           '   Sex');
   WRITE(Student.Name);
   WRITE(' ');
   WRITE(Student.SocSecNum);
   WRITE(' ');
   CASE Student.Class OF
      Freshman : WRITE(' Freshman');
      Sophomore : WRITE(' Sophomore');
      Junior   : WRITE(' Junior');
      Senior   : WRITE(' Senior')
   END;   (* CASE *)
   WRITE(Student.GradePoint:5:2);
   CASE Student.Sex OF
      M : WRITE(' Male');
      F : WRITE(' Female')
   END;   (* CASE *)
   WRITELN;
     .
     .

c. TYPE
   RollType = ARRAY[1..3000] OF StudentType;

   VAR
   Roll : RollType;

4. TYPE
   Part = RECORD
             Number : INTEGER;
             Price : REAL
          END;   (* RECORD *)
   PartsList = ARRAY[1..MaxLength] OF Part;

```
    VAR
      Parts : PartsList;
      Length, Pointer, I : INTEGER;
      Found : BOOLEAN;
      NewPart : Part;
        .
        .
        .
    LENGTH := 0;
    WHILE NOT EOF DO
      BEGIN
        READLN(NewPart.Number, NewPart.Price);
        Pointer := 1;
        Found := FALSE;
        WHILE NOT Found AND (Pointer <= Length) DO
          IF NewPart.Number < Parts[Pointer].Number
            THEN
              Found := TRUE
            ELSE
              Pointer := Pointer + 1;
        FOR I := Length DOWNTO Pointer DO
          Parts[I + 1] := Parts[I];
        Parts[Pointer] := NewPart;
        Length := Length + 1
      END;
```

5. **a.**
```
    TYPE
        TitleType = PACKED ARRAY[1..20] OF CHAR;
        DateType = PACKED ARRAY[1..8] OF CHAR;
        Class = RECORD
                    Title : TitleType;
                    UniqueNum : INTEGER;
                    Date : DateType;
                    Grade : REAL
                END;    (* RECORD *)
```

   b.
```
    TYPE
        TranscriptType = ARRAY[1 . . 100] OF Class;

    VAR
        Transcript : TranscriptType;
```

   c.
```
    PROCEDURE GetClass(VAR AClass : Class);

    VAR
      I : INTEGER;
```

```
      BEGIN    (* GetClass *)
        FOR I := 1 TO 20 DO
          READ(File1, AClass.Title[I]);
        READ(File1, AClass.UniqueNum);
        FOR I := 1 to 8 DO
          READ(File1, AClass.Date[I]);
        READ(File1, AClass.Grade)
      END;     (* GetClass *)
```

6. TYPE
```
      String = ARRAY[1..30] OF CHAR;
      CourseGrade = RECORD
                      CourseID : INTEGER;
                      Grade : CHAR
                    END;   (* RECORD *)
      GradeList = ARRAY[1..50] OF CourseGrade;
      Date = RECORD
               Month : 1..12;
               Year : 1900..2000
             END; (* RECORD *)
      ClassType = (Fresh, Soph, Jr, Sr, Grad);
      Student = RECORD
                  Name : String;
                  ID,
                  HoursCredit,
                  CourseCount : INTEGER;
                  Grades : GradeList;
                  EnrollDate : Date;
                  Class : ClassType;
                  GPA : REAL
                END;   (* RECORD *)
```

7. Statements c, e, g, h, and i are valid.

8. **a.** ARef := AMap.Chart;
    b. Guide[4] := AMap;
    c. Guide[10].MapCode := ACode;
    d.
```
        IF ACode[1] = Guide[2].MapCode[1]
           THEN
             BEGIN
               WRITE(Guide[2].MapCode);
               WRITELN;
               IF Guide[2].Style = Formal
                  THEN
                    WRITELN('Formal')
                  ELSE
                    WRITELN('Brief')
             END;
```

or

```
    WITH Guide[2] DO
      IF ACode[1] = MapCode[1]
          THEN
            BEGIN
              WRITELN(MapCode);
              IF Style = Formal
                  THEN
                    WRITELN('Formal')
                  ELSE
                    WRITELN('Brief')
            END;
e.  WITH AMap.Chart DO
      BEGIN
        FOR I := 1 TO 2000 DO
          BEGIN
            Match := (ARef.Token[I] = Token[I])
            IF NOT Match
                THEN
                  WRITELN('Token ', I)
          END;
        FOR I := 1 TO 20 DO
          BEGIN
            Match := (ARef.Symbol[I] = Symbol[I])
            IF NOT Match
                THEN
                  WRITELN('Symbol ', I)
          END
      END;
```

Chapter 12

```
1.  FUNCTION Length(Stringl : String) : INTEGER;

    VAR
      I : INTEGER;
      Padded : BOOLEAN;

    BEGIN    (* Length *)
      I := 20;
      Padded := TRUE;
      WHILE Padded AND (I > 0) DO
        IF Stringl[I] = ' '
            THEN
              I := I - 1
            ELSE
              Padded := FALSE;
      Length := I
    END;      (* Length *)
```

2.
```
PROCEDURE ReverseLine(VAR Data : TEXT;
                          VAR ALine : Line);

   VAR
     I, J : INTEGER;
     Temporary : Line;

   BEGIN   (* ReverseLine *)
     I := 1;

     (* Gets line *)
     WHILE NOT EOLN(Data) DO
       BEGIN
         READ(Data, Temporary[I]);
         I := I + 1
       END;

     (* Reverses line *)
     FOR J := 1 TO I - 1 DO
       ALine[J] := Temporary[I - J];

     (* Pads with blanks *)
     FOR J := I TO 80 DO
       ALine[J] := ' '
   END;   (* ReverseLine *)
```

3. This procedure checks for errors. If it didn't, it would be much shorter.

```
PROCEDURE GetSymbol(VAR DataFile : TEXT;
                        VAR ASymbol : Symbol
                        VAR Error : BOOLEAN);
VAR
   Character : CHAR;
   I : INTEGER;
```

```
    BEGIN   (* GetSymbol *)
      Error := FALSE;
      IF NOT EOF(DataFile)
          THEN
            BEGIN
              READ(DataFile, Character);
              IF Character <> '*'
                  THEN
                    Error := TRUE
          END
        ELSE
            Error := TRUE;
      IF NOT Error
          THEN
            BEGIN
              I := 1;
              WHILE NOT EOLN(DataFile) AND (I <= 5) DO
                BEGIN
                  READ(DataFile, Character);
                  ASymbol[I] := Character;
                  I := I + 1
                END;
              IF I <= 5
                  THEN
                    Error := TRUE
                  ELSE
                    BEGIN
                      READ(DataFile, Character);
                      IF Character <> '*'
                          THEN
                            Error := TRUE
                    END
            END
    END;   (* GetSymbol *)
```

4.
```
   PROCEDURE GetWord(VAR Filel : TEXT; VAR W : Word);

   VAR
     I, J : INTEGER:
     Character : CHAR;

   BEGIN     (* GetWord *)
     I := 1;
     READ(Filel, Character);
     WHILE (Character >= 'A') AND (Character <= 'Z') DO
       BEGIN
         W[I] := Character;
         I := I + 1;
         READ(Filel, Character)
       END;
     FOR J := I TO 25 DO
       W[J] := ' '
   END;     (* GetWord *)
```

5. **a.** False   **e.** True   **h.** False
    b. False   **f.** False   **i.** False
    c. False   **g.** False   **j.** True
    d. False

6.
```
WHILE NOT EOF(Data) DO
  BEGIN
    READ(Data, Person);    WRITELN(Person.Name);
    WRITELN(Person.Address);
    WRITELN('Class — ', Person.Class:1);
    CASE Person.Sex OF
      M : WRITELN('Male');
      F : WRITELN('Female')
    END;  (* CASE *)
  END
```

7. Statements a, b, d, h, j, and k are valid.

8.
```
RESET(Data);
Sum := 0;
WHILE NOT EOF(Data) DO
  BEGIN
    FOR I := 1 TO 10 DO
      Sum := Sum + Data↑[I];
    Average := Sum / 10;
    WRITELN('Average: ', Average:10:3);
    GET(Data)
  END;
```

9. **a.** `I IN [1..24]`
    b. `Ch IN ['A', 'J', 'K']`
    c. `X IN [1, 51..100]`

10. **a.** `SummerMonths := [June, July, August];`
    b. `WinterMonths := [December, January, February];`
    c. `SchoolMonths := [September..December, January..May];`
    d. `JMonths := [January, June, July];`

11. **a.** `[June, July, August, December, January, February]`
    b. `[June, July]`
    c. `[]`
    d. `[September..December, February..May]`
    e. `[December, January, February]`

12. **a.** TRUE
    b. TRUE
    c. FALSE
    d. TRUE

13. Assume the following global definitions and declarations:

```
TYPE
   ItemRecord = RECORD
                   Item : INTEGER;
                   Quantity : INTEGER
                END;  (* RECORD *)
   ItemFileType = FILE OF ItemRecord;

VAR
   ItemFileA, ItemFileB, ItemFileC : ItemFileType;
   .
   .


PROCEDURE MergeFiles (VAR InFile1, InFile2 : ItemFileType;
                      VAR OutFile : ItemFileType);


(**********************************************)


PROCEDURE WriteRest(VAR InFile : ItemFileType);

BEGIN  (* WriteRest *)
   WHILE NOT EOF(InFile) DO
      BEGIN
         OutFile↑ := InFile↑;
         GET(InFile);
         PUT(OutFile)
      END
END;  (* WriteRest *)


(**********************************************)
```

```
    BEGIN (* MergeFiles *)
      RESET(InFilel);
      RESET(InFile2);
      REWRITE(OutFile);
      WHILE NOT EOF(InFilel) AND NOT EOF(InFile2) DO
        IF InFilel↑.Item < InFile2↑.Item
          THEN
            BEGIN
              OutFile↑:= InFilel↑;
              GET(InFilel)
              PUT(OutFile)
            END
          ELSE
            BEGIN
              OutFile↑:= InFile2↑;
              GET(InFile2)
              PUT(OutFile)
            END;
      IF NOT EOF(InFilel)
        THEN
          WriteRest(InFilel);
      IF NOT EOF(InFile2)
        THEN
          WriteRest(InFile2)
    END;  (* MergeFiles *)
```

Chapter 13

1. **a.**

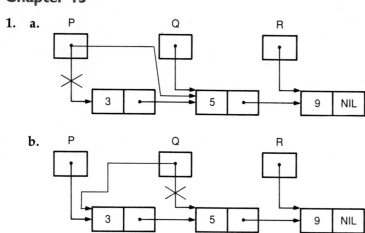

c.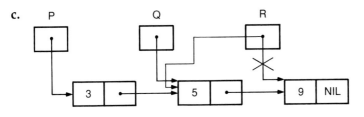

d.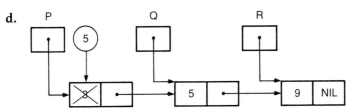

e.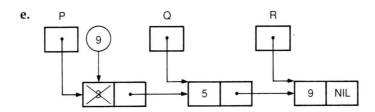

f.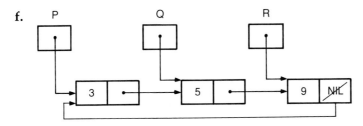

2. a. `P↑.Next := P↑.Next↑.Next;`
   b. `R↑.Next := S;`
   c. `List := P↑.Next;`
   d. `P↑.Next↑.Next := List;`

3. a. 1 1
   b. 2 0
   c. 0 0

4. False

5. a.
```
NEW(P);
P↑.EmpNumber := 0; (* 0 not actual employee number *)
P↑.Next := NIL;
Employees := P;
```

b.
```
VAR
   I : INTEGER;
   Character : CHAR;
      .
      .
      .
NEW(P);
WITH P↑ DO
   BEGIN
      FOR I := 1 TO 25 DO
         BEGIN
            READ(Character);
            Name[I] := Character
         END;
      READ(Department);
      READ(EmpNumber);
      READLN(Salary)
   END;
```
c.
```
PROCEDURE Insert(Employees, Emp : Pointer);

VAR
   Current, Back : Pointer;
   PlaceFound : BOOLEAN;

BEGIN   (* Insert *)
   PlaceFound := FALSE;
   Back := NIL;
   Current := Employees;
   WHILE (Current <> NIL) AND NOT PlaceFound DO
      IF Emp↑.EmpNumber > Current↑.EmpNumber
         THEN
            BEGIN
               Back := Current;
               Current := Current↑.Next
            END
         ELSE
            PlaceFound := TRUE;
   Emp↑.Next := Current;
   Back↑.Next := Emp
END;   (* Insert *)
```

Notice that there is a header node, so we never need to insert at the beginning of the list.

6. a.
```
FUNCTION Even(P : NodePtr) : BOOLEAN;

   BEGIN    (* Even *)
     IF P↑.Info MOD 2 = 0        Must be a
        THEN                     type identifier.
           Even := TRUE
        ELSE
           Even := FALSE
   END;     (* Even *)
```
Must be a type identifier. *(pointing to NodePtr)*

b.
```
PROCEDURE Successor(P : Pointer);

   BEGIN    (* Successor *)
     WHILE P↑.Next <> NIL DO
        BEGIN
           WRITELN(P↑.Info, ' is followed by ',
                   P↑.Next↑.Info);
           P := P↑.Next
        END
   END;     (* Successor *)
```
The original loop condition would make this an illegal reference when P↑.Next = NIL.

7.
a. True	**e.** True	**h.** False
b. False	**f.** False	**i.** True
c. False	**g.** True	**j.** True
d. True		

Index